THE GIFT
of VIOLENCE

Pitchstone Publishing
Durham, North Carolina
www.pitchstonebooks.com

Library of Congress Cataloging-in-Publication Data

Names: Thornton, Matt (Martial arts instructor), author.
Title: The gift of violence : practical knowledge for surviving and
    thriving in a dangerous world / Matt Thornton ; foreword by Robb Wolf ;
    afterword by Peter Boghossian.
Description: Durham, North Carolina : Pitchstone Publishing, [2023] |
    Includes bibliographical references and index. | Summary: "Based on the
    author's decades of experience teaching everyday people how to defend
    themselves and on a rational approach to the scientific data, The Gift
    of Violence provides the average person with the knowledge they need to
    reduce the likelihood of becoming a victim of violence-and to survive a
    violent encounter"— Provided by publisher.
Identifiers: LCCN 2022000895 (print) | LCCN 2022000896 (ebook) | ISBN
    9781634312301 (hardcover) | ISBN 9781634312318 (ebook)
Subjects: LCSH: Self-defense. | Violence. | Survival.
Classification: LCC GV1111 .T475 2023 (print) | LCC GV1111 (ebook) | DDC
    613.6/6—dc23/eng/20220317
LC record available at https://lccn.loc.gov/2022000895
LC ebook record available at https://lccn.loc.gov/2022000896

ISBN 978-1-63431-031-4 (pbk.)

THE GIFT

of VIOLENCE

Practical Knowledge for Surviving
and Thriving in a Dangerous World

MATT THORNTON

Foreword by Robb Wolf
Afterword by Peter Boghossian

Pitchstone Publishing
Durham, North Carolina

*To my mother, who gave me the greatest gift any writer can have,
the love of reading.*

To my wife, Salome. You are my everything.

To my children, to keep you safe.

To my Tribe, SBG. Build upon this.

*And to Karl Tanswell.
The one man who always knew what I was thinking better than I did.*

Contents

Section Three: Threats
The Who, What, and Where of Danger

Section Four: Prevention
How to Avoid and Outsmart Predators

Section Five: Preparedness
How to Not Be Easy Prey

Foreword

One might not be surprised to see the following headline: "We live in the most violent time in human history."

Surely this is true, as the near-instantaneous aggregation of news via both traditional and new media outlets paints a fairly bleak picture. It would appear that we are killing, raping, and maiming each other as if this were a high-stakes contest! But is this picture accurate? Or is "accurate" really the right word to consider here? Perhaps we need to think more about context.

With a bit of digging in publicly available databases, it would appear we live not at the brink of anarchy (yet, things could get worse) but rather in the safest, most prosperous period of human history with the lowest levels of interpersonal violence ever known (yet, things could get better still). So, what's happening here? Is the world burning down? Or is this all fake news? Are threats of physical harm from human predators of real concern, or are we actually living in a golden age that previous generations could only dream of? The answer to the last two questions, of course, is yes. These two realities are not mutually exclusive. The world has become (for most people, although unfortunately, not all) less violent (as measured by relative rates of activities such as assault, rape, and murder), but like infectious disease, violence is a co-traveler with humanity from our deepest evolutionary past.

Violence and infectious disease will likely be with humanity for as long as we exist. However, it's safe to say our lives are best when the magnitude of their influence is minimized. How does one reduce or mitigate the effects or potential of infectious disease or—more specifically, given the focus of this book—violence? We must keep the following in mind:

1. It exists.

2. It is inescapable but fairly well understood statistically.

3. It is largely manageable, both at an individual and societal level.

4. Some situations foster its expansion, and some its reduction.

5. We cannot lie to ourselves about point 4 and hope to realize point 3.

In *The Gift of Violence* Matt Thornton helps us come to terms with all of these points, which is itself a gift. If we properly and accurately understand a topic and its associated problems, we are provided agency in how to address them. The goal is to form a healthy awareness of and relationship with violence. Obliviousness to or denial of violence is just as damaging as the paralyzing fear or crippling anxiety violence sometimes invokes. Indeed, a sufficiently poor read on the potential for violence can cost you your life, but becoming a shut-in to avoid violent threats at all costs will severely diminish your quality of life. So we are not best served by living in unrelenting fear, nor are we wise to assume violence "only happens to other people." This is where understanding the statistical probabilities of violence helps us to take steps as individuals to avoid it, de-escalate it, or defend against it. I live in the mountains of Montana, and if I take a hike in the late fall, I am far more worried about bears than rattlesnakes. A little awareness of my environment and the likely risks I face help me focus attention appropriately. A smart, mindful individual will take the same approach no matter the season or surroundings. When we better understand where, when, why, and how violence occurs, we are in a much better position to make sound risk analyses. This requires situational awareness and self-defense knowledge.

At a societal level, understanding the mechanisms and statistical realities of violence provides us the proverbial "red pill" opportunity. The potential for violence in modern societies is *not* evenly distributed. This is a hot-button political topic that is not debated as to the facts of this reality—but the prescribed remedies we often encounter for this situation often cannot be more at odds. The standard narrative of societal disparities in violence is often addressed in a parts-and-pieces "treat-the-symptoms" fashion. Aside from the sound and sober guidance Thornton offers to individuals, his analysis of this topic offers us an opportunity to "treat the cause," but only if we are brave enough to follow the data and acknowledge the root-cause issues.

Violence is a tough, uncomfortable topic. Violence changes individual lives and societies forever. Given this reality, it is not surprising that *The Gift of Violence* is a tough and uncomfortable book. Tough and uncomfortable though it may be, understanding violence is our route to building agency. With agency, we can foster change. With change, we may create a better world—one that is less violent and even safer than the one we inherited.

Robb Wolf
biochemist and author of *The Paleo Solution* and *Wired to Eat*
BJJ brown belt

Introduction: The Gift of Violence

Violence is natural. In fact, violence is an essential part of our nature.[1] We wouldn't be here without it. Although no moral or ethical person would ever want to knowingly or intentionally inflict harm on others in the course of daily life, violence remains adaptive under some circumstances. To paraphrase Charles Darwin, we bear the stamp of our lowly origins.[2] Understanding those origins and becoming proficient in the language of violence will not only help us establish a healthy relationship with violence but also, ultimately, reduce the chances of it finding us.

Violence comes in many forms,[3] but for the purposes of this book, I am speaking specifically about physical acts of force committed by individuals against individuals so as to subdue, injure, or kill. It is true that violence as a whole has been trending downward for decades across much of the globe.[4] But this progress is incremental—and it is by no means assured. Violent crime causes four times as many deaths worldwide per year—nearly half a million fatalities—than all armed conflicts and terrorist acts combined.[5] While young men face the highest risk of homicide globally, largely due to the oversized effect of homicide rates in the Americas, women bear the highest burden of intimate-partner and familial homicide[6]—to say nothing of sexual violence.[7] Yet, while some characteristics and features of violent crime hold true across countries and cultures, other elements do not. For example, what I have to say about gun violence will be more relevant to readers living in or traveling through areas known for armed violence than to those living and traveling only in, say, Singapore or Japan. Regardless, this book is meant for all readers—no matter your nationality or location—because the traits of the violent criminals that I describe and the types of predators that you are most likely to encounter are universal, as are my recommendations for keeping yourself and your loved ones safe.

The world isn't suddenly going to become less cruel and violent tomorrow than it is today. Indeed, recent history provides all the evidence you need to understand the folly of such thinking. Effects of the pandemic and associated lockdowns led to a temporary drop in violent crime in much of the world,[8] particularly in violent criminal acts committed by strangers, but crime rates have slowly begun to return to pre–Covid-19 levels in many European countries.[9] Elsewhere in the world, there was a dramatic rise in violent crime during the pandemic. Homicide rates in the United States spiked more than 30 percent in 2020, and several major cities, including Philadelphia, Louisville, Albuquerque, and my hometown, Portland, Oregon, experienced their deadliest year on record in 2021. For the country overall, homicide levels were the highest they've been in a quarter-century.[10] And there's currently no sign of this trend reversing.

The causes of this particular spike in the United States are varied. Contributing factors include the death of George Floyd and associated protests, the so-called Defund the Police movement and prosecutorial activism, and other ingredients that are well beyond the average person's individual control.[11] But no matter where you live, whether in Los Angeles or London, Cape Town or Caracas, there are things you can control—specifically, *you* can become smarter, stronger, and more prepared for violent threats tomorrow than you are today. When it comes to violent threats, the best way to become safer still is to become more dangerous. Absorbing the lessons in this book, *The Gift of Violence*, can be the first step toward that end.

You're perhaps wondering, why not "lessons" in violence or "understanding" violence? Why "the gift" of violence? I have long come to realize that freedom from manipulation and exploitation by physical means is a gift, and it is available to everyone who is willing to learn and work for it. The first step is easy—reading this book. Indeed, the goal of this book aligns fully with the overall mission of Straight Blast Gym (SBG), the organization I founded in 1992: "To make good people more dangerous to bad people." The second step will require more work, but, as I will describe, it involves one of the most rewarding journeys a person can undertake. As I long ago came to understand through my professional work, making good people more dangerous to bad people doesn't just make safer people—it also makes better people.

When it comes to self-defense, it is easy to be led astray. Many people are. Seduced by the promise of street-fighting "secrets" and images of martial arts hocus-pocus, they get lost in nonsense. What has kept me on target is my overwhelming desire for truth. From day one, I had to know whether what I was doing worked. Training based on tradition, or extraordinary promises of future power, was never enough to keep me from trying out material against resisting opponents. When it comes to self-defense strategies and tactics, I have always held truth as a categorical imperative. And it is that impulse, more than any other, that unwrapped the gift of violence for me.

As of this writing, I have devoted the last thirty years of my life to the martial arts. For most of that time, I have actively trained in Brazilian Jiu-Jitsu (BJJ)—an art made famous by the Gracie family and popularized by the sport of Mixed Martial Arts (MMA).[12] I received my black belt in BJJ more than twenty years ago. Since then, I've become a husband and father to six children, and I've taught, coached, and trained some of the best fighters on the planet. I've traveled the globe—visiting Europe, Asia, Africa, and much of the United States—to give hundreds of seminars. Teaching people to fight has been my only career. I've been punched, kicked, thrown, kneed, elbowed, slapped, bitten, stabbed, and hit with sticks. I've "tapped out" (gestured my submission or surrender) to sparring partners due to a joint lock or stranglehold I was unable to escape from literally thousands of times. And I've made my training partners tap out to joint locks and strangleholds many times more.[13]

Straight Blast Gym was the first MMA/BJJ academy in Portland, Oregon, and thus far, I have awarded more than thirty-five black belts in the art of BJJ. Many of my students have gone on to have coaching careers that far exceed my own. My second black belt, John Kavanagh, was the first BJJ black belt in Ireland. As a coach, he had four of his own fighters from Straight Blast Gym Ireland compete on the same card at Ultimate

Fighting Championship (UFC) Fight Night 46 in Dublin. Participating in the world's premier Mixed Martial Arts competition, all four fighters won within the first two rounds. One of them, Conor McGregor, went on to become a double UFC champion. He's not only the highest-paid fighter in UFC history but was also the world's highest-paid athlete in 2021, beating out the likes of Lionel Messi and Cristiano Ronaldo.[14] My third black belt, Karl Tanswell, opened one of the first BJJ schools in the United Kingdom. His athletes also excel in MMA. My first crop of students, including Adam Singer and Chris Conolley, have also produced several MMA and UFC champions as coaches. Other early students of mine, including Paul Sharp and Raymond Price, have turned their attention toward teaching members of the military and law enforcement, where they have been instrumental in modernizing training curriculums, thereby saving countless lives. Others, like Travis Davison, have built large communities through thriving SBG gyms. All the coaches I have trained are world class.[15]

During my travels, I have spent time with murderers and maniacs, as well as with some of the kindest and most successful people on the planet. I have hung out in some of the poorest parts of the world and slept in some of the most expensive hotels. I have been in some of the strangest environments you can imagine. And I have experienced scenes so surreal that they would probably perplex even the weirdest among you. I've personally worked with all applications of hand-to-hand combat and all manner of students, from military operatives to Olympic athletes. I've taught soldiers to use knives and housewives to head-butt. Yet—despite my current assuredness and strength, my current proficiency and skill—I have not always been this way. In the 1970s and early 80s, I was an awkward, shy, bookish, somewhat effete, and skinny little boy to whom violence felt anything but natural. That may be why I ended up devoting my life to mastering it—or perhaps it was simply the result of a series of coincidences. Either way, I have evolved a great deal from who I was then, and much of that evolution was fueled by my disillusionment with the contradictions inherent in my own relationship with violence.

This book isn't about justifying violence. Indeed, I have a skill set I never want to use. Kindness, love, and compassion are a lot more enjoyable. But kindness and good intentions are never enough for being safe—intelligence and a sincere dedication to facts are also required.

Similarly, any ideals regarding your relationship with violence should not inhibit, distort, or confuse your ability to look at things as they actually are. Explanation and rationalization are two very different things.

Your goal should be to understand violence as it actually is—so that you can manage its role in your life. This will require analytical thought, not emotion. One of the largest impediments to solving much of the violence around us is our inability to see it as it is rather than how we would like it to be. This can lead to a failure to notice when it is near, or to recognize it when it is already upon us, and trigger a refusal to take decisive action when we are no longer in a position to deny it. The final part of this equation—decisive action—is the least understood and, as a consequence, the most fetishized.

I've spent my entire life teaching people how to fight. But violence is a much broader topic than fighting. When I began writing this book, I sent out a series of questions to people with extensive experience with this topic. I wanted to know what questions they still had. The responses were varied and fascinating, but everyone shared one thing—they had all established a relationship with violence. They all knew how to survive and manage violence as well as humanly possible. But they still struggled with the concrete questions of when, where, and, especially, why to use violence. It's harder to mitigate violence you failed to predict. The scars and pain—both physical and psychological—can stay with people for a lifetime. These men and women are problem solvers. They know how important prediction and awareness are, but they also know that there is always more to know. Their questions fueled my research.

Many people are drawn to self-defense strategies and martial arts because they have experienced bullying or abuse, whether as a child or as an adult. If you are one of those people, I want you to understand that you're not alone and that there is a solution. This book is my gift to those who need and deserve that solution—one I wish I could have given my younger self. I'll share the first and most important secret about martial arts upfront: most martial arts simply don't work.[16] That is a cold, hard fact. At best, they are of no use; at worst, they'll give you a false sense of security. Indeed, one of my goals in writing this book is to help give you a bullshit detector so that you might be better attuned to martial arts and self-defense nonsense—to immunize you against the boy-speak profiteers and to give you an indication of just how striking the differences can be between a healthy approach to violence and the path many martial arts offer. In this book, I explain how you can distinguish for yourself between the fantasy-based arts and the functional delivery systems that provide true self-defense benefits.

As already noted, my overriding goal is to help good people become more dangerous to bad people—or, to put it another way, to help you protect yourself and those you love. To that end, the book is primarily focused on the pre-physical aspects of self-defense, those that do not require in-depth training in a functional martial art or a high level of physical aptitude. Although I have much to say about the pros and cons of martial arts training in this book, this is not meant as a "fighting technique" book. That is a book I have yet to write. Yet, this is meant as a training book, even if the lessons I offer are more for the mind than the body. Only by understanding the true nature of violence, the types of threats you are most likely to face, and the warning signs you might encounter can you begin to protect and defend yourself and others.

At the heart of my message is one simple if paradoxical truth: the best way to reduce the risk of violence is to embrace the gift of violence.

Section One: Violence

How It Defines and Shapes Us

"The first rule is to keep an untroubled spirit.
The second is to look things in the face and know them for what they are."

—Marcus Aurelius

1 The Nature of Violence

Violence is natural, and we owe our very existence to it.

To understand the role that violence plays in our human story, we first need to understand the roots of violence, and to understand that, we first need to remember that we humans are, of course, animals. Like all animals, our relationship to and with violence has played an essential role in our evolutionary history. Violence is at the heart of who we are as a species. It shaped our past, defines much of our present, and molds our future. It is found within all our mythologies and religions.[2] It is front and center in our news and entertainment. Videos that feature it consistently go viral on social media. It is feared, desired, shamed, celebrated, glamorized, demonized, fetishized, idealized, romanticized, and, so very often, misunderstood. As neurobiologist Robert Sapolsky puts it,

> [W]e don't hate violence. We hate and fear the wrong kind of violence, violence in the wrong context. Because violence in the right context is different. We pay good money to watch it in a stadium, we teach our kids to fight back, we feel proud when, in creaky middle age, we manage a dirty hip-check in a weekend basketball game.... Our sports teams' names celebrate violence—Warriors, Vikings, Lions, Tigers, and Bears.... When it's the right type of aggression, we love it.[3]

In thinking about its place in the hierarchy of human life, few things match the dominance and centrality of violence and its ability to reach deep within us.

As long as there has been life on this planet, there has been violence. Violence is as natural as sex. Indeed, violence—along with sex—was one of the prime drivers behind the development of awareness itself—awareness about others and thus of ourselves.[1] All animal life feeds on other life. All animal life is, in one form or another, murderous. Violence is ubiquitous in nature. As Charles Darwin famously noted, "we do not see, or we forget, that the birds which are idly singing round us mostly live on insects or seeds, and are thus constantly destroying life."[4]

Violence can't be wished away any more than one could wish away hunger pangs. Nor can it be indulged inappropriately without leaving suffering in its wake. It needs to be seen as it is, without either the romantic glamorization of adolescent fantasies or the denial and repression found in the wishful thinking of idealistic hippies.

We need to make sure that what we think we know about violence is accurate. Rather than reflexively fetishizing or demonizing violence, we should seek to understand it and allow it its proper place within our souls. Every human being has a relationship with violence; the mission of an intelligent and pragmatic human being is to make sure that that relationship is a healthy one.

This reality can't simply be wished away.

Without violence, we wouldn't be sitting here today as living beings endowed with consciousness, capable of rational thought, and reading these words. Our DNA would be completely different—if we had managed to exist at all. In an effort to explain what Darwin meant by "evolution from natural selection," English philosopher Herbert Spencer coined the phrase "survival of the fittest." But what does *fittest* mean? Does that mean the strongest survive? Define strong. The average antelope has a far greater chance of reaching adulthood than the average lion. Our planet was once filled with creatures that possessed levels of physical strength that dwarf those of any species currently living. When Spencer said *fittest*, he meant those with the greatest ability to reproduce and to have offspring that survive to sexual maturity.[5]

In evolution, it isn't the strongest who survive but the ones most able to adapt to the environment, circumstances, and habitat in which they find themselves. Adaptation leads to longer and more successful lives. Longer and more successful lives lead to greater numbers of offspring. Heritable characteristics that increase an organism's likelihood of reproducing will be selected for from one generation to the next. This includes those characteristics that make an organism capable of committing—and defending against—violence.[6]

From the basic skills that help protect yourself and your loved ones to the most sophisticated methods of geopolitical warfare, the forms of violence vary enormously. Yet, if we look closely enough at how violence is utilized and deployed, we see patterns emerge. Expressions of violence are often predictable. And it is that predictability that gives smarter animals an advantage when it comes to survival.

There are two types of prediction. One involves conscious thought; the other is intuitive and relies on instinct, feeling, and emotion. Mice that run through open fields haphazardly tend to live shorter lives and therefore procreate less than mice more adept at staying hidden. The mouse isn't *thinking* in the analytical sense. It isn't summing up its odds in that field. Its form of prediction is innate. To consciously predict how something will behave, we need to know its patterns.

Education is where this process begins.

You have within you an extraordinarily powerful set of primal instincts that far exceed your conscious awareness.[7] They are there for the same reasons that a mouse recognizes that open fields are dangerous. But those instincts are only as good as your ability to recognize and process them, and those of us fortunate enough to be living in well-to-do communities in wealthy first-world nations may have lost touch with those instincts—our intuitive knowledge of violence—a relationship our bodies have always understood, but our conscious minds have long ignored.

Modern, civilized people in wealthy nations often think of violence as only a maladaptive behavior. Most humans alive today, in most parts of the world, stand far less chance of being murdered than they would have in premodern societies. Yet, though we may usually not want to admit it, violence is found within us precisely because it has been an adaptive behavior across evolutionary time.[8] Denying the evolutionary roots of violence will get us no closer to a solution to the problematic and maladaptive violence that exists today. We live in an age when nearly limitless information is available on our cell phones. We can travel across the world in a matter of hours, and we live longer, healthier lives than our ancestors could have imagined. But our minds—the grey matter in our skulls that creates the consciousness we call *I*—are still the product of our reptilian and mammalian predecessors.

I understand the hesitation many have about biological or evolutionary accounts of behavior. Genetic pseudoscience has a dark history. In the past, those who called themselves "civilized" were unimaginably ignorant about how much they got wrong or simply didn't know, an ignorance manifest in the mistreatment of women and people with different skin color under the specious reasoning that some groups were, somehow, inferior "by nature." But we can look at the evolutionary roots of violence without falling prey to the naturalistic fallacy. The more we understand violence, the better we can predict it. The better we can predict it, the more we can avoid it, thereby decreasing the frequency of violence in our lives.

Consider bar fights. People with higher IQs and greater emotional stability may see them as absurd. And while I agree with that assessment, bar fights are a means some males use to prove themselves "fit" in Spencer's sense of the word. If males require a certain status in order to gain access to females, and increased displays of aggression enhance that status,[9] bar fights are anything but a mystery.[10] An animal needn't be consciously aware of its own internal motivations in order to be moved by them. The human animal is no exception.

The farther back we go, the more homicidal our ancestors seem to have been. Most humans alive today, in most parts of the world, stand far less chance of being murdered than they would have just some hundreds of years ago. In the late medieval period, for example, the homicide rate in London was 50 per 100,000 inhabitants, more than thirty times today's rate, and up to a quarter of all deaths among English aristocrats were violent ones. Even so, according to all available data, England had the lowest homicide rate in Europe throughout the Middle Ages.[11] In the prehistorical period, homicide rates were likely higher still. Studies of existing isolated tribes provide some evidence for this. Anthropologist Napoleon Chagnon, who conducted ethnographic fieldwork among the Amazon's Yanomamö tribe in the second half of the twentieth century, estimated that 44 percent of Yanomamö men twenty-five or older had participated in killing at least one person.[12]

Stop and consider that statistic for a moment.

Yanomamö men reportedly gathered into raiding parties, invaded their neighbors' camps, murdered the other males, killed the infants by bashing them on the ground, and proudly frogmarched the women home to rape them. While Chagnon's research has had its detractors, even his fiercest critics admit that violence is anything but foreign to the Yanomamö.[13] An unsentimental look at life for many Native American peoples shows similar evidence of intercommunity violence.[14]

As with warfare, most interpersonal violence—assaults, rape, robbery, and homicide—is perpetrated overwhelmingly by men.[15] But this doesn't mean that violence is something that evolved only in, or due exclusively to, the male of the species. In the Yanomamö tribe, men who commit homicide achieve a special status known as *unokai*. They have, on average, more than twice as many children and twice as many wives as the non-*unokai* men.[16] Rape and forced marriages likely account for some of this difference. But we can't ignore sexual selection here, either. On a planet where female animals often have to rely on the strength and ferocity of their male mates in order to ensure the safety and well-being of their offspring, it would be surprising if human females—whether they wish to admit it or not—were not also deeply imprinted with a desire to secure a human male who is a good protector skilled in the art of violent deterrence.

There is nothing nefarious in that. This urge only becomes unhealthy when it is pushed to extremes. As with sexuality, if it is glamorized and indulged beyond its due or demonized and repressed to the point of hypocrisy, it may not manifest itself in a healthy way. As a husband and father of daughters, I recognize that my family's safety, which is my primary concern, isn't well served by a head-in-the-sand denial of our human instincts. Moral good and bad are irrelevant to this part of the discussion. Stow away your moral compass for now. It's a useful tool, but it can be deleterious when it comes to solving problems. As economist Steven D. Levitt and journalist Stephen J. Dubner put it: "When you are consumed with the rightness or wrongness of a given issue—whether it is fracking or gun control or genetically engineered food—it's easy to lose track of what the issue actually is."[17]

This is the issue with which we're faced: violence isn't unique; it is omnipresent wherever life on this planet is found. Your ancestors were tough, brutal, and sometimes savage people. You wouldn't be here today if they hadn't been. The need, desire, and ability for violence come from our very biology. And, while we must avoid the idea that what is natural is necessarily good, we cannot ignore our evolutionary past.

As risen apes, we may turn our noses up at violence,[18] but our indignation will not offer us protection from it. We may decry violence all we like, but when the punch lands on our nose, when we hear the sound and feel the pain, and when the aggressor is right there, face to face with us, even the most intelligent person becomes just another animal, afraid of being hurt, maimed, or killed, afraid of having its most precious belongings torn away, afraid of being extinguished forever—and in that moment, no amount of idealism, moral philosophizing, or wishful thinking will help you survive.

2 The Folly of Pacifism

Those determined to commit violence can only be dissuaded by violence. True power has always belonged to those who can offer security—or threaten it.

All healthy people oppose the *wrong* kinds of violence—for example, the types of violence that stem from naked aggression and harm innocent people. But some people actively oppose or demonize violence in all forms. The most extreme form of pacifism takes the position that the use of any form of violence is wrong, no matter the circumstances, including for purposes of self-defense. These pacifists typically oppose violence on ethical or religious grounds. They often view violence as something morally beneath them. While their commitment to principle is admirable, they are practicing a particularly dangerous form of denial.[1]

My mother was a pacifist from a very religious Jehovah's Witness family. Her version of Christianity relied heavily on Jesus' command from the Sermon on the Mount to turn the other cheek. Military service, or any job that might require the use of violence, was forbidden. My father, on the other hand, long maintained a relationship with violence, beginning when violence was forced on him as a child and continuing through his long career as a police officer.

As a young boy, I would attend church with my mother at least three days a week. Indoctrination through repetition was the teaching method the church preferred. Critical thinking was discouraged, and engaging in any form of combat was considered a serious transgression. When school was out, I would spend the day inside the police department, watching my father walk around with his holstered gun and listening to officers talk about the arrests they had just made. My understanding of violence was mired in contradictions from an early age.

I remember my first encounter with violence. I was somewhere between the ages of two and three, sitting in my front yard playing with a toy doctor's kit. It consisted of a cheap black Gladstone bag, a stethoscope, and vials filled with multicolored candy. Up walked a much older boy. Smiling, I held the doctor's kit out in an offer to play, as you do at that age. After a quick shove and grab, the boy took off down the street with my kit. I wasn't so much upset as confused. I had never encountered a stranger who would just take your things. My mother, who must have observed the event from the screen door or window, came tearing out of the house, screaming at the now-terrified thief. When she caught up to him, she yelled something unintelligible to me while waving her finger in his face. Then she returned, doctor's kit in hand. Few things in the animal kingdom are fiercer than a mother protecting her child.[2]

That was my first experience both with the problematic use of force and with its solution, but it certainly wasn't my last. The episode illustrated the inherent futility of pacifism. For the rest of my early childhood, I wrestled with the contradiction between pacifist teachings and practical reality. Kids who wanted my things, bullies, violent strangers, and the world at large seemed not to care about my mother's interpretation of the Bible. Over time, I learned that either you defend yourself and what is yours or you become a victim. And, given my mother's position on the matter, victimhood didn't seem like an involuntary situation: it seemed like an active decision.

My father came from a much rougher family life than I would ever be exposed to. My grandfather had been a combat medic and D-Day veteran—something he didn't discuss, though the experience had clearly changed him. He died young, leaving my dad fatherless as a young man in the 1960s. My dad respected many of the values of my grandfather's generation, things like establishing a work ethic, having civic pride, respecting your elders, taking personal responsibility, and being self-reliant, and thus he understood the flaws that permeated much of the hippie counterculture at the time. At the same time, like all good men, he wanted to make sure he didn't repeat the mistakes his father had made when raising him.

As a child, I would ask him why he carried a gun and why he did the job he did. He would patiently explain that, while he wore a gun and was trained to use it, he hoped that he would never have to. He would have preferred to live in a world in which that wasn't necessary. In my childish wisdom, I asked the obvious follow-up question: why did my mother's church teach that carrying a gun was wrong when it was necessary for men like my father to do their jobs? My dad patiently explained that if everyone believed what my mother did, he wouldn't need to carry a gun. And that was the end of the conversation.

By not participating in the protection of the neighborhood, city, state, and nation, the Jehovah's Witnesses—and pacifists in general—I came to understand, simply shift the burden of defense onto someone else. In terms of the only world I then knew, my mother's church had shifted the responsibility onto my dad and his colleagues while staking out some imagined higher ground for itself. Until we have the same level of control over other people's behavior as we do over our own, such a position represents a moral failing. People exist who would torture and murder us and those we love for pleasure. Their existence isn't our choice, but how we respond to this reality is. Arguing that we wouldn't need violence if we stopped all violence is about as useful as saying we wouldn't need doctors if we stopped all sickness.

When I engage in these discussions, people often reference Gandhi or Martin Luther King, Jr. and the demonstrated effectiveness of nonviolent resistance. My response is this: such a strategy yields positive results only when certain other ingredients are in place. First, there has to be some level of open and accessible press.[3] Without it, the marches, protests, and inevitable clashes with authority will be ineffective because they will go largely unnoticed by the broader public. Second, the broader public itself must possess a degree of goodwill.[4] Gandhi understood that direct military confrontation with the British Empire would be a bloody and unsuccessful strategy for the Indian people and that nonviolent protest would offer them a strategic advantage. But if the values of British culture hadn't led people to find the beating and murder of Indian protesters reprehensible, all the effort and struggle would have been in vain.

Gandhi once had the good sense to write,

> I do believe that, where there is only a choice between cowardice and violence, I would advise violence. Thus when my eldest son asked me what he should have done, had he been present when I was almost fatally assaulted in 1908, whether he should have run away and seen me killed or whether he should have used his physical force which he could and wanted to use, and defended me, I told him that it was his duty to defend me even by using violence.[5]

Yet, Gandhi became increasingly convinced over time that nonviolence was the answer in *all* situations. Thinking in terms of absolutes is rarely a good sign and often leads to utterly bizarre conclusions. For example, speaking after World War II, Gandhi made clear what he thought the Jewish people should have done at the beginning of the Holocaust: "Hitler killed five million Jews. It is the greatest crime of our time. But the Jews should have offered themselves to the butcher's knife. They should have thrown themselves into the sea from cliffs. . . . As it is, they succumbed anyway in their millions."[6]

Like Gandhi, Martin Luther King, Jr. and other leaders of the Civil Rights Movement in the United States also took a calculated risk.[7] They wagered that, in the end, the innate decency of the average American citizen would lead them to demand en masse an end to the dogs and hoses and attacks—an end to the injustice. Their strategy of nonviolence worked, but not without significant sacrifice and the strong and principled will of the protestors.

But these necessary dynamics and ingredients are not present in all countries at all times. Totalitarian governments, such as the one in North Korea, care little about nonviolent protesters or their followers. Wholesale slaughter, concentration camps, and state-enforced media silence would be the result of a misapplied pacifist protest there. In short, such an approach would be the equivalent of suicide, just as Gandhi recommended of the Jewish people. As Rabbi Shmuley Boteach has noted, "What Gandhi failed to realize is that when dealing with moral or at least somewhat humane governments, nonviolent resistance has its place. But when dealing with murderous barbarians such as ISIS or the Nazis, no level of nonviolent resistance will ever change their minds. Gandhi's philosophy would only guarantee that they take over the world."[8]

History has proven this to be the case for thousands of years. Power has always belonged to those who can offer security—or threaten it. As George Orwell pointed out, "Despotic governments can stand 'moral force' till the cows come home; what they fear is physical force."[9]

As I write, there is an ongoing battle in the Gaza Strip. Israel, facing rocket attacks from the Palestinian enclave,[10] has militarily engaged Hamas, an Islamist terrorist organization, in a repeat of multiple such engagements since Israel withdrew from Gaza in 2005. Although Israel is militarily far more powerful than Hamas, Hamas often relies on human shields in an attempt to gain a tactical advantage in the conflict by exploiting Israel's humanitarian impulses.[11] The great irony is that if Hamas were to use this tactic against another Islamist terrorist group instead of a Western-oriented country with a desire to minimize civilian casualties, it would be a total waste of time. Nonviolent tactics do work occasionally. But—like Hamas's use of human shields—they rely on enemies with a certain level of moral decency and concern for innocent life. Wise people should never base their strategy for safety on such an assumption.

Gandhi's earlier view against absolute pacifism—his call to reject it if you are left only with "*a choice between cowardice and violence*"—is the correct one. It is something he got right at the time. And he was certainly not the first intelligent man to recognize a categorical imperative against displays of spinelessness. English philosopher John Stuart Mill wrote:

> War is an ugly thing, but not the ugliest of things: the decayed and degraded state of moral and patriotic feeling which thinks nothing *worth* a war, is worse. . . . A man who has nothing which he is willing to fight for, nothing which he cares more about than he does about his personal safety, is a miserable creature who has no chance of being free, unless made and kept so by the exertions of better men than himself.[12]

There are times when the use of physical violence isn't optional: it is a moral imperative. We can debate how rare those circumstances might be. That is a complicated issue. But we cannot deny that such circumstances exist. As former military intelligence officer Tim Larkin correctly points out, violence is a tool, and sometimes it's the last and only tool available.[13] When other members of the tribe are unable to provide protection in those moments, pacifists who refuse their "duty to defend" will either cause their own slaughter or the slaughter of those in their care.

The boy who ran off with my medicine kit wasn't deterred by sudden moral misgivings at taking something that wasn't his; he was deterred by a larger, stronger animal filled with anger.

A show of force to deter a threat can be a useful tool when wielded appropriately. Yet, as with pacifism, showy machismo can also easily be taken to a dangerous and unhealthy extreme.

3 The Folly of Bravado

Nature, though red in tooth and claw, doesn't strut.
While violence is sometimes necessary, it shouldn't be glorified.

Those who glamorize, glorify, romanticize, seek out, or fetishize violence use what I call *boy-speak*.

Boy-speak is bravado. People who use boy-speak give away the fact that they don't know what they're talking about. They confuse the boldness of immaturity for the authority of experience. They mistake fear for respect. Boy-speak betrays a lack of real power. Boy-speak is loud and insecure—it stems in part from a state of weakness on the part of those who are still attempting to define their own sense of self and who want to be perceived as strong. Boy-speak is the opposite of true or traditional masculinity.[1] It represents an attempt to sound masculine, but it actually reveals that its user is insecure and scared. Boy-speak is evidence of unresolved adolescent issues. Boy-speak isn't bound to any culture, race, or time. It has been with us for as long as young males have attempted to navigate a threatening world. But it is always rooted in immaturity and feelings of inadequacy.

Outside the realm of religion and perhaps "alternative" medicine, few genres of human activity are filled with as much superstition and egregious bullshit as the martial arts.[2] It is those fantasy-based martial arts systems that tend to traffic in high volumes of boy-speak. For adolescent males, the lure of powerful fighting skills combined with a dash of mysticism is often too tempting to avoid. Absent a solid background growing up in a combat sport like wrestling or boxing, kids are easy prey for martial arts woo-woo.[3]

In his book *Leadership and Training for the Fight*, retired U.S. Army Delta Force operator Paul R. Howe writes: "I equate loud talk with foreshadowing of failure. This is my mathematical view of boasting: Loud talk = failure = impotence/cowardice."[4] Put another way, those who talk about violence the most often know the least about it.

The traditional martial arts often attract and encourage such culprits. The reality-based self-defense (RBSD) world is similarly filled with child-like bravado.[5] Frightened and insecure young men who lack proper male role models seek out relief for their neuroses in all the places that claim to offer a remedy for the ailment, such as in academies run by Kung Fu masters who promise magical fighting skills or self-defense instructors with nicknames like "The Animal" or "Beast Man" who happily boast about the time they subdued an attacker with their left hand—while never spilling the coffee in their right. We also see this in schools that traffic in "secret" Russian commando training methods, Israeli military arts, and "street-fighting" techniques. They are often accompanied by fancy gear, lots of jargon, army fatigues, and loads of boy-speak. These confused, immature, and emotionally stunted grown men serve this all up via advertisements that target vulnerable, insecure, emotionally needy young boys and promise a cure the instructors themselves have so clearly never received. It is a giant hamster wheel, served up with a heap of dysfunctional training methods and delusional concepts, thereby ensuring that the cycle of immaturity, confusion, and fear continues. Add a bit of "Oriental" hocus-pocus theater, and the scheme is almost fail-safe.

While my words may seem harsh, when you have had thirty years of watching the absurdity of it all, you cannot see it any other way. The great tragedy is that the cure these young men seek does exist, but the path they get placed on moves them farther from it rather than closer toward it. They simply go from being scared and insecure young men to being scared and insecure older men. No emotional growth is achieved. But if those same kids are placed in a proper combat-sports environment, they can quickly flourish. Why? Because the very process of training in a genuine combat sport and developing a practical fighting skill causes you to grow in confidence, maturity, strength, and self-awareness and improve your understanding, empathy, and health.

The problem of romanticizing violence is, of course, much larger than the world of fantasy-based martial arts. It is larger than any one activity, medium, or culture. It permeates our world. Whether mirroring or influencing reality, or—as I suspect—a bit of both, movies and television profit greatly from the boy-speak crowd. They portray violence in ways that range from cartoonish to pornographic. Arts journalist Ian Grey wrote one of the better short pieces I have read on this topic for RogerEbert.com. His essay titled "Blood on the Screen—Violence, Movies and Me" is one of the more raw and honest accounts of someone's life-long relationship with violence that you will find. He introduces the essay by writing:

> Nicolas Winding Refn, the director of *Only God Forgives* and the king of stylish wound-infliction cinema, said he's never experienced violence at all, that it terrified him beyond the telling, and that he'd fall to his knees and do what it took to stop it from happening to him. "I would just give them what they want: 'Please don't hurt me! Please, no!'"
>
> When I read that, I thought of how one of the very first things I remember of this world was being violently hurt in a flurry of action and left to weep in a dark room. That day, at the age of five or six, I learned one of my first big life lessons: that waiting for violence is often as bad as having it inflicted upon you. Alfred Hitchcock, of course, based his entire filmmaking career on this terrible truth.[6]

In this passage, Grey recognizes the dread any normal person feels as they wait for an inevitable clash. Instances of this are many: a young child anticipating the entrance of a drunk, abusive parent; a boy sitting in class knowing he will be "jumped" and beaten once the bell rings; a soldier sitting in a helicopter waiting to be dropped into a warzone; a professional fighter anticipating the moment he will walk into a cage to face his opponent; and a movie audience holding their collective breath as the hapless on-screen character makes the fatal decision to find out what that noise was in the basement. Of course, we don't want to equate these circumstances in terms of morality, intensity, or the stakes involved. There is nothing that justifies the beating of a child or the terror the wife of an abusive husband feels as she hears him return home from the bar. It isn't the situations that are related here; rather, it is the way the body responds to such situations that is worth noting. Grey continues:

> Fast forward, junior high, first day. I got it in my fool head to wear the tight purple flares and paisley shirt like I'd seen John Lennon wear on the sleeve for the "Lady Madonna" single. At lunch a plug-shaped boy hurled me to the cement and beat my head until my ears leaked blood, screaming 'f#@king faggot!' like it was a song request. For three years plug-boy and his acolytes bullied me, finally realizing that my mint copy of Robert Shekley's "Dimension Miracles" was my only prized property and, right there in Plastics Class, ripping it from my hands, slapping me, and tearing the cover and causing me to finally have the PTSD nervous breakdown I'd been working on since I was six.

Many of you reading this book can probably relate to that passage better than you would like to let on. I certainly can. As a young boy entering elementary school, I was somewhat effeminate. I don't mean that in a pejorative way. I was shy, had gentle mannerisms, a quiet demeanor, and a preference for my own company. One day, in first grade, a major fight was about to break out among the boys in the class. Sides were picked as if gym captains were picking teammates for a dodgeball game. I watched in curiosity, more like a journalist than a participant. The moment my name was mentioned, it was universally assumed that I would go and sit under a tree with the girls. I didn't feel angry or humiliated—I wouldn't encounter those types of emotional responses until later. I preferred the company of girls. They smelled better, and they generally made more sense. I sat with them and watched as aggressive group posturing broke out on the field until panicked teachers rushed in to stop the show. It was all very foreign to me.

As each school grade passed, encounters with bullies became more frequent. Sometime around fifth grade, an older boy walked over as I was sitting by myself at recess and, without uttering a word, punched me in the face. I don't remember crying or even being upset. I only remember being shocked—I felt just as I had when the boy stole my doctor's kit;

the senselessness of it left me confused and indignant. At some point, I figured that I would have to toughen up.

When I was twelve, our family moved to a different part of the state, and I entered a much larger, much rougher school. It took time to adapt. When I hit puberty, I looked as ridiculous as any very tall, very skinny, and very shy kid could. I quickly caught the attention of the school's worst bullies, and, since I hadn't made any friends or even acquaintances yet, I became a target.

Things came to a head one day after PE class. As usual in such moments, the teachers were nowhere to be found. A group of three older kids cornered me in the locker room. I was able to get out into the courtyard when one of them grabbed me from behind. While he held my arms, one of his friends rifled through my pockets. They tore my shirt open, laughed, and started punching me in the body and head. By this time, what was probably a small crowd—it seemed enormous at the time—had gathered to egg on my attackers. They had taken to calling me "stork" due to my gangly appearance. The students began laughing and chanting, "Stork, stork, stork!" as they watched the three boys beat me. I began to cry.

I had been humiliated in front of what felt like the entire school. For my persecutors, that signaled victory, and they let me go. As the crowd laughed and applauded their work, I made my way out of the courtyard and into the office, where I was admonished to take a seat. While I was waiting—ashamed, head down, and sobbing—the largest of the three boys walked through the hall and punched me in the face again before running out the door and off the campus.

The school's principal gave me obvious advice: I needed to fight back. This was not something you might expect to hear from a principal, but this was a depressed school in every sense of the word, and I think he was annoyed at even having to have this conversation with me. More to my surprise, my mother told me the same thing. The whole turn-the-other-cheek principle had been immediately dismissed and forgotten. "You need to beat these kids up next time they attack you," she said sternly. Once more, the incongruence of the messages I had been raised with began churning the question mill in my mind.

As I returned to school each day, I would mentally try to prepare myself to face my attackers. But I had no idea how to do so. My stomach was always in bits; I was a wreck. I looked forward to the evening and the safety of my bed. And I dreaded every weekday morning.

My grades dropped to solid Ds and Fs, but I did manage to make new friends—the kids who also cut school. The delinquents. And, best of all, the kids all the other students were most afraid of. My social group, and my newfound confidence within it, prevented anyone from harassing me. But I was still seething with anger. It wasn't the black eyes or bruises that were the problem—those healed quickly. It was the humiliation.

Aggression and fear are often two sides of the same feeling.

I didn't wait for them to attack me again. As the weeks progressed, I hunted down each person involved in my humiliation, using the power of hate-fueled aggression.

I found one in the library, and I hit him with a chair. It was not a very impressive performance on my part—but it was a decent use of tools.

I saw one in line in a hallway, waiting for a classroom to open. I had a large oblong fishing weight in my pocket. We were frequently stopped and searched by school police, so we had taken to carrying screwdrivers, bike chains, and other makeshift weapons we knew they would have to reluctantly give back to us a few days after confiscating them. I had no idea how to punch properly, but I did know that hitting someone with lead in my hand would hurt them. Without saying a word, I walked over to him and punched him in the face. He dropped to the ground. I walked away.

My third and final persecutor was unlucky enough to be found all alone at a pinball machine in a pizza parlor. I had a baseball bat hiding under my coat. Lots of stuff could be concealed in baggy 80s-style clothes. As I walked up behind my attacker, I asked him if he remembered who I was. I don't remember what he said, but I do remember the look on his face when he saw the bat.

After that was over, out of the corner of my eye, I spotted the pizza clerk rushing toward me. I sprinted out into the darkness. The police drove cruisers up and down the blocks looking for me. I had dropped down into a large field by a creek. The spotlights fell onto the weeds above my head. Thankfully, they didn't have a dog that night.

I am telling you all this for two reasons. First, I want you to understand that effective violence—successful violence—isn't about fairness. The art of intimidation depends solely on people knowing that you're

THE FOLLY OF BRAVADO • 39

not only capable of harming them but also willing to harm them.[7] It has nothing to do with performing or behaving in an honorable way. Second, I want you to understand that I had not discovered a solution to the fear and shame I felt. I had simply flipped the coin over and begun using its other side.[8] Though I freely admit that this other side felt better.

One lesson I picked up early was the value of staying quiet in threatening situations. This is important. All the bravado—the pushing, shoving, yelling, threats, and boy-speak that so often occur when two males begin to get physical with each other—is usually intended, whether consciously or not, to ward off the threat. In other words, it is usually an indication that they don't actually want to engage in physical conflict.[9] If they just act boldly enough and shout loudly enough, the other animal will simply back down and go away. That's the hope. It's a common survival mechanism found throughout nature.[10] I've talked my way out of more dangerous situations than I've fought my way out of, but I've never engaged in the kind of shirtless pushing and shoving games that are so common in immature violent conflict. I've always wanted my opponents to feel my attack before they were aware it was going to happen. Once you make the decision that physical conflict is inevitable, or is the best option for avoiding an even worse outcome from a predator intent on hurting you, don't give any warning. It's smarter that way—not just from a tactical standpoint but also a psychological one. Often, the lasting psychological effects of a violent encounter in which you fail to defend yourself are worse than the immediate physical effects of any violence you might experience.[11] As Grey wrote, "You wonder if early violence leaves a scarlet letter on people. If you're a survivor, please listen: this is not true. It. Just. Isn't."

Grey's words have haunted me. I understand them to my core. But they don't resonate with me in the same way they would have as a teen. The anxiety and humiliation people struggle with after violent encounters can be intense and lifelong. It has been my experience that those feelings manifest themselves later on in even more severe ways if the encounter occurs at a young age or if the person does not fight back. This is not a moral judgment. It is not about character. It is an observation of consequences. When those three boys attacked me in school, they held my arms. But they didn't need to. I wasn't fighting back. To fight and lose is painful, but it isn't usually humiliating. *To be attacked and not fight at all can be emotionally debilitating.* This is one of the main reasons I always advocate that children stand their ground against bullies, verbally as well as physically, if need be. A suspension may last a few days. The ripples from an undefended beating can last a lifetime.

I've talked a lot about extremes of violence—the two opposite poles—because I have lived through them both. It didn't take me decades or even years to go from a shy, skinny, effeminate, and scared little kid to a scrappy, ill-tempered, violent, and scared teenager. It took only a few months. If pushed far enough, any boy in his formative period, roughly between the ages of twelve and seventeen, is capable of doing the same.[12] And, while my reactions to circumstances went from one extreme to the other, what I felt inside never changed. By overreacting to threatening circumstances, by lashing out, I had not happened upon the proper, intelligent, or even pragmatic solution to problematic violence. I had just stumbled upon a more socially acceptable way to express my feelings among my male peer group.

When I entered high school, I was alone again. My group had all either gone to jail or to other schools or had ceased going to school altogether. The fights that followed were pretty unremarkable. I learned a few lessons, though. I quickly discovered that, unless you got in the first blow, fights usually ended up on the ground. I was on the receiving end of a few bashings while stuck in a headlock or underneath a kid who was mounted on my chest, raining down blows. I also had a couple of close calls involving weapons. If things had been even slightly different, the outcomes could have been grim. Some people wonder why boys do extreme things, like shooting or stabbing a classmate. I never have.

What I suspect Grey understood, and what I sensed when I read his short piece, is that the quotation from Nicolas Winding Refn, "I would just give them what they want: 'Please don't hurt me! Please, no!'" isn't expressing fear of violent actions themselves, in so much as it is expressing fear of how he might react to them. Having, by his own admission, no experience with physical violence at all, Refn's true nightmare is that the day he comes face to face with it he will discover himself a coward. I believe it is that terror, not the physical blows, that has haunted Ian Grey, too. That is the neurosis from which the boy-speak crowd profits. And since what the boy-speak profiteers teach is, in a very practical sense, based on a lie, they only ever further the suffering.

Insincerity, whether in displays of sexuality or violence, is almost always pornographic. Whereas sincerity, whether in displays of sexuality or violence, is rarely so. The most realistic depictions of violent combat—for example, the D-Day landing scene in the movie *Saving Private Ryan*—can be called a lot of things—intense, gory, troubling, those can all fit—but pornographic is not one of them. It is that authenticity that we want to give our attention to. That which is born of a process or a pedagogy devoted to factual truth that creates sincere reflections deserves our attention. Good writers, directors, and artists understand that truth deeply.

Members of the boy-speak crowd typically describe themselves and their heroes as *tough, angry, aggressive,* and *fearless*. Those traits represent their idealized version of a "fighter," one who can both take a beating and have a "killer instinct." By contrast, what I find important, and what I look for in my athletes, is the ability to remain *calm, smart, happy,* and *focused* when under pressure and to maintain a higher overall level of *maturity* and *self-reflection* in daily life. This list isn't based on a philosophical ideal; it is, first and foremost, pragmatic. The traits I listed produce better fighters and athletes. But—and this is good news—they also produce better survivors and better human beings.

The allure of "street fighting" disappears pretty quickly once someone sincere begins training in a combat sport. The idea of beating up the average man holds no glamor when you spend your days battling with fellow athletes who are at least as skilled as you are in the art of hand-to-hand combat. The fetishization of violence indulged in by so many men who have an immature relationship with it can gradually disappear in the proper environment. As Oscar Wilde noted, "As long as war is regarded as wicked, it will always have its fascination. When it is looked upon as vulgar, it will cease to be popular."[13]

When you are working in an environment that is based on meritocratic competition, when you tap people out and get tapped out daily, when you punch and get punched, and when you understand what physical conflict feels like, violence loses its glamor.

When you know the reality of violence, it ceases to feel *wicked*. And you truly begin to understand what *being tough* really means.

4 The Command of Safety

You are responsible for your own personal safety.

Violent crime is on a long-term decline in the West.[1]

This fact may come as a shock if you spend any amount of time scanning news sites, watching television news, or reading newspapers.[2] *If it bleeds, it leads.* Two weeks of immersion in the news would leave even the most optimistic among us filled to the hairline with toxic levels of pessimism. It isn't just the media that propels this misunderstanding. It is also well-meaning advocates who do so. Very few interest groups or charities for good causes would be able to collect money by telling people only how good things are getting. Setting off sirens of angst helps fill coffers. Thus, they fundraise not only off our goodwill but also our anxiety.[3]

The problem isn't that activists use such methods to bring attention to their causes. If I were responsible for fundraising, I would use the most efficient methods possible. The problem is that if we never pay attention to the areas in which we are doing well, if we never focus on what is working in addition to what is going wrong, we will miss many of the best solutions to the problems society faces and may even steer the ship of society away from calmer waters and toward rougher seas.

Often, our pessimism is uncalled for. As long as we insist on comparing the world today to an imagined utopia, we will remain blind to the incremental improvements that have made each generation better off than the one before it. Never has there been less hunger and disease—and more prosperity. These developments have been enabled, in large part, by increased levels of personal safety across much of the world. Without it, societies simply cannot advance or flourish.

Psychologist and author Steven Pinker has written extensively on the long-term decline of violence throughout the world. His book *The Better Angels of Our Nature* provides detailed evidence of this decline across centuries and offers multiple reasons for it. These include the rise of the nation-state, the increase in cross-border trade, the increasing role of women in modern society, rising literacy rates, and the Enlightenment. "If the past is a foreign country," he writes, "it is a shockingly violent one."[4]

There are often periodic spikes in violent crime, whether on an international, national, or even local level. For example, major cities in the United States have been experiencing a spike in homicides in the past few years. But we shouldn't confuse peaks and valleys with long-term trend lines. Most of us face less violence than our recent ancestors and much less violence than our ancient ancestors. That's a very good thing.

Violence is an innate tendency in humans,[5] just as it is throughout the animal kingdom. But that doesn't mean that we are fated to indulge that impulse. In fact—and this is extremely good news—each succeeding generation has become better at *not* acting on our violent tendencies. And, while even a modest amount of reflection will demonstrate that the cliché *violence never accomplishes anything* is a lie—after all, those who are determined to commit violence can only be dissuaded by violence—it is equally true that violence, when used in situations where it is unnecessary, is as counterproductive as it is vulgar.

With violence as a whole decreasing since the dawn of civilization, we should expect to find higher rates of homicide per capita the farther back in time we go, no matter where we are on the planet. The Americas are no exception. If we take into account all the murders of the twentieth century—all the homicides and genocides, the two world wars, the dictatorships, gulags, and bombs—there was still less violence per capita globally over that century than in Mesa Verde in the century prior to the arrival of the Europeans.[6] This doesn't mean that the Europeans did well by the native population there. It just means that the fourteenth century in Mesa Verde was more violent than the world was in the twentieth century when controlling for population size. We shouldn't lose sight of this reality.

Most mature adults living in wealthy nations today are blessed with a state of relative security about which our ancestors could only have fantasized. This is a wonderful thing. In the United States, for example, the chance of being a victim of a violent crime in any given year is relatively low (roughly 1 percent).[7] But this sense of relative security also presents two new and related challenges. First, many of us have been lulled into such a state of ease that our own healthy and robust primal instincts, hard-earned relics of our evolutionary past, can often end up being either ignored or misunderstood. And second, our conscious awareness—once concerned primarily with issues of survival—has been taken over by modern concerns and worries that don't usually relate to actual predators and threats in our midst. Yet, if you ever do find violence knocking at your door, the raw statistics will provide little comfort.

Even if the overall level of violence in society has been receding over time, and the world is safer now than in the past, the stakes of violence are the same as they've always been. Further, the chance of being a victim of a violent crime, when measured across a lifetime, is quite high.[8] We continue to live in a physical environment in which others of our own species pose a direct physical threat to us. All mature human beings understand that few things are as repugnant as a bully or predator precisely because such people have not only the capacity but also the intention to cause us harm. We can never become too complacent. We cannot allow our own comfortable circumstances to lull us into forgetting that if an attacker is determined to inflict violence, only force or the threat of force will stop him. If you wake up to find someone kicking in your front door, he won't be the least bit interested in your opinion of how wrong his behavior is. Only physical force will attract his attention—whether the force is imposed by you or someone else. When a situation becomes serious, skill in the use of violence becomes a necessity.

Those of us fortunate enough to live in wealthy democratic nations pass much of that responsibility on to others who are authorized to use force on our behalf. I am not advocating vigilante justice. The formation of national and local governments, with their various law enforcement organizations, is one of the major accomplishments of civilization and one of the many reasons violence in all its forms has been in decline. But I would urge those who are too eager to pass on to others responsibility for their own personal safety to remember a handful of key points.

First, *feeling* safe and *being* safe are not the same thing. You can feel safe, even though you may be in danger. And you can feel unsafe, even when you're quite secure. Without a proper education in violence, you may not be able to distinguish between the two until it's too late. I don't want to instill paranoia. Paranoia is counterproductive. The trick is to be able to distinguish between paranoia and the perception of real peril. I don't want you to waste your time worrying about nonexistent threats— but neither do I want you to be unable to recognize an actual predator when you are truly in danger.

Second, police can respond to a crime only once it has occurred or is in the process of occurring. As much as law enforcement personnel would love to preempt a violent attack by rolling up just before it happens, they usually find themselves arriving after it is already over. By passing on the duty for your personal safety to the authorities, you are taking a potentially fatal risk.[9] You don't have to walk around in a state of constant worry in order to avoid harm. But you do have to be smart enough to take responsibility for your own safety and maintain a certain level of education on a topic that is central to our reality.

Third, remember that those authorities charged with the safety of the community place themselves in harm's way on your behalf. Having been involved in fighting and hand-to-hand combat training for decades, I've run into many people who've turned up their noses at the mention of my career. Without exception, these people have been manifestly hostile in a repulsively passive-aggressive way. Indeed, some of the angriest people I've ever met have been self-proclaimed pacifists, and their open disdain for law enforcement personnel could only be possible in a society that provides a basic level of safety and defends their personal freedoms. While you may personally find the use of force distasteful, the police are not afforded the luxury of that opinion. If nothing else, they should be respected for taking risks on your behalf. Few things are as repugnant as human beings who sneer at the people charged with protecting them.[10]

Fourth, remember that by denying and repressing an essential aspect of human nature, you are isolating yourself from part of your own visceral connection to this planet.

All decent and healthy people prize kindness, compassion, and love and aspire to live by these qualities, but good intentions are never enough for preventing, avoiding, and surviving violence. Intelligence and a sincere dedication to the facts are required, as is knowledge about the language and methods of violence. The process we rely on to discover the truth about violence is the most important item in our toolbox for drawing accurate conclusions about violence—and for developing effective strategies and proven techniques that will help keep us safe from it.

Section Two: Truth

Why It Matters and How to Discover It

"Why is martial arts fraud so instructive?
It is faith and self-deception made visible."

—Sam Harris

5 The Search for Truth

*If you want to discover the truth, you must be more interested
in what is than in what you want "what is" to be.*

Your preferences do not determine what is true. If you are more interested in what violence *should* be than in knowing the truth about violence—what it is, where it comes from, and how to manage it—then nothing I can offer here will be of much help to you.

Reality isn't always comforting.

I did not begin my martial arts journey because I wanted to be an MMA fighter. MMA did not exist then. I did not start it because I wanted to be a BJJ black belt. Brazilian Jiu-Jitsu was unknown in the United States at that time. I started my journey for one simple reason: I wanted to learn how to fight. I later dedicated my life and my adult career to training and teaching functional martial arts because I wanted to know how to fight really well. Along the way, I discovered and learned many things far more important than my original intentions presumed.

After leaving the U.S. Army in 1989, my sole focus in life became training in "functional" fighting—real martial arts. This is something I had been interested in for as long as I can remember—something that became an obsession for me after losing one too many altercations. Then, as now, there were a lot of martial arts styles from which to choose. Based on what I'd read and researched, I decided to train in what's known as Jeet Kune Do (JKD), a phrase coined in 1967 and translated as "the way of the intercepting fist."[1] Many things drew me toward JKD, including, most notably, the writings and personal philosophy of Bruce Lee, the founder of the art: "Absorb what is useful, reject what is useless, and add what is specifically your own."[2]

For a pragmatist like myself, this precept made perfect sense. For the traditional martial arts world, Lee was proposing something radical: cross-training. He was telling martial artists not to be trapped by the limits of a rigid martial arts system and to utilize and integrate what works from all systems. This was the core idea behind JKD, which initially drew heavily from Wing Chun, Northern Kung Fu, and Western boxing and later incorporated Filipino weapons fighting (Kali/Escrima).

I was particularly attracted to this idea because, in theory, it meant becoming well-versed in the "four ranges of combat," a phrase used by JKD practitioners that is popularly attributed to Lee.[3] These four ranges refer to kicking, boxing, trapping, and grappling. Kicking was for when you could kick your opponent but not yet reach them with your hands. Boxing was for when you could kick or punch your opponent but not yet effectively grab them. Trapping was for when you could kick, punch, and grab your opponent, but you were both still standing. And grappling was for when you were both on the ground. It all made sense.

I'd been in enough fights to know that where you wanted to be in a physical confrontation wasn't always where you ended up. My skirmishes in the years following the baseball bat incident had varied in outcome and detail. Some I had won. Some I had lost. The losses almost always occurred on the ground. And the ground happened a lot. I knew wrestlers were dangerous, at least as dangerous as boxers. But most martial arts systems at the time contained little to no effective groundwork. The attitude at the time was simple: you don't want to be on the ground in a fight, so why train there? This, of course, meant that most martial arts systems missed the crucial point—just because you don't want to be somewhere doesn't mean you won't end up there. By definition, your opponent in a fight is not cooperating. You have to learn how to fight wherever you are, not just where you wish to be. Your preference won't always determine where you end up, but your opponent might.

Yet, despite the conceptual usefulness of the four-ranges-of-combat philosophy, I found the ground training in JKD to be quite limited in practice. Like the traditional martial arts from which it was drawn, JKD focused primarily on stand-up fighting. To its credit, however, JKD did offer one key advantage many of those same traditional martial arts did not. It incorporated Western boxing, and boxing, like other combat sports such as Muay Thai and Savate, involves sparring. I knew enough to know that any striking art that didn't involve sparring wasn't just missing the boat—it wasn't even in the water. The promise of this was enough to make me want to engage with the art.

As my exposure to JKD progressed, however, I began to develop doubts about some of its frequently used training methods. JKD people rightly derided things like kata—solitary karate patterns acted out in the air—as counterproductive. Yet, following Lee's death, many of the leading JKD instructors adopted a lot of one- and two-person forms, which in actuality were little more than kata themselves that had been taken from other, more obscure Southeast Asian martial arts. They would spend an inordinate amount of time on ineffective "hand-trapping" movements that bared no resemblance to anything that happens in an actual fight or within full-contact sparring matches—and little to no time on wrestling or grappling, something that did happen in almost every fight or full-contact match in which it was allowed. It did not make sense.

The unveiling of the JKD mystique began to progress exponentially for me when I moved to Portland in my early twenties. After several years of training daily at a boxing gym and teaching full-time at a JKD school, I realized my training philosophy and, above all else, my objectives were moving me in a very different direction from JKD. I would find myself daydreaming about the ideal training environment—the kind I wanted to be in, the one that did not yet exist. I imagined people fighting full contact at all ranges, with takedowns and ground fighting allowed, pushing the limits. I imagined athletes truly learning what it means to fight—intelligently—against a fully-resisting opponent and growing, changing, and adapting from each experience. After all, how else would we know if what we were learning and teaching actually worked? If our techniques aligned with reality? I wanted to test everything we were doing. All of this I saw clearly in my mind, down to the minute details. In retrospect, it's easy to realize that what I was, in fact, envisioning was something like an MMA gym. But the UFC, and the sport of MMA that followed, were still years away. At the most basic level, I simply wanted to know what was true.

And truth matters.[4]

If you don't value what is true, and if you don't have an accurate mechanism for discovering what is true, you can, and most likely will, create conditions external to yourself in which you believe you're flourishing when you are in reality floundering. Truth matters because if you don't accurately map the world around you, you may find yourself moving farther away from your intended goals rather than closer toward them. As American philosopher Daniel Dennett so succinctly put it when discussing the scrupulously investigated medical advances that had weeks earlier saved his life: "Good intentions and inspiration are simply not enough."[5] Faith is not sufficient. You also have to be right. This requires reason and open inquiry.

Let's consider the nonfunctional martial arts, such as Aikido. If the Aikido master is sincere with himself and others about his intentions, and those intentions revolve around maintaining a cultural tradition, getting exercise, or performing a two-person dance, then the activity of Aikido may be a very healthy thing for him. If, however, the Aikido master has the intention to learn functional self-defense, whether that intention is held privately or proclaimed publicly, then the activity of Aikido becomes something that moves him farther from his objective.[6] In both cases, the man is engaging in conditions designed to bring about an outcome. But if those conditions don't actually match the actions required to achieve that outcome in the world of noncooperating opponents, the activity itself can become deleterious to the goal. It becomes inauthentic. It becomes unhealthy.

I am not claiming that every truth is a fixed commodity, some object that remains unchanging, something stuck in time. But I am also not a believer in the postmodern idea that "science . . . is no more objective than Scientology" or a magical view of the universe that posits that no such thing as truth, as it relates to an external reality, exists.[7] Some hold the belief that "Truth is a pathless land," as Indian philosopher and mystic Jiddu Krishnamurti famously claimed.[8] Like many aphorisms that get repeated often within "spiritual" circles, this claim could be true in a narrowly defined context, but that would not make it some kind of universal truth. Absent further definition or context, it is little more than what Dennett calls a "deepity," which the Urban Dictionary defines as "Something that sounds profound but is intellectually hollow."[9] Like the phrase "Love is just a word," it's true in a trivial sense, false on a more meaningful level, and profound sounding only to those who lack an education in actual profundity.

Is the "true" distance from the earth to the moon something that cannot be approached by any path whatsoever? No, it isn't. It can be discovered. There is an objective answer. The same can be said for virtually every empirical question. The process and tools we use to arrive at that truth are what matter. What matters for determining truth is our epistemology—how we know what we know (see chapter 6). Are we taking scientific measurements, following scientific principles, and performing scientific tests, checking and verifying our results?[10] Or are we pulling an estimate out of a hat? Or are we accepting as truth a distance revealed in a dream hundreds of years ago by some presumed prophet and transmitted across generations from teacher to student?

Indeed, one fallacy committed too often, whether in religion or the martial arts, is what's referred to as the appeal to authority.[11] The argument from authority can take several forms. As a syllogism, it often has the following basic structure:

A says *P* about subject matter *S*.
A should be trusted about subject matter *S*.
Therefore, *P* is correct.

Person A may be correct, but a claim based solely on the authority we have granted this particular person as it relates to a particular subject is not evidence. In other words, just because the Pope or Albert Einstein or Ip Man says something does not make it true.

But let's be clear with our definitions here, so we don't fall into commonplace philosophical quagmires. For my purposes, I consider a statement to be true if it accurately describes or accords with the world—or, put another way, with facts and reality. When understood in this way, truth isn't a thing: it is a measurement of how well something we as humans believe or propose aligns with reality. By extension, this means that truth can admit to ever-increasing levels of refinement. For example, Einstein refined Isaac Newton's theory of universal gravitation with his theory of general relativity; he did not invalidate Newton's work. Today, Einstein's theory of general relativity is believed to be "truer" than Newton's theory because it has been shown over and over again to align more closely with reality both in experiments and in real-world applications, and not because of Einstein's IQ or reputation. But as with Newton's theory, Einstein's theory is also likely incomplete. This means some yet-to-be-born physicist may well refine our current understanding of gravity and come up with a new theory that even more closely aligns with reality.

From a practical standpoint, we are always better off thinking we don't have a good mechanism for discovering truth than thinking our flawed mechanism will lead to truth. We are always better served by knowing we don't know than by thinking we know when we don't. As Darwin noted, "To kill an error is as good a service as, and sometimes even better than, the establishing of a new truth or fact."[12]

When we pretend to know what we don't, we cannot grow. Once we believe that all epistemologies are created equal, we have effectively walled ourselves into the penitentiary called *doxastic closure*.[13] Our beliefs become fixed because we have no reliable way to revise them. Whenever someone is unwilling to admit that some methods are more accurate than others, they have tipped their hand: they are choosing willful ignorance over the sincere search for truth.

If someone has a callous disregard for the truth or adopts an attitude that either denies the possibility or importance of truth, no progress is possible. Even if someone is sincere in their beliefs, personally authentic, and honest to others about their objectives, meaningful progress is possible only if they have critical-thinking skills and a proper epistemology. Absent a proper feedback mechanism, a *self-correcting mechanism*, the best they can hope for is to stumble forward blindly through sheer luck. More likely, they will fall behind painfully. They will think and act as though they possess the truth even if they are dead wrong. Being willing to revise your beliefs and change your mind is the first step on the path called improvement.

In the traditional martial arts that rely on kata or forms, there is no self-correcting mechanism. More simply, there's no way to determine whether the movements being taught and performed are in any way effective. This is true even for those techniques or combinations that are only practiced against compliant or nonresisting opponents. Anyone can look like they have amazing martial skills with the right demonstration partner, but to truly judge the efficacy of a technique, you need to look at the behavior of the "feeder," or attacker, and not the demonstrator. Anything can appear functional when total cooperation is involved. And the first thing to notice about most traditional martial arts demonstrations, and a great deal of what passes for training methods within traditional martial arts, is that the attacker is almost always cooperating.

The Kung Fu student steps out with a forward-lunge punch, locking his arm in the air and freezing in a manner that no real opponent on planet Earth will ever mimic. The Kung Fu master looks amazing as he executes multiple deadly strikes against his frozen, immobile opponent. The student drops in a heap.[14]

The Aikido demonstration partner, known in Japanese as an *uke*, runs forward, his arms mimicking the downward strike of a sword in a manner and form that no modern, angry, violent attacker will ever use, and the Aikido sensei gracefully steps to the side executing a perfectly done—and perfectly choreographed—throw. The *uke* lands gracefully.[15]

The Kali guro stands ready, stick in hand. His partner swings wide, locking his arm in place in a manner no primate with a tree branch has ever mimed. The guro then deftly deflects, disarms, strikes, and sweeps his "opponent" in an impressive-looking display. His opponent falls, weaponless, defeated.[16]

All of this is very common. And all of this is very make-believe.

There are a number of rationalizations for this kind of dead-pattern charade. First, you will hear this is only the first step in the process. Once the movement has been "mastered," the students begin to use these techniques against resisting opponents. This is almost never true. If it were, everyone would quickly realize that the movements and responses themselves don't align with what happens when someone really resists, a reality every student who has ever tried to use these movements against someone who is actually fighting back quickly, and painfully, realizes. Next, you'll hear that the movements themselves are "too dangerous" to be used in live sparring. This, too, is a lie. There is no movement, no technique, no strategy, and no "art" that is too deadly to train against a resisting opponent in a manner that is functional and safe. (I will discuss this more in chapters 22 and 23.)

Regardless of how well-meaning our intentions, if we are wrong about the facts or deny them out of distaste for what they imply, we are inviting harm both to ourselves and those in our care. When it comes to the martial arts, truth cannot be avoided in the face of a malevolent attack.

Truth is the angry street fighter who doesn't give a damn about the Kung Fu master's reputation. The fighter has no intention of throwing a punch and locking his arm out in a typical Kung Fu pose, one that mimics the only types of punches the master has practiced against. That fighter is a vehicle of truth the moment he throws a real punch to the master's face, tackles, mounts, and pummels him into unconsciousness. Truth doesn't care about the Kung Fu master's opinion of what a fight should be or how many compliant demonstration partners he has beaten up.

Truth is the BJJ blue belt with two years of training who politely asks for a match with a larger, stronger Aikido sensei with twenty-plus years of training, and who then takes him down, holds him down, and quickly chokes him, forcing the Aikido sensei to submit by tapping out, time and again, until his ego can take no more. That truth doesn't care that the effective and gentle movements used to control the sensei were out of line with Aikido's utopian fantasies about what human movement "should be."

Truth is the man who grabs a large stick and swings it the way any human being with bad intentions will swing an impact weapon. Crashing through the Kali guro's block, cutting open his face, and repeating until the guro gives up. That truth won't care that the stick did not move in a manner that conforms to how the guro practiced, how the guro assumed it "should be."

The above scenarios are not speculation. All three have occurred. Admittedly, such anecdotal stories prove nothing, but they are illustrative of the problem. Thankfully, we can rely on a more rigorous method to discover truth in personal combat. The beauty of martial arts is that, unlike more theoretical subjects, the techniques and styles are all testable. The tests themselves are all repeatable. And the results are all very predictable.[17] Anyone can look amazing with the right partner. Anything can *look* functional when the person having the demonstration done on them cooperates with the person doing the demonstration to them. But for the martial artist seeking reality, it is the resisting opponent who offers them truth.

Unless you're foolish or a sociopath, you will want to experience that truth in a training facility—and not in a parking lot, where the stakes are much higher and the potential outcomes far more severe. You want to test that truth always, every day, every week, every month, and every year you train. That does not mean training needs to be rough or lead to injury. People who think it does haven't been exposed to the correct training methods yet.

Why does truth matter?

Because when it comes to self-defense, if your beliefs about reality don't correspond to reality, the end result will be painful at best or fatal at worst.

The world of traditional martial arts, like religion, is overflowing with superstition, creation myths, miracle stories, antiquated training methods, and all manner of woo-woo. This is exactly the type of thing Bruce Lee intended to change and wanted to move martial arts away from.[18] I have run into people who feel that explaining all of this is a waste of time, because they think those who fall for the fantasy-based martial arts, or for any con game or superstition, are stupid, lazy, or both and thus deserve their fate. I don't share this opinion.[19]

As relates to my own martial arts journey, why did I want a training environment with nowhere for the ego to hide, an ongoing experiment designed to give the most accurate feedback possible? Why did the functionality of what I was going to do, the authenticity of it, matter so much? The answer is a universal one, available to everyone: without authenticity, without self-honesty as it relates to our intentions or motives, we will not be able to see the world as it actually is. And unless we are willing to see the world as it is, we won't even know the right questions to ask, let alone find the right answers. Those questions, when matched with an accurate answer-seeking method, a practical epistemology, lead us ever closer to truth.

6 The Power of Method

When you pretend to know what you don't know, you cease to grow.

It isn't our conclusions that matter most. It's the method we use to arrive at those conclusions that matter—in other words, our epistemology.[1] Our epistemology is vital when we are discussing questions that admit of an objective answer, because if we cannot determine what is true, then we cannot have knowledge in any meaningful sense.[2]

What do I mean by "objective answer"? I want to be careful in defining my terms here because different fields will occasionally use the same words in different ways. Let's break this down.

If person A says, "There are chairs in that room," they are making an empirically testable truth claim about the nature of reality. If person B says, "There are *no* chairs in that room," they, too, are making an empirically testable claim about the nature of reality. Person A and person B cannot both be right. One of them is wrong. The question "Are there chairs in that room?" admits of a right or wrong answer. It is in this sense I am using the word "objective."

By contrast, if someone says, "I think there should be chairs in that room," and someone else says, "I don't think there should be chairs in that room," then we are discussing "subjective" answers to a "subjective" question. Each answer could be right according to one's values, objectives, or desires, but this would not equal objective knowledge.

People often fear clear, honest, blunt dialogue when what they ought to be concerned about are foolish and dangerous ideas. Clarity and candor are indeed virtues—especially within the realm of communication. And while someone will always be offended by something, it is worth remembering that very little human advancement has occurred through complete consensus. If you have never been criticized for anything, you have likely never stood for anything, and that isn't something to be proud of.

Objective questions admit to right and wrong answers, whereas subjective questions tend to be matters of taste. "There is currently rap music playing in this club" is an empirical statement. "Rap music sucks" is a subjective opinion. Similarly, some individuals may prefer hard chairs, other individuals may prefer soft chairs, and other individuals still may prefer the floor. Thus, whether someone thinks chairs "should" be in a room may depend on a whole host of variables. On such questions of opinion, the attitude that everyone may have their own truth may be quite appropriate. But for questions that admit of right and wrong answers—for objective questions—the idea that everyone is entitled to their own truth is nothing less than fraud. Our thinking that something is true does not make it true.[3]

There are, of course, objective questions for which we currently lack answers. For example, "How many planets in the universe contain life?" We simply do not know. But that we cannot currently answer a question does not mean the question itself doesn't have an objective answer. Indeed, back in the late 1980s and early 1990s, I had a lot of objective questions about martial arts, and only after years of experience and experimentation did I slowly begin to arrive at objective answers.

In those early days when I first started asking objective questions, I was fortunate to have had many positive experiences with JKD's top instructors. I learned a lot of important lessons from them, even if those lessons weren't necessarily their intended ones. Among these instructors was the man generally acknowledged as the leader of the JKD community, Dan Inosanto.[4] I liked "Guro Dan." He was affable and energetic. I would watch him teach seminars, and he would demonstrate hundreds of techniques, flowing from one style to another and looking sensational as he did so. He would talk about the beauty of boxing. He would teach Muay Thai and Jun Fan Gung Fu (Bruce Lee's art). He would even show a bit of Shooto (a branch of Japanese professional wrestling). Then, grabbing a stick or a knife, he would slip in some patterns drawn from Filipino martial arts.

Yet, for all their talk about functional sparring, when the training actually took place at those seminars, it was filled with dead patterns. The demo partner would swing the stick, throw the punch, or launch a kick, and then leave their appendage or weapon hanging, frozen, while the instructor executed chains of impressive-looking moves. The promise that those moves would be just as effective against a noncooperative opponent was always implied but never demonstrated. Giving them all the benefit of the doubt, we could say this was due primarily to the format. Once students advanced, so too would the training method. But the problem ran deeper than that.

In front of the seminar, Dan would always say, "All arts have something to offer." Everything depended on the context. There were no superior arts. It was all relative. But there were a few occasions when I had a chance to listen to Dan talk to his instructors privately, and he would be blunter when speaking with them. Backstage, he would tell them that some people were fighters and some people were not—and that they should teach piecemeal, one movement at a time. As I'd often hear in such circles in that era, "If you sell all the merchandise on your shelves, you'll have nothing left to offer."

Meanwhile, at the boxing gym, I worked with men like Jesse Sandoval. He had spent seventy years boxing, coaching boxers, and training athletes. And yet, he had, by his own admission, still only mastered one aspect, one kind of "style" within the sophisticated and complex art of boxing. When I taught a boxing class, I would teach a jab, cross, hook, and uppercut, with plenty of footwork. When I would watch a world champion like Riddick Bowe train, he would work a jab, cross, hook, and uppercut, using plenty of footwork. When I worked with Olympic wrestlers, I would watch them work level changes and penetration steps. When I took my son to his first pee-wee wrestling class, I watched the coach teach a roomful of seven-year-olds level changes and penetration steps. In short, there are no "advanced" techniques when it comes to learning how to fight. There are only fundamentals. Fundamentals that are done poorly identify beginners. Fundamentals that are done well identify experts. Ask yourself which boxing, wrestling, or functional combat sport coach on the planet would ever worry that they would run out of "merchandise" to offer?

If I said to you I was about to teach Canadian geometry, I hope that you would immediately view my claim with suspicion. Geometry isn't bound by any culture, location, or even time. Base angles theorem—that if the base angles of a triangle are congruent, then the sides opposite them are also congruent—holds true in Canada, China, England, and everywhere else. It was true before humans even had the capacity to recognize it as true.[5] The properties of angles and shapes don't depend on geography, culture, or time. So, too, with hand-to-hand combat. The bodies of *Homo sapiens* may vary in size and strength, but their properties—two arms and two legs, with a specific, measurable range of strength, speed, and agility—remain constant.

Just as there are better and worse ways to measure the properties of a circle, there are better and worse ways to attempt to cut off the blood flow to another human being's brain with your bare hands. Some methods will be more efficient and functional than others. And just as the properties of a triangle have a fixed set of parameters, so too does human anatomy. Fighting involves a variety of situations, but the core mechanics that make a move work remain the same across space and time. Just as the properties of angles are not limited by geography, the properties of a proper strangulation hold are not bound to any period or culture. And those properties—the appropriate movement, base, posture, connection, and angle—create the root delivery systems that underlie all functional styles of combat.

From my interpretation of Bruce Lee's stated goals, I truly believed that JKD *should* have been all about discovering those *root delivery systems* and refining them—and that the JKD world had strayed away from this focus in the years after his death. I took what I saw as Lee's core idea to heart. When I was still teaching JKD, and before I opened my own gym, I led a Friday night sparring class where I could teach and train how I wanted—where I could research, absorb, reject, and add. We used whatever equipment we could adapt from other sports: motorcycle helmets, baseball catcher shin guards, kendo gloves, lacrosse gear, elbow pads, and whatever else seemed to work. I would create different scenarios for the purposes of training and exploring. For example, I'd give a student the goal of making it through a door guarded by three other students. And we also did lots of what would later become known as Mixed Martial Arts.

A small crew of people who wanted to train as I did—as realistically as possible—soon began to accumulate. And I gradually began to recognize that these folks were different in character and integrity from those who would never have lasted through one of our Friday nights. My ragtag crew was rough and sometimes crude. But they were authentic human beings in search of the same thing I was: truth. We just wanted to learn how to fight, and we discovered more objective answers on those Friday nights than I ever did from my own more formal JKD training and instruction. Most importantly, it became increasingly clear to me that expertise in fighting meant mastery of fundamental skills and timing, which could really only be gained one way.

Whereas I wanted to develop better ways to throw a punch or stop a takedown, many of my peers were busy memorizing secret *djurus*—static movements or forms repeated over and over again, in the same solo patterns—patterns that bore no resemblance to anything that happens when fighting an aggressive, noncompliant attacker.[6] My idea of a workout involved sweat, athletic effort, and pressure. Theirs involved comparing stick patterns or memorizing some ornate hand-trapping sequence. Instead of a healthy diet of training in functional delivery systems with resisting opponents, JKD had become a buffet line at an all-you-can-eat exotic-foods restaurant. And that buffet was filled with a lot of junk food.

Most traditional martial arts share a similar arrangement and methodology. Their selling point is usually that their most efficient techniques are too deadly for sport fighting: they were designed for the street. Their mythologies all tend to follow the same story arc—a creation myth involving a founder who designed a novel system after overcoming some personal hardship that they then used to defeat scores of deadly attackers. Wanting the art to remain pure, he (or she) created patterns for his students to repeat after his death, thereby preserving the movements. Some patterns are aimed at the general public. But the more lethal combinations are secret and reserved for the top students only. And all of it is "too deadly to be tested."[7]

The fighting demonstrations are a con game in all these dead-pattern systems. All the choreographed dances fall quickly apart when you have to face someone who is moving around and actually trying to hit you or take you down. The moment someone attacks you the way any boxer, wrestler, MMA fighter, irate football player, or even drunken hooligan would, the con is up. Oz is revealed behind his curtain, pulling levers and putting on the show. And this is where the all-important "too deadly" part comes in. It serves as a useful adaptation that helps to prevent the hustle from ever being exposed.[8]

Then, as now, I do not mean to offend. Even so, I quickly discovered that whenever I speak these basic truths in plain, obfuscation-free language, I inevitably offend some people. These people are not offended because I am saying something that isn't true; they are offended because I am saying something that is true, and they don't think I should say it.

You will encounter this type of response from believers of any objectively bad idea or superstition—whether related to medical quackery, extremist ideologies, paranormal phenomena, or religious cults. Martial arts woo-woo is no exception. The practitioners often plead for "tolerance," which, in their case, means sheltering their bad ideas from criticism. The critics of their sacred cow are labeled intolerant, closed-minded, and cranky, while the purveyors of the deception portray themselves as enlightened, ecumenical experts who are able to rise above the fray and see the value in their dogma.[9] It's a great spin if it works. And it is profoundly dishonest.

The idea that tolerance is a virtue in itself is a dangerous fallacy. I am intolerant of all sorts of things: violence against children; the torture of animals; and people with bad hygiene who want to take a wrestling class. Real morality—the kind arrived at through concern for the suffering of conscious creatures—requires *intolerance*. Tolerance is neither good nor bad: it always depends on what one is tolerating.[10]

But the most hysterical criticism I have come to experience, the kind that really lets you know you are transgressing some taboo, is from people who claim I am being "disrespectful" to the master, guru, sensei, teacher, or sifu responsible for whatever method or concept I am criticizing. My response is always the same: ideas are not people.[11] Methods are not teachers. And concepts are not individuals. The mushy-minded blurring of distinctions between people and ideas can be fatal. People deserve respect. Ideas do not. When we afford any idea, method, system, ideology, or faith protection from criticism, we set ourselves up for disaster.

Nobody sensible would see criticism of a certain bridge-building technique as a personal insult to the engineer who developed it. Bridges need to be structurally sound—lives depend on them. In the same vein, self-defense methods need to work—lives depend on them. The distinction between people and methods has always been clear to me, but for those whose ideas are being scrutinized and who feel besieged as they attempt to defend an indefensible position, that distinction tends to get blurred. And that can literally be a lethal problem.

When it comes to asking objective questions, one of the beautiful things about the martial arts is that ideas about punching, kicking, wrestling, and grappling are all testable—you need only a resisting opponent to begin to discover objective answers and gain actionable knowledge.

7 The Power
of the Opponent Process

*Meritocratic competition is the self-correcting mechanism of actuality,
and the opponent process is the self-correcting mechanism of combat.*

When I first decided to teach others to fight, it was for a somewhat
selfish reason: I knew I needed to have good training partners if I ever
wanted to answer for myself the many objective questions about fighting
I was wrestling with. And, before I realized it, what began as a hobby
born of an obsession had morphed into a full-time career. Along the way,
sorting out what worked—that is, what was functional against strong,
aggressive, fully resisting opponents—from what didn't work consumed
a lot of my time.

One thing stood out immediately. If you consider the arts that demonstrably work within the realm they're designed for—boxing, wrestling, Muay Thai, Judo, BJJ, Savate, and Sambo, to name but a few—they
all have something in common.

They are all combat "sports."

It's here that people like to make a distinction between "street" and
"sport." They will say things like: "Those arts are designed for sports,
for one-on-one combat, with gloves, with a referee, with rules. Not for

the street, where multiple opponents, weapons, and banned techniques come into play!" The street-versus-sport fallacy is one of the most common defenses for all that is silly within the martial arts. I will address this issue in depth in chapter 23, but for now, remember, a boxer who can knock your head clean off in the ring can do the same thing in a parking lot. And a wrestler who can decide whether the fight goes to the ground in an MMA cage, regardless of where you want that fight to be, can do the same inside a crowded mall. Circumstances will dictate the appropriate tactics, always. But the root skills of striking, takedowns, and grappling—they remain the same regardless of the environment.[1] As Paul Sharp, one of the first coaches at SBG, says: "You can't beat us with rules. What makes you think you can beat us without them?"

People unfamiliar with this principle tend to ask questions about specific styles.

"Is Shotokan Karate better than Hung Gar Gung Fu?"

"Is Wing Chun more practical than Tai Chi?"

These are the wrong questions. It is not about any particular style.

Relativists will say things like, "Each art will work within its given context," but aside from being untrue, that response, too, misses the point.

Consider the question differently for a moment. Instead of wondering which styles work and which don't, consider the styles themselves to be technical answers to a physical problem—in this case, how to handle a particular kind of attack. Then remember that a physical problem like this is an empirical question. As walking, talking, and thinking creatures with two legs and two arms who all operate within a limited spectrum of physical capabilities, there will be better and worse ways to solve such a problem. This is not a subjective question with a subjective answer. This is not about whether or not there *should* be chairs in a room. This is about whether or not there *are* chairs in a room. Given that fact, what matters most is not the particular answer we arrive at. What matters most is the method we use to arrive at that answer. More specifically, it is not about "styles." It is about the *method* those styles use to arrive at their answers, the answers being the techniques applied as solutions to a particular attack. It is all about the epistemology. It is all about the training method.

The very nature of all sports is that they exist in a world of competition. The word itself is derived from the Latin term *competere* ("to strive together"). And while that root may at first seem counterintuitive, since the nature of competition seems to be "striving against," it makes perfect sense upon reflection. An athlete grows in skill through practice against a resisting opponent. Both competing parties grow together through a process that is, at its ideal, a form of meritocratic competition. The "styles" that work when tested against resisting opponents do not necessarily have a particular set of techniques, type of motion, or set of rules in common. Rather, what the styles that work all have in common is their training method, *competere*, a form of meritocratic competition—the opponent process.

If your child were diagnosed with cancer, would you take them to a witch doctor, or would you want them to see an oncologist armed with the most up-to-date scientific knowledge and training? Would you want to fly on an airplane built according to someone's dream, revelation, or faith, or would you prefer to fly on one built using the principles of science? If you were considering investing your entire life savings in a new business venture, would you consult a palm reader, or would you prefer getting advice from an expert who understands the market and numbers based on their long experience within the industry?

Whenever things really matter, it is science and reason to which we turn—the best methods we hairless primates have thus far conceived to arrive at accurate answers. As evolutionary biologist Richard Dawkins once wrote, "Show me a cultural relativist at 30,000 feet and I'll show you a hypocrite. Airplanes built according to scientific principles work. They stay aloft, and they get you to a chosen destination. Airplanes built to tribal or mythological specifications, such as the dummy planes of the cargo cults in jungle clearings or the beeswaxed wings of Icarus, don't."[2]

The scientific process is, at its core, a form of meritocratic competition. Done properly, science demands that all hypotheses be put into question.[3] Science accepts or rejects ideas based on evidence—and demands that any experiments or findings are replicated. Replicability is important because it gives credibility to results and allows us to make more accurate models of the world. Those models aren't always perfect; they just need to be more accurate than those of your competition, or more accurate than before, to facilitate the evolution of best practices, whether in medicine, engineering, business, or hand-to-hand combat.

Just as the scientific method guides the march of scientific discovery, the opponent process guides our discovery of truth in combat. It is the correcting mechanism we use in functional martial arts that lets us make gradual improvements in our timing, techniques, and delivery systems. When our proposed solution to a problem doesn't work, it lets us know. When it works well and produces repeatable results, it also lets us know. And when better methods or models evolve, as they inevitably do in any competitive process, the opponent process reveals them too.

As I became more estranged from the JKD community as a whole, little did I know that a revolutionary martial art had been evolving through this very opponent process for decades in Brazil and was just starting to establish a foothold in the United States: Gracie Jiu-Jitsu, or Brazilian Jiu-Jitsu, as it's more commonly known today.[4] I was finally introduced to it by a man named Fabio Santos in the early 1990s.[5]

Fabio had placed a classified advertisement in my local newspaper offering to pay anyone who could beat him up. When my friend showed me the ad, I immediately called the number. *I pay to train at the boxing gym, where I get beat up six days a week. Getting paid would be a nice change*, I thought. I remain thankful to this day that he answered my call.

When he arrived at the gym where I trained, I saw that Fabio, a Brazilian, was a smaller man, maybe 150 pounds. He looked to be in his forties. I was in my early twenties and weighed about 230 pounds. I laid out small foldable mats. He had me throw on gloves. Then he said, "Attack me." I thought I was about to make some easy money.

But I never stood a chance. For him, I was an easy mark. He simply wanted me to know that what he had to teach worked so that I would pay him for lessons. The bounty was just a marketing gimmick—a highly effective one. He wanted me to understand that he could beat me whether I cooperated or not—whether I was bigger and stronger or not. Such was the power of Gracie Jiu-Jitsu. And before teaching me any techniques, he wanted to prove that to me in no uncertain terms. And he did. No matter how many times we repeated the experiment, the results were the same. I'd try to hit him, but he would close the distance between us, clinch me, and take me down. Once on the ground, he would control my body, and there was nothing I could do to hurt him or escape. This happened over and over.

After I showed my genuine admiration for what his art could do, he began to teach me what it was all about, how it worked, and, more importantly, why it worked.

My first lesson started in what is known as "guard." With me on top, Fabio lay on the ground and used his legs to control me. Again and again, he would direct me to attack him. "Try to punch me, try to get past my legs, try whatever you want," he would say. And I quickly found myself being forced to submit, to "tap out," as he choked my neck with his legs or placed me in a position where he could easily break my arms.

Each time he would patiently explain what he had done. Then he would tell me to "relax a bit."

"Relax" is probably the most expressed piece of advice BJJ instructors give to new students. For someone unversed in what the BJJ player is doing on the ground, a feeling of helplessness quickly sets in—something author Sam Harris has compared to drowning.[6] You find yourself in the water with a great white shark, and you can't even dog paddle, let alone swim. That sense of vulnerability lends itself to frustration, which, more often than not, manifests in spastic, strength-based movements by the beginner. That doesn't help. Going harder, faster, and stronger on the ground against a good BJJ player simply means you lose more quickly while getting even more exhausted. It's the equivalent of panicking in the water—it only accelerates your drowning.

At the end of my first lesson, Fabio gave me a piece of advice that I've never forgotten. Something that now, three decades later, I still repeat often to my own students. "Relax," he said. "Jiu-Jitsu is about learning when to use energy and when to rest. And that takes time." Even then, Fabio had already had lots of time under his own belt. One of the original students of Gracie Jiu-Jitsu, he had received his black belt in Brazil from the legendary Rolls Gracie, the older brother of Rickson and Royce Gracie and adopted son of Hélio Gracie.[7]

What I experienced that day truly seemed like magic. I'd been beaten up in enough street fights by wrestlers and trained with enough "grappling" instructors to understand that the ground was my weakness. But I had never witnessed or experienced anything as advanced, technical, and intelligent as this. Gracie Jiu-Jitsu is pure genius. I was captivated by the efficiency of the entire system. Everyone talks about using technique to overcome power, using leverage to overcome strength, using an opponent's own force against them. It is the lofty ideal of arts like Aikido. But never before had I run into a martial art that could actually pull it off.

Gracie Jiu-Jitsu was, in reality, what those other arts falsely claim to be.

As Fabio left that day, he could see the wheels spinning in my head. "You're hooked now," he said. "I can see it. You've got the Jiu-Jitsu bug. Once that bug bites you, there is no turning back."

He called it early.

After only a couple of lessons with Fabio, he received a call from Rorion Gracie, who was starting to make a name for himself as a fight choreographer for films like *Lethal Weapon*.[8] Rorion told Fabio to "prepare himself"—that something big was coming and he needed his help in Southern California. That "something big" would eventually change my own life in profound and unanticipated ways, but at the time, Fabio's departure simply meant a delay in my own grappling development because opportunities for training in Gracie Jiu-Jitsu were so limited back then.

Indeed, very few people knew what Gracie Jiu-Jitsu was at the time. Outside of an article in *Playboy* magazine that featured Rorion promoting the now famous "Gracie Challenge," a $100,000 winner-take-all fight, and some publicity within martial arts journals, Gracie Jiu-Jitsu was something few Americans had even heard of.[9] What I didn't know at the time was that the "something big" Rorion had told Fabio about was the first ever Ultimate Fighting Championship (UFC)—the showcase that would introduce Gracie Jiu-Jitsu to the world, forever change the way the world viewed martial arts, and trigger the fastest growing sport in the world, Mixed Martial Arts.

Before that first UFC in 1993, martial arts still held a mystique among the public at large. Some arts were believed to be truly "deadly," and the idea that you could use them in a competition with "no rules" surely meant that someone was going to die. People's knees would be broken by kicks. Heads would be split. It would be a gruesome spectacle.

Of course, none of this was close to being true, but most of the public, including most practicing martial artists, didn't know that. And Rorion was smart. He understood that his brother Royce would win this competition, which would pit martial artists using various styles against one another. After all, they had been running this experiment for decades in Brazil. And like all good science-based outcomes, that experiment had returned results that could be predictably repeated time and again. Anticipating the flood of students that would arrive at his own school following the inevitable victory of Royce, Rorion was planning ahead, and he knew he'd need Fabio as an instructor to meet demand.

The first UFC may have been the first time such a large-scale and well-publicized martial arts experiment had been run in the United States, but at its core, it was nothing more than an extension of the opponent process long known to all functional martial arts. To illustrate this point, let's apply the idea of the opponent process, the self-correcting mechanism of a resisting opponent, to a specific physical problem within the realm of hand-to-hand combat: a headlock.

You've gotten into a fight. Your opponent is bigger and stronger than you. They tackle you to the ground, grabbing your head and squeezing hard with one arm and hitting you in the face with the other. If you've ever been in a grade-school fight, you've probably experienced this.

What are the best methods for escaping?

You could bite. But what if they're wearing a leather jacket?

What if you've also had enough experience to realize that inflicting pain on your opponent is one of the *least* reliable ways of gaining their compliance? Their adrenaline will be pumping. If you're in a bar or on the street, they may have been drinking tequila or smoking meth. They are not really feeling pain at that moment. What now?

This is a physical problem. And it admits of best answers.

You've made an observation. Being trapped in a headlock can be a problem. Now we need a possible solution, a hypothesis to test. The Gracie family and newer practitioners of BJJ have been conducting this and many other such experiments for decades, while Judo, wrestling, and every other grappling "sports" in which headlocks are allowed have been experimenting with headlock escapes for longer still. There are literally generations of experiments to draw from and improve upon. So while theoretically someone smart enough could come up with a rational technique based on physics and human movement to escape a strong man's headlock without using the opponent process, we already have a suite of techniques that are proven to work.

The planet is filled with old wrestling and other grappling coaches who are overflowing with such information—knowledge built upon generations of competition, centuries of experiments, millions of results that can be measured and repeated. That's where we need to look first for solutions. We take what those who came before us within the field have learned. We adopt and integrate their techniques, which, if what we are talking about is based in reality and not fantasy, will have been discovered through an opponent process, a process of competition, and we continue the evolution. That is how every combat sport on the planet has evolved.

At this point, you might be wondering, if martial arts that have no opponent process don't actually work, how have they managed to survive for so long?

There are many reasons these traditions pop up and remain prevalent. All of those reasons, in one form or another, boil down to incentives. The flourishing science of astronomy has been granting mankind glorious understandings about the nature of the universe since before Galileo Galilee put feather to quill. Yet, we still find the sclerotic tradition of astrology in nearly every newspaper in the world. It is a mistake to assume that because a tradition has existed for a long time, it must be necessarily useful. The only thing we can say about any tradition that has existed for generations is that it is good at replication. And many things that are good at replication are deleterious. We know astrology is silly because we can test it. We can observe its epistemology. And we can say, factually speaking and absent any hesitation, that it is nonsense.[10] So why do so many human beings get something so obvious so wrong?

One of three reasons:

1. They think they already know.
2. They don't know how to know.
3. They don't actually care to know.

First, they may already have their mind made up that astrology works. They think they know it is real. This is usually based on some faulty conception of what constitutes "evidence." But if they are already sure they're right, they will be unlikely to realize how they could be wrong.

Second, they may not yet understand *how* to know. They may think astrology works based on the Barnum effect—briefly, the tendency to see vague descriptions of themselves as accurate, such as in horoscopes.[11] If someone takes the time to explain to them what the effect is, and they then realize that they have been duped, they may be smart enough to change their mind. Which is why I said they do not *yet* know. There is always hope for people afflicted with this type of ignorance. These people have a chance at a better understanding and deserve one.

Third, they simply don't actually care to know what's true or false. There is little we can do about such people. People who don't care about truth can be as stubborn as those who are factually wrong but are convinced they're correct. In both cases, we must follow the basic rule laid out by the late polemicist Christopher Hitchens: "What can be asserted without evidence can also be dismissed without evidence."[12] People in this category must relinquish their seats at the adult table.

As critical as I have been so far, I have still given more credit to traditional martial arts than they deserve. It is not enough to say they stall progress; they are, in fact, "devolutionary."[13] They hold up someone, often some frail, old, mythological figure who is said to have lived years ago, as the pinnacle of martial prowess—despite all evidence to the contrary that has only grown that much more since the first UFC. They are also hypocritical in that they deify this make-believe icon because of the person's legendary fighting skill while deriding combat sports for stressing fighting functionality. All of it, from its posturing to its pecking order, is deeply retrograde.[14]

By contrast, BJJ—and, by extension, MMA—has evolved greatly in the almost thirty years since I started practicing it. And as much as I admire the toughness and technique of Jack Dempsey and other boxing champions from past eras, the modern boxer would eat them alive. This is as it should be. And it is the exact opposite of what you will find within fantasy-based, sclerotic martial arts systems whose methods, forms, techniques, and rituals remain fixed in time.

Without the opponent process, without *competere*, you simply cannot discover or evolve best martial arts practices. You must be willing to challenge and test yourself.

8 The Command of Strength

You cannot truly test yourself or grow
without first making yourself vulnerable.

To truly test yourself is to make yourself vulnerable: emotionally, intellectually, and physically. And by *vulnerable*, I don't mean *weak*. Vulnerability is the willingness to expose areas where your weaknesses may normally hide, precisely because you're strong enough to risk that exposure and to grow from it. This, in turn, creates a cycle that makes you even stronger.[1]

True weakness is being too frightened to allow yourself to be vulnerable, too scared to grow. True strength is the opposite of this. The strength to be vulnerable goes hand in hand with valuing objective truth. Each requires the other. Here are four principles I find useful for this process:

1. Be committed to reality as it is, as opposed to how you want it to be. (Want to know what is true.)

2. Be unwilling to make factual claims about reality that are not based on evidence. (Don't pretend to know what you don't know.)

3. Be willing to proportion your beliefs to the evidence. (Don't exaggerate what you do know.)

4. Be willing to revise your beliefs in the light of new evidence. (Don't ignore contrary evidence even when you think you already know.)

When we let our desire for something to be true supersede our desire to know the truth, we are being greedy. Our behavior suggests that reality isn't enough for us—that we need reality to be the way we wish it were. This is a recipe for suffering.

You can't break through such a cycle unless you are strong enough to be vulnerable. That vulnerability is cultivated in every combat sport, every time you step on the mat or in the ring. If you're not tapping out often in BJJ, you're probably not learning or growing much. Real growth is directly proportional to one's willingness to lose, to miss, to fail—and to engage in the opponent process is to risk failure.

You also can't learn or grow unless you ask questions. You won't ask questions if you're pretending to know the answer.[2] Boy-speak—the adolescent bragging that betrays a lack of maturity on the topic of violence—always signals unfamiliarity with the subject. There are a lot of men who pretend to know a lot about violence. The incentives to pretend to hold such knowledge are often very strong.[3] Acknowledging we don't know or were wrong about something requires bravery. Many ethical systems regard courage as the most important virtue because, without it, you will lack the fortitude to follow other important precepts when it matters—that is, when it isn't easy, when it involves risk.

To ask good, meaningful questions, we also have to fall out of love with *mystery for mystery's sake*. We must turn mysteries into puzzles. Some people would prefer certain mysteries to remain murky. Even if the water is perfectly clear, they will make it as cloudy as possible in an attempt to obscure what would otherwise be in plain view at the bottom. Religious apologists and their spiritual guru counterparts like obscure definitions for the same reason Bigfoot hoaxers like to keep their photos blurry. Until you begin to view mysteries as puzzles, you may not realize the extent of this common practice.

All combat sports, when done properly, teach you to see puzzles instead of roadblocks. Every puzzle has a solution, and the job of a great coach is to help the athlete find it. The opponent process presents challenges. We teach our athletes to see these challenges impersonally, not as enemies, threats, or roadblocks, but as objective questions, puzzles, and locks that have a key.

As discussed in the last chapter, my lessons with Fabio Santos didn't last long. After he moved to San Diego to assist Rorion Gracie, I searched for more exposure to BJJ. I had the good fortune to find it at the hands of BJJ and MMA legend Rickson Gracie.[4] Today, every BJJ instructor on the planet knows the name Rickson Gracie. But at the time, he hadn't yet fought his famous Vale Tudo and Pride Fighting Championship fights in Japan. His younger brother, Royce Gracie, hadn't yet fought in the UFC. And thus, Rickson was still relatively unknown outside of Brazil. A friend who ran a JKD school in a neighboring city was flying him in for a seminar. He invited me to attend.

I walked in on a Sunday to a room that had about two dozen men in it. They were large guys. Most of them were wearing gis, a common martial arts uniform, and they had on black belts. I recognized immediately that these were Judo black belts. These were grapplers. I had exposed myself to high-level boxers. I felt competent when it came to exchanging punches with another man. But wrestlers and grapplers always concerned me. I knew from personal experience just how easy it was to find yourself tackled to the ground. And I also knew that all the boxing, kickboxing, and striking in the world didn't help you when you were down there. A skilled grappler with experience in Judo, high school or college wrestling, or BJJ is a frightening foe. Anyone who says otherwise is either ignorant or foolish.

Rickson had just finished wrestling with someone as I walked in. He was kneeling at the edge of the mat. I was standing at the entrance. He looked up at me. No smile. No gesture. No pleasantries. He was sizing me up. He didn't seem overly large, but he was obviously an athlete. With a lean muscular build, a T-shirt, gi pants, a black belt tied around his waist, and hair that was pulled back into a ponytail, he looked more like a surfer than he did the typical martial arts "master." Those who came to know of the Gracies later through the first UFC saw a tall, skinny, unimpressive-looking Brazilian kid who dominated much larger, much scarier-looking men. But Rickson didn't share the unassuming average-man appearance of his little brother Royce. Rickson looked like a carnivore.

Rickson's eyes went back to the wall of grapplers, to the second man in what I quickly realized was a line. Rickson gestured him over. What I then observed was nothing short of wizardry. The large Judo black belt, a grappler with cauliflower ears and zero signs of intimidation at Rickson's offer, jumped on Rickson. With a few short, effortless-looking motions, Rickson placed him into a chokehold, using only his legs, and the larger man tapped out. An expression of consternation spread across the Judo practitioner's face. He walked, head down, back to his spot on the wall. I could see his wheels turning internally. His eyes said, "What the fuck just happened?!"

Rickson then motioned to the next man, again larger than himself, and did a similar thing, rapidly forcing that man to submit too. His movements were smooth and efficient. No detectable strain showed on his face. He was breathing normally. He appeared calm, always. It was obvious this was easy for him. About the third or fourth man in, I realized something even more awe-inspiring. He was doing all this without using his hands! He went through the entire line, forcing every one of the twenty-odd men to tap out, and he never once used his arms. He kept them folded in front of himself, hands jammed inside his own belt while making quick work of these fully resisting, competent grapplers.

When he finished the line, Rickson turned to me. I was sitting on the opposite end of the mat. I hadn't put myself in the queue. I was bewildered by what I had just observed. It all seemed miraculous to me. I had, at that point in my life, met and watched lots of martial arts "masters" teach seminars. My brief time with Fabio aside, I found almost all of their lessons to be pure nonsense. The seminars were always the same: a demonstration against a cooperating partner, followed by a bit of talk about how deadly it all was, followed by another demonstration against another cooperating partner. It was bullshit. This was entirely different.

"You, my big friend," Rickson said, gesturing toward me. "Come beat me."

I took off my baseball cap. I was wearing sweatpants, a T-shirt, and wrestling shoes, the uniform de jour for JKD people of that time. I walked over and squatted in front of him on the mat.

A tiny smile showed on his face. "For you, my friend, I will take one hand out."

He slipped only his right arm into his belt while reaching out to shake my hand with the other. Why he took one arm out, I don't know. He didn't need it. I leaped at him. I'd seen more than twenty men in a row lose to this guy.[5] I knew all of them had more grappling experience than I did. I figured my best bet would be to lunge on top of him and grab his head as hard as I could. So that's what I did.

I know what Rickson did to me only in retrospect, and that's because I've now trained in the art for three decades. At the time, I had no idea. All I knew was that within what seemed like a few seconds, Rickson had reversed the position, gotten on top of me, and placed me in an armlock. Recognizing I was a newbie on the ground, he put it on gently, and I immediately realized that if I did not tap, my arm would break. I also understood that there was absolutely nothing else I could physically do to stop that from happening. He let go. And seeing my expression, he laughed, not in a mean bullying way, but, rather, in a genuine and kind way. This was remarkable. I was amazed. And he could tell. I never once felt much muscle, much force, or even the hint of rough effort on Rickson's part. His movement was as smooth as the finest Scotch and much more powerful. Everything all the fantasy-based martial arts claimed to be but clearly were not was actually real—and, just as Fabio had predicted, I was forever addicted.

Rickson had performed an experiment with each man he called to the mat. The results were always the same. But if those results had been unique only to Rickson, then we wouldn't be talking today about the discovery, testing, and proof of a method, what you will often hear me refer to as a "delivery system." Instead, we would be talking about an anomaly, one that goes by the name Rickson Gracie. But the delivery system Rickson utilized that day, BJJ, has by this point been tested by many hundreds of thousands of people, and the results continue to point to its clear efficiency and effectiveness.

Few, if any of us, will ever be as good as Rickson was that day—just as few basketball players will ever be as talented as Michael Jordan. But we are not talking about one set of results, one event, one experiment, one legend, one myth, or one individual. We are talking about the delivery system itself, a method of movement that is continually tested, analyzed, refined, and retested. BJJ evolved through the opponent process—*competere*—and it has been proven functional in every hand-to-hand combat experiment yet designed.

I came back from my Rickson Gracie experience like a man who had just seen an alien spacecraft land in the center of town. This was it, guys.

This was the missing link. This was the piece we needed. This was real. This wasn't like Aikido, Kung Fu, Silat, or any of that. There was no choreographed motion. No *"too deadly to apply"* make-believe. No kata. As with Fabio, I hadn't been asked to attack him in a particular way. I had been allowed to try as hard as I could to really beat him—and he effortlessly beat us all. This was the future. This was clearly the way forward.

To my amazement, my enthusiasm wasn't universally shared.

My fellow JKD instructors talked about how hard it would be to take them down in an actual street fight. And, after all, who wants to fight on the ground? The reality that fights often go to the ground whether you want them to or not just didn't register with them.

It was then that I realized the systemic depth of the problem. First, many of them had no real fighting experience and didn't even enjoy the combat-sport aspects, the authentic parts, of what we did. In other words, they had no idea what fighting was. And second, many of them didn't care. They thought they knew all they needed to know, and they didn't care to discover that they didn't know. Developing real fighting skill wasn't their sincere reason for training. It wasn't what inspired them to begin with. In a nutshell, we were not on the same path.

I classify ignorance according to three levels,[6] from least to most dangerous.

Level 1: You don't know something, and you know you don't know it.

Level 2: You don't know something, but you think you do know it.

Level 3: Denial. You refuse to acknowledge the issue at all.

Imagine the following scenario: While on a camping trip, you wake up and find a snake with striped markings in your sleeping bag with you. If you suffer from level 1 ignorance, you don't know whether the snake is poisonous. While it would be better to know, at least you recognize that you don't know and act with extreme caution. If you suffer from level 2 ignorance, you think you know that the snake is harmless. But you're wrong. Depending on how far you are from medical attention, this could end badly for you. If you suffer from level 3 ignorance, you don't want to accept the situation, so you refuse to acknowledge the snake even exists. This probably won't end well, either.

While the third scenario may seem like a far-fetched response to a snake in your sleeping bag, that level of denial occurs all the time when people deal with violence and the violent human predators in our midst. As George Orwell once said,

> We are all capable of believing things which we know to be untrue, and then, when we are finally proved wrong, impudently twisting the facts so as to show that we were right. Intellectually, it is possible to carry on this process for an indefinite time: the only check on it is that sooner or later a false belief bumps up against solid reality, usually on a battlefield.[7]

Here's a story that perfectly illustrates this point: One day, a small-ish man walked into my gym in Portland. This was well after we had established ourselves as SBG. I had a crew of MMA fighters training under me, as well as BJJ students. The man, whose name I honestly can't remember, was angry over things I had said about Wing Chun and tra-ditional Kung Fu styles in an interview. He claimed to be a twenty-year veteran instructor in Wing Chun, and he wanted a challenge match. He was perhaps 5'4" tall and slender. I was at the time an in-shape 260 pounds, and I had more than a foot on him. I said I'd be happy to oblige, but he said he would prefer someone his own size. That was understand-able, and before I could even turn all the way around, there was a group of about a dozen or so smaller MMA fighters all chomping at the bit to get in the ring with this guy.

"It looks like you can have your pick," I said. "You just happened to walk in during team practice, and there are a number of guys your size here who would be happy to get in the ring with you."

The bravado he walked in with vanished as quickly as the blood did from his complexion. I don't think he had expected that reaction. Or, if he had, he had not thought out the potential consequences—until just then. "I'm not ready now," he replied. "I'll be back." He turned and left the gym.

I didn't think too much about this. We didn't do a lot of challenges in Portland, but we had a few.[8] It was never a big deal. In most cases, guys like him never set foot in the gym again. I was, therefore, surprised to receive a phone call at my house about a week later from one of my students, who nervously explained that this same Wing Chun instructor had shown up at the gym again, and he had brought a giant of a man with him. "This guy is about your height but probably 60 lbs. heavier than you," he said. "And he wants to fight!"

I jumped into my car, taping my knuckles as I drove. It took me about fifteen minutes to get there. As I walked in, I saw one of my purple belts in BJJ and an amateur MMA fighter, Rick Davison, in the ring with a guy who looked to be about 6'6" tall and a bit north of 300 lbs. The Wing Chun veteran, apparently his instructor, was in the corner.

Before I could walk from the entrance of the gym to the ring, the big guy was punched, taken down, mounted, and arm-locked. Then I saw the big guy step out and the Wing Chun instructor step in. Rick repeated the process. Punch, takedown, and submission. The instructor then stepped out, and the big guy stepped back in. Rick stayed in. Same result: punch, takedown, punch, and rear-naked choke finish. I stood on the apron of the ring and watched. Rick was having fun. One of my other students was filming it. I don't think Rick ever took a single punch.

The large man actually had a good attitude about the whole experience. How could this small guy, Rick, who was maybe 165 lbs., beat him like he was a little child? He was smiling, almost joyful. But his instructor was not of the same mindset. The anger and frustration on his face were unmistakable. He clearly thought his Wing Chun would work. Rick had allowed them to wear MMA gloves, which are designed so that fingers remain free to grab. The common excuse that they could not use their "trapping" hands just was not there for them, as it would have been with regular-sized boxing gloves.

I walked over to the instructor while Rick was manhandling the big guy in the center of the ring one final time. "Pretty amazing, isn't it?" I remarked. He had beaten each of them at least half a dozen times by this point, totaling maybe fifteen minutes.

"He's just doing takedowns. He doesn't want to stand and strike with us," the small Wing Chun instructor replied.

A bad case of ignorance had now become full-blown delusion. And delusion is the most dangerous form of ignorance.[9]

The big guy may have been a victim of level 1 or 2 ignorance. I don't know if he expected to win when he walked into the academy. He may have been unsure. But after the first five or six losses in a row, he accepted the reality that Rick knew something he did not yet know—in this case, how to fight. But the small instructor, while afflicted with a bad case of ignorance (level 2) when he walked in, moved straight down to level 3, and that is always very dangerous.

"I don't think you understand," I said to him. "Rick is taking you down to be nice to you. You're mistaking his compassion for weakness. You don't want to do that."

"Bullshit," he said.

Now, he had pissed me off. He had walked into my school, challenged my integrity and that of my students, returned with a much larger man, been granted his trial by fire, been dealt with compassionately, and was still too pig-headed to realize the truth.

"Don't take him down this time," I yelled to Rick as the little guy climbed back in.

The Wing Chun instructor's eyes went wide.

Rick was not as skilled a striker as he is now. But he could still box. And he threw his hands mercilessly until the Wing Chun instructor dropped down to his knees. "Okay, okay, you don't have to just punch!" the instructor yelled.

They touched gloves again. Rick, being kind, took him down again and mounted him. The instructor immediately lifted his arms straight into the air, offering an armbar. For those not familiar with the significance of this, it meant only one thing: he did not want to be punched in the face while mounted, so he was giving up a submission to Rick. This angered me even more.

Keep in mind what had been happening. Every time there had been a new start, the little guy and his big friend would swing as hard as they could, trying to hit Rick in the face. Granted, their Wing Chun striking style lacked the knockout power found in, say, Western boxing, and thus their hands were not really that dangerous, but still, it wasn't their ability that mattered but their intent. They had been trying to knock Rick out, while Rick, being kind, had only been submitting them with joint locks and chokes.[10] In reality, however, he could have simply sat on their chests and beaten them both unconscious. Neither had the knowledge or skill to escape from his mount. Up to this point, it had been only Rick's mercy that had saved their faces from demolition.

"From now on, make them submit with strikes," I called out to Rick as they started again.

The moment the little guy heard that, he raised his arms up. "I'm done," he said as he stormed off to the bathroom.

His large student sat on the ring and talked to Rick and me. He wanted to know our schedule and whether he would be welcome in the gym. This experience had been an eye-opener for him. And honestly, he seemed like a genuinely nice guy.

"Of course you would be welcome," I said. "We have beginner classes every day." I then asked how long he had been training Wing Chun.

"Ten years," he replied.

Wing Chun contains the typical mythology present in all sclerotic traditions, including various fanciful creation myths. It also has a hierarchy and a whole host of anecdotal stories—just like Aikido, Silat, Escrima, and every traditional martial art on the planet.[11] But, and this is an important point, if these traditions are challenged, you will only ever hear the same three sequential responses from their guardians: (1) it works; (2) it may not work, but it's useful; and (3) you are a [insert ad hominem here]. These responses are embellished with three forms of "evidence": (1) anecdotal stories; (2) an appeal to authority; and (3) the claim that what's being discussed is "beyond empirical testing." While martial arts woo-woo is an extremely useful vehicle to help teach people how to calibrate their own bullshit meters, we have to remember that all forms of nonsense and superstition follow this same truth-avoidance formula.

The burden of defending an image and a position that is built upon delusion isn't, in the long run, going to be healthy. The basic truth is this: there are better and worse ways to learn how to fight, and given the right training, anyone can be taught to fight. And that includes you.

I imagine the Wing Chun student felt a bit like the way I had felt years earlier when I first trained with Fabio and watched Rickson tap out a room full of large men without bothering to take his hands out of his belt. The experience must have felt like magic to him. Yet he obviously knew there was nothing supernatural or mystical about Rick's abilities. He was simply experiencing what martial arts were supposed to be. Indeed, the ease with which Rick had handled him and his instructor was no accident, because the gym they had walked into that day was inspired in large part by my early experiences with Fabio and Rickson.

It was also established in opposition to the prevailing martial arts environment of the time. Many people have asked me over the decades why I decided to name my school Straight Blast Gym. To understand the meaning behind the name, you first have to understand the type of martial arts instruction then being offered elsewhere. When I left my JKD practice to open something new, something that had not been done before, there was no such thing as an "MMA gym." Those did not yet exist. Everything was called an "academy"—for example, the name of the school I was leaving was Portland Martial Arts Academy. And the training methods at such schools tended to revolve around, as I have said, the replication and memorization of physical patterns. These were not "gyms." This is why I intentionally used the word "gym." Gym denotes a place you go to sweat, to push yourself, to work out. Gyms were not about collecting certificates, or clicking sticks together, or discussing magic spells. They were places of physical exertion. So gym it was.

Next, I chose the term "straight blast," which is a striking technique initially brought over by Bruce Lee, modified by the JKD community, and later modified again into a more powerful boxing-related technique. The straight blast was one of the few techniques from that old-school JKD training that we still used in full-contact sparring. By prefacing "gym" with these two words, I meant to communicate that this would be a place where martial arts techniques, and Bruce Lee's original idea of training and fighting at all ranges, would actually be tested—and questioned—rigorously and nondogmatically.

The first Straight Blast Gym, a tiny 800-square-foot room, opened its doors in Keizer, Oregon, in 1992. I finally had a place I could run my own way, a place to discover truth. It is what Bruce Lee was searching for, and it is what SBG was created to find: truth in combat.

Section Three: Threats

The Who, What, and Where of Danger

"A wise man proportions his belief to the evidence."
—David Hume

9 The Real Bogeyman under the Bed

*You have the power to dramatically increase
or decrease your odds of survival.*

On a warm Sunday evening in Connecticut in July 2007, twenty-six-year-old Joshua Komisarjevsky spotted Jennifer Hawke-Petit and her eleven-year-old daughter, Michaela, picking up dinner items at a local grocery store. Michaela liked to cook for the family, which also included her father, Dr. William Petit, and her seventeen-year-old sister, Hayley. As they settled in for the evening that night, none of them realized that Komisarjevsky had followed Jennifer and Michaela home and that he was texting his friend, forty-four-year-old Steven Hayes, about them.

At 3 a.m., Komisarjevsky and Hayes entered the family's stately Colonial home through an unlocked door. They found William asleep in a chair on the first floor. After standing silently over William for a moment, the intruders swung a baseball bat into William's face. They then bound him before ultimately tying him to a post in the basement.

With William restrained and incapacitated, they went upstairs, where they found Jennifer and her two daughters asleep. They woke them, tied them to their respective beds with rope and pantyhose, and started to ransack the house. Komisarjevsky then returned to Michaela's room, where he cut off her clothes with a pair of scissors and, as she lay helpless, raped her. He snapped a few photos of her with his cell phone. By this point, Jennifer had been moved to the living room, where Hayes raped and strangled her to death.

When Hayes and Komisarjevsky were finished with their fun, they dowsed the dead mother with gasoline. They then poured gasoline over Hayley and Michaela—the two girls still strapped to their beds, very much alive—and set them on fire. Of the four family members, only William survived. Bound and bloodied, he had managed to escape out of a basement door shortly before the flames engulfed the house.[1]

The two predators had met in rehab. Komisarjevsky had been breaking into homes since he was fourteen. He was fond of wearing night-vision goggles and latex gloves. Hayes, meanwhile, was a smash-and-dash car thief. He liked to break car windows with a rock and run off with whatever was on the seat. Both men received the death penalty for their crimes that night, but due to subsequent legislation and a ruling by the Connecticut Supreme Court that put an end to capital punishment in the state, they remain alive. Both are serving six consecutive life sentences for the rapes and murders. Hayes has since made news by revealing in an interview that he is transgender and is receiving hormone therapy in prison.[2] Speaking about their acts that night in an earlier interview, Hayes claimed that, a "couple of minutes" aside, he and Komisarjevsky were "nice to everyone." He added, "I was trying to keep people calm. I got them water. I let them go to the bathroom."[3]

It's hard to imagine that there are adult males among us who, given the chance, would tie an eleven-year-old girl to a bed, rape her, take pictures of her, and then burn her alive. But there are. That rightly scares many people. I don't want to frighten you. What I'm after here is truth. While animals like this exist, and I will discuss how to protect yourself and your family from them in great detail, they are not the bogeymen you should be most concerned with.

In order to assess real-world threats to our health and safety, we *always* need to consider our own habits, behavior, and environment when thinking about general probabilities. With this in mind, one of the questions I often ask students at self-defense seminars is why they are interested in training in self-defense in the first place.

Looking around the room, I always see a lot of quizzical expressions. "Because I want to be able to defend myself," someone will offer.

"But why do you want to defend yourself?" I respond.

Someone will usually answer in a perplexed manner and say something like, "So I don't get hurt" or "So I can go home to my family."

"So you can live longer?" I ask.

The students in the crowd nod their heads in agreement, wondering why I am stating the blindingly obvious. "Then," I continue, "why are some of you fifty pounds overweight? Why don't you always buckle your seatbelts? Why are you constantly slamming down forty ounces of sugar? Why do some of you still smoke?"

It isn't unheard of to stumble into a street-fighting seminar—in which people are talking about tactics, ammunition, and serial killers—to find the room full of grossly out-of-shape paranoids, all pretending that their main motive for being there is to live longer. The irony and incongruence are telling. Men often try to cultivate a fearsome *image* based on what they think a person who is capable of handling and surviving violence looks like, but they often do so for reasons that don't have anything to do with actual, real-world threats. If they truly wanted to live longer, they would proportion their energy and behavior to the risks. Almost all of us are far more likely to die of heart disease or a car accident than to be killed by a knife-wielding sociopath in some dark alley. If you don't put physical fitness at the top of your self-preservation list, self-preservation probably isn't the thing that really motivates you.[4]

I didn't fully appreciate this fact until after I opened the first branch of SBG, when my sole focus became functional fighting: boxing, grappling, Brazilian Jiu-Jitsu, and full-contact sparring, with and without weapons. I felt liberated because I was no longer burdened with having to teach the impractical movements and techniques that served as ornamentation in much of the Jeet Kune Do and traditional martial arts world. Yet, all my former JKD associates gave me the same warning: people don't want to sweat, get hit, and wrestle on the ground; people want certificates, patterns, uniforms, and rituals.[5] What I was doing was, from a business perspective, suicidal, they told me. I believed them. Newly married, with a pregnant wife, I even took on a full-time job with the assumption that I would have to treat my teaching solely as a hobby. I resigned myself to such a life because I could not bring myself to teach anything I didn't think was real. Maybe I wouldn't be able to make an actual living by teaching, I figured, but at least I would be doing something *true*.

Thankfully, within a few months, all that changed. Word spread. My 800-square-foot room was soon packed. There was no such thing as a Mixed Martial Arts coach back then. Indeed, there were no MMA gyms of any kind in the area when I started SBG, so students drove from downtown Portland and Vancouver, Washington—forty-five minutes each way—several nights a week to take part in classes. It turned out that a lot of people wanted the same thing I did: reality.

Yet, in those early days, it didn't look like MMA would stick around as a professional sport, at least not to me. As I was getting my gym off the ground, the sport itself was on the verge of collapse due to a powerful political campaign against it. Notably, Arizona Senator (and later presidential candidate) John McCain famously called it "human cockfighting."[6] Because we were learning as we went along, training was much rougher in those early years. We evolved over time. As my own skills increased, better training, drilling, and teaching methods started to emerge. Best practices revealed themselves through *competere*. Every class was a little better than the one before. One core lesson that was repeated day in and day out was just how important physical fitness is to actual fighting.

Why has every successful military fighting force known to man— from the ancient Greeks and Romans to the modern Combat Applications Group (CAG), Navy Sea, Air, and Land (SEAL) Teams, and Special Air Service (SAS)—made physical fitness a priority? There are five primary reasons:

1. When you run out of physical energy in combat, you are as good as dead.

2. Physical exertion helps mimic the way your body will feel when it is actively engaged in a fight and your adrenal glands are raging.

3. Proper physical training tests your mind, heart, and body.

4. Excellent fitness allows a warrior to travel longer, faster, and farther.

5. A fit soldier will be able to fight longer, faster, and harder than an enemy who isn't in the same shape.

While the average person doesn't necessarily require that same elite level of fitness when training in a martial art, we also have to maintain bodies like athletes, or we will eventually break, succumb to injury, or simply gas out during a long and strenuous match. And sure, when you move perfectly and completely outclass your opponent, you can achieve a lot without much exertion, just as Rickson had on the day I met him. But even with his world-class technical ability and proficiency, Rickson still committed himself to an intense hour-long calisthenics routine every morning in order to maintain peak fitness. I attempted to do it with him once, failed miserably, and was sore for a week. When I asked him if he ever took a break, he replied, "I cannot take a break. If I do, they will catch up to me." I didn't understand who *they* were until years later when I realized that, when he said *they*, he meant *everyone*. But even for those of us who would never be able to catch Rickson, a commitment to some level of physical fitness does a lot more than improve our performance and health. It also improves our quality of life.[7]

I once gave a seminar in New York City, and, as I was coming back from lunch, I ended up walking behind a couple of the students from the seminar, young men who had told me earlier that day that their main motive for attending the seminar was to learn how to defend themselves on the street. Yet, a couple of hours later, here they were, blindly wandering through the packed city streets, totally unaware of their surroundings. As I heard them discuss color-coding options for various forms of imagined threats, I actually had to put my arm out to stop one of them from being killed by oncoming traffic. Feeling rather annoyed, I dropped my *why-are-you-eating-chips-while-driving-without-your-seatbelt-on* speech as soon as the seminar resumed, only to realize that an obese man was sitting in the audience. He was attending my class in an effort to get into shape—he wanted to do exactly what I was telling everyone to do. I grew up knowing what it's like to be picked on, so I've always felt mortified when someone makes an unkind comment about a stranger who may be within earshot. I softened my message a bit after that. It's never made sense to me why some people make fun of morbidly obese people who are jogging or exercising in a gym. Isn't that what they should be doing? The answer is obvious because it's what we all should be doing.[8]

Most human beings are terrible at assessing risks accurately.[9] We tend to pay a great deal of unwarranted attention to risks that are both beyond our control and highly unlikely. Terrorist attacks, airplane crashes, nuclear power plant disasters, and viruses like Ebola all occupy far more space in our minds than is justified for people who are not actively engaged in jobs meant to combat those threats. We pay far less attention to things like smoking, poor diet, lack of exercise, and car accidents—all of which are far more likely to kill us and all of which we have much more control over. If we are serious about self-defense and self-preservation, we need to recognize this human tendency and direct our efforts, energy, and time toward things that we can immediately affect or control.

Let's look at what actually kills us (see table 1).

The data vary depending on your age, gender, location, and other factors, but the main causes of death that we face tell an important sto-

Table 1. Causes of death in the United States by percentage of total deaths, 2019

CAUSE OF DEATH	PERCENTAGE
Heart disease	23.1
Malignant neoplasms	21.0
Accidents	6.1
Chronic lower respiratory diseases	5.5
Cerebrovascular diseases	5.3
Alzheimer disease	4.3
Diabetes mellitus	3.1
Nephritis, nephrotic syndrome, and nephrosis	1.8
Influenza and pneumonia	1.7
Suicide	1.7
Chronic liver disease and cirrhosis	1.6
Septicemia	1.3
Essential hypertension and hypertensive renal disease	1.3
Parkinson disease	1.2
Pneumonitis due to solids and liquids	0.7
All other causes	20.5

Source: Jiaquan Xu et al., "Deaths: Final Data for 2019," *National Vital Statistics Report* 70, no. 8 (U.S. Department of Health and Human Services, July 26, 2021), 10, www.cdc.gov/nchs/data/nvsr/nvsr70/nvsr70-08-508.pdf.

ry.[10] In the United States, less than 1 percent of the population dies in a typical year. Thus, with a population of 330 million people, we might expect just over 3 million deaths per year.[11] The fifteen leading causes of death in the United States account for nearly 80 percent of all deaths in the country. Looking at data from 2019, to choose the last year for which pre-pandemic data is available, we see that more than 23 percent of all deaths were a result of the biggest killer, heart disease. Deaths from our number two killer, cancer, stood at 21 percent. The two biggest preventable risk factors in both of these categories are smoking and obesity. At number three were accidents, or unintentional injuries, which accounted for just over 6 percent of all deaths. Speeding, drunk driving, and failing to wear a seatbelt are all obvious risk factors in this category. I could go on, but the important point here is this: you can reduce your chances of death across all fifteen leading categories of death by simply monitoring your environment, modifying your behavior, and staying active. Yes, some things are out of our control, such as hereditary factors and age, so lifestyle changes do not guarantee good health or longevity. But, even if the behaviors under our control—not smoking, eating healthful food, exercising, etc.—only increased our odds of survival in any given year by 20 percent, that would be of substantial benefit statistically speaking.

Notice what didn't make the top fifteen causes of death for an average American in 2019? Homicide.[12] If we add up *all* murders, including terrorist attacks, they accounted for roughly 0.67 percent of all deaths in the United States that year.[13] The bottom line is this: if you're not focused on staying healthy and in shape, you're not serious about self-preservation—no matter how many self-defense seminars you attend or guns you buy. Pontificating about which type of ammunition has greater knockdown power or which form of deadly martial art will render a more lethal strike will not statistically increase your chances of survival.

An obese, out-of-shape chain-smoker who doesn't wear his seatbelt, drives fast, drinks thirty-two-ounce sodas, and spends his time worrying about what type of firearm he should carry isn't really concerned about self-preservation. He's worried about humiliation. He doesn't want to be beaten up in front of other people. The cure for this guy isn't another street-fighting class or a concealed carry permit. That won't save him from the bogeyman under his bed. The real solution to what threatens this man is a solid regime of combat athletics and exercise.

10 The Predator Next Door
(or Already Inside)

Your home is your haven—don't invite the vampires in.

Once our behavior and lifestyle choices have demonstrated that we are sincerely motivated by a desire for self-preservation, we can genuinely begin to talk about the boogeyman that causes us to lock our doors and keep our porch lights lit: *human predators.*

When it comes to homicide, there are three key things to remember—no matter where you live. First, you are more likely to be killed by a family member than by a stranger. Second, the homicide victim personally knew the killer in roughly 80 percent of homicide cases in which the relationship between them could be determined. Third, the killer is male in more than nine out of ten homicides.[1] Yet, many precautions taken in the name of personal safety focus exclusively on threats from outsiders, even though strangers commit only 20 percent of homicides in which an offender is identified (in roughly half of all homicides, the relationship between the killer and victim is unknown).[2] Basic safety measures against external threats, such as deadbolts, alarm systems, and motion-activated lighting, will do nothing to stop our closest predatory threats—the ones who freely enter the home.

According to one Bureau of Justice Statistics study, the average American's overall lifetime odds of being murdered is about 1 in 133.[3] This rate certainly isn't negligible, but if we know that strangers account for one in five murders in which the relationship between the offender and victim is known, and family, friends, and acquaintances account for the remaining four out of five murders, this means the lifetime odds of being killed by a stranger might be as low as 1 in 665 and the lifetime odds of being killed by someone you know might be as high as 1 in 166—all else being equal.[4] Therein lies a problem. It isn't the masked stranger waiting in a dark alleyway who is most likely to kill you—it is the man you think you know and invite into your own home.

Don't invite the vampires into your sanctuary.

If you're a woman, this is an even more salient point. Female homicide victims are far more likely than male homicide victims to be related to or in a relationship with the offender, and females are far less likely than males to be killed by a stranger.[5] In fact, when a stranger commits a murder, the victim is male more than 80 percent of the time.[6] Roughly 50 percent of women murdered in the United States are killed by intimate partners, whether husbands or boyfriends—if not current then former ones.[7]

Yet, on balance, women in a stable, monogamous marriage are generally far safer than their single counterparts, at least in the West. According to one Department of Justice study, never-married women are more than three times more likely to be victims of violent crime than married women,[8] and married women as a whole are less likely to be assaulted, robbed, or raped than single women.[9] For young single women, life outside the family home can be particularly dangerous when it comes to the threat of sexual violence.[10] This is especially true when alcohol or drugs are involved.[11]

Time and again, I have watched, attended, or read a transcript from a women's self-defense seminar only to discover that the instructor is focused exclusively on the violent stranger in a ski mask or the psychopath in the parking garage. While the instructor inevitably provides solid information and sound advice to the attendees for those specific scenarios, they fail to make any mention of the greater potential threat women face: men already in and around the home.

This failure to prioritize is especially true when it comes to thinking about and discussing threats to children. When I was a kid in the 1970s and 80s, I thought the world was full of kidnappers. You couldn't open a paper or turn on the TV without hearing about a kidnapping or a child abduction. Stories about missing children from families that weren't rich or famous began making national news in the United States for the first time, and Hollywood cranked out television shows like *Starsky and Hutch* and *CHiPs* and films like *Dirty Harry* and *Death Wish* that often revolved around a kidnapping or child killing. Even at breakfast, kids across the United States came to be reminded every day of the dangers that awaited them outside their doors as milk cartons began displaying photos of missing children—an analog version of today's Amber alerts. But even when I was nine, when violent crime, including kidnapping, was statistically more prevalent than it is today, the odds were significantly higher that I'd suddenly die from cardiac arrest than that I'd be kidnapped by a stranger.

In any given year, roughly a half-million missing children cases are recorded in the United States. Well over 90 percent of these cases get resolved the same year, either because the child returns home or because law enforcement locates the missing child. Of the children reported missing in the United States, nearly 95 percent of them will be runaways. In far fewer cases (around 1 percent), they will have been taken by a non-custodial parent. Only about 0.1 percent of missing children—one out of every thousand children reported missing—will have been abducted by a stranger. In 2021, there were 331 such cases recorded in the United States.[12]

Of those children abducted by a stranger, the majority will make it home. In any given year, somewhere between 40 and 150 won't. Three out of four of those killed will be murdered within three hours—usually after being abused, raped, or tortured. Nearly nine out of ten will be killed within the first twenty-four hours. The typical victim in such cases is a white girl just over the age of eleven. The child will have been abducted within a quarter mile from her single-family home, where she had been leading a normal life in a low-risk family. The typical child abduction murderer, meanwhile, is a single, white, unemployed twenty-seven-year-old male who lives with his parents.[13]

I don't want to minimize the importance of these children or the terrible suffering they and their families endure. Nothing would horrify me more as a father than knowing my child had been abducted, raped, and murdered by a stranger. But for the purposes of assessing risks and taking steps to protect ourselves and our families, the key point is this: 99.8 percent of all missing children are found alive.[14] As a young teen pouring milk onto my Frosted Flakes and staring at yet another photo of a missing kid, I wish I had known that.

Here's the scarier fact of the matter: roughly 67 percent of all murdered children are killed by a family member.[15] The majority of these cases are classified as filicide, the killing of a child by a parent, stepparent, or parental figure. It's popularly believed that stepparents are more likely to kill a child than biological parents. We see some evidence of this in our fellow primates,[16] and there are evolutionary explanations for why this might be the case.[17] Indeed, children who live in a home with a stepfather or surrogate father may be ten times more likely to suffer abuse and eight times more likely to suffer neglect than those who live with both biological parents.[18] And according to psychologists Martin Daly and Margo Wilson, a child is up to *a hundred times* more likely to be killed by a stepparent than by a genetic parent.[19]

Yet, other researchers argue that this so-called Cinderella effect is either vastly overstated or nonexistent, at least when it comes specifically to filicide.[20] For example, one group of researchers found that the raw number of filicides committed by stepfathers and genetic fathers are roughly equal, which suggests stepfathers are roughly five times more dangerous than biological fathers when we account for the proportion of children who live with stepfathers versus biological fathers.[21] But other researchers who conducted the first comprehensive study of filicide in the United States, which identified 94,146 filicide cases between 1976 and 2007, found that stepparents were *no more likely to kill* a child than biological parents. Interestingly, the study did find that "the proportion of biological children killed was inversely related to victim age (i.e., 78.6% of adult victims, 87.4% of child/adolescent victims, and 98.2% of infant victims were biological offspring)" and that stepparents were twice as likely to use a firearm, suggesting stepparents and biological parents may on average have slightly different motives for killing. More significantly and perhaps shockingly for the purposes of determining personal risk, the study determined that filicide accounted for 15 percent of *all* murders committed during that thirty-year period.[22]

Let that disturbing fact settle in.

The intentional killing of a child by a parent, stepparent, or parental figure accounted for nearly one in six of all murders over the course of three decades. Two-thirds of the victims were age six or less, and dads and moms made up 57 percent and 43 percent of the offenders, respectively. The mothers who killed were typically younger than the fathers who killed.[23] Notably, when it came to infants, dads and moms killed at equal rates.

Infanticide is arguably the only area in which women are on par with men in terms of their rates of violence. All other forms of physical violence, including all other violent crime, is overwhelmingly a male problem.[24] Indeed, when it comes to other forms of intrafamily homicide—whether patricide, matricide, fratricide, or sororicide, a teenage boy in the family is roughly five times more likely to be the killer than a teenage girl in the family.[25]

Facts:

1.   Most violent attackers are male.

2.   Most violent attackers are aged 15–34.

3.   Most violent attackers are known to their victims.

Despite the overall statistics, people tend to worry more about violence from strangers than from family members or acquaintances. Why? One possible explanation is that they simply do not know the data. People commonly see violence as being external to their family and social circle, something perpetrated by violent outsiders—strangers. They thus don't consider closer possible threats already in their lives. Another possible explanation is that they do know the data but that they assess the data in the context of their own lives. After all, if no one in your immediate family or circle of friends is a genuine threat, strangers may indeed represent the greater danger to you. In short, all else *is not* equal—your age, location, gender, class, race, marital status, and job all matter for determining your overall homicide risk.

The Petit family didn't have any close acquaintances who were recidivist violent criminals. They didn't have buddies frequenting their home between stints in prison. The young Petit daughters were not drug addicts who brought their new boyfriends over to visit. And the Petits didn't live in a low-income, high-crime neighborhood. If the father of the family, a doctor, had sought out self-defense classes, attended a self-defense lecture, or looked for material on the topic, he wouldn't have been unwarranted in his desire to focus on outside predators. His family wasn't typical of the majority of victims of violent crime. One of the reasons self-defense experts focus on violence by strangers is that their audiences do not see themselves as fitting into a troubled demographic.

Even if the above description of the Petit family describes your family as well, it is vitally important to know the basic facts about violent crime as they relate to all aspects of your life. Without having factual information about the forms of violence you might one day face, or the types of predators you might one day encounter, you will never acquire the practical knowledge required to defend yourself, no matter the context.

When violence is committed, it has identifiable features that reflect, among other things, the underlying motive, the choice of target, and the psychology of the offender. For the purposes of self-defense, I divide violence into three major forms. These forms of violence are listed below from least to most common:

> *Moralistic violence:* violence that is motivated by ideological or religious beliefs and committed in the name of some cause.
>
> *Instrumental violence:* violence that is rationally planned and designed to achieve a specific goal.
>
> *Expressive violence:* violence that occurs spontaneously and represents an aggressive nonrational response to tension or emotion.[26]

These three major forms of violence line up well with the three major categories of human predators that I refer to when discussing self-defense, listed below from least to most common and from most to least dangerous.

> *Moralistic criminals*
>
> *Violent criminals*
>
> *Character-disordered individuals/criminals*

Although these forms of violence and categories of predators are not mutually exclusive, each is identified by certain characteristics. For example, when it comes to large-scale murder, the moralistic form of violence definitely wins the prize. Moralistic criminals commit violence for what they consider *moral* reasons and are thus often willing to inflict tremendous widescale damage.[27] Violence committed by Islamist radicals, Timothy McVeigh, and the Unabomber all fit into this category. While dangerous at the macro level, this form of violent attack is the least likely to occur to an average citizen living in most parts of the industrialized world.[28] Although individuals or groups are at times directly targeted in brutal and shocking fashion by terrorists due to their profession, profile, religion, nationality, or location,[29] the average Western citizen living in an average town is so unlikely to experience a random terrorist attack that the stress incurred from worrying about one is arguably more damaging to their individual health than any potential future attack. If you're in a profession or in a location that puts you at high risk, you're likely already taking sensible protective steps against moralistic criminal actors. When traveling internationally, research the areas you'll be visiting and monitor relevant travel advisories.[30] Otherwise, let the professionals in the military, FBI, CIA, and other international law enforcement and intelligence agencies worry about the terrorists whose ideology informs their choice of targets and attacks.[31]

For purposes of prioritizing, know that the assailants most likely to target you and your family directly will not be moralistic criminals acting for some religious or ideological cause. They will be violent criminals and/or character-disordered individuals. Violent criminals are those professional criminals who use violence primarily for instrumental purposes—that is, in pursuit of a specific objective. They account for most of the violent attacks committed by strangers. Instrumental violence committed by violent criminals tends to arouse more fear and attract more media interest than the expressive violence of character-disordered individuals. The attack on the Petit family falls in this former category, which is often marked by raw brutality. The crimes committed by Komisarjevsky and Hayes that night and morning may have had many expressive elements, but the violence was instrumental. They planned the home invasion with clear goals in mind.

Character-disordered individuals exhibit antisocial behaviors but rarely show their true malevolent or even violent faces at first. They usually enter your life disguised as sheep and may not have yet even been arrested or committed any prosecutable crimes. There are many such individuals, and they are thus encountered frequently. They may be related to you, but they will always be deleterious to your well-being. The most common type of violence they use is *expressive*—the spontaneous release of tension through aggressive behavior. But their violence can sometimes also be *instrumental*—the utilization of force to achieve a specific goal. At the more extreme end of the character-disordered spectrum are *sociopaths* and *psychopaths*. Many forensic psychologists, psychiatrists, and criminologists use those two terms interchangeably, while others draw a distinction between the two, and some don't use them at all.[32] For the purposes of this book, I make no real distinction between these terms.

In terms of frequency, no form of violence ranks higher than expressive violence. It is spontaneous and erupts in the heat of the moment.[33] Yet, when this type of violence leads to murder, it often represents the final beating in a long string of brutal, emotional, and violent outbursts by someone within the home. In such cases, the killers are generally not lifelong violent criminal actors. They are rage-filled primates, the product of millions of years of evolution, doing what we animals have done since the species began: killing in the heat of passion or killing off potential mate poachers who have encroached on what we believe to be the source of that passion.

While visiting a prison to transport a criminal, my father once noticed that the prisoners were wearing different colored jumpsuits. The ones freely walking around the prison grounds, doing yard work and maintenance, were all wearing yellow. When he asked a guard why, he was told that yellow was the color given to murderers. "Why would the murderers be the ones allowed to roam freely?" my father asked. "They're the least likely to be violent," the guard responded. "Most kill once, in the heat of the moment, and don't do it again. It's those who are in here for assault and armed robbery you have to worry about." Put another way, the ones who committed instrumental violence are the ones most likely to be planning and plotting.

When it comes to violent crimes against children, character-disordered individuals in or around the home represent the greatest overall threat. A staggering 1 out of every 7 girls and 1 out of every 25 boys in the United States will be sexually abused by the time they are eighteen.[34] Approximately 30 percent of the time, the offender is a family member, and more than 50 percent of the time, the offender is someone the victim knows who is outside of the family, whether family friends, boyfriends of the mother, babysitters, priests, or neighbors. Only in 11 percent of cases is the offender a stranger to the child.[35] As with most violent crimes, child sexual abuse is committed primarily by men. One study based on the National Incident-Based Reporting System found that males are the offender in 96 percent of such cases reported to law enforcement and that the attacker is over the age of eighteen 77 percent of the time.[36] As already noted, children living with a single mother or a mother with a live-in boyfriend who is not genetically related to them are at much greater risk.[37]

Outside of the United States, the core threats and risks to women and children remain the same—no matter the country—but a lack of legal protections or a cultural or religious tradition that sanctions abuse can create situations in which abuse is neither recognized nor punished, making it difficult to determine the extent of violent and sexual crime against women and children in various parts of the world.

Consider, for example, large Islamic countries like Pakistan and Iran, where it is legal for a girl to be married once she's had her first menstrual period, which can occur in a child as young as eight.[38] In many Arab states, women and girls who report being raped are themselves put on trial for "lewdness" or adultery and cannot secure a conviction without four male witnesses or a confession from the rapist.[39] In Saudi Arabia, women are considered the property of their husbands or father.[40] And in countries like the United Arab Emirates, live-in-maids have little recourse if they're assaulted by their employers.[41] Then we have places like India, where child marriage is illegal yet rampant and rape is legal within marriage,[42] and China, where the communist regime rarely releases crime statistics and likely fabricates the data it does release. And finally, we have impoverished nations like Guatemala, Equatorial Guinea, Sudan, and Nicaragua, to name just a few, where corruption, lack of resources, and nonexistent infrastructure make the recording and reporting of reliable crime data extremely challenging.

All of these issues and more make compiling an accurate worldwide list of the violence against women and children a task that ranges somewhere between extraordinarily difficult and impossible. But for the purposes of our discussion—personal self-defense—we don't need precise figures. Anyone with an ounce of common sense should know to proceed with caution when visiting impoverished nations like Sudan, El Salvador, or Liberia—no matter their gender. And the fact that women do not have the same legal rights in Islamic theocracies as they do in a liberal democracy should be all the information you need in order to stay wary when visiting those countries. But what about developed democracies—or, more specifically, a region like Scandinavia, with its world-leading standard of living and quality of life and highly touted political and social progressiveness? Are those countries safe?

No. Safety is always relative. Wherever you find humans, you will find human predators. Here's the key point: don't be fooled by glossy brochures or glowing travel articles into thinking you are ever completely safe, no matter where you are, because that's when you let your guard down and risk inviting a vampire in. Indeed, the highest rates of child rape in the Western world are found—surprisingly to many—in Scandinavia.[43] And within Scandinavia, Iceland faces an epidemic of sexual violence, with twice as many reported rapes per capita as other Nordic countries.[44] According to a survey conducted in 2018, a quarter of Icelandic women have been raped or sexually assaulted.[45] In Europe overall, the reported figure is 1 in 10.[46] Iceland's consistently high rates of violence against women—and its legal system that doesn't seem to take such violence with the seriousness it deserves—should be a major embarrassment and a major wake-up call for all good Icelandic men.[47] Reported sex abuse against children is also much higher in Iceland than in other Nordic nations.[48] One study showed that more than one-third of Icelandic girls and nearly 18 percent of Icelandic boys are sexually abused before their eighteenth birthday.[49]

Iceland is a tiny island in the middle of the North Atlantic most people will never visit, but I mention it here because—unlike places like Pakistan, Honduras, and India, where most visitors know the risks—most people who associate Iceland with glaciers, hot springs, and northern lights would likely give very little thought to possible predatory threats if they ever went on holiday there. I like Iceland, I have family in Iceland, and I've been to Iceland many times. But just as a responsible person traveling from a Western nation to a place like Pakistan would understand the need for increased caution, so too should they maintain the need for caution elsewhere, even in a quiet and idyllic place like Iceland.[50] It's easy to let your guard down when on vacation, especially in a place referred to as the "best place to be a woman."[51] Even if much of the violence committed against women and children occurs within the home, you should understand not just the universal risks but also the local ones when traveling—and stay aware and alert.

The violent crimes discussed thus far—from sexual abuse and rape to kidnapping and homicide—are not the only forms of wickedness in which the predators are usually known to the victims. The same is true for victims of burglaries, defined as the unlawful entry of a structure to commit a felony or theft, with or without the use of force.[52] Burglars make threat assessments and generally take into consideration the same factors most predators consider:

1. Range (ease of access)

2. Risk (likelihood of injury or capture)

3. Reward (potential benefits)

After all, breaking into a house when someone is at home is a potentially fatal endeavor for the burglar, especially in a country like the United States, which experienced an estimated 1,117,696 burglaries in 2019.[53] This is why most burglaries occur during the day,[54] when the burglar suspects or knows the dwelling is empty. Even if there's not a gun in the house, the police are far more likely to be called immediately when someone is home, which for the burglar means—at best—less time to steal. Either way, burglars typically act fast—usually within minutes.[55] As a result, no one is home in more than 70 percent of home burglary cases.[56] (In places like the United Kingdom, where there are far fewer guns in the home, nighttime burglaries are more common.)

Thus, even with more than a million home burglaries per year, only about 266,000 individuals—or roughly 0.08 percent of the U.S. population—will actually run into a burglar in their home in any given year. In nearly two out of three such cases, the homeowner knows the burglar.[57] A lot of these crimes happen in inner-city neighborhoods, trailer parks, and other impoverished places when "friends" sneak in to steal any miscellaneous items they can find to fund their next dose of fentanyl, meth-amphetamine, crack, or heroin. They either often do not realize anyone is home or don't intend to be discovered by the people in the house. This is partly why violence occurs in only about 25 percent of burglary cases when someone is home.

While such statistics won't be of any comfort to the person who suddenly finds herself woken in bed by men like Joshua Komisarjevsky and Steven Hayes, we, as smart primates, should portion out our attention and energy in a way that grants us maximal benefits. If we don't want to misalign our priorities, we must learn to think statistically, not just intuitively or emotionally. And statistics can be deceptive. While only 0.02 percent of the U.S. population will have a violent encounter with an intruder in their home in any given year, those odds vary dramatically depending on who you are, where you live, and what your habits are.

Precise data on this type of home invasion is hard to come by—largely because of differences in legal codes across states.[58] This means the same crime can be defined and classified differently from one state to the next. Data is also difficult to parse because the FBI does not directly track home invasions specifically but rather home robberies more generally.[59] As written in a 2020 Bureau of Justice Statistics report,

> "Home invasion" has been used broadly to describe any crime committed by an individual unlawfully entering a residence while someone is home. More narrowly, home invasion has been used to describe a situation where an offender forcibly enters an occupied residence with the specific intent of robbing or violently harming those inside. The limited numbers of states incorporating the term "home invasion" into their state statutes include the intent on the part of the offender in their definition.[60]

States that do not use the exact term home invasion may instead refer to this type of crime as aggravated or first-degree burglary.

While parsing exact numbers is difficult, there are a few things we do know. First, unless you run a drug house in the South Side of Chicago or some other inner-city neighborhood, the odds of becoming a victim of home invasion or aggravated burglary are low. Second, even in those cases in which you might encounter a burglar in your house, you'll likely know them. And third, the elderly are disproportionately singled out for this particular type of crime—because they are physically less dangerous to the predator and often easier to trick or overpower.

The typical image of a home invasion involves hooded thugs kicking down a front door or sneaking in through a basement door. That *does* happen, as the Petit family tragically discovered, but it is uncommon. They are more likely to first ring the bell with a question.

"My car broke down. May I use your phone?"

"Hi, is this Jim's house? I'm supposed to pick him up, but I lost his address."

"Sorry, but my dog is lost. Have you happened to see a yellow lab?"[61]

Sometimes they are checking your house out.

Is anyone home?

Is there a back patio door?

Is there a security system?

Is there a dog?

Sometimes they are checking you out.

Do you look like you'll put up a struggle?

Are you aware they are a threat?

Are you alone in the house?

Do you look like a threat?

Are you assertive?

Predators assess all this information rapidly. As soon as you answer the door, they'll size you up as a potential victim and peek past you for potential threats. If you look like a soft target, they will push the boundaries. If you fail to say *"No!"* to any attempt of theirs to push those boundaries—or if you let them ignore your first *no* as you keep the door open—it sends a clear signal that they can take advantage of you. And then, before you know it, they're in your house.

Much of this can be addressed by remembering the rule about vampires from the beginning of this chapter: *don't let them in*. Never let them in! No means no. If you ever have to say *no* more than once, call the police. Remember that you never, ever need to open the door to speak to someone. In violent home invasions, the attacker often begins by playing the role of someone harmless who needs or is offering help in an attempt to sneak past your lines of defense in their search for easy prey.

All predators, whether unknown violent criminal actors or known character-disordered individuals, give clues to their violent intentions well in advance—you just have to know what to look for. Even if you don't see any potential threats in your life now, your failure to recognize those threats when they enter your life may be your undoing or the undoing of those you love. Not all predators will enter your world wearing the costume of a bad guy—a high percentage will try to slip beneath your radar as sheep.

11 The Stealth Predator

Deliberate error isn't an error; it's a character flaw.

The literature on violent criminals is extensive. By contrast, very little has been written on those character-disordered individuals who victimize their own families and friends. If character-disordered individuals intentionally remain covert until they have a chance to victimize you or your loved ones—until they turn violent—how do you spot them?

One of the few researchers to have worked in this area is George Simon, author of the books *In Sheep's Clothing* and *Character Disturbance*.[1] Simon is a practicing clinical psychologist who noticed a common pattern in many of the stories his patients told him. They were all experiencing ongoing problems with individuals who regularly attempted to manipulate, abuse, or exploit them. His patients often felt guilty, ashamed, and anxious about their experiences with these individuals. The people who plagued his patients shared certain character traits. Over time, Simon determined that many of these manipulators had defective or deficient characters. A *character disorder*—a term I borrow from Simon—affects personality, virtue, values, and conscience.[2]

A character-disordered individual operates from a place of desire and manipulation. If their attempts at manipulation are successful, they acquire a sense of domination and supremacy. They feel very little guilt or shame for their actions and tend to externalize blame for their failures. Unlike neurotic individuals, who worry about how they might have affected others, character-disordered individuals fixate on how others have affected them. They portray themselves as victims, betray a deep-rooted sense of entitlement, and are quick to anger and prone to lashing out, often childishly, with aggressive verbal attacks designed to strike at the emotional weak spots of their victims—often their spouses, children, lovers, or "friends." When that doesn't work, they may launch a violent attack, particularly if they have a physical advantage over their victims.

Character-disordered individuals are sometimes acknowledged—and even admired—for their assertiveness. This is a mistake. There is a distinct difference between being assertive and lashing out. Assertive behavior is one of the healthiest and most useful traits a human can have. Reactive aggression is not. To ascribe to a character-disordered individual the noble trait of assertiveness is to mistake a bully for a leader—an error that can be fatal to an organization, tribe, or family.

The core traits of a character-disordered individual include:

- a false persona (insincerity);

- a failure to take responsibility;

- an attitude of entitled victimhood;

- a propensity for childish reactive aggression; and

- consistent attempts to manipulate through covert aggression.

Put another way, character-disordered individuals tend to be inauthentic and manipulative, generally avoid taking responsibility, often adopt a pretense of victimhood, and are quick to lash out if questioned. If this type of behavior sounds familiar, it should. Most families and social groups contain individuals who fit this category, and understanding who they are, why they are unlikely to change, and what you need to do to defend yourself against them is a first step in the direction of safety.

There is considerable overlap between the character-disordered individual and certain Cluster B personality disorders, as outlined in the DSM-V—namely, narcissistic personality disorder, which is often characterized by grandiosity, a lack of empathy, and aggression, and antisocial personality disorder (APD), which is often characterized by irresponsibility, impulsiveness, deceitfulness, lack of emotional depth, manipula-tiveness, and sometimes extreme antisocial behavior (think sociopaths and psychopaths).[3] I prefer the term character-disordered individual for one principle reason: my focus is on self-defense, and when we think about self-defense, we're thinking about protecting ourselves from pred-ators—that is, those who demonstrate a clear lack of virtue, honor, re-spect, ethics, and conscientiousness. This concerns character.[4] As such, what I want you to remember is that regardless of what you believe about free will, regardless of how damaged someone may be because of their past, it is *character* that defines what they do and how they act—and knowing this will help keep you safe. More simply, understanding char-acter is critical to maximizing personal safety.

Character-disordered individuals tend to remain in a state of arrest-ed development. Although their exploitation skills improve over time, character-disordered individuals typically do not mature as they age and thus remain immature indefinitely. Since their sense of power comes primarily from manipulation and intimidation, they are often trying to convince you of something, yet their actions, behavior, and words are forever insincere. When in doubt, ask yourself: *does this person sound like she is trying to sell me something?*

Philosopher Daniel Dennett offers wonderful guidance on how to protect yourself against being manipulated:

One thing we require of moral agents is that they are not somebody else's puppet. If you want the buck to stop with you, then you have to protect yourself from other agents who might be trying to control you. In order to fend off manipulation, you should be a little bit unpredict-able. So having a poker face is a very big part of being a moral agent. If you can't help but reveal your state to the antique dealer when you walk into the store, then you're going to be taken for a ride. If you can't help but reveal your beliefs and desires to everybody that comes along, you will be a defective, a disabled agent. In order to maximize getting what you want in life, don't tell people exactly what you want. . . . You see a woman and you fall head over heels in love with her. What's about the worst thing you can do? Run panting up to her showing her that you've fallen head over heels in love. First of all, you'll probably scare her away, or she'll be tempted by your very display of abject adoration to wrap you around her little finger. You don't want that, so you keep something in reserve.[5]

In other words, the key to being free from control and getting what you want is to maximize the uncertainty of other agents. Don't just show your hand. Use the element of surprise to your advantage—not theirs. That's the kind of advice a wise grandfather passes on to his grandson or granddaughter just before they enter the fray in any tough field. And it sums up most of what you'll need to remember when defending yourself against people whose intentions you remain unsure of. When dealing with manipulators, maximize their uncertainty. Never reveal anything inadvertently. Keep a poker face. Trust your gut. And never let anyone make you feel guilty for protecting yourself.

So how do you know whether someone is trying to manipulate you or whether they are simply being *nice?*

This is the kind of question only decent people ask. That hesitation to judge others is exactly what character-disordered individuals are looking for. Such an individual's natural prey is a nervous and preferably lonely person, separated from the herd. Niceness is a strategy we hairless primates use to manipulate others. It is also the bread and butter of every con artist on the planet. True goodness reveals itself through kindness, which is different from niceness, in that it is born of sincere empathy and not motivated by personal gain.[6]

One of the main things that can cause many people, especially women, to hesitate to be assertive in situations in which assertiveness is called for is the fear of being *mean.* In neurotic individuals, the people most often targeted by character-disordered individuals, that fear is magnified. Sadly, this can leave victims frozen, unable to act decisively, allowing the character-disordered individual to make his move.

Salespeople are nice because they want your money. Sexual players are nice because they want to use your body. Con artists are nice because they want to steal your resources. And character-disordered individuals are nice because they are trying to manipulate you. The end goals of character-disordered individuals can vary, but whatever their goals are, know that they are not acting in your best interests. If they were, sly manipulation wouldn't be necessary. The moment you show a character-disordered individual that you've seen through their false persona, the costume designed to manipulate—the first core trait of a character-disordered individual—you'll get a direct peek at the kind of human you're dealing with, and it won't be pretty.

This brings us to the second core trait of a character-disordered individual: a failure to take personal responsibility. You can't change a trait or habit that you refuse to acknowledge. Think about the battered wife of an abusive husband who, after one late-night beating too many, finally gathers the strength to get herself and her PTSD-diagnosed children out of the house but later decides to take him back, yet again, after he promises to change his behavior. It's a promise that is always preceded by a laundry list of excuses incorporated into an elaborate story about the "stress" he has been under. She returns in a full-blown state of delusion, and within ninety days, she is beaten so severely that she dies.

Think about the battle-weary parents of a twentysomething son—who has lived on and off the streets for several years, taking methamphetamine and racking up a three-foot-long arrest record—who take that son in one more time only to wake up to find every item of value in the home stolen and the son gone. The mournful parents still keep a light on for him, praying nightly that their boy may yet turn his life around. He won't.

Think about the adult daughter of a negligent, angry, abusive, alcoholic father who finally confronts him after years of therapy, personal struggle, and self-reflection, only to be flippantly told by the man who was charged with protecting her when she was little that you can't change the past—you have to live in the now. Or perhaps she is met with the simple yet ever-popular excuse that he was drunk and doesn't remember any of that. The daughter, distraught and hopeless, comforts herself with the delusion that one day the man will change. He won't.

Think about the octogenarian father of a fifty-five-year-old man-child with a temper problem who has to tell the postman that he tripped and fell in order to explain the black eye he suffered at the hands of his own son—who then takes his son back into his home for the umpteenth time after his boy put on a long display of crying over his most recent "unjust" dismissal from a job—only to be hospitalized two weeks later after suffering a broken hip because his son threw him down the stairs. The elderly father still holds out a hope that one day, if his boy can just find the right calling, his son will turn the corner and become a decent man. He won't.

What do all these predators—the wife beater, the junkie, the degenerate father, and the elder abuser—have in common? None of them have ever—or will ever—take responsibility for their actions. This failure to take responsibility goes hand in hand with the character-disordered individual's third core trait: a sense of entitled victimhood. By externalizing blame, such individuals relinquish responsibility for their past actions or current state while laying the entire blame on someone or something else. They always concoct a story in which they are the victims. Everything is always someone else's fault.

> *Do you have any idea of the stress I was under at the time?!*
>
> *I was struggling with my disease back then!*
>
> *You can't change the past! Let's live in the now.*
>
> *I had just lost my job! I was suffering!*
>
> *It was his/her/their [not my] fault!*

Anyone who consistently says such things is signaling two things loud and clear. First, he has a high likelihood of being a character-disordered individual. And second, he will not change. These are not easy things to realize about anyone, especially if it is someone you love. However, if your personal safety and the well-being of those you are tasked with protecting are really at the top of your agenda, then you have to accept this coarse reality.

Few things are as debilitating and infantilizing as viewing yourself as a casualty of your own life rather than as its author, but not all miserable, self-pitying people qualify as character-disordered individuals. To qualify, they must not only possess the first two core traits of character-disordered individuals but also demonstrate some kind of aggression. Of the three major types of aggression, they typically exhibit the first two types, but they sometimes also exhibit the third type:

1. *Reactive aggression*: irrational, spontaneous, highly charged, emotionally abusive behavior that often leads directly to expressive physical violence.

2. *Covert aggression:* rational, surreptitious, psychologically manipulative behavior that often precedes expressive (and sometimes instrumental) physical violence.

3. *Proactive aggression:* rational, deliberate planning to inflict harm through instrumental physical violence.[7]

Reactive aggression, the fourth core trait of character-disordered individuals, undergirds most common forms of physical attack—those defined by expressive violence. It tends to be directed at people the character-disordered individual already knows, is usually spontaneous or the result of unplanned circumstances, and ends with an eruption of brutality. Examples include a jealous lover's fit of rage, an honor-based status dispute between two males on the street, and the tantrum of a man that ends in the beating of his wife and children. It is commonly called *losing one's temper*. Reactive aggression is the product of both nature and nurture.[8] An outburst of reactive aggression that leads to expressive violence is frequently preceded by various periods of covert aggression that have previously slipped under the victim's radar.

While character-disordered individuals are highly prone to exhibiting childish reactive aggression and committing expressive violence under certain circumstances, they tend to be masters of covert aggression in their daily lives, the fifth and final core trait they exhibit. This should not be confused with passive-aggressive behavior. Whining, pouting, sulking, sighing, and acting in other similar types of attention-seeking ways are examples of passive-aggressive behavior. Character-disordered individuals can often be passive-aggressive, especially if that tactic has proven effective for them, but covert aggression isn't passive at all. It is an active form of manipulation that the predator tries to keep secret. It isn't the result of a bad mood or disappointment. It is planned, rational, surreptitious, malicious behavior. Covert aggression is abusive, but unlike reactive aggression, it is not conspicuous.

Since covert aggression, even if hidden, is active, why don't people recognize it sooner? Ultimately, they are "hoodwinked," to borrow a word from the ancient sport of falconry in which a small hood is placed over a falcon's head in order to deceive the bird into believing it is nighttime and to calm it under the pretense that it is safe. Working with patients over the course of many years, Simon has discovered some common reasons why victims of covert aggression are hoodwinked:

1. *Denial:* The victim refuses to see the nature of the abuser.

2. *Subterfuge:* The aggression is hidden; no smoking gun can be found.

3. *Guilt:* Aggressors act as though they are the true victim and play on the guilt of others.

4. *Vulnerability:* Aggressors learn their victims' weak spots and push those buttons.

5. *Naïve psychology:* Victims make excuses for a malevolent agent.

Place yourself in the mind of a typical victim. Your predator is a cousin. You grew up together. You love him. Time and again, you try to put what you consider negative or judgmental thoughts about this cousin's behavior out of your mind. When your cousin finally hurts another family member through a series of emotionally abusive and exploitative actions, you call him on it, only to discover that your cousin has carefully crafted the story in such a way as to leave no obvious evidence. He turns the tables on you, playing the victim, and asserts that you are the one in the wrong. Lashing out aggressively, he brings up an unrelated issue about which you are very sensitive—perhaps something you suffered through in years past—playing on your guilt, shame, and conscience until you back off. A week later, you tell a friend about the whole thing. She offers various explanations: your cousin is ill, confused, misguided, and probably the casualty of past abuse. You go to bed wondering what the truth really is.

This is a common scenario. With each passing incident of covert aggression, the abuse often becomes more acute, culminating in an outburst of reactive aggression and expressive violence. Remember that character-disordered individuals gain their sense of power by successfully manipulating others. For them, this isn't abhorrent behavior; this is domination. *This isn't an error—it's a character flaw.*

Neither character-disordered individuals nor those who exhibit reactive aggression more generally tend to be good at listening to reason or adult discourse. The reactively aggressive individual who doesn't exhibit other character-disorder traits might lash out emotionally the moment they sense disagreement, but theirs is simply the reflex of a taunting schoolyard bully. The true character-disordered individual, meanwhile, will regard any discussion or argument as an opportunity to manipulate you. For them, conversation is a zero-sum game. If lashing out will make you capitulate, they'll do that. If bringing up some disturbing experience from your past or a personal insult that strikes at your deep-rooted insecurities will get you to back down, they'll do that. For them, the tactic doesn't matter. What matters is that they hurt you. That's their victory. They are locked into what Peter Boghossian has defined as *doxastic closure*—they won't question their behavior or change their beliefs. Reasoned analysis isn't a path that they can take.

Because the character-disordered individual cares less about tactics and more about hurting you, covert aggression can also be a precursor to proactive aggression, which in turn presages instrumental violence. While reactive aggression is defined by lashing out, flying off the handle, and losing control, proactive aggression is marked by deliberate plan-making behavior and a desire to get even through the infliction of direct physical harm. Those individuals who exhibit proactive aggression are, by definition, able to keep their cool even when insulted and may at first respond with a witty or sarcastic retort instead of a blow. Those prone to reactive aggression become highly emotionally stimulated whenever they perceive a threat or sign of disrespect. Reggie Kray, of London's infamous Kray brothers, is the perfect example of such a person. Serial killer Ted Bundy, on the other hand, is the perfect example of a predator known for proactive aggression. Reactive aggression is emotional, unplanned, and unregulated. Proactive aggression is purposeful, planned, and measured.

Most violent criminals within the penitentiary system are far more likely to have a propensity for reactive aggression than proactive aggression, just as they are more likely to have committed expressive violence than instrumental violence.[9] Many of those who exhibit most, if not all, of the core traits of character-disordered individuals are themselves the sons of violent criminals with the same set of traits. Do fathers who commit violent crimes tend to have children who commit violent crimes because violence is a learned behavior? Or do fathers whose brains are wired in a reactive-aggressive way tend to have children who are wired in a similar way? And is this necessarily an either-or choice?

The scientific evidence suggests that some percentage of this behavior is a product of genetics—that is, due to nature.[10] Given the fact that genes play a significant, if not major, role in the behavior of all animals and that we ourselves sit squarely in the animal kingdom as primates, this reality is anything but surprising.[11] Just how large a role do genes play in violent behavior relative to socioeconomic, sociocultural, and other environmental causes—that is, due to nurture? The subject is not without controversy,[12] but twin and adoption studies suggest that correlates of character-disordered behavior, such as impulsivity, are from 20 to 62 percent heritable, and other studies estimate that conduct disorder in children is 27 to 78 percent heritable.[13] In other words, the reason some of us are more aggressive and violent than others may be partly due to genetics. Every law enforcement officer I've ever spoken with knows that character-disordered parents often have character-disordered children. "You know, I used to arrest your dad," the older officer says as he cuffs his young prisoner.

Yet, even if we accept that our genes are responsible for our impulse control to varying degrees, we must be careful not to prejudge any specific individual—or, indeed, ignore the important role of nurture and its potentially transformative power. After all, rotten trees can produce healthy fruit. It is in everyone's best interest to make sure every child gets every chance to make a better life and to break the cycle of any antisocial, dysfunctional, violent, character-disordered behavior within their family. In such cases, this usually involves getting the fruit as far away from the tree as possible. After all, genes are by no means destiny. Many other powerful forces—most notably environmental ones—are at work.

Our aggressive impulses emerge from activity deep within the limbic system. How and whether our aggressive impulses are expressed, however, depends largely on our prefrontal cortex, which moderates our social behaviors, reigns in our impulses, and modulates our decision-making.[14] Someone who engages in proactive aggression may get just as angry as a reactive aggressive, for example, but he has enough control to be able to hit the metaphorical pause button before that anger erupts. A reactive-aggressive individual has very little impulse control. Such individuals have a faulty pause button. Once rage builds, they explode and burst into violent action.

The prefrontal cortex, which is located behind the eyes, not only plays a key role in our executive functioning but also in our development, facilitating the growth of remorse, empathy, and conscience. Given its role in our higher brain functions, it's not surprising that antisocial behaviors are often associated with abnormalities in the prefrontal cortex.[15]

Such abnormalities often have environmental causes. Drug and alcohol abuse during pregnancy can negatively affect the brain development of the fetus. Lead exposure in children can reduce grey-matter volume in the prefrontal cortex,[16] and alcoholism in adults can profoundly impact the functional and structural status of the prefrontal cortex.[17] Head trauma can also have adverse long-term effects on brain function. For example, prefrontal cortex lesions that occur early in life can dramatically affect social behavior later in life,[18] and clinically significant focal frontal lobe damage might lead to a 10 percent increased risk of violence over the given population's base rate.[19]

While damage to the prefrontal cortex does not inevitably lead to violent crime, why might poor prefrontal functioning predispose one to violence?

1. There is less control over the limbic system, which regulates emotions like rage.

2. It leads to increased risk-taking and irresponsibility.

3. It increases impulsivity and loss of self-control.

4. It lowers the ability to modify and inhibit inappropriate behavior.

5. It generally results in poor social judgment.[20]

The combination of nature and nurture is powerful. Just as children subjected to abuse display higher rates of antisocial behavior, so too do children with prefrontal cortex damage, whether caused by prenatal injury or childhood trauma. Yet, while such environmental factors may account for 50 percent of the variance in antisocial behaviors and psychopathic traits in humans,[21] as cognitive psychologist Steven Pinker has shown, there is also no such thing as a blank slate.[22]

This may all sound highly pessimistic, even fatalistic. But think of this as analogous to diabetes. Some people need to be administered insulin in order to stay healthy. We recognize that diabetics suffer from a biological problem. Similarly, the more neuroscientists discover about the brain's function, the more we will be able to offer help to people who, for example, lack impulse control due to prefrontal cortex damage. As psychiatrists Alexandra Junewicz and Stephen Bates Billick write,

An expanded understanding of the impact of environmental factors on the expression and behavioral manifestations of genes may lead to improved interventions to curtail the development of antisocial behavior and psychopathic traits. Further, research revealing the importance of gene-environment interactions in the development of antisocial behavior and psychopathic traits may encourage expanded supports and more rehabilitative policies for youth in the juvenile justice and social welfare systems.[23]

Yet, while we should always support science in its pursuit to help people, we must also become comfortable with the fact that when people repeatedly do bad things, we must treat them as agents with intent, regardless of what we believe about free will. It is their character that is the problem. This is a crucial point—our *minds* are who *we* are. Knowing the core traits of character-disordered individuals helps us differentiate between those who might simply have problems with attention, focus, and impulse control due to prefrontal cortex damage and those who are truly character-disordered. For example, many people display symptoms of both attention-deficit/hyperactivity disorder and impulsivity, but they do not necessarily exhibit the other definable traits of character-disordered individuals and are thus not necessarily antisocial. They may have trouble concentrating or restraining their behavior, but unlike the character-disordered individual, they show no signs of manipulativeness, malice, or enmity. Here are the key questions to ask yourself when assessing whether someone is truly character-disordered:

When you confront a person about his past actions, does he portray himself as the victim?

When you question him about his behavior, is his first response an outburst of adolescent insults?

When you discuss the past, does he respond with a laundry list of excuses?

Does he attempt to portray himself inauthentically, in a manner designed to manipulate the image other people have of him—for example, does he spuriously portray himself as someone who has recently found God or as some form of enlightened guru?

Is he more prone to physical aggression when dealing with children or women?

Is he constantly trying to get something from you?

If the person is male, does he socialize well with other strong, stable males?

Posing as a victim, externalizing blame, hurling verbal insults, and attempting to play on your guilt, shame, and other sensitivities are all forms of malicious manipulation. They indicate not only that the person in question lacks maturity and has trouble acting responsibly but also that he is character-disordered.[24]

In the context of this discussion about identifying character-disordered individuals, I want to pivot back briefly to functional martial arts—a term that you now know means "combat sports." Combat sports can offer much more than just a means of self-preservation and self-defense against violent criminals. They can also be vehicles for increased empathy, impulse control, and self-awareness—for growth and maturity—and they can not only shape but also reveal character. This is especially true for a combat sport like Brazilian Jiu-Jitsu.

All full-contact sports leave few places for the ego to hide, no matter how they are trained, but in the striking arts—boxing, kickboxing, and Muay Thai—sparring usually needs to be paced and is generally kept at a light to moderate intensity. Smart athletes and intelligent coaches don't bang out a full-contact striking session every day—that would just lead to a major loss of brain cells and would rapidly weed out anyone who cared about their future cognitive function. A grappling art like Brazilian Jiu-Jitsu, on the other hand, offers a different experience because practitioners can "roll"—that is, spar competitively—with full use of power and force on a regular basis without a significant risk of suffering major injuries or cognitive impairment.[25] Because of this, everyone on the mat quickly knows exactly where they all stand relative to others. They know who can beat whom and who can successfully challenge whom. If someone is a bully, prone to picking on smaller or lesser-skilled players, those with a higher skill level will quickly sort them out, laying down loss after humiliating loss until the insecure aggressor has gotten the point. At a proper BJJ school, someone who pushes others around will quickly find themselves pushed around until they change their ways or leave.

The Brazilian Jiu-Jitsu dynamic is as beautiful in its honesty as it is powerful. Over the decades, I've seen students cry, throw their water bottles across the room, shake with anger, rant uncontrollably, and pout after being tapped out. I've seen others actively avoid facing those who can challenge them on the mat, only to recognize over time that, by doing so, they have allowed everyone else to advance while they have steadily fallen behind. One of the highest compliments I frequently receive from guests who visit my school is how *kind* everyone is. "There are no dicks!" That's because people with character disorders don't last long on my mat. When we notice them, they're immediately asked to leave, and even if we don't catch them right away, the process of learning Brazilian Jiu-Jitsu eventually weeds them out of the community.

Maintaining a safe and healthy training environment is the single most important duty of any coach or head instructor. In the past, I have kept troubled individuals around much longer than I should have: these are some of the career mistakes I most regret. Just as a good father's first job is to provide safety and stability for his family, a good coach's first job is to provide safety and stability for his athletes and students.

I've become much better at detecting character-disordered individuals as time has gone by. My career has trained me to quickly recognize when something is off—particularly in a male. But you, too, have that ability—a beautiful gift from your ancestors that helped them survive and made it possible for you to be alive today—and can easily further develop that skill, just as I have.

The first step is to simply listen to your instincts.

12 The Traits and Characteristics of Predators

Recognize the true threat: dumb, desperate, and dangerous.

A mugger, armed robber, or home invader—any stranger who makes physical threats against you or causes you physical harm—is, by definition, a violent criminal actor. But remember that roughly 80 percent of all violent crime is committed by someone the victim knows. When the character-disordered individual moves from displaying only covert aggression to committing actual expressive or instrumental violence, they become a violent criminal. Identifying character-disordered individuals and getting them out of your life before they get the chance to make that final costume change is a crucial step toward greater personal safety and well-being. But what if you encounter someone new who would make you a statistic in that remaining 20 percent? What if a violent *stranger* entered your life five minutes ago—or even five seconds ago?

As security specialist Gavin de Becker explains, survivors of violent attacks by strangers frequently relate how shocked they were by what seemed to them a *sudden* event.[1] Given the relative safety of modern twenty-first-century society and the remoteness of violence for most humans in such societies, this impression isn't surprising. But it also isn't accurate. From the conscious perspectives of the victims, the violence probably did *feel* like a sudden attack. But, in almost every case, the assailant gave a series of pre-incident indicators that were either unseen or ignored by the victim. (I will detail these indicators in chapter 15.)

There have been approximately twelve thousand generations of human beings on this planet so far.[2] You are the product of an unbroken streak of success. Each of your ancestors—with each generation of ancestors doubling in size as you go back in time—lived long enough to have children. To accomplish such an improbable feat required unimaginable sacrifices. Most of your ancestors saw the majority of their children die. Many of your ancestors were murdered defending their babies or their tribes so that those who survived could procreate in their own time, and many more killed others so that they could remain alive. High levels of intelligence, nurturing love, social guile, adaptability, awareness, and violence were required for survival. These were people who could fashion a spear and kill an eight-ton wooly mammoth—these were people who could protect and feed their families through the long winters that never seemed to end. So remember this: *you come from that!* You are the product of millions of years of evolution and thousands of generations of gifted human survivors.

This evolutionary journey of biological and cultural change was accompanied by an unending arms race between predator and prey. If your ancestors had been prey more often than predator, you wouldn't be here. They knew how to read the intentions of other *Homo sapiens.* Cooperation was required for survival because we humans are social primates. Parasites and perverts were quickly weeded out. Your ancestors didn't just keep a watchful eye on what was roaming around outside the cave; they were also vigilant about who was inside the cave. Those primal instincts that tell you when a predator is near are as much a part of you as love, fear, jealousy, rage, curiosity, hunger, lust, and humor. But our instincts give us an advantage only if we listen to them and apply our intelligence.

When it comes to character-disordered individuals, for example, your instincts might tell you something is wrong before the person turns violent against you or your family. Knowledge of the five core traits of character-disordered individuals—traits like a consistent failure to take personal responsibility and a propensity to adopt the role of the victim—will help you define the threat. Statistically speaking, you likely know such individuals; some of them may even be related to you. This will give you a chance to distance yourself before a "sudden" event occurs. After all, the most common type of violent criminal actor is the one you know.

There is a tendency in the self-defense world to describe violent criminals as fearsome creatures. In reality, they are often just dumb, desperate, and dangerous. Legendary Brazilian Jiu-Jitsu champion Rickson Gracie once told me that he was unafraid to step into a ring or cage with any man, no matter how tough. If the opponent was worthy and the money commensurate, anxiety wouldn't stand in his way. What scared him, he said, was a thirteen-year-old with a gun. His greater uneasiness at the prospect of an armed and out-of-control teenage boy—as opposed to a strong, skilled, trained man—is smart. Almost all violent crime is committed by men, and these "men" are often literally boys.[3]

We have all heard the stories of wealthy gangsters with mountains of cash and enormous political clout—Hollywood often romanticizes the malignant parasites who engage in violent organized crime—but the truth is far less glamorous. Most violent criminal actors

- are male;
- are between the ages of 15 and 34;
- have multiple prior arrests, including one felony conviction;
- have low intelligence; and
- come from fatherless homes.

The first three bullet points in this profile are not controversial and require no further explanation, because they are easily observed and measured,[4] so I will focus on the last two points and what they imply.

There is some debate about the correlation between low intelligence and violent criminal behavior. For example, individuals with below-average cognitive functioning make up a disproportionate amount of the prison population, but this could just mean that smarter criminals are not as likely to be caught or sentenced. Even when controlling for confounding variables, however, multiple studies in various countries have found that criminals tend to have an intelligence quotient (IQ) that is at least 8 to 10 points lower than noncriminals. In short, lower cognitive ability is almost certainly related to an increased risk for antisocial and violent behavior.[5] But ultimately, this isn't simply a matter of IQ scores. What makes many criminals especially dangerous is something even high-IQ people can fall victim to: *stupidity*, whether in thought, action, or behavior. By their nature, most violent crimes reflect an inability to make smart decisions or to see beyond one's own immediate needs—let alone the needs of others. If violent criminals acted smartly or even wisely, they'd do a better job of weighing the costs and benefits before making potentially life-changing decisions. They'd think more like economists.

To better communicate my point here, let's take a look at a few common types of violent crime. In the United States, robbing a bank is a federal crime. If the amount stolen exceeds $1,000, the penalty can be up to ten years in prison. Additional charges, such as gun-related felonies, add more time, often doubling the term to twenty years. Bank robbery has among the highest clearance rates of any crime—nearly 60 percent in a typical year.[6] To choose an arbitrary year, the average amount stolen in bank robberies in 2006 was $4,330. This means that the average bank robber in 2006 had a better than 50 percent chance of being caught, faced up to ten years in prison if caught, and netted less than $5,000 if they managed to get away. How much are ten years of your life worth? What about your whole life?[7] That same year, the average commercial robbery netted the criminal $1,589, and the average convenience store robbery netted them $769.[8] Any robbery in which a weapon—even a fake one—is used is considered an armed robbery, for which the penalty varies by state. In Georgia, for example, the minimum sentence for armed robbery is ten years, and the maximum is life imprisonment. So, at best, the typical convenience store robber in Georgia in 2006 was risking at least ten years of his life for an average of $769.

Unlike robberies, some violent crimes offer no immediate financial or economic benefit at all, such as drive-by shootings. These are often little more than dick-measuring moves for young gang members who want to display their credibility. Many of these shooters are caught—in some cities, arrest rates have reached 90 percent. Often no one is hit. When someone is hit, it's an innocent bystander up to half the time. Based on data from Los Angeles, roughly 95 percent of those hit by a drive-by bullet survive.[9] Penalties for a drive-by shooting vary by state but generally range from seven to thirty-five years behind bars. How much money is gained in the act? Usually none. This crime is about *pres-*

tige. The stated motive may be revenge or the defense of territory, but for the shooter, the principal gain will be in reputation. The perpetrators are usually caught. And even when no one is killed, the perpetrator is still looking at decades in prison.

In *Freakonomics*, Levitt and Dubner include a chapter on gang culture aptly titled "Why Do Drug Dealers Still Live with Their Moms?"[10] Here is what they report: over a four-year period in the 1990s, the average foot soldier in a Chicago gang was arrested 5.9 times and incurred 2.4 nonfatal wounds (not including those inflicted by his own gang). These kids—most of whom were aged between twelve and twenty-two—also had a 1-in-4 chance of being murdered by other gang members, easily making their "job" the most dangerous in the nation. So how much money did these gangsters earn for such an incredibly high-risk endeavor? On average, $3.30 an hour—less than a typical McDonald's worker would have made back then. What about all the bling and expensive cars? Most of that is fake. The oversized bling is often little more than costume jewelry, and most of the cars are rented or leased. Like the late-night infomercial hucksters who rent Lamborghinis and mansions for the day in order to pitch their get-rich-quick schemes to a gullible, bloodshot-eyed audience, these gangsters know that a tacky display of property can seduce fatherless young boys into suicidal jobs for slave wages.

Does any of this sound anything but stupid to you? Violent crime is a loser's game. If you're dumb enough to consider a life of crime, you're too dumb to pull off a life of crime. But again, statistics related to IQ don't reveal the full story here. After all, the vast majority of people with low intelligence will never commit a violent crime. The real danger comes when we couple *stupidity* with *immaturity* and *desperation*. The formula is as simple as it is straightforward:

Stupidity + Immaturity + Desperation = Danger

I've already explained what I mean by stupidity. What of the other two addends? To understand immaturity, we must first understand what it means to be mature. Maturity implies three basic traits:

1. *Self-awareness:* the inclination and ability to take responsibility for oneself.

THE TRAITS AND CHARACTERISTICS OF PREDATORS • 127

2. *Empathy:* the inclination and ability to put oneself in the shoes of others.

3. *Impulse control:* the inclination and ability to restrain negative emotions and delay gratification.

As a measurement of self-awareness, empathy, and impulse control, maturity admits to ever-increasing depths. With maturity, we are talking about someone's character and capacity, and unless a person has hit a state of arrested development, a person's character and capacity should always be growing. A healthy person naturally matures as she experiences more of the world around her, expands her relationships, challenges herself, learns, loves, and ages. Character is earned. We don't earn it by being better than other people but by being better than we used to be. That leads to humility and maturity. A life well-lived. (See chapter 16 for a more in-depth discussion of this.)

Immaturity is the opposite of all this. A lack of self-awareness is the first sign of an immature person. Immature individuals are irresponsible, blame others for any of their failures, do not see how their behavior affects others, are lacking in empathy, are rarely able to restrain their impulses, and often seek immediate gratification. For most of us, our adolescent and teen phases are the low-water mark of our maturity (and thus the high-water mark of our immaturity). That was certainly true for me. Our emotions seem closer to the surface, our hormones are raging, our tempers are more likely to flare, and our impulses are less easily restrained. Our lack of experience handicaps our ability to observe how our behavior affects those around us, and the nuances of a complicated world anger us because they don't fit neatly into the black-and-white thinking of a know-it-all teenager. This is the age at which the likelihood of engaging in or becoming a victim of violence reaches its zenith.

This likelihood is elevated further still when the teenager comes from a family or environment that fails to provide a strong sense of self. A lack of identity breeds insecurity, which is often expressed in exaggerated displays of aggression and antisocial behavior. These are desperate attempts by young men to solidify their status and identity within their peer group, something all boys desperately seek, especially if a proper foundation is not provided at home. They traffic in boy-speak, and it is found everywhere you find groups of immature, lost young males. Most of the arguments and disputes that these young males have involve other aggressors low in maturity and impulse control. They fight over petty, trivial, and irrelevant issues. When such young men are caught doing something they shouldn't, they often fail to take personal responsibility. Things are always someone else's fault: society, the father who wasn't there, a teacher, a rival gang, a girl, another guy—you name it, anything and anyone else is to blame.

An early lack of guidance and stability at home will mean a later lack of resources for support and growth when they most need it. This will only heighten their lack of hope—their *desperation*. As a result, their violent outbursts will start to become more common. Within their peer group, this will further elevate their status. They will learn that violence breeds fear, but because they are still immature, they will mistake fear for respect. They soon begin to rack up arrest records. Eventually, a felony conviction is added to the resume. Within a few years, the lucky ones will end up in prison. The unlucky ones will already be dead.

This can lead to a vicious cycle across generations because the very conditions that caused this triad of stupid, immature, and desperate criminal behavior will be repeated. Why? Because this cycle is fed by arguably the single greatest predictor of future violent criminal behavior: parental absence or, more specifically, *fatherless homes*.[11] Most violent criminals had absent fathers who were often reactive-aggressive individuals themselves, were raised by single mothers or grandmothers, and attended failing schools in poverty-stricken neighborhoods with high levels of truancy. It isn't easy to get good data on the family background of violent criminals, and the distinction between stepparent and no parent is often blurred, but whenever the data can be tracked, we see that the majority of those involved in violent crime generally come from fatherless homes.

The effects of fatherless homes extend well beyond questions of violent crime. Here is what we know:

- 85 percent of children with violent behavior disorders come from fatherless homes.
- 63 percent of youth suicides come from fatherless homes.
- 71 percent of high school dropouts are from fatherless homes.
- 90 percent of all homeless/runaway youths are from fatherless homes.

- 70 percent of youth in state reform institutions grew up in fatherless homes.

- 75 percent of adolescent patients in substance abuse centers are from fatherless homes.

- 85 percent of rapists motivated by displaced anger are from fatherless homes.[12]

While no *single factor* is the cause of violent crime, it's clear that children of single mothers are more likely to commit violent crime than children who grow up with both parents. This is true not just in the United States but also worldwide.[13] But it's not just the individual fatherless homes that can affect the child—so too can the overall neighborhood-level family structure. For example, one study showed that for every 1 percent increase in single-parent homes within a given area, a 3 percent increase in adolescent violence could be predictably measured. When controlling for other factors, this means that neighborhood-level family structure explains 58 percent of the variance in violence between neighborhoods.[14]

Former New York senator Daniel Patrick Moynihan, a scholar on urban ethnic politics and the poor, understood this idea well:

> From the wild Irish slums of the 19th Century Eastern Seaboard to the riot-torn suburbs of Los Angeles, there is one unmistakable lesson in American history: a community that allows a large number of young men to grow up in broken homes, dominated by women, never acquiring any stable relationship to male authority, never acquiring any rational expectations for the future . . . asks for and gets chaos.[15]

Notice what neither Moynihan nor I have named as a meaningful predictor of violent behavior or "chaos"? Skin color.

While it's true that there are large discrepancies in crime rates across races and ethnic groups in the United States, these discrepancies are not some natural outcome of a particular racial or ethnic category. Yet, neither are they necessarily the result of poverty, unemployment, or low education levels within those same categories. As criminal-justice scholar Barry Latzer writes, "Throughout American history, different social groups have engaged in different amounts of violent crime, and no consistent relationship between the extent of a group's socioeconomic dis-advantage and its level of violence is evident."[16] Rather, as already sug-gested, the discrepancies are largely due to the relative rates of fatherless homes found within those categories and the cascading negative effects caused by fatherless homes on children, neighborhoods, and communi-ties. This point becomes even more salient if we look at a related statistic that is more easily tracked than the rate of fatherless homes and that similarly correlates with the large gaps we find in crime rates: unmarried or out-of-wedlock birth rates.[17]

If unmarried birth rates correlate with violent crime, and a high per-centage of violent crime is committed by young men, we should see high rates of homicide in areas that had high rates of out-of-wedlock births twenty years earlier regardless of other factors, such as poverty rate.

And we do (see table 2).

Consider a state like Louisiana. In 2020, it had the highest inten-tional homicide rate of all U.S. states, at 15.8 homicides per 100,000 people. Any guesses as to whether Louisiana ranked high among states in percent of births to unmarried mothers in the year 2000? It shouldn't surprise you when I say it did, ranking second, with 45.7 percent of all babies in the state born to unwed mothers that year. We see this same trend when looking at specific cities. New Orleans, for example, had a staggering 51.0 murders per 100,000 people in 2020, the second highest in the United States.[18] This suggests that the city's out-of-wedlock birth rate is higher than the state's rate, and the data bears this out. Although I could not find birth data specifically for the year 2000, the New Orle-ans Health Department put the figure at 64.1 percent in 2011–2012.[19] When we control for specific neighborhoods, this same trend holds. We see that out-of-wedlock births within Orleans Parish in that period ranged from 5.3 percent to 100 percent, depending on the neighbor-hood. If you wanted to know which neighborhoods produce the high-est rates of violent crime in New Orleans and which ones produce the lowest today, you wouldn't need to consult the city's crime statistics: the out-of-wedlock birth rates from past years would tell much of the story.

I will discuss the connection between violent crime and out-of-wed-lock birth rates in greater detail in chapter 16, but I'd like to make one final point here. The link between out-of-wedlock birth rates and crime is perceived by some as ideologically inconvenient. Because of this, the link is often denied, and when the link can no longer be denied, it is marginalized.[20] That, of course, doesn't change the truth of it, or the data.[21] When there is no positive male role model at home to impart wisdom, help cultivate a meaningful identity, or offer love, support, and resources, young males look to the dominant culture around them to develop their values and sense of self—that is, they look to their peer group to fill those voids. When the homes of most of their peers also lack male role models, violent chaos inevitably ensues. Given this reality, we can rewrite our earlier formula to something far simpler:

Fatherless homes = Danger

Table 2. Unmarried birth rates in the year 2000 and poverty rates in the years 2016–2020 of U.S. states with the top ten highest homicide rates in 2020 (by 1–51 numerical rank from highest to lowest)*

STATE	HOMICIDE RATE IN 2020 (BY RANK)	UNMARRIED BIRTH RATE IN 2000 (BY RANK)	POVERTY RATE IN 2016–2020 (BY RANK)
District of Columbia	1	1	8
Louisiana	2	3	2
Missouri	3	14	20
Mississippi	4	2	1
Arkansas	5	12	6
South Carolina	6	5	10
Alabama	7	18	7
Tennessee	8	16	11
Illinois	9	16	27
Maryland	10	14	50

* This list includes the District of Columbia.

Note: Rankings based on data in Crime Data Explorer, FBI, crime-data-explorer.app.cloud.gov/pages/explorer/crime/crime-trend; "Births: Final Data for 2019," *National Vital Statistics Report* 70, no. 2 (March 23, 2021), table 6, 21, www.cdc.gov/nchs/data/nvsr/nvsr70/nvsr70-02-508.pdf; and "2020: ACS 5-Year Estimates," American Community Survey, U.S. Census Bureau, table S1701, data.census.gov/cedsci/all?q=S1701%3A%20POVERTY%20STATUS%20IN%20THE%20PAST%2012%20MONTHS.

While this fundamental formula might account for most common forms of violent crime—especially the expressive violence of character-disordered individuals in ego-based disputes—it doesn't account for all violent crime. Although rarer, there is a type of character-disordered criminal who demonstrates proactive aggression and uses violence as a means to an end. These are the violent criminals often referred to as sociopaths and psychopaths.[22] Though they may have a temperament prone to fury and the same violent tendencies springing from the limbic system, unlike their reactive-aggressive cousins, their prefrontal lobes are capable of cooling those passions—even hiding them—until a more opportune time to attack.[23] According to neuroscientists Kent Kiehl and Joshua Buckholtz, they tend to commit crimes more frequently and more violently than others, often from a young age, and their recidivism rate is four to eight times higher.[24] The term psychopath especially tends to strike fear into the general population. Yet, many remain nonviolent. After all, violent crime is usually a fool's game. A decent percentage of CEOs, Wall Street traders, and politicians may have this disorder.[25]

Even when psychopaths are nonviolent, that doesn't mean they're necessarily noncriminal. Con artists, lonely-hearts scammers, and other fraudsters like televangelists and New Age healers are also likely to exhibit psychopathic behaviors and traits. Some of these include a parasitic lifestyle, superficial charm, sexual promiscuity, manipulativeness, pathological lying, and a lack of remorse. Estimates suggest that psychopaths constitute 0.5 to 1 percent of the population at large and 15 to 35 percent of the prison population. Males are roughly twice as likely as females to be psychopaths, and they are found in all cultures.[26]

Most of the traits I listed for character-disordered individuals in chapter 11 are the same for those referred to as sociopaths or psychopaths. In 1970, Canadian psychologist Robert D. Hare developed what he called the Psychopathy Checklist, which remains the standard diagnostic tool used by mental health and law enforcement professionals when diagnosing the condition.[27] Hare's fundamental finding was that psychopaths are egocentric, narcissistic personalities who are incapable of feeling guilt, remorse, or empathy. They view other human beings solely as resources to be manipulated, used, and dominated for their own personal gain. Their inability to recognize that they have anything psychologically or emotionally wrong with them renders them totally unresponsive to treatment. In Hare's assessment, psychopaths cannot be fixed. The Psychopathy Checklist is interesting, and I would encourage readers to take the test themselves. Inevitably, most of us will end up scoring high on certain questions. This leads many people to wonder if they themselves are sociopaths. If you're the type of person who worries you're a sociopath, you probably aren't. True sociopaths rarely ask themselves that kind of question. They may recognize their own condition, but they are incapable of worrying about it.

Some of Hare's criteria are less subjective. In his lectures, Hare will sometimes suddenly show a picture of horrific human slaughter, and most of the audience will immediately feel the physiological response that all humans share, except for sociopaths or psychopaths. To check whether you are dealing with one, ask yourself the following questions: Does the person possess a glib, superficial charm? Is he insincere? Does he have a grandiose sense of self? Is he a pathological liar? Does he constantly try to manipulate those around him? Does he show a lack of remorse, compassion, or empathy? Is he parasitic? Does he live off other people? Does he frequently cast himself as the victim? How does he treat others, especially service workers, strangers, and people from whom he stands to gain nothing?

Though they constitute only a small percentage of the general male population, when the sociopathic or psychopathic criminal turns to violence, the results can be savage. Kiehl and Buckholtz described one such predator, a violent criminal named Brad who kidnapped a young girl, took her out to the woods, tied her to a tree, raped her for two days, and then slit her throat and left her to die. As horrendous as those actions were, that is not the remarkable part of the story, because it doesn't necessarily take a true psychopath to commit that kind of crime. What Brad told the interviewer after relating that story gives his psychopathy away. "Do you have a girl?" he asked. "Because if you do, I think it's really important to practice the three Cs: caring; communication; and compassion. That's the secret to a good relationship. I try and practice the three Cs in all my relationships." As Kiehl and Buckholtz report, "He spoke without hesitation, clearly unaware how bizarre this self-help platitude sounded after his awful confession."[28] True psychopaths cannot feel empathy, but they can fake it. Or, as in Brad's case, they can at least try.

At this extreme end of the sociopath and psychopath spectrum are serial killers, defined by the FBI as someone who's committed two or more killings that are separated by event and time.[29] In part due to their relative rarity, however, we know less about them from a scientific standpoint. As author Adrian Raine notes:

> If I could perform brain scans on a significant group of serial killers, I might expect a brain profile similar to our proactively aggressive killers—a hotbed of seething limbic activation bubbling under the good prefrontal functioning that allows them to carefully plan their actions. Yet even within this pack of serial killers, make no mistake—there will inevitably be several shades of gray lurking in the etiological shadows.[30]

Indeed, rather than displaying the kind of prefrontal damage commonly seen in reactive-aggressive individuals during brain scans, high-functioning sociopaths often display prefrontal cortices that are brightly lit. In other words, that part of their brain is highly active and functional, meaning the difference between an extremely high-functioning sociopath and an extremely low-functioning violent criminal may very well lie in the prefrontal cortices of their brains.

Someone who has all the hatred and malice a human animal can possess, along with a high-functioning prefrontal cortex that allows him to remain calm even if pulled over during a traffic stop with the body of a young dead boy in his trunk, is a very scary prospect. In his book *Without a Conscience: The Disturbing World of the Psychopaths Among Us*,[31] Hare gives examples of infamous killers who possessed these exact traits, such as Ted Bundy and John Wayne Gacy. But just how likely is it that you, an average citizen, will come into contact with a predator like them?

The FBI estimates that serial killers commit fewer than 1 percent of all homicides in the United States. Although it's difficult to determine exactly how many serial killers are active at any given time, some experts estimate there are as many as four thousand in the United States today.[32] Even so, the number of serial killer arrests has been steadily falling over the past few decades, and they can often be profiled based on their murders. Despite popular Hollywood renderings of serial killers, serial killers, like other violent criminals, are slightly less intelligent than noncriminals on average, but they generally have a brain that allows them to be more methodical in their plotting and planning. Serial killers want to get away with their violent crimes and typically handpick their victims accordingly. Thus, prostitutes, the homeless, and other vulnerable members of our society are usually the preferred targets of these sorts of predators, who typically act alone.

While serial killers in the Ted Bundy or Jeffrey Dahmer sense who commit murders over a protracted period of time are almost always psychopaths, not all mass or spree murderers are psychopaths. They generally do not plan on getting away with their acts of violence, which they see as the ultimate revenge for some perceived deep-seated grievance, whether against girls, bullies, or society at large.[33] Even if they kill in a paroxysm of violence until they are stopped, many of them had demonstrated empathy at earlier points in their lives, suggesting they suffered from a severe mental disorder other than psychopathy. For example, in the case of the two Columbine shooters, experts believe that Eric Harris was a true psychopath but that Dylan Klebold was psychotic.[34] In the case of the Isla Vista massacre, Elliot Rodger may have been both a psychopath and psychotic.[35] Such distinctions may give little comfort to the families of the victims or survivors, but we can't address root causes—or determine the most effective protective measures—without understanding what motivates these killers.[36]

We can make similar distinctions between serial killers and contract killers or paid assassins. Although they, like serial killers, may commit multiple murders over an extended period of time, their motives are typically extrinsic as opposed to intrinsic, and they are, by definition, committing murder at the request of some third party.[37] That is, they are rewarded and even praised for killing. While psychopaths are likely drawn to such a "profession," and many hitmen exhibit psychopathic traits, such as callousness and manipulativeness, this doesn't mean all hitmen are necessarily psychopaths in the true sense. As one study found, even if mafia members as a whole exhibit significant antisocial traits, they also tend to exhibit a capacity for emotional connection, suggesting the possibility of resocialization and rehabilitation for some.[38] Take, for example, Salvatore "Sammy the Bull" Gravano, who was the right-hand man of John Gotti, the then boss of the Gambino crime family. Before turning state's witness against his former don, Gravano once lived and thrived in a world filled with cold-blooded violence.[39] Yet today, he has a popular YouTube channel and podcast called *Our Thing*.[40]

Gravano is known to have murdered nineteen men, but the actual number is probably higher. In one such incident, Gravano ambushed a man by the name of Frank Fiala. When Gravano caught him, Gravano is reported to have said, "Hey, Frank, how you doing?" as his partner came up behind Fiala and shot him in the back of the head. They then put a bullet in each of Fiala's eyes, and Gravano pulled his pants down and pissed in the dead man's mouth. I mention this to give you a picture of the world in which Sammy Gravano lived. Surrounded as he was by men just like him, any weakness would have been an invitation to be killed. Whether he and the majority of those around him were full-blown psychopaths, totally incapable of empathetic emotions, is debatable.[41] What isn't debatable is the skill at proactive violent aggression these sorts of violent criminals must have in order to survive. Losing your cool and being unable to trick or manipulate your prey would render anyone in that filthy ocean little more than fresh meat.

Just how likely is it that the average person will have a run-in with a man like Gravano? Unless you are involved in organized crime, exceptionally unlikely. Gravano and his ilk represent the kind of problem the FBI has to worry about—not the average citizen. Most gangsters make low wages while performing high-risk jobs. The few who reach the upper levels, like Gravano, tend to live out short careers in a hellish realm of never-ending stress and suspicion.

Serial killers and mob hitmen are arguably the most fetishized and even romanticized violent criminals of all.[42] They might make for terrifying characters in movies, but unless you are a drug-addled prostitute living on the streets or operating as a snitch within the world of organized crime, the odds you will ever face either are minuscule. Your fear of them should end as soon as the end credits roll.

Mass shootings are also rare relative to other violent threats, accounting for roughly 0.1–0.2 percent of U.S. firearm deaths in any given year.[43] In 2021, there were 693 mass shootings (303 of which resulted in zero deaths) and 28 mass murders in the United States,[44] with two mass shootings resulting in ten or more deaths.[45] Sixty-one shootings were designated as "active shooter incidents" by the FBI, up by nearly 53 percent from 2020.[46] Due to their somewhat random and sporadic nature, there's very little you can do on a day-to-day basis to protect yourself from mass or active shooters. Just as you should be aware of any character-disordered individuals in your life, so too should you be aware of any friends, family members, coworkers, or employees with newly acquired negative personality traits that suggest an externally directed end-of-the-rope anger. Many mass or active shootings could likely have been avoided with early mental health intervention, especially in those cases related to psychosis.[47] Beyond that, my simplest advice is to train yourself to always be aware of possible exits and hiding places when in public should you suddenly hear gunshots (for more, see chapter 15). This is true whether you are in the crossfire of a drive-by shooting while waiting at a bus stop, or in a crowded building or public square when a psychopath with a semiautomatic weapon has decided to enact their revenge on the world.

So about whom exactly *should* you be concerned?

I'll repeat again: the primary threat you need to address is always the character-disordered individual you let into your home and around your family—the family friend, the stepfather, the boyfriend, the uncle, the cousin, or the acquaintance. Statistically speaking, these men pose the greatest threat to you. Most exhibit covert and/or reactive aggression. Some exhibit proactive aggression. All are dangerous. You will know most of them personally before they begin to express their violence.

The next—far more distant—threat you need to concern yourself with is the unknown violent actor. They may be in your neighborhood, town, or city, are usually poor, dumb, and desperate, and are already known to local law enforcement. And they are almost always detectable, avoidable, and manageable, even at the individual level.

Joshua Komisarjevsky and Steven Hayes were petty criminals with typical backgrounds and criminal records featuring basic burglaries and smash-and-dash vehicle thefts. Nothing about them was all that unusual. They were both witless losers. Neither of them had a well-thought-out strategy for escape. When the police surrounded the Petit residence, the two became desperate. Dousing the Petit house with gasoline was their idiotic scheme to erase DNA evidence.[48] Yes, these people are extremely dangerous, but they are not criminal masterminds.

The violent criminal actors you're most likely to meet are not bogeymen who should keep you awake at night. They're usually little more than boneheaded parasites who are desperate. As the philosopher Seneca observed two thousand years ago, all cruelty springs from weakness.

So even if they are dangerous, you can beat them—never forget that.

13 The Methods and Motives of Predators

*By understanding the role that means, motive, and opportunity play
in homicide, we can forecast threats and risks.
Prediction leads to preparation—it keeps you safe.*

Once you learn to listen to your primal instincts, your chances of surviving a violent encounter increase dramatically. When you combine those biological instincts with accurate knowledge, the kind that makes for good predictions, you become an even harder target. We've covered *what* kills us and *who* kills us. Now let's analyze *how* they kill.

There are three necessary components to any homicide: means, motive, and opportunity.[1] Let's start with the easiest to quantify: means. Year in and year out, handguns are far and away the most common murder weapon in the United States (see table 3). Although the absolute numbers vary from year to year, the relative percentages found in the data have been fairly consistent over time. For example, according to data compiled by the FBI, there were 17,813 murders in the United States in 2020. Nearly half of the victims—8,029 people—were shot with a handgun, with another 4,863 shot by an unspecified type of firearm. A few years earlier, in 2016, there were 15,070 recorded homicides

Table 3. Means of homicide in the United States ranked by number of victims, 2020

RANK	MEANS OF DEATH	NUMBER OF VICTIMS
1	Handguns	8,029
2	Firearms, type not stated	4,863
3	Knives of cutting instruments	1,739
4	Bare hands	662
5	Rifles	455
6	Blunt objects	393
7	Shotgun	203
8	Narcotics	113
9	Other guns	113
10	Fire	106
11	Asphyxiation	71
12	Other weapons not stated	983

Source: "Murder Victims by Weapon," Crime Data Explorer, FBI, crime-data-explorer. fr.cloud.gov/pages/explorer/crime/shr (accessed May 12, 2022).

in the United States, 7,105 of which were recorded specifically as handgun-related deaths. Another 3,077 homicides that year were attributed to an unspecified firearm. Rifles, meanwhile, including those labeled as assault rifles, account for only a small fraction of homicides by firearm in any given year. In 2019, there were 455 homicide victims by rifle, and in 2016, the number was 374, or roughly 3 percent of all homicides by firearm.[2] Even if we assume that some small percentage of unspecified firearm homicides are also due to rifles, more Americans are likely to die in any given year by falling out of bed than by rifle.[3]

Shootings typically account for roughly two-thirds of all murders in the United States.[4] Male offenders between the ages of eighteen and twenty commit nearly one-quarter of homicides by firearm,[5] and most gun victims are males between the ages of 15 and 24.[6] Gang violence rightly gets a lot of attention when the subject of gun violence arises. According to one well-regarded study, it can account for as many as 67 percent of all homicides in highly populated areas. Gang violence is also "contagious," with each act of violence more likely than non-gang violence to trigger further acts of violence.[7] But let's not forget that the prevalence of gang-related shootings varies greatly by city and state, and law enforcement agencies report that gang activity occurs in only 30 percent or so of all jurisdictions. As a result, no matter how acute the gang situation might be in certain areas, gang shootings account for only 16 percent of all U.S. homicides annually.[8]

Your location matters—a lot. This is true on both a local and global scale (see figure 1). The overall murder rate in the United States was 6.4 murders per 100,000 people in 2020, the highest rate since 1998. In Chicago, which gets a lot of attention in the press for its high violent crime rate, the murder rate was "only" 28.6 per 100,000, more than four times the national average. Compare that to Detroit and Memphis, which had murder rates of 49.7 and 44.4 per 100,000, respectively, roughly seven times the national average. St. Louis, meanwhile, topped the chart with an astounding 88.1 murders per 100,000 people.[9] Vermont, Idaho, and Wyoming, all states with high rates of gun ownership,[10] had 2.2, 2.2, and 3.1 homicides per 100,000 people, respectively, making those states safer

Figure 1. Homicide rate by region (per 100,000 population), 2017

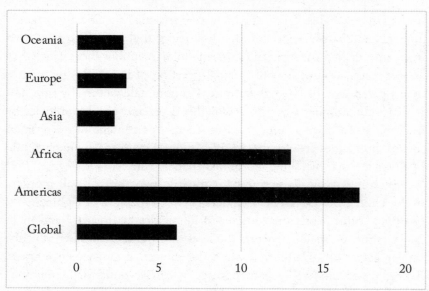

Source: United Nations Office on Drugs and Crime, *Global Study on Homicide* (Vienna: UNODC, 2019), 11, www.unodc.org/documents/data-and-analysis/gsh/Booklet1.pdf.

than many European countries. By contrast, St. Louis had more murders per capita than any country in the world.

In 2020, you were less likely to be killed in New Hampshire or Maine (0.9 and 1.6 per 100,000, respectively) than in Canada (1.97 per 100,000), and much more likely to be murdered in St. Louis or Detroit than in Honduras (36.3 per 100,000) or Jamaica (44.7 per 100,000), the countries with the highest reported murder rates in the world that year.[11] But as with all statistics, murder rates per 100,000 people tell only part of the story in any given country or city. Consider a place like Chicago, for example. Its homicide rate (28.6 per 100,00) may have been higher than that of Mexico (28.4 per 100,000) and Colombia (22.6 per 100,000), but that overall rate tells us nothing of the risk in any particular neighborhood. Depending on which zip code you live in, the odds of becoming a victim of violent crime can be radically different.[12] Writes criminology professor Lawrence W. Sherman,

> Even in cities like Chicago, the homicide rate in middle-class neighborhoods such as Hyde Park is comparable to that of Sweden and is 80 percent lower than the national average. Yet 100 yards to the south of Hyde Park lies Woodlawn, where the homicide rate in 1996 was 12 times the national average. The cumulative effect of neighborhoods like Woodlawn on the overall homicide rate is similar to the effect of the Rocky Mountains on the mean elevation of the United States.[13]

The same effect is seen when it comes to U.S. gun deaths, which stood at 6.1 per 100,000 people in 2020.[14] Yet when broken down by race, we find that black Americans are twelve times more likely to die from gun violence than white Americans, and nearly six times more likely than Hispanic Americans (see figure 2). This striking effect explains why, as Sherman notes, more than 90 percent of Americans likely live in neighborhoods where the homicide rate is well under the national average.

Once you immerse yourself in the facts, you can't help but wonder whether the major problem in much of the United States is gangs rather than guns. Such a point of view is supported not only in the profile of the predators but also of the victims. Between 75 and 90 percent of homicide victims in high-crime cities like Baltimore, Chicago, and Philadelphia have criminal records.[15]

Beyond the question of *how* predators kill, there is also the question of *why* they kill. Motives, which aren't as easily quantifiable as means when it comes to homicide, vary greatly depending on the demographic. Age, profession, relationship status, and geography all matter considerably. Among the three broad categories of motive—pride, passion, and profit[16]—murders due to misplaced pride reign supreme. Suspects and witnesses frequently tell police the victim showed *disrespect*. Often this sense of personal injury is set off by a couple of words, or even the wrong look (e.g., mean-mugging).[17]

The Chicago Police Department released a comprehensive study detailing the characteristics of all murders that occurred in the city in 2011. Of the 433 recorded homicides that year, the most common motive, by far, was a category called "street gangs," accounting for 118 of the murders. Most of the crimes in this category involved altercations related to status (armed robbery accounted for less than 10 percent of murders that year, and fights over narcotics accounted for less than 7 percent of murders).[18]

Figure 2. U.S. gun deaths by race (per 100,000 population), 2020

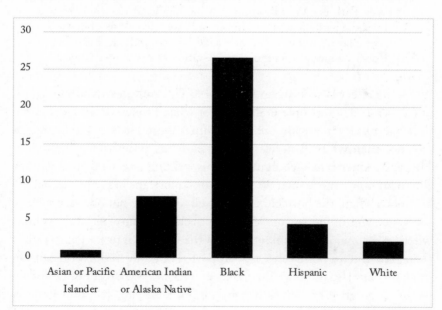

Source: "Supplementary Table 1," *Morbidity and Mortality Weekly Report* 71 (April 19, 2022), CDC, https://stacks.cdc.gov/view/cdc/116520.

Although absolute numbers ebb and flow, the motives of killers are fairly predictable no matter the year or city. In Houston in 2005, for example, there were 336 killings. Of those, 113 were the result of petty disputes.[19] In Philadelphia that same year, 208 of the 380 murders were the result of frivolous disagreements. Drug-related killings—murders directly connected to profit as opposed to pride—accounted for less than 13 percent of total homicides. The city's police commissioner Sylvester Johnson put it this way: "When we ask, 'Why did you shoot this guy?' it's, 'He bumped into me,' 'He looked at my girl.' It's not like they're driving around doing drive-by shootings. It's arguments over stupid things."[20]

Who are the suspects arguing over "stupid things," as Commissioner Johnson worded it? They fit the exact profile we've already outlined. They tend to be young males (aged 15–34) with previous criminal records who come from fatherless homes and live in poor neighborhoods full of other fatherless homes. A lack of rooted identity and economic prospects or resources sends immature young men in search of the only currency they know that purchases selfhood: status, also known as *respect*. To earn the counterfeit cash of respect, young men must participate in the culture of their peer group. As a result, the culture of the group will determine, in large part, the behaviors and actions of the young men that wish to be a part of the group. This sometimes includes committing murder.

Culturally specific idiosyncrasies aside, one motive for murder that transcends time and space is passion. Crimes of passion include murder by the jealous ex-husband, abusive boyfriend, or even drunken uncle. Between 1985 and 2020 in the United States, more than 40 percent of murders in which a motive was identified were a result of arguments (other than drugs or money). It's difficult to parse how many of these arguments were due to pride and how many were due to passion, especially since their boundaries overlap, but a closer look at the data offers some hints. Of the murders in which the relationship between the murderer and victim was known, roughly 18 percent of the victims were listed as wife, husband, boyfriend, or girlfriend in the FBI's expanded homicide data from 2011 to 2020, and roughly 22 percent were listed as son, daughter, mother, father, other family member, or friend (see table 4).[21] Many of the killers in these cases are the ones in the yellow jumpsuits my father saw doing yard work in the penitentiary. They are the impulse killers who didn't wake up that day with a plan to murder. We see this reflected in the fact that more than half of all U.S. homicides occur in the home (see table 5).

Together, pride and passion account for the majority of homicides. For most people, a single argument or fit of rage that leads to an outcome that can never be reversed is the biggest threat they face. But we are still left with one other major motive: profit. Just over 20 percent of murders between 1985 and 2020 in which the circumstances were identified involved money, drugs, or property.[22] Homicides due to this motive typically involve criminals killing other criminals and only rarely involve people uninvolved in criminal activities. That said, if your husband decides to take out a large insurance policy on your life after an argument, you might want to be careful. If you are a witness in a long court battle with millions of dollars at stake, you might need some form of security. If you work for an armored car company picking up deposits, you might be killed in pursuit of profit. But, generally speaking, if you're not involved in illegal activities, and you're not in a profession that is at high risk for armed robbery, being murdered for profit is relatively rare.

Relatively rare, of course, does not mean such murders never occur. Muggings and burglaries happen. Sometimes they lead to murder, whether the offender initially intended to kill or not. Profit was almost certainly a motive for Komisarjevsky and Hayes. But their horrific acts were headline-grabbing precisely because the event itself was such an

Table 4. U.S. homicides by victim's relationship to the killer (as a percentage of all homicides), 2011–2020

RELATIONSHIP TO KILLER	NUMBER OF HOMICIDES
Relationship unknown	47%
Acquaintance or otherwise known	21%
Stranger	11%
Boyfriend/girlfriend or spouse	9%
Parents or siblings (including step)	6%
Friend or other family	5%
Other	1%

Note: Percentages based on data from "Expanded Homicide Data—2011–2020," Crime Data Explorer, FBI, https://crime-data-explorer.app.cloud.gov/pages/explorer/crime/crime-trend.

outlier. When a brutal attack on an innocent family in their own home occurs, it stands out as an exceptional crime.

No matter the overarching motive—pride, passion, or profit—homicide victims usually know their killers, and when they don't, they are usually from the same race as the predator. In 2019, for example, 90 percent of black murder victims were killed by a black offender when both victim and offender were known, and 81 percent of white murder victims were killed by a white offender when both victim and offender were known (see table 6).[23] Yet, such statistics tell us nothing about the extent of violence or victimization within racial categories. For that, other data paints a tragically lopsided picture. Specifically, black-on-black murders have accounted for approximately half the homicides in the United States for decades, and black males kill each other at a rate that's roughly ten times higher than that of white males.[24] Indeed, murder is by far the leading cause of death for black males between the ages of 15 and 34 in the United States, while accidents are by far the leading cause of death for white males of the same age in the same country.[25] Not surprisingly, the victimization rates within a racial or ethnic demographic are often a direct reflection of offender rates within that same demographic. Looking at data from the 2020 Bureau of Justice Statistics National Crime Victimization Survey, which accounts for both reported and unreported violent crime, we can estimate that there were roughly 23.9 violent crimes committed by black offenders per 1,000 black people age twelve

Table 5. U.S. homicides by location (as a percentage of all homicides), 2011–2020

LOCATION OF HOMICIDE	PERCENTAGE OF HOMICIDES
Residence home	53%
Highway/alley/street/sidewalk	23%
Parking garage/lot	7%
Field/woods	3%
Bar/nightclub	2%
Other or unknown	12%

Note: Percentages based on data from "Homicide Victim Demographics—2011–2020," Crime Data Explorer, FBI, https://crime-data-explorer.app.cloud.gov/pages/explorer/crime/crime-trend.

Table 6. Race of U.S. homicide victims by race of offender when both are known (as a percentage of total), 2019

| RACE OF VICTIM | TOTAL | Race of offender | | |
		WHITE	BLACK	OTHER
White	3,216	81%	17%	2%
Black	2,843	9%	90%	1%
Other	235	24%	17%	59%

Source: Percentages based on data from "Expanded Homicide Data Table 6," Crime in the United States 2019, FBI, https://ucr.fbi.gov/crime-in-the-u.s/2019/crime-in-the-u.s.-2019/topic-pages/tables/expanded-homicide-data-table-6.xls.

or older in the designated survey period; that there were roughly 10.5 violent crimes committed by white offenders for every 1,000 white people age twelve or older; and that there were roughly 11.1 violent crimes committed by Hispanic offenders for every 1,000 Hispanic people age twelve or older.[26]

While victims of violence are typically the same race or ethnicity as the offender, this, of course, does not imply that the rate of interracial violent crime is identical across or between all races and ethnicities (see table 7). Of the estimated 437,894 interracial violent crimes involving white and black individuals reported in the 2020 National Crime Victimization Survey, for example, black offenders purportedly committed nearly 84 percent of them (approximately 367,589 black-on-white incidents vs. 70,305 white-on-black incidents), and of the estimated 170,348 violent crimes involving Hispanic and black individuals, black offenders purportedly committed roughly 65 percent of them (approximately 111,511 black-on-Hispanic incidents vs. 58,837 Hispanic-on-black incidents).[27] Yet, even with this apparent disparity, black offenders accounted for only 17 percent of violent incidents in which there was a white or Hispanic victim (479,100 of 2,786,240 incidents), according to this same survey.[28] Collectively, these are the types of stats that inevitably get butchered or misrepresented in widely shared memes meant to disparage, create division, or invoke fear—particularly those that grossly exaggerate the threat of interracial violent crime relative to intraracial violent crime.[29]

While sociologists, economists, criminologists, and historians can

Table 7. Violent incidents in the United States by race or ethnicity of victims and offenders (as a percentage of incidents), 2020

RACE OR ETHNICITY OF VICTIM	NUMBER OF VIOLENT INCIDENTS	Race or ethnicity of offender			
		WHITE	BLACK	HISPANIC	OTHER
White	2,214,390	69.2%	16.6%	11.1%	3.1%
Black	498,620	14.1%	65.7%	11.8%	8.4%
Hispanic	571,850	33.2%	19.5%	41.3%	6.0%

Source: Rachel E. Morgan and Alexandra Thompson, *Criminal Victimization, 2020—Supplemental Statistical Tables*, NCJ 303936 (U.S. Department of Justice, February 2022), 6 (table 5), https://bjs.ojp.gov/content/pub/pdf/cv20sst.pdf.

provide important insight into why such statistical differences exist across racial and ethnic groups in the United States,[30] this book is specifically about self-defense. And anyone serious about self-defense, or intent on giving those they love accurate information about real-world threats, must acknowledge these basic facts. Indeed, people living and working within black communities regularly urge me to speak openly about the high rate of violent crime within them so that the victims might receive the attention and assistance they need—and so that productive steps might be taken to lessen the violent crime rate in those communities. In fact, at the height of the #DefundThePolice movement in the summer of 2020, the vast majority of African Americans (81 percent) wanted police to spend the same amount of time or more time in their neighborhoods.[31] It should also be a surprise to no one that African Americans are more likely than white Democrats to support increased spending on local police.[32] After all, it is the good people within black communities who are victimized and suffer the most. Given the stakes, silence and self-censorship on this topic for fear of offending polite society, committing an act of sacrilege against the new "religion,"[33] or saying something deemed taboo strikes me as a form of cowardice.[34]

But regardless of your race, gender, or age, if you're not selling or buying drugs or living in a neighborhood where a lot of drug trafficking occurs, if you're not in a gang or spending time with gang members, and if you're not prone to getting into emotionally charged confrontations over the wrong look or because you feel "disrespected," you're not at anywhere near the same level of risk as those involved in such activities and behaviors. A *mature* person who associates with other mature people and engages in mature activities is in an entirely different category from an *immature* person who is stuck in a rudderless environment full of other immature young men—no matter their race.

One of my good friends is a professional who, like many educated and mature adults in modern Western society, has little experience with actual violence. His wife, also a professional, devotes a great deal of her life to those who are struggling. She is also very sensitive to other people's feelings. One evening, the two of them—both white—were walking back to their car when they noticed a group of young black men ahead of them on the sidewalk. Taking his wife's hand, my friend led her across the street. This upset his wife, who asked, "Would you have wanted to cross the street if they were white?"

My friend gave it sincere thought. His conclusion was that he would have wanted to do so—assuming that the young white males were dressed like average teenagers and not wearing three-piece suits or looking like Mormon missionaries. But this felt like an unacceptable answer to him. He began questioning his own judgment, so knowing my research interests and professional work, he asked for my opinion. I told him that he had done the right thing. Any group of teenage boys or young men can be a threat, and if you're feeling uneasy about a situation, whether due to the time of day, the geography of the street, poor street lighting, a lack of other pedestrians, or *any* other factor, you need to honor and act on those feelings, not override them for fear of appearances. I know that my friend isn't a racist. Yet he risked second-guessing his own gut reaction in some future situation regarding basic personal safety. That kind of self-doubt helps no one—and can be extremely dangerous in true life-or-death situations. Had the group of young men on the sidewalk been white, would my friend's wife have similarly questioned his decision to cross the road? Almost certainly no.

It's important to remember that all intelligent animals profile. We wouldn't be here today if our ancestors hadn't been successful at avoiding threats. Our innate detectors are often oversensitive, so we often see a threat where none exists, but as long as we're not causing harm to anyone, it's always better to be oversensitive in our threat detection than to have no sensitivity at all. Writes Richard Dawkins, "A rustle in the long grass is statistically more likely to be the wind than a leopard. But the cost of a mistake is higher one way than the other. Agents, like leopards and burglars, can kill. Best to go with the statistically unlikely guess."[35]

You might occasionally see rustling grass, but thankfully the vast majority of people you will encounter in your life will be good. Most young men, for example, would never commit a violent crime, even if they knew they could get away with it. But you should not allow that understanding to override your body's biological warning signs if you think or feel someone in your presence might be a threat. When you find yourself frightened and your primal instinct is calling out to you, but you're concerned about appearing rude, disrespectful, or even racist—*that's when those instincts matter most*, because that's when you might ignore them at your peril. Due to our evolutionary history, we instinctively make rapid decisions—using what psychologists call *thin slicing*[36]—when assessing our environment for potential threats. Predators, both character-disordered individuals and violent criminal actors, do it when they pick out their victims. Human animals who don't want to find themselves on the predator's shopping list need to pay heed to their detectors too.[37]

I speak from experience here. I was once one of those young men at the end of the sidewalk, full of misplaced pride. My friends were a mixture of black and Hispanic teens, but we were all immature delinquents. We fit the profile. We were males between the ages of fifteen and seventeen, and I was the only one who didn't come from a fatherless home. While we would have never struck a woman or child in the face, it would have been smart to cross the street to avoid us. Indeed, as a young teen, if I had observed you crossing the road to avoid me with visible apprehension on your face, it would have been a source of pride for me. Boys often mistake anxiety for respect. But as an adult male—especially one who is large and tattooed—seeing someone actively trying to avoid me out of fear immediately makes me self-conscious. It forces a rapid self-assessment. Do I seem aggressive? Am I dressed oddly? I become concerned. But concern is not anger. I don't get mad when I see a look of trepidation on a woman's face as I am about to enter an elevator with her. I know I am a sizeable animal. I know that can scare people—and rightly so. So my natural reaction is to play that down. I stand as far from the woman as possible. I'm polite. I do what I can to ease people's fears, even if that means taking the next elevator. Decent, strong, mature men—regardless of their appearance or race—understand when people betray anxiety in their presence. A gentleman will always seek to respectfully calm that fear.

You should be concerned when someone like me begins to play on the uneasiness you feel and fails to empathize with you. That's a sign that you are dealing with a character-disordered individual or violent criminal. But this isn't about being scared of certain kinds of people. I don't advocate paranoia—quite the opposite. I want to hammer home the message that you should trust your own primal instincts when those instincts are telling you to watch out. Anyone who follows my advice regarding threat assessments will be *less—not more*—likely to falsely assume the worst of someone based on their immutable characteristics.

While we should listen to our instincts, we must always make every effort to treat individuals as individuals in the course of our daily lives. Even if there are measurable and sometimes substantial differences in violent crime rates across different groups, whether defined by gender, age, or race, there is even greater variance in the behavior of individuals within a given group.[38] The behavioral gap between an individual who is stupid, immature, and desperate and an individual who is wise, mature, and content is ultimately the one that matters most when it comes to identifying and assessing threats. As evolved humans, we are fully capable of both learning statistically accurate information about who is most likely to commit violent crime and treating all people as individuals worthy of respect, dignity, and kindness—until they prove otherwise.

Being armed with the right knowledge about violent crime and the characteristics and traits of those who commit it allows us the ability and confidence to interact with others in just such a way. It allows us to see when an individual is crossing a line and is in the process of proving otherwise, because knowing *how* and *why* predators attack gives us better vision of the environment we're in and those around us. Knowing the means and motives of predators also allows us a chance to make small adjustments in our own life that can help keep us safe and informed judgments so that we avoid high-risk situations to begin with. By doing so, we maximize our ability to deny the third and final necessary piece for any violent attack or homicide to occur: opportunity.

Predators assess their prey by examining range, ease of access, risk, potential liability, and potential gain. This is true no matter the city, state, or country. Our job is to limit their opportunities to attack. This means we need to know our environment, or at least trust someone who does. As an example, the first time I traveled to South Africa, violent crime was soaring. In the immediate aftermath of apartheid, murder rates were exploding. Armed robberies and carjackings were common. Predators walked the streets with bicycle spokes designed to penetrate under the rib cage. Public service announcements on televisions, billboards, and buses made it known that having sex with a virgin doesn't cure AIDS. Why the education campaign? Witch doctors had promoted the notion that sex with a virgin could cure AIDS, which led to HIV-infected men raping young children and infants, sometimes as gangs.[39]

Depressing? Absolutely. Dangerous? You bet. How did I arm myself in such a foreign environment with a high risk of violence? I didn't—at least not with a gun. I couldn't legally carry there, so my best method of self-preservation was my driver, a young 130-pound man named Nuno. He had the most important self-defense skill there is: knowledge. Nuno knew where to go and where not to go. He knew the safest way to get from place to place and which routes to avoid. Nuno's local knowledge helped keep me safe by minimizing opportunities. You can't make accurate or reliable threat assessments based solely on countrywide or citywide data. You can't just travel around aimlessly in a place like Cape Town or Chicago or Caracas without putting yourself at extra risk. In the United States, roughly a quarter of all homicides occur in cities with a population of one million or more, and half of all homicides occur in cities with a population of a hundred thousand or more.[40] You have to know the neighborhoods, often street by street and block by block. Even the safest city can have pockets with high crime rates.

It's also important to keep in mind that assessing risk in the places and spaces we're in can change dramatically depending on the time of day, day of the week, and even season. Based on murder data from Chicago, for example, we know that nearly 40 percent of the city's murders occur between 9 p.m. and 2 a.m., and less than 1 percent occur between 7 a.m. and 8 a.m. Further, we know that roughly 50 percent of murders occur on the weekend (Friday, Saturday, and Sunday) and that violent crime increases in warmer months and decreases in colder months, with 31 percent of murders occurring in the summer (June, July, and

August).[41] Other broader-scale studies demonstrate similar findings: (1) rates of "serious violence" (violent crimes other than simple assault) are highest in summer, with rates in fall, winter, and spring standing 3 percent lower, 6 percent lower, and 5 percent lower than in summer, respectively;[42] and (2) the chance of violent crime is lowest at 6 a.m. and slowly increases throughout the day before peaking at 9 p.m., at which point it slowly decreases. The one exception to this nearly universal trend involves violent crime committed by juveniles, which peaks between 3 p.m. and 4 p.m. in the afternoon—the time when schools typically end for the day.[43]

Such statistics are informative and can help us make better decisions in our day-to-day lives that can lower our risk of encountering violence, but we still have lives to live and can't ever erase all risk. We work, raise families, travel, and socialize. This is all part of the human experience, and we thus can't deny predators opportunity in all places and at all times without completely removing ourselves from society. All the knowledge you have about risk assessment and threat avoidance will be worthless once you find yourself in a dangerous situation against a predator with a clear opportunity to strike. That's when it's time to be more proactive. Although I will discuss this subject in depth in chapter 19, I'll briefly share an encounter I once had in Northern Ireland to illustrate my point.

One evening after a martial arts seminar, I was wandering through Belfast in search of a drink with John Kavanagh, one of my first black belts and the head of SBG Ireland, and John Frankl, the head of SBG Korea—two skilled grapplers and solid fighters. We found a nightclub. As it was still early, the club was almost empty. I was surveying the bar when a short, ill-tempered little fellow in a stocking cap approached me and said something I couldn't understand. The music was loud, and his accent was so thick that nothing he said registered as English. When my lack of understanding and interest became obvious, the guy became even angrier. Seeing the trouble from a distance, Kavanagh stepped in to interpret. Apparently, I had placed my foot on a chair, and the guy didn't appreciate that. His subsequent attempt at conversation with me left him even more unsatisfied, as he mistook my inability to understand him as a sign of disrespectful indifference to his presence. In truth, he was correct about my indifference, but after speaking with Kavanagh for a few more moments, he finally took a step back, told us to enjoy ourselves, and walked back to the other side of the room. I quickly realized he wasn't just some irritated vagrant, though he dressed the part—he was an employee. From across the way, I could see him busily chatting on his phone. Moments later, he approached me again.

"Would you be so kind as to step outside," he said. "It's loud in here. Let's have a chat."

There is no way to do justice to the hatred I felt radiating from him in that moment. Missing teeth appeared through his insincere smile. His tone was calm and his eyes were clear. No weapon was visible. But everything about him suggested pure, unmistakable malice. All the hairs on my body stood on end. All five senses went on alert.

I politely refused his offer, then signaled to Frankl and Kavanagh that it was time to go. I could see from their expressions that both of them recognized what was happening. We went out together. Five of them followed us. Just as our feet hit the sidewalk, a van pulled up, and we kept walking. I turned back to see at least ten of them. But we had by then reached a busy street, so they retreated back into their cave.

No guns had been brandished. No knives had been drawn. No one threatened any violence. No one began announcing loudly and publicly that they were about to commit a felony. This wasn't boy-speak. This wasn't the bravado of young, insecure gangstas. This was calculated enmity, as I later discovered when John Kavanagh told me about the short conversation he had had with the man. The call and the van had nothing to do with where I had put my boots; it had to do with Kavanagh. As soon as Kavanagh opened his mouth to interpret on my behalf, the man could tell what part of Ireland he was from. That was when the man stepped back to use his phone. It was then that his goal changed from getting us out to keeping us there a little bit longer. We had wandered into an Ulster loyalist bar, where someone with Kavanagh's accent wasn't welcome. This wasn't about me. This was about sectarian hatred.[44]

When you understand why an attack occurs and the factors that make it easier for a bad guy to do bad things, you can consciously structure your life in a way that allows you to minimize threats. You deny them opportunity by staying out of range. When you're far enough out of their range, you're safe. After all, predators are lazy. Energy conservation is written into their DNA. In South Africa, Nuno knew where that line was. In Northern Ireland, we didn't. Had Kavanagh or I been alone,

I have little doubt that we would have been attacked there and then. But because there were three of us, and because we showed signs that we were aware of the threat, they either needed to separate us or bolster their numbers to ensure their advantage. Our demeanor and communications also warned them that that might not be easy. That's why the little man got on his phone, and that's why we had time to exit the scene and make it to a more populated area.

When we fail to be aware of the environment and its potential threats, we fail to predict and avoid those threats. We needlessly give the predator an opportunity. If you are a fully functioning adult, you are always the person most responsible for your own safety. Although our movement toward a busy street helped protect us that evening in Northern Ireland, you can't always rely on bystanders to discourage an attack, let alone to help you, especially today, when average citizens on subway cars and street corners often seem more likely to pull out a phone to record an assault than to intervene to stop it.[45] Research confirms this isn't just a matter of perception. According to one study, 70 percent of fights, 50 percent of robberies, and 30 percent of sexual assaults have onlookers.[46] In a best-case scenario, you might come upon a police officer in your greatest moment of need, but a police officer just around the corner won't be able to save you from a quick and decisive attack once you're targeted.[47] While you should never rely *only* on law enforcement for your own personal safety, you should also never be shy about calling 9-1-1 for help when warranted. That's what the police are there for—to protect and serve the public.[47]

As I will show, don't be fooled into thinking otherwise.

14 The Police as Threat?

If your intentions don't lead to actions that map accurately onto the world around you, you may move farther away from your goal, rather than closer toward it.

One issue that cannot go unmentioned in any honest discussion about violent crime, especially in today's highly charged climate, is the role of those authorized by the state to use deadly force when necessary: police. What, specifically, does the data tell us about fatal shootings committed by police officers against the very citizens they are sworn to protect and serve? Are police officers actually targeting people for murder based on their skin color, as sometimes claimed? Is this a horrific epidemic, or something else? If you've relied only on what major media headlines infer or activist celebrities tell you about the subject,[1] the answers might surprise you.

We have a good idea about how the public at large might have answered such questions in the wake of George Floyd's death thanks to a survey conducted in 2020 by the Skeptic Research Center.[2] They asked a nationally representative sample of Americans two questions:

1. "If you had to guess, how many unarmed black men were killed by police in 2019?"

2. "If you had to guess, in 2019 what percentage of people killed by police were black?"

They also asked respondents to say whether they considered themselves to be "very liberal," "liberal," "moderate," "conservative," or "very conservative."

Before reading on, any guesses on these two questions?

For the first question—"how many unarmed black men were killed by police in 2019?"—the survey offered a set of possible answers ranging from "about 10" to "more than 10,000." Roughly 31 percent of survey respondents who identified as very liberal estimated that police had killed about 1,000 or more unarmed black men the previous year, with an additional 22 percent believing the number to be at least 10,000. For those who identified as liberal, just under 27 percent believed the number to be about 1,000, with an additional 12 percent believing at least 10,000 had been killed. For those who identified as moderate, conservative, or very conservative, 16 percent, 9 percent, and 13 percent, respectively, guessed about 1,000 had been killed, with an additional 9 percent, 4 percent, and 7 percent, respectively, believing the figure to be at least 10,000.

In response to the second question—"in 2019 what percentage of people killed by police were black?"—those who identified as very liberal gave an average estimate of 60 percent, and those who identified as liberal, moderate, conservative, and very conservative gave average estimates of 56 percent, 46 percent, 38 percent, and 45 percent, respectively.

Did the wisdom of the crowd correspond in any way to reality here? The short answer is no.

Arguably the best available public data on police shootings, found in the *Washington Post*'s comprehensive database of fatal police shootings,[3] reveals the following: police shot and killed 54 unarmed people in 2019, of whom 26 were identified as white, 12 as black, 11 as Hispanic, and 5 as other. Of these 54, 49 were male (23 of whom were identified as white, 11 as black, 10 as Hispanic, and 5 as other). Two caveats here: First, this data doesn't include those extremely rare cases in which an officer killed an unarmed person without shooting them, such as through a stranglehold or car strike. George Floyd's death, for example, would not have been included in these numbers. Second, although classified as "unarmed," many of these police shooting victims were actively trying to hurt or kill an officer or some other party when they were shot. Keep in mind that unarmed never means "not deadly." In any police action in the United States, there is always a gun involved—the officer's—and, in many cases, an unarmed suspect is fighting to take hold of it. Perhaps the most well-known and highly publicized case involving this exact scenario occurred in Ferguson, Missouri, in 2014. At the time, it was claimed that the young victim, Michael Brown, had his hands up when Officer Darren Wilson shot him, in cold blood, in the middle of the street. This account led to a protracted period of unrest marked by waves of protests and riots. Upon investigation, however, the forensic evidence, as well as a half-dozen black witnesses, confirmed Officer Wilson's account: Brown had tried to gain control of Officer Wilson's gun and was charging at him when he was shot. The widely adopted and repeated "Hands up, don't shoot!" slogan was based on a lie.[4]

If we look closely at the twelve fatal police shooting cases in 2019 involving unarmed black individuals, we find the following: in one case, a suspect was killed as he was trying to run over an officer with a car;[5] in a second case, a suspect grabbed an officer's taser and used it on him;[6] in a third case, a female officer was hit in the head and knocked to the ground by a suspect before she fired;[7] in a fourth case, a suspect led a trooper on a car chase before fighting with the trooper;[8] in a fifth case, police shot a domestic violence suspect who stated, "I'm gonna kill every last one of them mother f——s!" before waving an object at them, which those on scene mistook for a gun;[9] in a sixth case, a teen fought with officers after "flipping out" on his girlfriend, running naked through a neighborhood, breaking into a house, and knocking out an officer who had been unable to subdue him with a taser;[10] in a seventh case, a deputy was hit by the rear door of a moving car as a suspect tried to drive away;[11] in an eighth case, a mentally ill man stealing food was shot after a short foot pursuit and struggle on the ground with a deputy;[12] in a ninth case, an officer shot a suspected drug dealer high on methamphetamine who the officer believed was reaching for a gun in his waistband after a brief struggle.[13]

When you set aside those cases in which the suspect is actively trying to harm or kill an officer, or officers have a legitimate reason to fear that their own or some other person's life is at risk, you are left with just a few deaths of unarmed black individuals per year in which the police are demonstrably at fault. To date, only two of the twelve cases from 2019 recorded in the *Washington Post*'s database have led to an indictment for the officer or officers involved.[14] An indictment is possible in a third case.[15]

Just how misinformed was public perception on this issue?

Let's allow for a moment that the *Washington Post*'s database is incomplete and estimate that the actual number of unarmed black males killed by police was 25, more than double the database figure. Even with this allowance, roughly a third of those who identified as very liberal would be off in their estimates by a factor of 40, and almost a quarter of them would be off by a factor of 400! For those who identified simply as liberal, just under a quarter would be off by a factor of 40, and roughly one in eight would be off by a factor of 400. Those who identified as moderate, conservative, or very conservative would have fared the best, with 74 percent, 87 percent, and 80 percent, respectively, estimating the total at about or under 100. They would be off by roughly a factor of 4.

(Remember, the actual number in the database is 11, not 25.)

Similarly, when it came to estimating the proportion of people killed by police who were black, those who identified as very liberal or liberal fared the worst, though moderate, conservative, and very conservative respondents did not guess accurately either. The average survey respondent guessed 50 percent of those killed were black, but the actual figure was just over 23 percent.

Again, my focus is on self-defense, so I'll leave it to others to determine the causes of this disconnect between public perception and demonstrable reality when it comes specifically to this subject. But now that we know the actual data, we can adopt a perspective that maps onto reality. And the reality is this: in a nation of roughly 330 million people, where police have more than 60 million contacts with civilians per year and an arrest is made every three seconds,[16] officers shot 12 unarmed black individuals and roughly twice as many white individuals in 2019, almost all of whom were men. When considering that white males make up roughly 33 percent of the population and black males make up roughly 7 percent, we can easily calculate that—holding all else equal—black victims are overrepresented in these figures.

When it comes to crafting a strategy for personal safety and survival, what assessment can we make given these numbers? Should black people necessarily be more fearful of the police than white people? Is this the evidence that proves beyond doubt that police are intentionally targeting black citizens? Indeed, many in the media point to this discrepancy as glaring evidence of racist policing. However, could variables other than racism account for the overrepresentation of black males in police shootings involving unarmed suspects?

Let's take a closer look at the numbers. In 2019 there were 13,927 homicides recorded in the United States. In that same year, police fatally shot 1,004 suspects, most of whom were violently resisting arrest, armed, or otherwise dangerous. About a quarter of those killed by police that year were black, or roughly double what we might expect if looking *only* at U.S. population percentages (roughly 13–14 percent of the population is black). Yet, if we consider crime rates rather than share of population across demographics, the fact that roughly one in four of those killed by police in 2019 were black is actually less than what we might have predicted. In 2019, black Americans accounted for more than 55 percent of homicide arrests and, assuming statistics from 2018 remained about the same, committed approximately 36 percent of serious nonfatal violent crimes.[17] Given these numbers, you could argue that black Americans were actually *underrepresented* in police shootings in 2019, if you make the basic assumption that the number of police shootings corresponds to violent crime rates. The logic is simple: a group or community with a high crime rate will have more police contacts than a group or community with a low crime rate—especially when it comes to violent crime.[18] The greater number of police contacts or arrests a group or community experiences, the greater chance for a violent or even lethal outcome.

I want to stress here again that the questions we ask are of primary importance, because if we're not asking the right questions, we can't hope to find the right answers regarding important questions involving public safety and civil rights—and we as a society certainly won't be able to protect ourselves or help those who deserve our attention the most: the victims. Of the homicide cases in the United States in 2019 in which the victim's race was known, 54.7 percent were black and 42.2 percent were white.[19] Given this reality, for all those who would still argue that the police are intentionally targeting black males because they are racist, what percentage of police attention do the victims and the communities in which they lived and died deserve? What percentage of police attention should be given to getting violent criminals off the street so that there will be fewer future victims in those communities?

These questions are vital for determining how, when, and where police should operate, given their finite resources. Let's take New York City as an example, where roughly 24 percent of the population is black.[20] In 2021, 67 percent of homicide victims were black, and 61.7 percent of those arrested for homicide were black. In 2020, 65.0 percent of homicide victims were black, and 60.2 percent of those arrested for homicide were black. In 2019, 56.6 percent of homicide victims were black, and 58.0 percent of those arrested for homicide were black. In 2018, 62.6 percent of homicide victims were black, and 60.1 percent of those arrested for homicide were black. I could go on, but the pattern is clear.[21] Every year in New York City, a demographic that makes up just under a quarter of the city's population makes up roughly 60 percent of its homicide victims. We also know that roughly 90 percent of all homicides in which the victim is black are intraracial.[22] Again, this is not surprising, as the vast majority of all violent crime is intraracial.[23] So let me ask, if a group that makes up one-quarter of the total population in New York City accounts for roughly 60 percent of the homicide victims, year after year, what percentage of police attention should that group receive? Is giving that 60 percent of victims anything more than 24 percent of police attention racist? No, of course not. And homicide isn't the only violent crime where this same pattern of violence occurs. If we look at reported rapes in 2021, for example, 37.7 percent of reported victims were black, and 45.4 percent of those arrested for rape were black.[24] Do those rape victims not deserve police attention? Does the community not deserve any meaningful protection from future murders and rapes?

If we apply the logic that every disparity in policing is due only to racism, how do we account for the fact that more than 95 percent of people shot by police in any given year are men,[25] when women account for half the population? Does this imply that police forces everywhere are sexist against men? Or consider this: Asian Americans make up roughly 6 percent of the total U.S. population,[26] but they account for less than 2 percent of people shot by police in the United States. Should we infer from this that police are uniformly racist against whites, given police shoot white Americans at a far higher rate than Asian Americans?[27]

If we use post hoc reasoning, assume that only systemic sexism and anti-white racism are at play, and reason backward from there, we could indeed reach a predetermined conclusion that cops hate men and that cops hate white people. This would be the identical reasoning process used by those who routinely assert that the disproportionate shooting of black suspects is incontrovertible proof of racist policing. The Creationist fallacy of the "God of the gaps,"[28] in which any holes in our current scientific knowledge are seen as evidence of God's existence, has never reflected a serious attempt at finding the truth. Similarly, assuming any disproportionality in police shootings to be evidence of racism only, without bothering to control for any other factors, is no more than a "racism of the gaps."[29]

I don't say any of this to make light of the issue or to detract in any way from the pain and suffering caused when an individual is harmed or killed by a police officer, especially when they are unarmed or an innocent bystander.[30] In an ideal world, there would be no police shooting deaths, and we should take sensible, evidence-based steps to reduce them. But in the real world, there's no reason to believe police shootings should, or even could, correlate perfectly with U.S. Census Bureau data. Believing so is a failure to reason honestly about the best available evidence.[31] This includes accounting for crime rates, particularly violent crime rates.[32]

Any honest look at most of the police shootings anti-police activists commonly cite, and I strongly suggest readers take the time to read the facts about each event, will find little to no evidence for racially motivated murders.[33] Instead, you'll see cases like the one involving Michael Brown, in which a half-dozen black witnesses and forensic evidence confirmed that the initial popular narrative about the case was false.[34] Put simply: if Michael Brown had not attacked a police officer that night and had not tried to grab his gun, he'd be alive right now. And I think most Americans, no matter their race, understand that.

Even in those cases that involve a terrible mistake, such as in the death of Daunte Wright,[35] or when there are legitimate questions about whether a suspect's rights were violated, such as in the case of Freddie Gray,[36] there's usually very little direct evidence of racism. When Gray died in police custody in Baltimore in 2015, three of the six officers involved were black.[37] This was also at a time when the United States had a black president and a black attorney general; Baltimore had a black mayor, a black police chief, and a black deputy police chief; Maryland had a black state attorney general; and a black Circuit Court judge oversaw the trials of the officers. Can Gray's death be directly attributed to police racism? Might the case just show that police brutality, misconduct, and negligence sometimes occur, regardless of race, and that's the challenge in need of a solution?[38] And, as the ensuing trials demonstrated, that due process often reveals facts that clash with the public's prejudgment? Indeed, for every case involving a black suspect that causes justifiable outrage, you can usually find a comparable case in which a white suspect is treated with the same coldness or malice—those cases just don't lead to weeks of front-page headlines. If you honestly believe that white suspects are immune to poor or even dehumanizing treatment, or that justice always rewards white victims of police violence, look up the Tony Timpa case or the Daniel Shaver case.[39] The officers involved in those cases usually end up walking free, too.

When mainstream media and anti-police activists tell us that black Americans are targeted or shot by police at higher rates than white Americans without also mentioning relevant violent crime rates, they are saying something that is half-true and wholly dishonest. The same is true when they filter news stories and we adjust our levels of condemnation and credulity according to the race of the victim(s) and perpetrator(s).[40] Telling half-truths, believing falsehoods, and framing every event through the lens of race has pernicious and dangerous consequences.[41]

The constant attacks on law enforcement, whether through ill-advised budget cuts, regressive anti-policing policies, or the climate of hatred fueled by irresponsible media, have effectively halted proactive policing in many American cities. What makes matters worse from a public safety standpoint is that many violent offenders are either not being charged with felonies or are being put back on the streets in various cities thanks in part to far-left district attorneys, activist judges, and reckless government agencies.[42] As a result, more than a dozen U.S. cities saw record-breaking levels of murder in 2021. Thousands more innocent victims will needlessly die in the years to come from such "progressive" policies. The people who will suffer most from these changes won't be the upper-middle-class urban elites who foolishly push them through. Most of the victims will be poor, many will be children, and the majority will be black.[43] Our most vulnerable populations will also be at elevated risk. Indeed, we have already seen a dramatic uptick in brutal and sadistic assaults on the elderly, especially against the Asian American community.[44] The blood that covers the media personalities, policymakers, activists, and donors who've pushed the defund-the-police narrative will never wash off.[45]

But don't just take my word for it. Listen to what the communities most at risk and in need of protection are saying. When asked to identify the single most important issue facing the community they live in, 17 percent of black Americans answered violence or crime—by far the most common answer (only 3 percent answered racism, diversity, or culture).[46] It's no wonder that black Americans want increased police spending and a greater police presence in their cities and towns.[47] The good people who live in high-crime neighborhoods know better than anyone that cutting police funding doesn't solve our violence problem; it only increases it.[48] And that's exactly what we've all watched happen. I would also caution everyone to remember that in many cities and towns, a sizeable percentage of police officers are themselves black,[49] many police chiefs are black, many mayors and city council members are black, and many attorneys general are black.

Once you actually look at the evidence, read past the headlines, and ignore the current moral panic about our legal and judicial systems, you see that George Floyd's murder isn't an indication of any kind of trend or bias. George Floyd's death stands out precisely because it's an aberration—an incredibly rare, if tragic, event.[50] An officer with his knee on George Floyd's head no more represents the honest and hard-working men and women of American law enforcement than a single black gang member represents black Americans or a single white school shooter represents white Americans. We shouldn't let the media or activist groups that fundraise by stoking divisions ever cause us to forget that.[51] As political scientist Wilfred Reilly wrote *before* the murder of George Floyd, "A remarkable irony of the modern American conversation is that while race relations have empirically never been better, many members of different races are terrified of one another."[52]

In today's tense political and cultural environment, you would think some caution as it relates to stirring up racial animus would be appropriate. And yet, our media shows little to no self-awareness about its own culpability in eroding trust in our most vital public institutions. Heather Mac Donald, who has written for years on this topic, has called this the "high-volume delegitimization of American justice." As long as the mainstream media remains determined to recklessly repeat half-truths and outright lies—regardless of the facts—you can expect these attacks on our poorest and most vulnerable populations to continue.[53]

The core truth is this: the police are a threat to your life—but *only* if you are engaged in criminal activity and you resist arrest, no matter your race. Of the 5,787 known white homicide victims in 2019, before the giant spike in 2020, at least 388 of them were armed white suspects killed by police, accounting for roughly 6.7 percent of all white homicide victims that year. Of the 7,484 known black homicide victims in 2019, at least 238 of them were armed black suspects killed by police, accounting for roughly 3.2 percent of all black homicide victims that year.[54] For those of you who aren't in an armed gang or involved in illegal activity, you're much better off taking simple precautions against lightning strikes than worrying about getting shot by the police. (Note: the average American has about a 1 in 500,000 chance of being hit by lightning in any given year.[55])

Beyond that, when it comes to interactions with police, the best guidance I can offer for avoiding any type of physical harm is to simply comply. This means: (1) obey any and all orders; (2) show your hands; (3) move slowly; and (4) be as respectful as possible. If you're being stopped for some reason or arrested, definitely don't try to run or drive away, and definitely don't resist. Those acts are crimes themselves and will greatly increase the likelihood of a violent response by the police. As any lawyer will tell you, compliance doesn't mean you have to answer police questions, at least in the United States. You have every right to remain silent.[56] But I'm not giving legal advice here—I'm giving *safety* advice. Even if you believe that you are being arrested for unlawful reasons, or that the police are abusing their powers, save your fight for the courts.

And remember, police officers aren't mind readers. In a country like the United States, where there are more guns than people,[57] they have an especially dangerous job and want to get home safely—just like you. In 2019, police died on the job at a rate of 11.1 per 100,000 full-time workers, more than triple the rate for all occupations combined (3.5 per 100,000). That same year, in which police shot and killed 54 unarmed individuals, 86 police officers died while on duty.[58] Also, keep this fact offered by Mac Donald in mind before having a knee-jerk reaction about the next tragic police shooting in which an officer mistakenly kills an unarmed black man due to a poor split-second decision in a moment of chaos: "a police officer is 18½ times more likely to be killed by a black male than an unarmed black male is to be killed by a police officer."[59] I certainly don't say all of this to excuse every police action in which an innocent person is killed, but these statistics should give us pause. The prudent, sensible, and measured approach is to reserve judgment until all relevant facts are known about any given shooting—and not to reflexively shout racism with every breaking news story involving the police.

Given all the data, are you better off with an active and engaged police force in your community, or without one? The answer couldn't be clearer, and it's shameful that so many innocent people have to die simply because people are often too cowardly to state it.[60] This doesn't mean that policing can't be improved, training can't be modified,[61] tactics can't be adjusted, law enforcement policies can't change, and tragic mistakes can't be addressed.[62] After all, any police shooting of an unarmed innocent is one too many, but a strong, well-funded, well-trained, well-supported, accountable, ethical, and responsive police force—one that has the backing of local government, is engaged with the community, and is visible—is vital for the healthy functioning of any society.

Now, what of those very rare instances in which an individual officer assaults or, worse, kills an unarmed suspect on purpose, whether for personal gain or due to rank racism? Can this ever be fully avoided? Sadly, probably not. After all, police officers are human, and some assuredly fit the very profile of a severely character-disordered predator. No amount of initial screening will be able to weed out all bad actors—racists included. In a nation of 330 million people, we will likely always have a few such cases per year. But remember, if you point to those rare cases of police brutality or racist misconduct to generalize against all police officers and enthusiastically march under a banner that reads, "All Cops Are Bastards,"[63] then the bigot with the character disorder might just be you.

15 The Command of Knowledge

Circumstances dictate tactics, and plans change upon contact.

I was once told a story about a self-defense instructor who explained at a seminar that he had a prepared line for whenever a stranger stepped too close to him. It was something like, "You are entering my space—back away now." This might be an appropriate thing to say when approached by some strangers under some circumstances, but according to the students who went to lunch with him after this particular seminar, he used that very line on the hostess who came to seat them. As the story goes, any time anyone he didn't know got too close to him that day, his response was a robotic, *"You are entering my space—back away now!"*

The story is funny, but it left me feeling a little sad—not just for the students who presumably paid to hear him. Imagine spending every waking moment guarding the immediate space around you. In addition to being a miserable way to live, it would undoubtedly cause a lot of anxiety to almost every person you encounter. Imagine how that hostess must have felt.

One simple lesson could have saved this gentleman a lot of misunderstanding and paranoia: the *initiation principle*. It's simple to understand. You need only make a distinction between those *you approach* and those who *approach you*.

Magician Penn Jillette of the famous duo Penn & Teller describes a scenario that perfectly illustrates this principle. If you were to run into a random Starbucks and throw the first man you saw the keys to your Mercedes, while excitedly explaining that your wife is having a baby, that you need to jump into her car to rush her to the hospital, and that you need him to please move your double-parked car, the odds are high that when you return a few hours later, you'll find your keys with the barista along with a note saying where the car is.[1] With this scenario, Jillette is making the point that most humans are good, decent people—just like you. But let's tweak the circumstances a bit.

What if, instead of you approaching a random stranger, a random stranger approached you as you quietly sipped a coffee in Starbucks and asked to borrow the keys to your car because of some emergency? If you were to hand the keys over under those circumstances, you'd likely never see your car again—or find it completely stripped in an abandoned lot.

As simple, commonsensical, and obvious as the initiation principle may seem, people tend not to think about it when interacting with a stranger. Always ask, did the stranger approach you, or did you approach the stranger? Did this person call you, or did you call them? Any time a stranger approaches you, you need to be more aware of personal distance and attuned to certain cues than if you are the one initiating contact.

Unless you're a criminal, a person of interest in an important investigation, an intelligence agent, or in possession or control of something valuable enough for others to be tracking, concern over initiating normal human contact in public is usually misplaced. Just be assertive, clear, kind, and respectful when approaching others. The person you are initiating contact with is probably a decent human being, just like you, and you're likely even asking something of them. In such cases, paranoia is just additional noise, making it harder for you to recognize other possible threat signals. But when strangers initiate contact with you in unexpected ways and places, there is always reason for suspicion. This is when we must heighten our awareness to stay safe.

How can we sort out the innocent contacts from the potential threats? Knowledge is key.

First, remember that nothing is as powerful as your ever-present, highly evolved primal instincts. When your hair stands on end, your skin crawls, or your senses tell you something is off about a person or situation, *TRUST THAT FEELING*. Don't second-guess yourself or worry about being overly judgmental, suspicious, or irrational—or being perceived as classist, racist, or sexist. Always trust your gut. When you hear that voice inside your head attempting to rationalize the creepy vibes you are feeling, ignore that voice. Your primal instincts have been set off. Listen to them instead. Your ancestors did. That's how they survived long enough to create an unbroken lineage stretching back millions of years.

Second, recognize the signals that security specialist Gavin de Becker and others call *pre-incident indicators*.[2] The most important ones to look for in the stranger are:

1. A *nervous demeanor* that is alert for possible witnesses.

2. Too much *unsolicited detail* or freely offered information or an unsolicited promise.

3. The contrived use of first-person plural pronouns like "we" and "us," which is known as *forced teaming*.

4. The failure to take *no* for an answer

5. Aggressive or covertly aggressive behavior, such as *throwing insults*, *pushing boundaries*, or *guilting or shaming* to generate sympathy.

Let me give you two examples from personal experience that illustrate these indicators:

Example 1: While waiting at my family doctor's office with my wife, a nervous (*#1, nervous demeanor*) and sketchy-looking white male came in and asked where the doctor was. I explained that he was in the back with another patient and should be out soon. The man then began to tell us details about his life, including why he had come to this doctor instead of his other doctor and why he had visited this doctor three times in the last month. On and on he went, without any encouragement or even acknowledgment of interest from us (*#2, unsolicited details*). Soon he began saying things like, "Man, he sure keeps us waiting a long time, right?" (*#3, forced teaming*). A few minutes later, while the man was still rattling on, the doctor came out, said a few abrupt words to him, and tried to send him on his way. The man's attitude changed instantly. At first, he refused to leave (*#4,* *failure to take no for an answer*), then he became more belligerent (*#5, aggressive behavior*).

In less than ten minutes, our villain had managed to exhibit five of the most common pre-incident indicators. Once the doctor adopted a sterner tone, the man nervously glanced about the room (*#1*) one final time before fleeing the office.

After he left, I asked the doctor, "Pill junkie?"

"Yep," he said. "He comes in about once a week, but I cut him off quite some time ago."

Example 2: Walking back to my car one night, I was approached by an older man who said that he was stranded because he'd run out of gas, and he hoped I'd be kind enough to give him some change to help him find his way home to his family. As the man was telling me an elaborate story about where he had traveled from and why and where he was going, he pulled a hand-drawn map out of his pocket to show me the location of his car. In his mind, that constituted some form of proof. I share this particular story because this man exhibited pre-incident indicator *#5*, an attempt to generate sympathy. Don't fall for it.

Both of these incidents were harmless enough. Neither man was looking to hurt me physically. One was a desperate addict, the other a con man. All predators—whether their aims are financial or physical—are liars. And most liars use the same generally easy-to-read tactics.

Third, figure out what the person wants. Whenever a person initiates contact with you, they want something. This is true whether their intentions are good or bad. If you can figure out what the person wants, that will help you determine their intentions. Those who initiate contact with bad intentions will always want at least one of the following five things:

1. Money
2. Compliance
3. Information
4. Distraction
5. Movement

And they will attempt to get them using one of two tactics:

1. *Persuasion*—by charming, fooling, or convincing you.[3]
2. *Power*—by forcing you through threats or physical means.

A stranger's level of "niceness" is largely irrelevant when it comes to determining their true intentions. In fact, niceness can be a red flag in many scenarios. Charm is a strategy that hairless primates use to manipulate others, and it's the bread and butter of every con artist on the planet.[4] The man with the map wanted money. He was attempting to use persuasion to get it. Had he come up to me with a gun or a knife and demanded money, he'd have had the same intentions, but he would have been using power instead. Power and persuasion are all any predator has at his disposal, and attacks that end with the use of power often begin with attempts at persuasion.

Money and material items are simple goals. Power and persuasion are the tactical instruments used to acquire them. The rules for dealing with people attempting to use persuasion on you are simple: *be clear and assertive,* and *create distance.* The tweaker in the doctor's office was seeking compliance. He, too, was attempting to use persuasion. He was hoping to make my wife and me allies in his poorly thought-out plot to obtain oxycodone. He could have tried to rob or steal the drugs (using power rather than persuasion), and at some point he might very well try to do so.[5]

With regard to compliance, someone who feels that you've "disrespected" him in front of his peers might want you to comply with some form of threat so that he can save face. But compliance need not require a physical threat; emotional or psychological threats can also be used. For example, it can even be demanded by a young girl at school, who might use the threat of social isolation—"Do this, or no one will play with you"—to make another girl go along with her attempts to humiliate someone else in their classroom. No matter the context of the push for compliance, the same simple rules always apply: *be clear and assertive,* and *create distance* between you and the perpetrator.

When a predator wants information—such as your social security number, credit card number, or maiden name—it is always in order to exploit or harm you.

"Is anyone else home right now?"

"Do you live alone?"

"Do you always come here by yourself?"

"How much did that watch cost?"

"Do you work at night?"

"Are you and your mommy close?"

Don't give any stranger who has approached you out of the blue this information, whether they are at your door, on the phone, or online.[6] If they are asking in person, and you can't simply hang up or delete their query, don't be afraid to let them know that you know what they're trying to do. Start asking them questions.

"Why do you want to know that?"

"What's your full name?"

"Don't I know your mother?"

Be prepared for them to feign offense, declare their good intentions, or insult you. That simply tells you exactly who and what they are and lets you know that you were right to be suspicious. *Genuinely well-intentioned people get embarrassed, not offended*, when they realize that they've been asking inappropriate questions.

Also, be sure to pay attention to the context. Are you being approached in a moment when it would be difficult for you to properly assess the situation, whether due to daily distractions or inebriation or general confusion? If so, this is the moment you are most open to victimization by predators and should be extra wary. The elderly, the vulnerable, and the inebriated are targeted by predators all the time for this very reason. Sometimes these predators work in pairs or even rely on multiple accomplices to create a distraction. Thus, read any obvious attempt by someone to distract you as a *serious* signal that demands your immediate attention. Try to determine the incoming threat, because, I promise you, it's already close.

I witnessed how a game of distraction works to great effect on a visit to Bangkok in the early 2000s, when I spent the better part of a night in an outdoor bar in the center of a strip of nightclubs. A uniformed officer was pacing through the middle of the complex, armed with a long stick. There was also a pack of barefoot children, aged between five and ten, running wild throughout the area. Little kids running around bars in packs at midnight isn't something I typically see in the United States, so they immediately caught my attention.

After a while, their game became clear. One kid—usually a five- or six-year-old, would approach a drunken tourist and try to sell him some chewing gum. Just as the tourist leaned down to hear what the child was saying, another kid would come up from behind to try to pick his pocket. If the kid managed to steal the target's wallet without being noticed, the kid would dutifully walk over to the cop and hand him the wallet as soon as the unaware tourist had stumbled away. But if the tourist happened to notice the kid trying to take his wallet, or reached for it and noticed that it had just been snatched, the kids would scurry off in random directions, hooting and hollering, while the uniformed officer made a show of chasing them, screaming, waving his long stick, and ensuring they stayed hidden until the victim had gone angrily back to his hotel. At which point, the whole show started all over again.

It was a fairly successful scam. The kids took all the risk. After a few hours of observing them, I made the very unscientific estimate that they had a roughly 50 percent success rate. The cop acquired a lot of wallets and who knows how much money over the course of his nightly graveyard shift. Whatever he managed to steal with the aid of the children was likely a lot more than his regular wage. Of course, the locals who worked there all knew the deal. When I asked the bartender why this cop was allowed to exploit the children, keeping them out all night stealing wallets amid all the prostitution and debauchery, she replied flatly, "They're Laotian and Cambodian, from the orphanage."[7]

A more severe variant of this type of distraction game is often played by preteens and teenagers on city streets in the United States. One of my friends in the gang unit in Chicago calls it "the raptor." It starts with a person jumping in front of the intended target.

"Got the time?"

"Where you going?"

"Hey, let me ask you something!"

The question doesn't matter: all that matters is successfully distracting the mark's attention. As the target engages in dialogue with the person in front of him, another person, hidden off to the side, runs at the target, blindsiding him and tackling him to the ground. Once he's down, more people emerge and stomp, kick, and punch him as others rip off his watch, jewelry, wallet, keys, and anything else of value.[8] The strategy is simple if brutal. It also works. For every group assault like this that leads to homicide, there are many more that lead to months of recovery or end in severe, irreversible brain damage for the victim.

So, if someone is trying to distract you, what should you do?

LOOK AROUND!

Step back and away at an angle, and examine your surroundings. Where are this person's accomplices? Where is the ambush? Don't focus solely on what the person trying to distract you is saying or doing: *create space* and look around. Be prepared to run or fight.

The final thing a stranger with bad intentions might want—to move or transport you somewhere else—is arguably the most dangerous. It generally means that the person wants to take you to a secondary crime scene. You should never go to a secondary location. They want to get you away from witnesses, isolate you from the pack, surround you, and ultimately hurt you. In Belfast, they wanted to move me to a back alley, alone. Had I been cocky enough—dumb enough—to follow the angry little man out there alone, his friends would have tried to hurt me seriously, so seriously that this book might never have been written.

The advice for dealing with people who are attempting to move you from one spot to another is fairly straightforward. Don't go. *Never* go.

If you can get away, as we did in Belfast, always do so. If a stranger tries to force you into a vehicle or tries to move you someplace else against your will, fight—*always fight*. Even if they have a gun pointed at you, run or fight. Never, ever comply with a stranger trying to abduct you.

But if a gun is pointed at me, won't I be shot if I don't comply?

Possibly. There's obviously no way to eliminate that risk, but the greater risk almost always lies at that secondary destination. This is a question of relative risk. If someone is demanding that you move to another location at gunpoint, that generally means they don't want to hurt you right then and there. If they did, they wouldn't be asking you to move. There might be too many witnesses, too many cameras, too many cops in the area, etc., so they want to take you somewhere more private first—somewhere more isolated. This is especially true when their plans include rape and sexual abuse. If they point a gun at you and demand you get into a vehicle, and you take off at a full sprint, there's a decent chance they will not fire a shot. And even if they do fire, the odds are good that they'll miss. Most of these goofs have no idea how to properly handle a gun. They may be holding their hand sideways, with absolutely no concept of trigger pull, grip, or sight alignment. The vast majority of predators have had little to no weapons training and would have trouble hitting a stationary target, let alone a moving one.

And if you do get hit by a bullet in a populated public area, the odds of survival are better than you might think. The success rates of U.S. emergency rooms are phenomenal, especially those located in cities like Detroit, Chicago, Memphis, and New Orleans, which have the highest rates of gunshot wounds in the country. Thanks to amazing doctors, nurses, and emergency medical technicians, the chances of dying from an interpersonal gunshot wound is—on average—22 percent. That means that if you get to the ER within a reasonable amount of time after being shot, your chances of surviving are around 78 percent.[9]

However, if you get into that car, you'll probably never be seen again—at least not in one piece.

Either get away or fight: compliance will end only in misery.

If you decide to run, don't simply *flee from danger—run to safety*. Running away, in and of itself, isn't always sufficient. Fleeing from danger implies running off haphazardly in a panic. That is better than simply freezing up or, worse, complying, but fleeing without a plan isn't the most intelligent strategy. There is an art to retreat:

1. *Run toward people* and *open spaces*. Don't run toward isolated positions where you will be alone or could be pinned down.

2. *Run light*. Drop anything you may be carrying—books, groceries, etc.—that isn't a child or a weapon. Light travel is fast travel.

3. If you are asked to get into a vehicle or chased by someone in a vehi-

cle, *run in the opposite direction*. Forcing your pursuers to turn around buys you time. Humans can change direction much faster than cars.

Still, when it comes to dealing with violent predators, no rule or recommendation is ever black and white. It isn't always easy to know the right move in advance, especially if you're not already being dragged into a van or forcibly moved at gunpoint. In some situations, for example, such as when you are confronted by a group on the street, turning to run isn't always the best strategy if things haven't yet turned physical. As SBG coach Paul Sharp reminds,

> Predatory chase drive, aka prey drive, exists in humans just like it exists in just about every other species. Unless your decision to run is strategic and part of a contingency plan that will put you in a superior position, you're rolling the dice on making a non-physical encounter into a physical encounter by running. Standing your ground in that circumstance is a deterrent and might give you time to de-escalate things.[10]

The key is to have a strategy and tactics in mind that you know you can realistically execute, even when your mind is clouded by fear. This is true not only when you are walking on a sidewalk but also when you are driving on a road. When in a car in an urban environment, the main threat you face will be from carjackers, which have quadrupled in number in many U.S. cities over the past few years.[11] They typically occur quickly (within 15–20 seconds) and involve a deadly weapon (gun or knife). Carjackers often act in pairs or as a group. They will either be on foot or in another car that bumps into or blocks yours. They are also usually young, either looking for a "joyride" or planning to use the car in the commission of some other crime.[12] But whether you are out in the country or in the heart of a city, here are some basic strategies and tactics to keep in mind when it pertains to your car and driving:

- Have your car serviced regularly and always have at least a quarter of a tank of fuel in your car.

- Leave any valuable items in the car out of view or keep them in the trunk.

- Always leave plenty of space between your vehicle and the vehicle in front of you, whether you're at a stop sign, a traffic light, or even a drive-thru restaurant. That way, if someone begins aggressively pounding on your window or starts pulling at your doors when you're stopped, you won't be boxed in.

- When time permits, reverse park your car into parking spaces so that the front faces outward. Accidents are much more likely to occur when backing out of a parking space, and you will be able to drive away more quickly upon your return if your car has been left front facing.

- After parking your car, pay attention to your surroundings before getting out of the car. If you spot someone lurking suspiciously nearby, park elsewhere, especially if you are alone.

- When returning to your car, have your car keys out and in your hand. Do not waste any time entering the car. Once in the car, lock the car doors and start the engine immediately.

- If necessary, don't be afraid to make noise if threatened while in your car, whether by honking your horn or engaging your car's alarm.

- If you have a flat tire while driving, pull over to a safe area, call your roadside assistance plan (such as AAA if you are in the United States) or a nearby service station, and wait inside the vehicle.

- If you're in a minor traffic accident with someone and they approach and request information, you can show them your license and insurance information from inside the car if your instincts tell you the person is an immediate threat. If no one is in need of immediate assistance and you are not endangering yourself or others by staying in the car (e.g., if there is no risk of fire and the car is to the side of the road), you don't need to roll the window down or exit the car. Tell the person you are calling 9-1-1 and waiting for first responders to arrive.

Strategy is your overall plan—for example, running to safety or staying in your car. Tactics are your means of achieving that plan—for example, running in the opposite direction of the car your attacker is trying to force you into, or blaring your car horn and driving away if someone starts banging on your car window. If our primal instincts are the best tool we have for recognizing a threat, being able to adapt and think on our feet is our single greatest tool for conquering violence. No matter how well thought out our strategy, no matter how superior our tactics are, the moment we make contact with the enemy, we need to be prepared to change them.

We don't want a sudden attack or the sudden need for a change in plans to render us indecisive or frozen. If you're stuck in a situation in which someone is aggressively demanding something of you and decisive action is needed before things turn even more violent, you'll need to make some quick calculations based on the following questions:

1.   What is their *objective*?
2.   What is in *my* interest here?
3.   What are the available *means*?
4.   What is the *best* possible result?
5.   What is the *worst* possible result?[13]

Some of the answers to these questions can be preprogrammed in advance. This will save you precious time when determining your response. Is my wallet worth my life? No. Therefore, is it in my interest to risk my life, if all the attackers really want is my wallet or even my car? Almost certainly not. Is your child or spouse worth your life? For me, the answer is always an absolute yes. I will engage physically if they are threatened, with a weapon if I have one. If I don't have a weapon, I will look to see if there is anything around I can use as one. There almost always is, even if it's just a pencil or a pen or a set of keys that I can hammer grip or set in my fist. Finally, consider the odds. Can you walk away? If so, should you?

I'd be lying if I said it's always best to walk away from a fight if you are able to. There are times when that option only leads to more suffering. But don't let your ego, your stupidity, or your misplaced confidence be the thing that goads you into an unwise conflict. Remember, two-thirds of drowning deaths involve people who know how to swim—many of them are highly experienced.[14] If an increase in your knowledge leads to an increase in risk-taking due to overconfidence, that knowledge won't necessarily lead to the desired results—your safety and survival.[15]

Knowledge improves our chances of safety and survival only to the extent that we adjust our beliefs and actions to align with reality.

The ultimate goal, of course, is to never have to run or fight at all. When it comes to self-defense, having basic knowledge about predators and how they operate is our first line of defense. It's what allows us to take simple and effective steps before threats arise—to prioritize. All of the small commonsense details you know matter. Pay attention when someone approaches you. Lock your doors. Close your curtains at night. Listen to your primal instincts. These are not complicated recommendations or difficult skills to acquire, but they are vital to your safety. If you don't prioritize these things, everything else you might do to bolster your self-defense capabilities—such as training in the martial arts or carrying a weapon—will offer protection only once the situation has advanced, often avoidably so. In the case of the Petit family, the creatures who raped, murdered, and burned the mother and daughters didn't disable an alarm system and then kick down the front door or break a side window. They quietly entered through a back entrance that had been left unlocked.

What do predators always assess when choosing their victims? If you've read this far, you already have this knowledge: *range, risk*, and *reward*. They generally aren't looking for prey that's out of easy reach or risky to catch. On the whole, predators are lazy. The lion doesn't chase the gazelle that runs well. Turning a door handle only to find it locked is often enough to deter a burglar.

If a locked door wouldn't have deterred Hayes and Komisarjevsky, what if the Petits had had an alarm system? A broken door or jimmied window would have triggered an alarm that would have immediately alerted the family and their neighbors, and likely even the police, and those two idiots would have probably fled in a panic. If an alarm wouldn't have deterred them, what if the Petits had had a dog? A large, loud dog is kryptonite to the kind of creeps who invaded the Petits' world.[16] Sometimes, a large dog bowl placed by a back door is enough to cause a predator to move on.[17] These are all simple measures that can deter men like Hayes and Komisarjevsky—but they need to be in place in advance.

Such basic measures should never be skipped in favor of a gun. Indeed, having a weapon in your home is all the more reason to keep your home locked and secure. In the case of the Petits, a gun would have done little good because those two lowlifes were able to enter completely undetected. Dr. Petit was asleep when they found him. The gun would have allowed the Petits to better defend themselves only if they had also had some warning of an active home invasion, whether in the form of a smashed window, an alarm system, or a dog.

Prioritizing isn't just important—it's everything, no matter the type of violent crime. For example, you are unlikely to ever find yourself in a position where you can prevent a child molester from hurting your kids by physically fighting them. If you are physically fighting them to protect your kids, it likely means you are at least one step too late. It likely means the molester already had access to your kids and was caught either in the act of molestation or in a molestation attempt. The key here is prevention, which needs to occur much earlier. The first thing you need to worry about is the person who offers to babysit your kids for free or who wants to spend more time with them because they're "special"—that person might just be a degenerate. Prioritizing what we need to be concerned about, and addressing those concerns in a rational way, keeps us, our families, and our children more secure.

Another example of prioritization involves school shootings, a subject about which I'm often invited to speak. Some safety experts recommend arming teachers and placing armed police on every campus as a possible solution. While I wouldn't necessarily rule out those options, they are not the priority. Just as denying child molesters access to kids is step one, so too is denying armed killers easy access to schools. The Columbine shooters, for example, managed to enter the school armed with rifles and large, body-sized bags filled with explosives before anyone was alerted to the threat. Fixed points of entry, locked doors, and security monitors might have been enough to stop their attack or greatly reduce the number of casualties. Prioritizing children's safety in school means prioritizing the ways in which we control access to the school.

But prioritization, of course, isn't always enough. You may have prioritized your threat responses. You may eat well, work out regularly, behave maturely, have intelligent friends, and keep character-disordered creeps out of your home and away from your kids. You may lock your doors, own a dog, have an alarm system, and train your kids to understand boundaries and defend them assertively. You may understand the distinction between someone who initiates contact with you and someone you initiate contact with, have well-thought-out plans to tackle common threats, and be armed. But you still might find yourself having to engage in a dangerous situation that you hadn't previously considered. At this point, you will need to rely on other forms of knowledge to survive—you will need that knowledge that will help you improvise. This includes having basic tactical knowledge and sociocultural knowledge. I'll give two examples to illustrate this skill in action.

> **Example 1:** In many small towns and rural areas, officers often have to work alone, and police backup is often far away. That means that the officers there have to be especially smart and careful because they will sometimes have to improvise solutions to problems they cannot solve using sheer force of numbers. As a police officer in a rural California town, my father understood this fact well.
>
> One evening, my dad received a call about a knife fight at a wedding in the local park. Large celebrations weren't uncommon in the park, and, for the most part, they were peaceful. This one was an exception. Few situations are as dangerous for an officer as family or domestic disputes. The officer may arrive at the home of a wife beater, witness him hitting his wife, wrestle the attacker down, and then find himself hit over the head, stabbed, or even shot by the abused wife as he tries to cuff the man who was trying to bludgeon her to death with a whisky bottle just seconds earlier. As my father pulled up at the park, he was concerned that he might find himself in a similar situation.
>
> My father exited his vehicle to find that a large crowd of screaming people had formed around two men—who were probably related—squaring off with knives. He tried to take command of the crowd, but the growing mob surrounding the two armed men wouldn't budge.
>
> Thinking quickly, my father popped the trunk of the squad car, pulled out a flare, lit it, and moved toward the crowd, ordering them to part. Not wanting to get burned, they complied.
>
> Arrests were made, and no one was hurt.

I'm not advocating this as standard operating procedure. These days, such a tactic might get an officer fired. But it serves as an excellent example of someone using his intelligence to improvise a solution to a problem involving violence.

At the most basic level, this means knowing how to gain a tactical advantage, such as by finding cover, taking high ground, identifying access and exit points, or grabbing an object that can serve as a weapon. When improvising in this way, do not filter your actions based on how you would behave in an ideal or normal situation. By definition, the situation you are in is an extraordinary one involving violence—or at least the strong potential for violence. I am not suggesting that you intentionally break the law. But what I am saying is that violent criminal predators don't care about the law, and you don't want them to discover an advantage that you overlooked simply because you're spending time thinking about ethics when you should be focused on the immediate threat in front of you.[18]

Example 2: I was once at a nightclub in Alabama when a fight began to look inevitable. We had been training in BJJ all weekend and were relaxing and having some drinks at the hotel bar. It was dance night, and many people there that night were locals, many of whom were overweight and middle-aged. After one too many bourbons, one of the other coaches made a couple of jokes about the nature of the crowd, which one of the locals overheard. Words were exchanged, and it was obvious a fight was about to go down. There were about four of us, but this man was a regular, and, looking around, I could see that he had the support of quite a few friends.

I felt bad for the fellow. This was his spot, we were strangers, and he had been insulted. I told him that we meant no offense, explained that we had just come from a long work weekend, and engaged him in a conversation about identity. "Isn't it interesting," I asked, "how we can all sometimes adopt habits and locations as a form of personal identity and then find ourselves getting wound up over something that really isn't personal?" I was sincere, so he listened. Within a few minutes, everything had de-escalated, and we went back to enjoying ourselves. Had I been too drunk to talk sensibly, I would not have been able to improvise like this—and this would be just one more story about a pointless bar fight. Remember that most violent interpersonal conflicts in developed nations are not about money: they are about status. When you're comfortable in your own skin, a little verbal improvisation can go a long way.[19]

Like anything else, this is a skill you can develop. You know one of the best ways to improve your verbal improvisation abilities—and thus your ability to de-escalate?[20] Talking to strangers.

Unless you are in the service industry, law enforcement, or sales, it may be rare that you talk to someone you don't know. Change that. Engage people in conversation. Watch their body language. Observe how your positioning causes them to relax or tense physically. Talk about the weather, and try to keep them talking without annoying them. It's a skill, some would say an art, but it's definitely going to force you to become verbally agile and mentally adaptable.

SBG has branches all over the world. If you were to walk into the one in Manchester, England, on any given morning during team competition practice, you would witness a lot of banter, much of it slang and—especially if you're not used to the accent—much of it difficult to understand. Some of it is self-deprecating, some caustic or sarcastic. This atmosphere was established by the late Karl Tanswell, who, as coach there, made it part of what they did, part of team culture. If you pay attention, you'll find that much of the banter is extremely clever. If your mind isn't quite alert, if your wit is a bit slow, you might be run over with words. Coach Karl taught that way because he saw banter as a tool. It creates camaraderie, builds focus, and keeps everyone on their toes—that is, it helps keep the fighters mentally sharp.

If you then traveled to the SBG location in Birmingham, Alabama, you'd find a very different accent and group of athletes, but if you watched and listened carefully, you'd hear the exact same kind of thing. The head coach there, Chris Conolley, uses banter the same way. His athletes are mentally quick. His team is close. For them, too, verbal sparring is both a tool and an art.

Despite being thousands of miles apart, Karl Tanswell and Chris Conolley promoted the same learning culture in their athletes. They developed the knowledge to defend their boundaries not only physically but also verbally. That's a valuable skill. And, as with physical skills, verbal skills can be trained, improved upon, and mastered.

Most of you are not MMA fighters or coaches. But I would like you all to begin developing the art of what I call *stranger banter,* the everyday conversations we all have with the people who sell us groceries, pump our gas, or ask us to sign petitions outside the mall. This is what police officers do every shift when they pull up on a scene and get out to talk to people. Police officers who are great at their job tend to do this very well. It needn't be insincere, and it shouldn't be impolite. But it should always convey strength—not through threats, but through the conviction and presence underlying the words, expressed in their tone.

I don't want you to avoid talking to strangers (or even avoid strangers altogether). I want you to become *good* at talking to strangers. The more practice you have, the more obvious it will be when the person you are speaking to has bad intentions. When you are nervous and haven't had a lot of practice with stranger banter, it is especially hard to accurately read the intentions of those who might engage you in conversation. You'll have too much noise in your own head to pick up on any subtle but important signals they might be communicating. But once you're comfortable with such banter, a predator's signals won't be as easily drowned out by any social anxiety you might have.

You should view stranger banter as a real-time training ground for developing effective nonphysical self-defense skills. Just as with physical skills, timing requires practice under pressure. If you don't work with the public and are especially socially anxious, start with totally safe interactions: chat with the person making your coffee or cutting your hair. As time goes on, become a little bolder. Learn to engage in banter. Learn to be comfortable talking from a position of strength.[21] Put your shoulders back and look people in the eye as you speak.[22]

- Be loud enough.
- Be clear enough.
- Be confident enough.
- Be PRESENT enough.

If you're scared at first, just fake it.[23] You'll become better at this in time.

The importance of knowledge for our survival and for the survival of our society, our children, and our children's children cannot be emphasized enough. Seeing the world as it really is gives us the ability to prioritize, strategize, and improvise effectively. Take care of your brain. Nurture curiosity. Value education. Learn. Engage in small talk. Hold in disdain the anti-intellectualism that is so often prevalent in dysfunctional families or communities. And remember that strength and knowledge are never at odds. They are synonymous.

Using our knowledge to be safe and survive is something our species has always been good at. Our ancestors excelled at it, and we have the same ability to excel as well.

We just have to use our *minds*.

Section Four: Prevention

How to Avoid and Outsmart Predators

"The final weapon is the brain, all else is supplemental."
—John Steinbeck

16 The Importance of Maturity

*You recognize that a lack of maturity
is at the heart of most problematic violence.*

In building a healthy relationship with violence to keep yourself and those you love safe, the first thing to understand is that the most important aspects of self-defense have very little to do with actual combat and a whole lot to do with everything that precedes it. One of the most frequently heard clichés about instructors of combat sports is that we don't understand, teach, or emphasize this all-important pre-physical pedagogy. This is simply not true. It would be a mistake to assume that—because what we do physically is so superior to our traditional martial arts competitors—what we do strategically must somehow be lacking.

It's all about your mind.

In fact, everything you need to know about the nonphysical aspects of violent altercations can be found in the simple acronym MIND: maturity, intelligence, noticing, and distance, deterrence, and determination. The acronym reflects the order of prioritization for proper self-defense, with each element leading logically to the next. It starts with maturity for good reason. *Anyone who studies problematic violence and does not conclude that issues related to maturity are at the core of it has not understood the data.*

To recap:

1. Most violent crime is committed by males.
2. Most of those males are aged 15–34.
3. Most violent criminals are not genetically related to their victims but are known to them (e.g., strangers commit less than 20 percent of all homicides).
4. Most violent criminals have prior arrest records, including, in many cases, at least one felony conviction.
5. Most violent criminals come from fatherless homes.

These general trends, which we see in statistics worldwide, demonstrate the central role of maturity in violence—or, more correctly, the central role of a lack of maturity.[1] Profiles of the victims of violent crime give further support to these general findings. Just as predators typically target those within their own communities, they also, more often than not, target those of a similar age. As a result, young adults between the ages of 18 and 24 are more than twice as likely to be a victim of a serious violent crime (which includes murder, rape, sexual assault, and aggravated assault) than adults over the age of 25,[2] and people over the age of 40 make up less than 20 percent of victims of serious violent crimes, even though they represent roughly half the population. A young woman aged 18–21 is nearly four times more likely to be raped than a woman between the ages of 35 and 49. Women over the age of 50 account for only 3 percent of rape or sexual assault victims.[3]

As discussed in chapter 12, I define maturity as a function of the following three traits: *empathy, impulse control,* and *self-awareness.* By *empathy,* I mean the ability to recognize and care about whether you are harming others. I am not talking about sympathy—or, worse, sentimentality, a trait found in abundance within most abusive and dysfunctional families. While sympathy is often a sign of disconnection and sentimentality is often a symptom of codependence and nostalgia born of denial, true empathy promotes deeper connections. It signals that we understand another person's emotional state. It communicates solidarity. When a person lacks maturity or has an impaired prefrontal cortex, his ability to feel empathy is damaged. This makes human connection harder. And this lack of connection to others, to the world around them, and to themselves fuels the emptiness that leads to violence.

Impulse control is managed by the prefrontal cortex (see chapter 11), which doesn't fully mature in humans until the age of twenty-five.[4] Impulse control problems are marked by high levels of emotional over-stimulation and aggression, which cause people to lash out verbally, behaviorally, and violently. An inability to delay gratification is one of the most common traits among character-disordered individuals and violent criminals.

The Latin root of "emotion" is *motere*: "to move." People who lack compassion remain unmoved by the suffering of others. At the extreme end, we call this sociopathy or psychopathy—but it doesn't take a sociopath or psychopath to laugh in the face of someone who's been hurt. When lower levels of empathy are combined with poor impulse control, then the thought, *"Wait a minute, what the hell am I doing to this person?"* may not arise until much too late. This reflects a lack of *self-awareness*, the ability to manage your emotional state and align your actions and behaviors with the standards of action and behavior you set for yourself.

Empathy, impulse control, and self-awareness are inextricably interlinked due to our wiring as humans. As intelligent primates, we have two different paths that our nervous system uses to process stimuli. In his book *Thinking, Fast and Slow*, Daniel Kahneman categorizes these as system one and system two.[5] We can call them the *low road* and the *high road*. We need both paths. The complete absence of a low road would mean an inability to respond to rocks or spears thrown at our faces or to swerve to avoid hitting a deer. A complete absence of a high road would leave us creatures of impulse, more wild animal than human. Both can be fatal. Maturity requires the healthy integration of these two paths, and that must be learned.

I once spent time in Pilanesberg National Park in South Africa, where I slept in a room in the trees, well off the ground. While we were on safari, our guide told us that they had experienced problems with gangs of young male elephants. The animals tore up trees, chased jeeps, and even murdered a few rhinos. Short of killing them, there isn't much you can do to stop angry teenage elephants on a rampage. Our guide was alert to the threat and carried a loaded rifle by his side. What was the cause of the delinquent elephant problem? Nearby Kruger National Park had been struggling with elephant overpopulation. The elephant ranks had grown larger than that park could sustain, so they needed to cull the herd. The decision was made to send some of its elephants to Pilanesberg. Rangers chose to transport them by helicopter, using a special harness. But, of course, moving a 13-foot-tall, 15,000-pound elephant isn't that simple. The harnesses could handle the girth of adult females and younger males but not the weight of massive, full-grown bulls.

By moving out many of the females and children, the rangers successfully thinned out the herd, and the situation at Kruger National Park improved. However, that's when the problems began at Pilanesberg. Rangers began to discover gruesome crime scenes. Mutilated bodies of rhinoceroses started to appear. There are not many things in nature capable of killing an adult rhino. Poachers were the first culprits that came to mind, but these huge animals had not been shot, and their valuable horns—desired by so many who subscribe to superstition and quackery—were still intact. The rhinos had been stabbed—deeply, forcefully, and repeatedly.

Stakeouts were set up, cameras were placed around the park, and the rangers waited. They quickly discovered that they had a gang problem. The young males, the ones that had been transported to Pilanesberg with the adult females, had banded together. They were roaming the park, terrorizing and killing anything in their path. They teased the rhinos, chased them, knocked them over, and then, together, stomped and gored them to death with their tusks. Gang behavior of this kind has been known to happen with chimpanzees, but in elephants, it is extremely rare.

There were young male elephants all over Africa—including in Kruger National Park—but this was only happening in Pilanesberg. What was different? The answer was as obvious as it was hard to fix. Due to the limits of the helicopter straps, mature adult males were missing from the transferred herd. In a healthy pachyderm community, the mature males act as mentors to the younger males. They teach them how to behave and how to treat the females: in short, they civilize them.[6] Young males on the verge of mating season go through a process known as *musth*. Energized by surging testosterone and absent dominant bulls to mentor them, the young, horny male elephants became a violent menace to everything around them.

As I later learned, the rangers eventually managed to design a stronger harness and flew in the big males. The result? In less than a month, all the belligerence, rampaging, and violence stopped. The old bulls had shown the young males how a mature male elephant acts. The gangs of young marauders broke up, and the teens began following the authority of the bulls.[7]

What happens when we switch from bulls to boys?

The prevalence of violent criminals who come from fatherless homes, while factually true, is often disputed by people who don't like its perceived implications. Three arguments are often put forth to invalidate the connection between out-of-wedlock birth rates and violent crime. The first invokes Scandinavia, where the out-of-wedlock birth rate is high but violent crime is low.[8] The second points out that violent crime rates have been steadily dropping while out-of-wedlock birth rates have remained stable or increased. And the third maintains that children raised by single fathers fare worse in life than those raised by single mothers.

I'll address each argument in turn.

First, at a superficial glance, Scandinavia appears to falsify any theory linking out-of-wedlock birth rates to violent crime rates. Indeed, Sweden has a low annual homicide rate (approximately 1 per 100,000 people),[9] even though it has a high out-of-wedlock birth rate (roughly 50 percent). But this isn't the whole story. As Swedish economist Tino Sanandaji notes,

> [O]nly 10 percent of children in Sweden are born to couples who are not either married or co-habiting at the time of birth. Even that exaggerates, since many couples start cohabitation after birth. Obviously what we are interested in is the child having two parents, not if they are in a Christian marriage or secular Swedish cohabitation. Only 3 percent(!) of children in Sweden are born to single mothers. Swedes can afford to be so politically liberal ideologically because they are so socially conservative in their private behavior.[10]

The Swedes call this form of cohabitation *samboförhållande*, and it is identical in practice to marriage in the United States.

The key statistic to examine here is the 3 percent of Swedish children living in fatherless homes. In those cases, we find the same problems we see in the United States. Sanandaji explains:

In both Sweden and the United States, children of single mothers earn less and are less likely to go to college. We don't know for sure to what extent this is caused by single-parenthood itself or by confounding effects. In both countries single-parenthood is correlated with less social capital and other problems that both cause single-parenthood itself and other undesirable outcomes. This does not change the fact that population groups characterized by single parenthood have worse outcomes even in welfare states.[11]

Other researchers have made similar conclusions.[12] Put simply, ignorance of cultural differences between Scandinavians and Americans helps perpetuate the belief that single-parent homes do not negatively affect child outcomes, whether related to future education level, job earnings, or crime rates.

Second, some researchers point to dropping crime rates—despite steady or rising out-of-wedlock birth rates—as evidence that fatherlessness plays little to no role in quelling violent crime. For example, the Liz Library, a feminist website sponsored by the law offices of attorney Elizabeth J. Kates that deconstructs "fatherhood propaganda," calls the idea that "juvenile delinquency is caused by 'fatherlessness'" a myth. The site "debunks" this so-called myth by noting that crime rates have been on a downtrend while the number of single-parent birth rates have been on an uptrend and stating that there is a "consistent relationship between juvenile delinquency and large family size, marital disharmony, alcohol abuse in parents and overall social deprivation.[13]

Unlike the Scandinavian argument, which would, if true, offer a case against my thesis, this argument warrants no serious attention. You can't refute the problem of fatherless homes by pointing to data on dropping crime rates *as a whole* and highlighting other causes of delinquency. I am not disputing the fact that things have generally been improving or that there are other causes of delinquency. I'm interested specifically in the effects of *fatherlessness*. On average, are children living in fatherless households doing as well as children living with both parents? The answer, of course, is that they are not. It is the differences in outcomes between these two groups of children that we are talking about.

Has violent crime been decreasing over the decades? As a whole, yes. Does that mean that out-of-wedlock birth rates are not linked to crime rates because out-of-wedlock birth rates are not also decreasing?

Of course not. There are many possible explanations for the overall drop in violent crime in the United States despite steady or even increasing out-of-wedlock birth rates. One is the legalization of abortion in 1973. As Levitt and Dunbar note in *Freakonomics*,

> Decades of study have shown that a child born into an adverse family environment is far more likely than other children to become a criminal. And the millions of women most likely to have an abortion in the wake of *Roe v. Wade*—poor, unmarried, and teenage mothers for whom illegal abortions had been too expensive or hard to get—were often models of adversity. They were the very women whose children, if born, would have been much more likely than average to become criminals.[14]

In 1980 alone, 1.6 million abortions were performed in the United States.[15] Statistically speaking, this means there were 800,000 fewer fifteen-year-old males in 1995 than there otherwise might have been, many of whom would have been born to poor, single mothers. Wherever a sizeable population of young men from fatherless homes exists, you will find higher rates of crime. Anything that decreases the size of that demographic will thus also decrease crime rates.

Imagine for a moment that we take 100,000 people, all of whom smoke three packs of cigarettes a day, and that, through multiple studies, it is determined that smoking three packs a day is harmful. Then imagine that over time we become better at early diagnosis and treatment as it relates to cancer, heart disease, and other sicknesses that are exacerbated by smoking. Now imagine that other studies are done, and the rate of death and disease among a population of 100,000 smokers was found to be decreasing, even though these smokers still smoked three packs a day.

"Voila!" we say. "Cigarettes clearly can't be the cause of these diseases. After all, we smoke just as much as before, if not more, yet the death toll is decreasing."

That, in a nutshell, is as deep as the argument gets. This is the same type of subterfuge a tobacco company apologist might attempt. And given the subject matter, it's potentially just as dangerous to public health.

There are many economic, educational, legal, political, and cultural reasons why crime rates can fall. The question of abortion aside, one fairly obvious one is the incarceration rate of repeat offenders. If more repeat offenders are being locked up today than yesterday, for example, we would expect to see a drop in the violent crime rate. When you make no effort to control for any other factors or any macro-level changes in society, you're not making an honest attempt at discovering the truth.

Third and finally, some researchers argue, "Well, single dads are bad, too!" when trying to advance the idea that fatherlessness is not connected to violent crime rates. This "defense" is equally silly because pointing out negative statistical data regarding motherlessness is not a rational defense of fatherlessness. Nor does it contradict the thesis. If a father gains sole or even primary custody of a child, it often means the mother has been severely negligent. The fact that children also do poorly in motherless homes is *not* an argument in support of children being raised in fatherless homes.

When it comes to the connection between out-of-wedlock birth rates and crime, the scientific evidence is substantial and has been growing for decades.[16] As researchers Cynthia Harper and Sara McLanahan report, when controlling for income and other factors, "youths in father-absent families (mother only, mother-stepfather, and relatives/other) . . . [have] significantly higher odds of incarceration than those from mother-father families."[17] Multiple studies support this finding. One study, for example, observed that boys in mother-only households exhibit higher levels of aggression than boys in households with both parents,[18] and another study found that future murder rates increased 5 percent for every 1 percent increase in out-of-wedlock births between the years 1965 and 2002.[19] Indeed, the dramatic collapse of the family unit across all demographics correlates with a sharp rise in violent crime rates in the late 1960s, 1970s, and 1980s, but this finding also helps explain changes in the rates of violent crime within demographics across time. As you might therefore predict, when we control for out-of-wedlock birth rates, the large differences in violent crime rates across demographics begin to disappear. The same is true when we look specifically at homicide rates, which track closely with the percentage of nonmarital births across demographics (see figures 3 and 4). Today, more than 70 percent of black children in the United States are born out of wedlock (up from 25 percent in 1964), which is nearly double the rate of white children born out of wedlock and more than quadruple the rate of Asian children born out of wedlock in the country.[20] As a U.S. presidential candidate, Barack Obama understood the significance of this fact:

If we are honest with ourselves, we'll admit that too many fathers are ... missing ... from too many lives and too many homes. They have abandoned their responsibilities, acting like boys instead of men. And the foundations of our families are weakening because of it. You and I know how true this is in the African-American community. We know that more than half of all black children live in single-parent households, a number that has doubled since we were children.[21]

The implications are clear: young men with absent fathers in poor areas with failing schools and little hope, surrounded by other fatherless young men just like themselves, often have no idea what being a man actually means.[22] This is true no matter their race. They confuse cowardice for masculinity and weakness for power. They don't know what strength, respect, and dignity look like, so those things remain beyond their grasp. They mistake behaving like a clown for being cool. They mock other males for studying, for being considerate, or for speaking properly. At the same time, they're taught to view themselves as victims and to see society at large as the enemy. And they leave high school either as graduates or dropouts without any of the skills necessary for becoming a productive member of society or for earning a livable wage. Why would they *not* turn to crime?

Multiple studies show that, by the age of nine, a child's peer group tends to be a stronger influence on them than their parents. Yet we also know that one of the most common traits among violent offenders is the lack of a father in the home. How do we reconcile these two facts?

A good father, like a good coach, helps control the environment within which the child or student operates. He provides a level of safety and stability that allows the key elements that propel maturity and growth—a willingness to be *vulnerable* and to accept the *opponent process*—to operate. At the same time, he weeds out the predators and parasites who seek to exploit and denigrate anyone who appears accessible and defenseless.[23]

While I admire and respect teachers, social workers, youth coaches, and police officers, they cannot ever fully replace fathers. Replacing fathers with more X simply isn't a sustainable solution for individuals or communities.[24] No matter how many police are hired and trained, for example, they will quickly be outnumbered if they are operating in an area that lacks a critical mass of fathers in homes. Real men don't assault

Figure 3. Percent of live births to unmarried mothers in the United States by race, 1980–2005

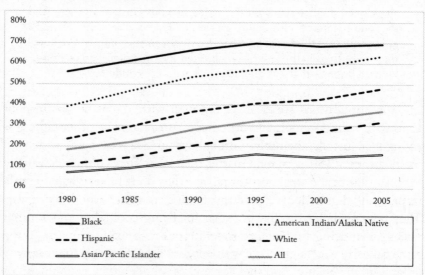

Source: "Table 7: Nonmarital Childbearing, by Detailed Race and Hispanic Origin of Mother, and Maternal Age: United States, Selected Years 1970–2008," CDC, https://www.cdc.gov/nchs/data/hus/2010/007.pdf.

the vulnerable: they protect them. And teaching that most basic tenet of manhood is the job of dads.[25] When the only male role models young men have are their peers, not their fathers, boy-speak prevails, and violence over petty issues of *respect* ensues. The desire not to be "disrespected" is directly correlated with a lack of status within society.

When young fatherless males lack the guidance of older men, they turn to their peer group for role models. If those other young males are affected by the same issues, a large number of police will be required to maintain public safety. And it isn't just the males within the peer group who will influence them. As with so many things in nature, much of their behavior will be geared toward accessing mates.

If tacky displays of property lead to increased sexual access to females, young men will be vulgar. If demonstrations of aggression and violence lead to increased sexual access to females, young men will be brutal. No matter how minor or petty a dispute might seem, if the young

Figure 4. Crude homicide rate per 100,000 males in the United States by race, 2000–2020

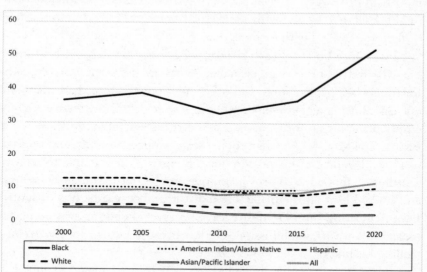

Source: National Center for Health Statistics, CDC Wonder, https://wonder.cdc.gov/Deaths-by-Underlying-Cause.html.

Note: Post-2015 data for American Indian/Alaska Native is incomplete.

males involved have reactive-aggressive tendencies, lack maturity, and are competing over mates, they will end up having a violent altercation. If you drop those males into an environment that mistakes aggression born of fear for power deserving of respect, then you will get wholesale slaughter. Making matters worse, pop culture often glamorizes and valorizes this type of kill-or-be-killed lifestyle, which is actually just a gathering together of the afraid, the ignorant, and the misogynistic.

Being mature means knowing when to take the high road and knowing when to take the low. This means knowing when to use violence *(rarely, but only as demanded)* and how much to use *(just enough, but no more)*. This is not always an easy course to navigate, but the mature intuitively understand the rough contours of the two paths. If your only choice is between becoming a victim and fighting, you should *always* fight. Yet, many situations that might require the use of physical contact don't legally—or even ethically—warrant gouging someone's eyeballs.

Gropey drunk uncles at family events, mentally unstable cousins throwing fits in driveways, or even pushy character-disordered individuals all might deserve to be met with some level of physical force, but not disfiguring force applied with extreme malice.

I was once hired to teach airport police how to safely extract someone who refuses to leave an airplane. Planes are not great environments for things like pepper spray, and other solutions the force had tried—in one case, hitting a guy with a flashlight—were deemed excessive. On an empty plane set up for training, I asked those assembled to show me a typical situation. A large man took a seat, gripped it tightly, and refused to move. I looked at his posture for a moment. Then, I squatted down a little bit, applied a control technique from Greco-Roman wrestling, and walked him off the plane. He didn't leave because he was in agony. I wasn't hurting him. He didn't leave because something was going to break. This wasn't a submission. He left because he had to. I was controlling his body.

Those at the training looked at me as if I'd used magic. Granted, I myself am a large man. If you needed to be my size to execute this particular move, however, it wouldn't be considered a fundamental of the delivery system of clinch. It would be a peculiarity of my personal "style." (When I use the word "fundamental," I don't mean what's most *basic;* I mean what's most *important.*) If you recall my discussion about epistemology, this action—to be truly testable and functional—would need to be one that everyone could perform and repeat. Within an hour, I had everyone at the training performing the move efficiently and effectively.

Contrast this with fantasy-based martial arts and self-defense curricula that are purportedly designed for "life-threatening" situations *only.* You're thrown to the ground? Gouge the attacker's eyes. You're cornered in an alley? Kick the groin. You're forcibly grabbed? Bite whatever flesh you can. Setting aside the fact that none of this is easy to do—especially if you're out-of-shape, overweight, and unathletic, with little to no skill in any combat sport—it also represents the extreme.

The key point here is that not every confrontation warrants inflicting brain trauma or taking out an eye. Combat sports give us options. Skill in combat sports, grappling in particular, gives us lots of options. To better put this intuitive concept into practice, John Frankl, head of SBG Korea, developed a program he calls Appropriate Response Training, or ART, which involves learning to regulate force according to the situation. As a highly experienced Brazilian Jiu-Jitsu practitioner, Frankl knows how to handle bigger, stronger, uncooperative men without kicking them in the groin. There is a scale of force and a litany of functional, tested, and proven methods we can put into play before we need to resort to the graver options.

But it isn't just good self-defense trainers or BJJ coaches who teach appropriate responses—fathers teach them too. Young men who've yet to prove themselves, who lack maturity, and who have no mature and loving male role models in their lives are the most likely to go straight to those graver options. They exaggerate everything they do. That's how a young man might come to pull a gun on another kid who has done nothing more than verbally berate him.

The list of things boys learn by watching their dads interact with others is enormous. Most involve how they naturally behave, not what they say. A good father will model shaking hands properly, speaking forthrightly, conducting oneself honestly, treating women respectfully, and standing up for others firmly, when appropriate: all the elements of what we often call *chivalry*. By watching their dads, boys learn when they should stand their ground and when they should remain gracious. The ability to be both assertive and polite is critical to success in life, and acquiring that skill set requires a good mentor.

Learning how to respond appropriately is a civilizing process. It involves controlling your emotions, especially those that tend toward violence. It also involves learning delayed gratification, self-discipline, and moderation. Finally, it requires learning to respect sincerely and—when appropriate—to obey authority. Manners that express these lessons communicate character, and a lack of manners signals not only a current lack of dignity but also a future lack of upward mobility.

Most of the mannerless anti-authority rhetoric of immature adolescents and the lazy burn-it-all-down mentality of their adult counterparts can be dismissed with one question: "What would you do instead?" Few things in this world are easier than criticizing long-standing institutions in which you are unqualified to participate. Ineligible commentators have the luxury of abstract theory, never having to face the far more difficult world of practice. Tearing things down is easy; building things up is hard. Good fathers save their sons from wasting precious time and energy by passing on that truth early—well before they leave home.

While most of my focus thus far has been on boys, who grow up to commit nearly 90 percent of all homicides and more than 99 percent of forcible rapes, let's not forget that girls need mentorship and strong role models as well. While boys are more likely to move straight to physical aggression—usually demonstrating reactive aggression—girls are more likely to display *relational aggression* before turning physically violent. This type of aggression can be covert, reactive, or proactive, depending on the exact context. Given the necessity of our ancestors to protect themselves and secure resources, this makes sense. Men fended off competition for mates and materials with the threat of physical force. Women fended off competition for protectors and providers through social bullying and by manipulating relationships. The evidence for this is substantial and growing.[26]

Relational aggression is defined by the exploitation of relationships to harm. For people who exhibit relational aggression, relationships are seen as tools—they are pawns on a chessboard that are moved, adjusted, and withdrawn in order to hurt others or to gain an advantage. Think *Mean Girls*. Social isolation, ridicule, gossip, rumors, secrets, lies, and cliquishness are the weapons of relational aggression, and they tend to precede the use of physical violence in female offenders.

Psychologists working within the juvenile justice system see relational aggression in girls all the time. Some use this knowledge to help train foster parents, who will need to be able to spot these tendencies before they become more severe. Others, like psychologist Stephen S. Leff, use the information to address problems within the public school system.[27] Understanding what relational aggression is, how it is displayed, and when it is likely to occur increases our ability to deal with it. Like all violence, the heart of the problem lies in a lack of maturity.

All social primates—both males and females—need the advice and direction that more mature mentors can provide. A safe community requires strong families. And a healthy population must recognize the dignity and duty inherent in being a parent, whether a father or a mother.[28] When only 20 percent of the parents of children at a given school show up on parent-teacher night, the teachers—no matter how smart, strong, and kind—cannot fill the gap left by the parents' absence.

The human need for a societal framework can't be overcome; it can only be replaced—often with deleterious consequences. Just as fatherless children born in poverty often fall for the costume-jeweled con artists who market themselves as "original gangsters," so too do yuppies born into privilege make easy prey for the sociopathic predators who thrive off the exploitation of the vulnerable. It is no coincidence that many middle-class kids who moved away from their ultraconservative or abusive parents in past decades gravitated toward autocratic and controlling gurus—even sleazy ones, like the late Bhagwan Shree Rajneesh, whose works can still be reliably purchased under the pen name "Osho" everywhere banal tripe is pedaled to the credulous.[29] No matter the targeted demographic, it is all the same sucker's game.

Each of us needs to recognize the areas in which we may lack maturity and the times when we lack impulse control—and be self-aware, compassionate, and willing and able to understand and sincerely connect with other human beings. Without this type of recognition and effort, we—as evolved apes—are vulnerable to acting immaturely and committing violence. But we should also understand that we can take active steps to become more mature.

My inclination to disengage from potential fights has increased with every passing year. While this type of maturation often comes with age, it can also be accelerated through functional physical training. I've put in thousands of hours being beaten up by some of the most skilled fighters on this planet. I know where I stand—something that might have been a mystery to me had I spent the last thirty years of my life behind a desk, dutifully avoiding physical conflict because I had been told that I always should. While the office worker and I might both walk away from a fight, the difference is that my knowledge of my ability to handle physical confrontation if necessary allows me to sleep well at night afterward, because I would not be questioning my manhood—or worrying about the next time such an event might occur.

There is no moment in my day when you would be less likely to goad me into a fight than right after a hard training session—not because I am tired or sore, but because I am calm, centered, and composed. Walking to your car after two hours of wrestling, choking and being choked, and taking down and being taken down by another trained, strong, and committed athlete, you will not feel a need to prove anything should you encounter some emaciated meth head with his hat on crooked, waving his arms in a primal display of aggression born of fear. You might smile, ignore him, and drive away, but you will never wonder if you have been a coward; the thought simply won't arise. You might be annoyed or concerned that he will harass someone else. You might even decide to remove him from a place where he could pose a threat to others. But you will realize that he is, in a very tangible way, beneath your physical level. That confidence, which comes from tested, verifiable, ingrained skill, cannot be faked any more than you can fake physical strength. You carry it with you. You always know it's there.

Ask yourself: how likely are you to allow yourself to be coerced into an avoidable conflict? If you found yourself being harassed, having your manhood questioned, and you walked away, would you beat yourself up over it? How negative would your internal dialogue become? How weak would you feel? The degree to which you would feel *punked* in such a situation is the degree to which you might be suckered into a status-based dispute. Be honest with yourself. If you know you are thin-skinned on this topic, get yourself to a combat sports gym. I don't care if it's a wrestling club, a Judo dojo, a Muay Thai gym, or a Brazilian Jiu-Jitsu or MMA academy. What matters is that the training must be *real*.[30] It must involve physical contact and athleticism and promote physical conditioning. It should challenge you. Over time, you will become stronger and more self-aware in violent contexts. You will improve your relationship with the topic. You will carry your tested skills with you everywhere you go. They will become like a second language, a proficiency that cannot be faked. And they will help keep you safe.

Real self-defense is the art of self-preservation, and it begins with the individual. You have to take personal responsibility for your own safety and well-being. It is your job. And that job begins with deep, internal, honest, brutal self-reflection. Your awareness of your own relationship to violence is the first sign of advancing maturity—and that maturity is more likely than any other factor to keep you safe. Your impulse control and your ability to empathize with others will increase as you become more in touch with your body. About half of you reading this will die not from a predator's knife or drive-by shooting but from heart disease or cancer. Most others will die from other health problems. Getting in touch with your internal, primal, physical animal self through contact sports will not only strengthen your relationship to violence and make you skilled at its application but also get you into healthier physical and mental shape. And getting in better shape is the single best thing you can do by way of self-preservation.

Increasing your maturity through combat sports training can also help you better assess external threats, because you will more clearly see the immaturity in others that you no longer express. Self-defense largely involves recognizing those around you who haven't yet matured internally. When animals become frightened, they try to make themselves appear larger. Cats and dogs will puff out their fur, bare their teeth, and arch their backs. Bears will stand upright with their arms wide open, gesturing with large, expansive motions. In the human animal, where do we see these same mannerisms? Look for a person trying to look larger than they are. Look for a dramatic gait and oversized clothes,[31] for theatrical gestures and obvious attention seeking. Where we find that we find fear, fear born of a lack of status, dignity, and power. You know this type of immaturity when you see it, and you need to recognize it as a threat. Not because it is strong, smart, or brave but because it is dumb, desperate, and—as a consequence—dangerous.

In his prime as a fighter, Rickson Gracie could have easily choked 99.999 percent of the men on this planet unconscious within seconds. Yet, he was more frightened of an armed and scared thirteen-year-old on the street than of a brave 280-pound trained fighter in the cage. He understood that the boy's immaturity made him a far greater physical threat. You must understand this, too. Gaining in maturity—and recognizing its absence in others—is your most important asset when it comes to self-defense.

17 The Importance of Intelligence

When it comes to survival, being smart matters—a lot.

Apart from maturity, nothing will help keep you safer from predators than intelligence—specifically, applied intelligence—the second foundational element in our MIND acronym.

Young men commit most violence, and they are also its chief victims. But young women are especially vulnerable to violence and need to learn to stay safe.[1] While the last chapter was mostly about boys, much of this one is about girls. I want my daughters to be smart about how they interact with and navigate the world. This means being realistic about the threats they might face without getting caught up in what columnist Joanna Williams calls "the feminism of fear."[2] This means being uninhibited about having normal interactions with boys and men, knowing when and how to be assertive, and being unafraid to speak their minds and defend their boundaries. This type of assertiveness requires confidence, which, in turn, requires maturity. All three of these traits must be nurtured for children to act intelligently.

No child will be able to defend their boundaries if they have no understanding of them. While sons often need boundaries to keep them in line, daughters often need them just to feel safe. Young girls who grow up without the safety that a strong father provides are less likely to develop the trust required to tell an adult when someone is trying to harm them. If they lack a safe, stable, loving, connected family environment, they will be more vulnerable to sexual predators and character-disordered creeps. They will be more likely to be picked out as targets and less likely to fight back. In short, they will be more likely to become victims,[3] if for no other reason than they will lack the confidence to say no.[4]

The type of confidence I'm talking about cannot be faked.[5] A girl might be able to mimic the appearance of confidence, and there are circumstances—athletic competitions, for example—when doing so might be useful, but that's not true confidence. True confidence is the product of maturity—which, as discussed, involves empathy, impulse control, and self-awareness and is built by observing other strong, mature people and committing oneself to disciplined practice.

One of my black belts, Leah Taylor, is a world-champion competitor.[6] She trains every day, teaches at an SBG, and spars and wrestles with men all the time. She knows what it feels like to escape when a large man is trying to hold her down. She knows what it feels like to choke someone who doesn't want to be choked. And this knowledge does two things. First, it makes her less likely to become selected by your typical street trash as a plausible victim—due to how she carries herself. And second, it makes her less likely to escalate a situation that doesn't warrant it. Why? Because she harbors no fantasies about what she's capable of doing, and she has no reason to prove anything outside the arena she competes in daily. In other words, she's way more likely to stay safe and be smart than a person with no combat sports experience.

This type of confidence should not be confused with the modern, scientifically questionable, and culturally damaging concept of self-esteem that is widely promoted.[7] As cognitive psychologist Steven Pinker wrote:

> Perhaps the most extraordinary popular delusion about violence of the past quarter-century is that it is caused by low self-esteem. That theory has been endorsed by dozens of prominent experts, has inspired school programs designed to get kids to feel better about themselves, and in the late 1980s led the California legislature to form a Task Force to Promote Self-Esteem. Yet . . . the theory could not be more spectacularly, hilariously, achingly wrong. Violence is a problem not of too little self-esteem but of too much, particularly when it is unearned.[8]

I am talking about the type of confidence someone feels on the mat after a decade of training in BJJ. I am talking about something substantial and authentic. Someone with ten years of training in an art like BJJ doesn't have a grandiose conception of their own ability. Nor does he harbor anxiety that some beginner may walk in off the street and show him up in front of the rest of the class. Someone with ten years of solid training knows exactly what he can and—more importantly—cannot do. The sort of comic-book fantasies some people indulge in about the nature of violent physical conflict after a two-day crash course on self-defense, or even after a lifetime of throwing around cooperative opponents in a make-believe martial art like Aikido, can lead to the opposite of confidence: delusion. And delusion can be deadly.[9]

A young woman who thinks she knows but really doesn't is in greater danger than she otherwise might be. She might think she knows someone's character—despite having been warned that she is wrong—and thus ends up trusting them when she shouldn't. She might think she knows something is safe, even if it is unsafe, and thus her misplaced confidence ends up causing her harm. Honesty with oneself and with others is a vital aspect of a strong character. Kids need to be shown that saying *I don't know* when they, in fact, don't know is a sign of strength, not weakness. And by *shown*, I mean that we must model this in our everyday behavior, not just preach it as a goal.

A young woman who, finding herself in a bad situation, ignores her instincts, rationalizes the behavior of her exploiters, plays along, or simply *locks up* is a vulnerable target who will be abused. She is displaying the most dangerous level of ignorance: denial. Girls who have suffered sexual abuse or have character-disordered parents (two things that frequently go together) can easily fall into this trap. Predators know precisely how to spot these girls. When they find a girl who lacks the defenses of a strong father and a stable home life, they zero in.

The first step in making sure that our daughters never fall into this category is to help them build confidence. Like physical strength, grappling skill, musical talent, or any other trade, art, or form of expertise, confidence is a skill set that grows through consistent practice and proper training methods. If someone said she wanted to build leg strength but was limited to just one exercise, I might have her do squats. The first step would be teaching her how to perform the skill with the correct mechanics so that she doesn't injure herself. Next, we would create a routine. No exercise—no matter how amazing—works if it isn't performed regularly. *Consistency is the least applied and most important factor* when it comes to the acquisition of skill. Finally, with increasing time and skill, we would increase the weight. Increase, fail, practice, success. Failure is an essential part of the process of learning any skill. *Winners fail frequently—and winners fail better.* They reach new plateaus and become stronger. The increase in performance ability gained through this process cannot be faked, and true confidence in its application cannot be faked either. If you throw one thousand pounds onto a squat rack and ask me to squat it, I will have zero confidence in my ability to do so. If you throw fifty pounds onto a squat rack and ask me to squat it, I will have total confidence in my ability to do so. I know what I can and cannot squat. If I were wrong, I could severely injure myself. But that won't happen because I know what I can and cannot do. That knowledge is true confidence. Confidence isn't faith, hope, or wishful thinking.

True confidence is the ability to accurately predict performance in a measurable skill. This can be attained *only* through experience and practice.

I want to raise confident, assertive, mature, smart, and physically, emotionally, and intellectually strong daughters, and I want the students I coach to have those qualities too. Once I know that they have the right hardware to defend themselves—the right intellectual, physical, and emotional strength—I need to make sure they are given the correct software, too: an ability to spot predators and an understanding of how to respond to them.[10]

How would you tell your daughter to respond to the types of relational aggression—such as social exclusion and emotional manipulation—described in the last chapter?

Here is what you shouldn't do:

- Never say *I told you so* (that betrays your own weakness).
- Never call her weak (that's projection).
- Never tell her that crying or displays of emotion are a sign of weakness (that's a lie.).
- Never lie to her (that also betrays your weakness).

- Never encourage delusional thinking about the nature of conflict, human beings, or life in general (teach her to value truth and evidence).

Here is what you should do: (1) teach her that relational aggression is a form of bullying—a tool used to get what the bully wants ("I won't be your friend if you don't give me the toy," "I'll make sure nobody is your friend if you don't do what I want," etc.); and (2) then give her some ART, or appropriate response training, which teaches her to confront, rather than appease, the bully. Assertiveness isn't just the best deterrent—it's also the best form of defense once a bully has picked you.

Saying how you feel bluntly, clearly, and loudly is where assertiveness starts. "It's not okay for you to speak to me that way!" is a great response, especially when the child who says it is using the correct physical posture and tone of voice. It's your responsibility to teach her that, too. Have her practice standing tall while speaking up. She needs to know what behaving from a position of personal strength looks like. Kids love to play games, and there is no reason this can't be fun. You want to make sure she is trained in how to do this *before* she is called upon to do it. So start now.[11]

While boys usually fear physical isolation (being smothered, pinned, or trapped), girls tend to fear social isolation (being alone, unwanted, or stigmatized). Bullies know this. It is always better to train your child to resist bullies *before* you see any signs that she might be being bullied.

This brings us to what I call the Safety ABCs (the only acronym aside from ART and MIND that I'm going to ask you to remember).

A is for *awareness:* be aware of what is going on with your child, and make sure your child is aware of what's going on around him or her. Nothing matters more than awareness. When awareness is deficient, parents might not learn about their child's victimization until it's too late. Developing awareness requires hard work, patience, and time. An immature parent who belittles, ignores, abuses, or competes with his or her own children will be incapable of teaching awareness. Aside from being a loving, mature, and responsible parent, there are three ways you can help foster awareness in your child:

1. The child should feel *absolute trust* that she can come to you with any problem, situation, or incident and that you will listen to and love her. Children who have that sort of relationship with their parents are not usually selected by predators. Children who don't are. Selfish parents can never achieve this type of trust. As a consequence, their children are more vulnerable to predation.

2. The child should *know*, deep down, from experience, that you will help her. You won't tell her that she is weak or that it was her fault. You won't lash out or blame her for feeling a particular way. You will listen and respond with wisdom born of maturity and love. And you will help your child solve the issue by giving her solid advice. The child will know not only that she can approach you with a problem but also that you will offer a smart solution. Children who have observed their parents or guardians making one poor decision after another may not believe that they will have much to offer by way of help—even if they trust them—and will avoid seeking their counsel. This is another important reason to start working on yourself.

3. The child should sincerely believe that if she ever *has to fight*, you will always have her back. Regardless of what the school system says or what another adult wants, the child must know that you will always support her when she defends herself. Despite the zero-tolerance bullying policies of some schools, administrators and teachers can be some of the worst offenders when it comes to ignoring or downplaying bullying. Teach your children to *defend themselves* and to depend on themselves.[12] Let them know that you will always back them up, regardless of what some teacher or vice principle might say. This is vital to your bond with them. And that bond matters much more than anything else.

Your child's awareness that she can trust you with any secret—and that you will listen to her, honor her feelings, and support her if she fights back—is the cornerstone of protection. The nature of a child's relationship with her parents is the one thing every pedophile and pervert will try to find out when he interviews her as a potential victim.

Is she isolated?

Is she close to her parents?

Does she trust her parents?

Will she tell her parents?

Will they believe her?

Will they even notice?

An isolated animal is a vulnerable animal. An isolated young animal is easy prey.

B is for *boundaries:* make sure your child understands boundaries and *asserts them* in a healthy way. In addition to her close, trusting relationship with you, your child's own ability to understand and defend healthy boundaries is critical. She can do this by using assertiveness, which, for a child, means the ability to *say what she feels out loud.*

Here are three ways to foster that skill:

1. Teach the child that assertive behavior is healthy behavior. Teach your child that being strong and assertive is good. Help them distinguish between assertiveness and aggression, strength and anger, boldness and bullying. These are valuable lessons that will help her for the rest of her life. Remember that your child is always watching you and that the best way to teach this behavior is to model it in your own life. If you frequently lash out childishly or are unable to distinguish between reactive aggression and healthy assertiveness yourself, you won't be much help. As always, start with yourself.[13]

2. Teach the child that it is okay to say *no* to adults and to defend her boundaries against anyone, whether older or younger, a relative or a stranger. You want your child to understand what is and is not appropriate. This means explaining it to her. What is inappropriate touching? Is it okay if it is done by an adult? Don't assume that the child automatically knows these things. Remember that predators are good at selling their ideas to kids. You need to teach your child that just because a person is a teacher, uncle, or adult doesn't mean

it's okay for him or her to touch her inappropriately.

3. Teach the child *how* to be assertive. Teach your child how to stand tall, speak loudly and clearly, and carry herself with confidence. Walk them through what that looks like in application. That may seem redundant, but there are distinctions between teaching your child that it's *healthy* to be assertive, that they can be that way with *anyone*, and teaching them exactly *how* to do it.

> Is an adult asking her to leave with them?
>
> Is mom's boyfriend telling her to keep a secret?
>
> Is she being bullied by a boy, who is using instrumental violence, or a girl, who is using relational aggression?

Discuss these scenarios and let your children know that it isn't just okay to be assertive—*it's what you want them to do.*

C is for *conflict:* help your child become comfortable and skilled at handling conflict. In our culture, conflict is too often reflexively derided, while tolerance is too often reflexively lauded. The worth of both is entirely dependent on the context. A mother who tolerates her boyfriend beating her child isn't displaying nobility. And a father who comes into conflict with that same boyfriend isn't displaying a moral failing.

When bad people are doing bad things to good people, good people have an obligation to engage in conflict with them. When bad people try to hurt you, you have an obligation to engage in conflict with them. *Conflict can be one of our highest moral duties.*

No matter who you are, where you live, and what you do, some form of conflict is inevitable.[14] This presents you with a choice: either you can just wing it when conflict occurs, or you can prepare for conflict and become more skilled at handling it. Only one of these choices is intelligent.

Here are three skills in which every child should be trained:

1. *Verbal conflict:* being clear, assertive, and, if need be, very loud. Standing tall, speaking bluntly and clearly, and not being afraid to say how she feels out loud are all important. And so is banter. One of the least

useful pieces of advice is *don't talk to strangers!* This advice is impossible to follow. As your child grows and ventures out into the world, she will run into situations in which she'll have to talk to strangers every day. She needs to be taught *how* to do so. (See chapter 15 for more on stranger banter.)

2. *Escape*: knowing when and where to run. Once the child feels afraid or recognizes that things are about to turn bad, she needs to escape. Simply telling her to *"run away"* isn't sufficient guidance. Run where and to whom? If someone tries to talk your child into getting into a car, where should she go? Running to safety is different from running away aimlessly. Here is what I teach my own children: run to where there are other adults and *find a woman*, preferably a *mommy*, and make lots of noise while running from a threat.

   As great as it would be to have a police officer within running distance any time our child is in danger, that isn't realistic. She will likely have to rely on whichever men and women she can find. Women are more likely to take the time to help a child who is seeking aid. A woman who is also a mother is even more likely to pay attention to a lost child. And, while the odds of a random man being a sex offender or predator are extremely low, the odds of a random woman being a sex offender or predator are lower still.

   When my own children get lost, they know they need to find a mommy. Once, while visiting the Oregon Aquarium, my youngest daughter, Una, was separated from the pack. She was three. My wife and I ran around all the tanks looking for her, only to find that she had found a mommy in the next room. She had explained who she was and that she was lost. While my wife and I were distressed to have lost sight of her, we were both happy to see how she had responded. She did what we had taught her to do.

   If facing a threat, the child should yell as she runs to safety. For example, screaming, *"This is not my daddy, help, help!"* is enough to make a lot of predators scurry back under their rocks. She should be loud, hard to catch, and defiant—difficult prey for any predator looking to attack unnoticed. It's vital to teach your child when to behave this way: any time someone asks her to go somewhere, tries to touch her inappropriately, or grabs or hurts her, and any time the child feels scared. We want children to recognize and honor their primal instincts—their fear—and we want them to act on that fear by running away loudly.

3. *Physical conflict:* knowing when it's necessary to fight. If words don't work, and running isn't possible, it's time to fight. One of the most important things you can teach your child is that sometimes it's *necessary* to fight. Physical confrontation is the simplest part of self-defense. Once a conflict becomes physical, the hesitation that often arises as a result of ambiguity disappears. Now, there are clear and obvious goals. If someone is trying to grab you, you need to break free and get away. If someone is trying to hold you down, you need to escape, get up, and get away. We want children to be comfortable with themselves and their bodies and with physical conflict in general. Contact sports, wrestling, Judo, and BJJ are all great ways of teaching children what being physical feels like.

If you want your children to grow up confident and strong, don't shield them from these types of activities. Instead, introduce them into their lives.

Let's summarize the ABCs of keeping your children safe:

1. You are *aware* of what's going on with your child, and your child is aware of what's going on around them.

2. Your child has a solid understanding of *boundaries* and skill in defending them.

3. Your child is comfortable with *conflict*.

Years ago, I gave a talk on martial arts and skepticism sponsored by the Portland branch of the Center for Inquiry. The talk was held in a pub. My family and I were all seated at a table with other people. The venue was small, and folks were packed in tight. At some point during the talk, a man sitting next to my oldest daughter, Anika, who was then about four years old, put his hand on her shoulder. She immediately shrugged it off and gave him an angry look. I could see that the man was startled and didn't care for her reaction. He started to say something by way of explanation, but my wife put her arm around Anika to let her know that her reaction was okay. The man slumped back.

Having witnessed the whole thing from my vantage point on the stage, I deemed it probably harmless. I don't think the man meant anything by it. But I was proud of how my daughter responded. She didn't know him, she didn't want him touching her, and she let him know that very clearly. My wife's reaction was also excellent: she let Anika know that what she had done was okay. She backed her up. Had my wife apologized to the man for my daughter's reaction, my daughter might have learned something terrible that day. Instead, Anika received a mini-lesson on trusting herself, being assertive, and trusting that her mother would stand with her. The last thing any adult should ever do is scold a child because she doesn't want another adult putting their hands on her. As far as I was concerned, this was a perfect learning experience for my daughter. And it was also a great test for us as parents.

The ABCs cover most of what you need to know to keep your children safe. But here are five more specific lessons that you can also pass on directly to your kids. These are the boundaries that your children should know shouldn't be crossed:

1. *I am the boss of my body!* If I don't like something or get the "uh-oh" feeling, I will stand up for myself! I don't need to be polite if I am scared or uncomfortable.

2. *Everyone's bathing suit areas are private.* If someone is touching me there or asks or wants to touch me there, I will tell my parents.

3. *Grownups don't ask kids for help.* Not even to find a lost puppy. And they never ask kids to go somewhere with them. If this happens, I will tell my parents.

4. *I don't keep secrets from my parents.* Especially if another adult has asked me to or made me feel scared, uneasy, or uncomfortable.

5. *I will always check in first before going anywhere.* If I get lost, I'll find a mommy with kids.

Beyond this, be sure they know not only their full name and birth date but also your full name, address, and telephone numbers should they ever get lost. Equally important, be sure they know as well as they know anything that you will always love and support them—and that if they should ever get lost—or worse, go missing—you will not stop searching for them until they are safely back at home.[15]

18 The Importance of Noticing

You are the product of generations of survivors,
and you know when things "Just Don't Look Right."

While maturity and intelligence are the two most crucial factors in proper self-defense, they are not sufficient for ensuring safety and survival if we have poor situational awareness—if we fail at *noticing*. A mature and intelligent human that fails to notice a violent threat can easily become a mature and intelligent dead human.

Even if maturity and intelligence help keep you away from most of the environments in which lowlifes roam, lowlifes may still find their way into your space, and you need to notice them as quickly as possible. To notice things effectively, to be fully aware of what's happening around you, requires letting go of anxiety and paranoia and embracing implementation and action. This takes practice.

Planning is not the same as worrying. Worrying is only useful if it inspires us to plan better. Anxiety and paranoia can make us less safe because they make it difficult for us to identify true internal threat signals amid our own internally generated noise. Like all unnecessary subvocalizations, they bias our attention and perception.[1] This clouds our awareness. Anxiety is fear of what *could* happen (or *has* happened); true fear is an immediate response to something that *is* happening.[2] Paranoia is like dragging our feet on the muddy bottom of an otherwise clear pond. It makes it harder for us not only to see real threats but also to recognize our own true fear, which—unlike worry—is not the result of imagined future threats or remembered traumas, but the involuntary effect of present danger.

Unlike anxiety or paranoia, true fear is always involuntary. It grabs you. It's effortless, authentic, and related to the present moment. True fear is always a gift that we will embrace if we are in tune with our primal instincts. It is literally what allowed each and every one of your ancestors to survive to a reproductive age. As evolutionary biologist Richard Dawkins writes,

> All organisms that have ever lived . . . can look back at their ancestors and make the following proud claim: not a single one of our ancestors died in infancy. They all reached adulthood, and every single one was capable of finding at least one heterosexual partner and of successfully copulating. Not a single one of our ancestors was felled by an enemy, or by a virus, or by a misguided footstep on a cliff edge, before bringing at least one child into the world. Thousands of our ancestors' contemporaries failed in all these respects, but not a single solitary one of our ancestors failed in any of them. These statements are blindingly obvious, yet from them much follows: much that is curious and unexpected, much that explains and much that astonishes.[3]

Keep in mind what Professor Dawkins is saying: *you come from an unbroken chain of success.* This astonishing fact explains why our genes carry with them an unbelievable set of predator-avoidance instincts. The evolutionarily evolved predator-detection system that is innate within us requires no effort other than the strain that exists within the act of listening—listening to our own body—paying attention to what our own nervous system is screaming out to us.

At a number of moments in my life, I have begun to feel the fight-or-flight response prior to making contact with a threat. If I were more superstitious, I'd be tempted to attribute this to a sixth sense. But that would be a mistake. As an animal, you take in far more information about your environment and everything in it than your conscious mind is aware of. This information processing is a biological event—like growing your hair or aging. It requires no effort—it just happens. Things like movement, posture, and tone can set off alarm bells long before you recognize the nature of the creature that is threatening you. When those internal bells ring, don't ignore them.

The fact that primal instincts are involuntary, they are "choice-less," is one of their greatest advantages. Like all forms of intuition, primal instincts always occur in response to something and always serve your best interests. The most important thing you can do to become more attuned to these natural survival instincts is to practice *not* ignoring them.

The command not to ignore your gut instincts may seem simple. But people who are victimized by violent crime often fail to follow their instincts. In such cases, had they listened to their gut, they wouldn't have become victims. As Gavin de Becker rightly points out, violence is not a stand-alone event, but a sequence of events that begins much earlier than most victims recognize.[4] And, while the victim often claims that the violent attack occurred suddenly, the process probably started much earlier than the victim remembers. Usually, the victim was busy rationalizing away what was occurring, and a clever investigator can bring that to light during an interview.

General Douglas MacArthur once said that *all* military defeats could be summed up in two words: *too late*.[5] When conflicts have turned physical and the predator has managed to hurt the victim, the victim's last error can almost always be summed up in those same two words: *too late*. What's the opposite of being late? Being early. This is a key component of BJJ. The earlier you execute your movement, the less strength and energy it requires. The earlier you are, the more effortless the technique. Being early is as important in physical self-defense as it is in situational awareness. To be early, you have to *notice*. Notice what? Notice what your own nervous system is telling you. If you're in touch with your primal instincts and you know the pre-incident indicators, you may have time to plan ahead before the conflict gets physical.

There are three primary reasons people fail to heed their own internal safety warnings. First, there is pride. The fear of being afraid runs deep. One of the great advantages of combat sports is that practitioners develop a healthy relationship to fear through training. Every combat athlete knows that an adrenaline rush—far from being something you should be ashamed of—is simply your body's way of preparing for intense physical activity. It's as normal as feeling hungry.

In many fantasy-based or "street"-orientated martial arts, men who don't have a lot of experience boxing, wrestling, or fighting with resisting opponents will speak of how "calm" they remain during violent physical altercations. Remember that the more someone talks in this way, the less experience they are likely to have. Men who actually do have a lot of experience with violent physical contact know that the feelings that arise within the nervous system don't go away. No one who truly understands physical combat tries to prevent this natural reaction—instead, they try to manage it. People who haven't yet understood this will often feel ashamed when their body begins displaying involuntary signs of external threat recognition. That shame will lead either to bravado (boy-speak), a verbalized form of denial, or self-talk, a subvocalized form of denial in which they begin rationalizing away their physical sensations. This type of denial is why sometimes, when events do turn physical, the assault victim feels that it all occurred "suddenly."

Second, our primal instincts often go ignored because we desire to be a "good" human and wish to be "above" fighting. While, at first glance, this may seem like the more moral approach, moral indignation toward certain acts never provides protection from those acts—as many a pacifist who's been hit in the face has been forced to realize. Of course, there is nothing wrong with trying to live your life in a kind manner. After all, being kind is at the heart of all real morality. But the desire to be kind in all circumstances and at all times can be fatal. Predators feel no such longing. Being kind just isn't a core part of their character. Recognizing that kindness is a core part of yours, they'll prey upon your kindness, use it against you, and try to take advantage of the sense of guilt you feel about being too assertive or abrasive. This type of guilt- and culture-induced restraint—to be "good" at all costs and to be "above" fighting—is the flip side of bravado.

The prescription for this ailment is to teach yourself, your children, and those you're charged with protecting that assertiveness is healthy. Kind humans don't need to be told "*No!*" more than once. Kind humans who recognize that they are making someone else uncomfortable or scared back off. Predators push the envelope. Recognizing your desire to be polite, they will attempt to manipulate you through persuasion or threat. So remember this: *being kind to yourself and those you love means being clear and assertive when faced with threats.*

220 • THE GIFT OF VIOLENCE

Third, people often fail to heed their primal instincts because they've never learned how to listen to them. Children who've grown up in an abusive, alcoholic, character-disordered family often live a life of denial as a coping mechanism. They grow up having to rationalize their parents' stupid and hurtful actions. They learn to lie, and they learn how to numb themselves. This often makes them perfect targets for other predators. Character-disordered individuals and violent criminals can spot these folks. They themselves are often the products of the same sort of broken family structure. These kids grow up skilled at denial. Nothing is more dangerous than denial. They don't willfully ignore their gut out of shame or indignation: they do it out of habit.

In all three instances, the solution is the same: exposure—to conflict, to banter, to physical contact, and to stress. That kind of exposure can be found in every combat sport. Stepping onto the BJJ, MMA, Judo, or wrestling mat and having to deal with another human being who is really trying to choke you, or put you in a position from which you cannot escape, while your peers watch, your coach observes, your mind lights up with self-talk, and your body surges with hormones, heals the human animal. It teaches you that being ashamed of how your body reacts is silly and that ignoring the intentions of others because you don't want them to be true is anything but helpful. It makes you stronger.

As you gain more practice through increased exposure to various forms of healthy stress, such as combat sports, you'll also become more in tune with your own body and better able to read your own primal instincts more clearly. Rather than waiting until your internal alarm bells are at full volume, you can catch the signal earlier while it is still faint.

We can divide our primal instincts into three stages, in order of increasing danger:

Stage one: Suspicion and doubt

Stage two: Concern and hesitation

Stage three: Fear

Stage one is when a thought such as "Isn't it a bit odd that uncle Joe likes to spend so much time with little Lisa?" arises in your mind. Or, "Uncle Joe is sending me creepy vibes." None of these thoughts is evidence of Joe's guilt. But that doesn't mean they should be ignored. The more you find yourself rationalizing Joe's behavior—making excuses as to why you might be biased or why Uncle Joe would never do *that*—the more you need to pay attention to your early-warning detection system. And if you have a healthy relationship with this topic and with your own instincts, you may quickly move on to stage two of our primal instincts: concern and hesitation.

Now let's say Uncle Joe wants to take Lisa to the park. You find yourself hesitating. You find yourself *concerned*. Listen to your gut. If you listen to your instincts, the consequences of being wrong are likely to be minor. Uncle Joe may get his feelings hurt. But if your assertiveness and honesty are expressed with care, even that outcome can be avoided or managed. Explaining your concerns to Uncle Joe will afford you the perfect opportunity to assess his character. Remember that decent human beings don't feel offended when you explain that their behavior is causing you concern. How he takes it will give you a better gauge of who Uncle Joe is—and that's important.

But if you ignore your concerns and your natural hesitation, and your primal instincts were right, then the consequences for little Lisa and yourself could be devastating. Putting your own selfish desire to appear kind to others above the safety of the children you are charged with protecting is nothing short of a moral failure. Don't be that person. I understand the general desire to spare someone's feelings, but sparing Uncle Joe's feelings isn't close to being the priority here. The worst possible response to your concerns about Uncle Joe is denial.

Denial protects you only from unwanted information. But *protect* is the wrong word here, because the kind of information that keeps you and your loved ones safe is precisely the kind we humans tend to try to avoid or rationalize away. Denial is an attempt to hide things we don't want to acknowledge because they make us uncomfortable or worried. This is dangerous. When you notice this happening, ask yourself, *what am I choosing not to see or feel here?* Remember that suspicion comes to you—you don't go to it. It isn't something you choose, it isn't an insult, and it is never something to shove aside or feel ashamed of.

Gavin de Becker tells a story that highlights how suspicion can work within our minds:

Even when intuition speaks in the clearest terms, even when the message gets through, we may still seek an outside opinion before we'll listen to ourselves. A friend of mine who is a psychiatrist told me of a patient he'd heard of whom reported, "Recently, when my wife goes to bed, I find some excuse to stay downstairs until she's asleep. If she's still awake when I get to our room, I'll stay in the bathroom for a long time so that I'm sure she's asleep by the time I get into bed. Do you think I'm unconsciously trying to avoid having sex with my wife?" The psychiatrist astutely asked, "What was the unconscious part?"[6]

Once you have moved from stage-one primal instincts—suspicion and doubt—to stage-two primal instincts—concern and hesitation—a decision becomes necessary. You must now respond with *action*. Whether that means telling Uncle Joe "no" and ignoring him, or having a blunt and clear conversation with Uncle Joe and physically distancing yourself and those you love from Uncle Joe, the time for action has arrived. If you fail at this task, if you instead succumb to denial or continued hesitation, then you will find yourself moving into stage three of our primal instinct hierarchy—fear, or, more precisely, true fear.

As already noted, true fear isn't worry. True fear isn't anxiety. True fear isn't hesitation. True fear isn't concern. True fear is a biological response to a threat that is present. And that's why you want to address your primal instincts at stage one or two. By the time you reach stage three, you're already in the presence of a threat. Your only option now may be physical conflict.

Here are a few other points to keep in mind as they relate to primal instincts:

1. *Women's primal knowledge is often different from men's.* It picks up signals men may not recognize as keenly. If you are a man and a woman tells you she is getting weird or creepy vibes from another man, keep an eye on him and trust what she tells you.

2. *If someone with consistently inappropriate behavior doesn't set off your own primal instincts, that doesn't mean they are okay—it just means you probably grew up around them.* Remember, the repetition of abusive behavior isn't an accident—it is a character flaw. If you find yourself having to rationalize an individual's poor behavior time and time again, distance yourself and those you love from that character-dis-

ordered individual, even if it is a parent, sibling, relative, or close friend.

3. *Nurture your child's primal knowledge as well as your own.* In fact, nurture the primal knowledge in everyone you care about. Nurture their reactions. Do not scold them for feeling uncomfortable around certain people. Remember the story of my daughter Anika and the stranger at my talk. If we don't want our children or those we love growing up to second-guess themselves, we have to help them learn to listen to and trust their own primal knowledge.

Along with our primal instincts, our ability to read our surroundings is one of the single biggest evolutionary advantages we have when it comes to noticing. We are able to assess our environment and the threats, allies, advantages, dangers, tools, and opportunities therein. When it comes to this type of situational observation and awareness, success begins with you: you must know what you are looking for. As an example, an infantryman, sniper, or secret service agent might be looking for, among many other things, positions from which the enemy can shoot. For most of us, most of the time, that isn't the main concern. When it comes to protecting ourselves and our families, our main concern, first and absolutely foremost, has to be identifying the character-disordered individuals who are already in our lives.

Let's now say you've patrolled the perimeters of your life well. You've culled the character-disordered individuals from your sanctuary. What about outside the house? What about strangers and strange environments? How do we manage unknown contacts? Here we circle back to the initiation principle: understand the distinction between those you approach and those who approach you. Those who initiate contact with you want something, and your job is to figure out what that is (see chapter 15).

Keep in mind, however, that proper situational awareness begins before contact is ever even made. Let me begin by giving you a scenario that's very common. You exit work and notice a stranger walking down the sidewalk in your direction. Where do you look, and what do you look for? Here is my simple order:

1. Face
2. Hands
3. Waistline
4. Face
5. Environment

I look them directly in the face, then at their hands, then at their waistline and torso, then back to their face, then around the environment itself—all within seconds or fractions thereof. It's a simple technique.
Let's break it down.

1. *Face.* We are remarkably skilled at reading facial expressions. The tiniest cues give much away, whether we consciously recognize them or not. Almost all of us, even in our more unaware moments, are pretty good at reading aggression and hostility on a human face. Are they hostile, worried, intense, frightened, bored, joyful, high, mentally ill? You would be surprised how much information you can take in within a fraction of a second when you look at someone's face.[7] Looking at their face also lets them know you see them. Predators don't like prey that see them coming. Knowing you've "clocked" them may be enough to dissuade them from selecting you.

   From a technique standpoint, as you look, offer no personal expression. And don't intentionally avoid or seek eye contact. I'm not talking about mean-mugging somebody here—to the contrary, just cast a quick, clear, direct look at the face.

2. *Hands.* Are they carrying a weapon? Are they carrying anything? Are their fists clenched? Are their hand gestures nervous or erratic? If they have a weapon or something that could be concealing a weapon in their hand, you want to know. Primates will hurt you using their hands. Human primates are no exception. Where are their hands, and what's in them?

3. *Waistline.* Are there any places where they could be concealing a weapon?[8]

4. *Face.* You've just taken a quick look at them in a manner that any experienced predator would recognize as intelligent. Does that concern them? If they noticed you noticing them, did that change their facial expression and overall demeanor? It only takes one more rapid glance to know.

5. *Environment.* What direction are they going? Are they alone? What is around you? Who is around you? If you're in a building, where are the entrances and exits? Are there physical barriers between you and them, such as tables or cars? Could you escape to safety if need be? Are there improvised weapons you could grab? If you're armed, is there cover nearby? The depth of your environmental observation will vary based on the threat.

You can practice your awareness in any public setting. While strolling in a mall, for example, just noticing whether someone is alone or accompanied by others will make for good drilling. Once you've clocked and evaluated someone using this technique, follow them for a bit with your peripheral vision as practice. Learn to develop and use that. We want to show awareness, not anger or insecurity. You'll get it in no time. Then take your loved ones out and have them practice as well.

This entire general scanning technique should take but a brief second, and I'd like you to make it a habit. It will help you become someone who is consciously aware of your surroundings, as well as someone whom predators will notice as being alert and mindful. And all of that will make you safer.

What if you're scanning and you do notice someone coming directly toward you? What are the next signs to look for or stages of a potential attack? Prepare to react if they are:

1. Closing in on you
2. Coordinating their movement with one or multiple other people
3. Hiding their hands
4. Looking out for potential witnesses
5. Self-grooming or weight shifting

The first four signs are self-explanatory, but what do I mean by self-grooming and weight shifting? Self-grooming includes scratching their chin, running their hands through their hair, and fidgeting with their nails—just about any like action on their part in which they are trying to look casual. And weight shifting refers to movement of their upper body to one side or movement of a leg toward the back (often called "blading"), signaling they're about to hit you.[9] By the time you've gotten here, it's usually time to fight or escape, as I will discuss in the next chapter.

But even if the approaching stranger isn't exhibiting any of the five signs, the best way to deal with him almost always involves you not stopping. If you're walking in public and not already at your destination, keep moving, even if he just tries to speak with you. You are under no obligation to engage with him. In fact, let me make this simple.

Don't stop!

Be short, be blunt, and keep moving the entire time. Stopping to speak to him only increases the odds of an attack, and if his intentions were innocent to begin with, he shouldn't mind your brevity. You might even help him learn a valuable lesson about appropriate boundaries.

It's almost inevitable, especially in larger cities, that some of the strangers who approach you will be mentally ill. When dealing with the mentally ill, remember mental illness is illness. You're not their doctor. You can't help them in any meaningful way at that moment. If you do feel compelled to assist, definitely don't pause to open your purse or take out your wallet. Rather, save your five dollars and donate it instead to an organization that helps the homeless and those with mental illness get off the streets, which ultimately is a place far more dangerous to them than to you.

One more thing, *never* say, "I'm sorry."

To say I'm sorry, in the subculture of violent criminal actors and immature "boy-speak" males, signals weakness. To predators, *weakness is always provocative.* They will perceive you as submissive. In environments where being cultured might matter, go with, "My apologies." In areas where you're surrounded by the criminal class, say only, "No offense."

If a stranger continues to badger you after a curt response, then you should follow the ask-tell-make formula. Consider this example:

"Hey man, you got a dollar?"

"No."

That's a back-and-forth. It isn't a problem. It is a conversation.

"Come on, man. I just saw you leave the store. You gotta have change."

He has now failed to respond to the word "no." That's the beginning of a problem.

"No, would you leave me alone, please?"

That's step one: *Ask.*

"Come on, man. Just ONE dollar?"

"No! Back off."

That's step two: *Tell.* You've now issued a command.

A well-executed step two, one that is clear, loud, and decisive, ends the vast majority of these confrontations. When it doesn't, that's a huge warning sign. At that point, it's time for step three: *Make.* You're drawing a line and making yourself extra clear, which should involve a further escalation in tone. "Back the FUCK off NOW!" is a nice example. Practice saying that out loud a few times. Preferably in private.

At that point, if he doesn't back off, you need to take action: leave, run, move him, or fight. I can't tell you which to do, but I can tell you that the ask-tell-make formula is something you need to ingrain. Here is a simple drill that you can do with a friend or family member to help you do that.

Step one: *Ask.* Begin by having someone approach you and ask for money. Make space, step *offline* (flanking the aggressor), and *ask them* to back away in a firm and confident tone: "No, would you back off, please?" As simple as that sounds, for some people, this action takes practice.

Step two: *Tell.* Have the aggressor continue to press the boundaries, invading more space and ignoring the word "no." Maintain distance and *tell* them to back off: *"Back up, now!"* As the intensity increases, this drill becomes harder for people who are not good at being assertive. And those are exactly the kind of people who need this practice.

Step three: *Make.* Have the aggressor continue to invade more space and ignore your commands. Keep maintaining distance and *make* yourself clear: *"Back the FUCK up, NOW!"*

At this point, if the attacker continues to press forward, attack or escape. I'm not opposed to hitting first. In fact, in many circumstances, *I recommend it*. But we're not at that stage of the book yet, and that's not the point of this drill. The point of this drill is to help people who are not naturally assertive become assertive—and that talent needs to be practiced prior to, or alongside, anything physical we teach. This is especially true when what we teach involves a weapon that can be taken away.

Keep in mind that the exact techniques that we use to manage unknown contacts like aggressive panhandlers or road-raging commuters are not necessarily the same as the ones we may need to employ to handle an angry customer in a restaurant who is upset because your party was seated before his. To make these distinctions, we need to really understand body language, voice inflection, and pacing. This takes practice. We also need to have knowledge of the various cultures and communities we move through across time and space to understand the full impact of certain words and gestures. This means there's always more to study and learn. It also means getting out of our comfort zone and engaging in regular, strenuous, competitive activity, like combat sports, which helps us build the strength and mental stability required for all of this.

But you should know what's normal and what's not normal in the environments you typically occupy. If you don't, you need to start focusing on such things. Wake up, pay attention, and look around. Notice your daily environment and the people in it. Does anything catch your attention as out of the ordinary? My long-time student and fellow SBG coach Ray Price taught me an old-school cop initialism for just such a thing: *JDLR*.[10]

Just. Doesn't. Look. Right.

A man alone in a crowded playground, a teenager in a large jacket on a hot summer day, someone loitering for no apparent reason, men sitting outside in a car in front of a neighbor's house—all these things can catch your eye. Most of these things will turn out to be innocent. The man in the park could be waiting for his wife. The teen in the coat could be a victim of vanity. The person loitering could be getting some fresh air. The men could be resting from a long road trip. This isn't about assigning guilt; it's a simple acknowledgment of the presence of something that *just doesn't look right*. For the present moment at least, that's all it is—*noticing*.

19 The Importance of Distance, Deterrence, and Determination

You know that weakness is provocative, distance management wins fights, and no matter what, you'll be the one going home to your family.

You are mature. You spend your time with worthwhile people, engaged in equally worthwhile things. You are smart. You understand that you are a product of an unbroken chain of reproductive success. You listen to and trust your primal instincts. You have taken the time to educate yourself about your environment and the predators and threats within it. You don't live in denial, and you seek to have a healthy relationship with violence. You have prioritized your responses, and you are prepared. You are healthy. You stay in shape. And you notice what is going on around you. Now it's time for the fourth and final aspect of the MIND acronym: D.

D stands for distance, deterrence, and determination. Each element is critical, and, as with everything else in the MIND formula, each element is part of a cohesive whole. Properly understood, they form a loop. You begin with distance, progress to deterrence, and, if necessary, conclude with determination. Then, if the engagement turns physical, you return to distance.

Distance

There is a maxim in BJJ that applies to all forms of combat: *position before submission*. What gives a BJJ player an advantage on the ground is the increased leverage they can achieve from their positions. It is structure, not strength, that gives you power in Jiu-Jitsu. When it comes to violence, much of our advantage will depend on our position—on the space between us and the threat. In everything from street fights and home defense to terrorism prevention and geopolitical warfare, distance management is key.

Think for a moment about the animal kingdom. Many evolved physical traits, things like the placement and structure of eyes and ears and the camouflage of fur, feathers, and scales, all contribute to controlling distance. They are built-in survival mechanisms. But we can also take practical measures to manage distance by controlling access and space—think reinforced cockpit doors on airplanes. Whether you are in an MMA cage, a battle for control of a handgun, or a late-night raid on a terrorist compound, control the distance and you control the battle. Distance determines what can affect you—and how you are affected.

Whoever controls the distance controls the experience.

Just as with BJJ, being technical when it comes to distance management means being early—early in the movement and early in responding to our opponent. Distance management ideally means seeing the threat so early that you can avoid it completely. Failing that, it means noticing a potential threat early enough to prepare for it, giving you an advantage. Finally, it means being able to control the physical distance once the threat is upon you.

Tests have shown that assailants can cover *at least* twenty-one feet in about 1.5 seconds, which is about the same amount of time it takes a trained police officer to draw and fire one round from their weapon.[1] Once that gap closes, things become hands-on, and once that happens, it's all about controlling space. Speaking of which, when was the last time you saw a police officer talking to someone from twenty-one feet away? Recall here the point I made in chapter 14 that a suspect always has a gun within reach whenever a police contact is made: the officer's.

Managing distance is the single most important measure when defending yourself from violence—both before and after physical contact occurs. Although we martial artists train for physical altercations, our ultimate goal is always to win the fight before it happens by putting space between ourselves—and those we love—and the threat.

I witnessed something when I was a young boy that illustrates this point perfectly. One evening my parents and I were walking down the sidewalk when a man came up behind my mom and grabbed her bottom. She let out a scream. He said something I couldn't hear and kept walking. My dad, who had witnessed the act, chased after the man, pushed him into a doorway, and had words with him. I have no idea what he said or exactly what he did, but as soon as my father let go, the man ran off. But a few minutes later, we spotted the man again. This time, he was on the other side of the street, moving toward us with one of his hands hidden behind his back. My dad yelled at us to run into a store. My mother, disregarding his warning, asked him what was going on, so she and I wound up standing in place on the sidewalk, witnessing the ensuing events.

Needing to act quickly, my dad separated from us, drawing the man away. As he moved away, the man pulled a large knife out from behind his back. As the man tried to close the distance on my dad, my father moved to the other side of a parked car and began trying to talk the man down over the top of it. The man would make a brief sprint around the vehicle, and my dad would do the same—always keeping the car between himself and the man with the knife. This movement involved the exact same pattern you might see in a game of tag. It works.

After a few minutes of this, the man, who was likely becoming increasingly aware of the fact that he was committing a felony in broad daylight and who wasn't able to get close to my dad, sprinted off. We all hustled back to our car and drove around downtown until my dad spotted a police officer in a patrol car. He left us in our car while he hopped into the patrol car, which then sped off. They returned about ten minutes later with the knife-wielding man under arrest in the back seat.

As we made the long drive home, I asked my dad why he hadn't disarmed the man. All I knew about knives was what I had seen in Kung Fu movies. My dad patiently explained that I had no idea how dangerous a knife is, what it can do to a human body, and how fast that can happen. He then spent the remainder of the drive talking about how mad he was at himself for not having carried a concealed weapon that day. Even when he was off-duty, he usually carried.

As I look back on that day now, some forty years later, I know he made the exact right call in using the best tool at his disposal—the car. It put a barrier between himself and a man with a deadly weapon. That's the smart move whether you are carrying a gun or not. My dad noticed the threat, was mindful of his environment, and used the few seconds he had to prepare by putting a large piece of metal between himself and his attacker—all hallmarks of the MIND principle.

Distance management, the cornerstone of physical combat, requires that you're able to orient yourself. On the ground, you orient yourself to your opponent primarily through feel. On your feet, you do it primarily with your eyes. No matter where you are, fully engaging all your senses and positioning yourself relative to the threat are critical. This is something Air Force fighter pilot Colonel John R. Boyd understood well. He earned his nickname—"Forty Second Boyd"—due to a bet. He wagered that he could turn any disadvantageous position in a dogfight around and be on his opponent's tail within forty seconds or less. But that wasn't what secured his fame within military circles. It was his method.[2]

He called it the OODA loop: observe, orient, decide, act.

At first glance, the method seems self-explanatory: you observe the threat, orient yourself to it, decide on your action, and perform it. But bear in mind that Boyd was a combat pilot. If he performed every action consciously, his reactions would be far too slow to survive. He is describing four steps that needed to occur almost simultaneously to be effective in typical flight-combat circumstances. But Boyd took things even a step further by applying the logic of the OODA loop to reverse-engineer his opponent's decision-making process. He knew if he could find a way to get into his opponent's head and interrupt their loop, he could gain the advantage. As Boyd said, "Machines don't fight wars, terrain doesn't fight wars. You must go into the minds of humans. That's where the battles are won."[3]

Most of us are never going to fly a combat jet, yet everything Boyd articulated applies to any individual self-defense scenario. We've already discussed the process of "observing"—the quick scan that takes in face, hands, waist, and demeanor. Based on your observation of the potential threat and the situation as a whole, you must now take decisive action. That is what my father did when he put a large metal object between himself and the man with the knife.

For purposes of self-defense, the OODA loop will very often occur almost simultaneously, but it may take anywhere from a fraction of a second to a minute or more. The amount of time available may not be under your control. This loop doesn't end until the physical altercation itself ends. Combat sports offer a terrific model for understanding this. In BJJ, for example, you can feel your opponent's grip, pressure, and general intentions. Rickson Gracie refers to this as *"connection,"* which he describes as the most important principle within BJJ.[4] This isn't some sort of mystical power, but simply the tactile sense that any combat athlete will develop over many years of training with resisting opponents. When training in this way, you are constantly observing, orienting, deciding, and acting. For your movements to be effective against a skilled opponent, you must make your adjustments without conscious thought. If you first think to yourself, "Aha, this person is trying to get on my back," they'll likely already be on your back by the time you react.

This process is part of what makes BJJ so pleasurable and addictive. It forces you to get out of your own way. You must let go of the conscious reins and let your body react in real time to your opponent's movements. You have to let your body perform the OODA process fluidly. As Prussian Field Marshal Helmuth von Moltke (the Elder) noted, "No plan of operations extends with any certainty beyond the first contact with the main hostile force."[5] Or, as heavyweight boxing champion Mike Tyson more memorably and succinctly put it, "Everyone has a plan until they get punched in the mouth."[6]

They are both making the same point: *Plans change upon contact.*

Every match you have with your opponent will be different. Every opponent you face will bring a different game—and a different set of potential solutions to the problems they encounter with your game. And every human body will present different challenges related to the movements you tend to favor. Creating a pattern where opponent X executes move Y and you respond with counter Z sets you up for failure for a very simple reason: as a dead pattern, it lacks timing. Similarly, a military unit that has no experience adapting on the battlefield will also be setting itself up for failure—regardless of how well thought out the initial plan—if it cannot adapt. This is why you first learn the fundamentals of the delivery system, making sure your movements can be executed smoothly and properly, then create an environment where you can drill those movements against a resisting opponent, with the all-important elements of timing and progressive resistance factored in, and finally integrate the movements in live sparring—over and over again. (I will discuss this "Alive" approach to training in chapter 22.)

When training correctly in this way, you will eventually find yourself performing Boyd's OODA loop all at once. Not because you've memorized a pattern or repeated some form of kata a thousand times, but because you have been in that position against various resisting opponents a thousand times and have a set of ingrained fundamentals to draw upon. You have the timing, you have the raw knowledge, and you have the feel. This process is no different from the process Colonel Boyd used to become a world-class combat pilot. What he described is, by definition, what every good BJJ or combat athlete in the world intuitively does. Athletics and the OODA loop go hand in hand.

Control the space and distance, orient yourself within that space, and control the encounter. No matter the objective of the criminal actor, the best solution for you in *every* case involves managing the *distance* between you and the threat. Often, this is done through deterrence.

Deterrence

In nature, predatory animals tend to attack the weakest prey.[7] The same is true for predators on the street. For them, weakness is provocative. Deterrence can thus take many forms, but for the purposes of self-defense, it typically involves some combination of assertiveness and awareness that is communicated through posture, tone, and appearance. These elements are all factors in the *range-risk-reward* assessment predators make when they pick a target. This doesn't mean that you have to look like a professional MMA fighter with cauliflower ears to deter a predator. More often than not, it just means that you have to have the presence of someone who will fight if they have to. That's usually enough to get you "unselected," as the late self-defense educator William Aprill used to say.[8] You'll be taken off the scumbags' attack list.

A person walking along head down, slumped over, unsure, and anxious is like catnip to degenerates. While the vast majority of human beings are decent and kind and truly disgusting predatory creatures are few and far between, the bad guys *are* out there. While a woman walking alone who appears uncertain or timid tends to bring out my protective instincts, when predators see that same person, they don't see someone who needs protecting; they see something they want to exploit.

Some years ago, a young woman called my academy. She was paralyzed from the waist down and thus confined to a wheelchair. She had been repeatedly victimized and was hoping to learn some self-defense. My general approach to these sorts of situations is to get the individual onto the mat, evaluate her range of motion, and take it from there. If you give me five minutes on the mat with someone, I'll know exactly what she will able to achieve given enough training—and what she won't be able to achieve.

When the disabled woman came in, I wanted to see whether she could get out of her chair and onto the mat by herself. She could. I next wanted to see how she moved. Her mobility was extremely limited. She could crawl a bit but lacked meaningful upper-body strength. As I watched her, we talked about her experiences with attackers. What she shared was emotional and grim. In the previous year alone, she had been groped multiple times by strangers, and she had been forcibly pushed out of her chair twice. On one occasion, a man had attempted to rape her, but her screams drew attention he didn't want and frightened him off. She was now terrified of going outside.

To experience so many attacks within such a short time is statistically very rare, even in Portland. But I quickly realized that this wasn't about Portland; it was about her. Given her extreme vulnerability, she was a magnet for human garbage. She was a safe and easy victim for predators, and she had no quick or effective means to create all-important distance when out in public. If it sounds like I am blaming the victim here, you've missed the point. This has nothing to do with blame—it is about selection. The attackers had picked her.[9]

A small segment of the population—upon finding a vulnerable woman or child with no witnesses in sight—will assault them, whether to harass, grope, or rob them, or rape, torture, and kill them. A woman with no mental or physical disability is less likely to be targeted by these creatures than a woman who is unable to create distance or defend herself. Firearms are often the best solution in such situations, but this woman's ability to confidently hold objects was also compromised, and

236 • THE GIFT OF VIOLENCE

she didn't feel comfortable taking that route. Pepper spray and other weapons can also offer some protection, but her impaired ability to hold and control things similarly made these less-than-optimal solutions for her. I suggested a guard dog.

The troglodytes who attack women in wheelchairs will cross to the other side of the street to avoid a dog.[10] The dog could be her companion, travel with her everywhere, and help keep her safe. I know a world-class dog trainer, and I passed his details on to her. There is only so much a person with her type of disability can do by way of deterrence. The dog would help even the odds for her. I don't know if she took my advice. I hope she did because without a visible means of deterrence, she would continue to be seen as a near-perfect target when out in public.

Criminal predators pay attention to specific things when selecting their targets. In one research study, convicts were shown footage of a busy New York City street, then asked to pick out their potential victims on a scale of 1 (easy day) to 10 (too risky to attack). Almost every inmate chose the same targets.[11] In another study, male students were asked to assume the role of a mugger and pick out potential victims from videos of people walking, and those students with high psychopathic traits were most likely to select those who had previously been victimized. They did this without seeing the faces of any of the walkers.[12]

What kinds of things do predators look for?

- Timid walking style
- Clumsy or injured gait
- Arms pressed to the body
- Slumped shoulders
- Lack of general awareness[13]

Walking in a confident and attentive manner, head up, shoulders back, will help keep you "unselected" from the dirtbags' to-do list. You can and should practice this posture and gait. You should also keep in mind that solid training in any form of combat sport, be it wrestling, Judo, or BJJ, will help you acquire that sort of body language organically. You will develop a more assured walk born naturally from hard training—true confidence. Yet again, this is one of the many, often overlooked benefits of functional training.

Still, a confident physical presence isn't a substitute for everything else I've discussed up to now. You don't get to act immaturely, engage in immature activities, hang out with immature people, fail to notice what's happening around you, and fail to put distance between yourself and a threat and still expect to remain safe simply because you look like you'd be a pain in the ass to fight. In such cases, the jackals will just make sure the odds swing in their favor by using weapons and multiple assailants.

Don't rely on the judgment of degenerates in order to stay safe.

The boy-speak crowd often fails to tell the difference between deterrence and machismo. To a smarter predator, machismo projects panic. Panic is weakness, and weakness is provocative. A huffing, puffing, preening, angry-faced male doesn't project deterrence. That behavior betrays fear. As noted in chapter 3, it signals an attempt to avoid a fight. Yet, when joined with alcohol, drugs, peer encouragement, and an opponent caught in the same chest-beating display, such behavior inevitably leads to a lot of unnecessary and stupid fights.

The deterrence I am talking about projects the kind of confidence a well-seasoned athlete displays when he steps into an arena. This quality is often described as *cool*. It is the noticeable absence of both desire and fear. It's the certainty radiated by professionals who are very good at what they do as they ply their craft. I've seen that cool in world-class fighters, talented artists, ruthlessly prepared attorneys, tiny but bold women, and effeminate gay men. It isn't about machismo. It's a signal that that person isn't going to make things easy for a character-disordered loser.

Remember: *predators are lazy.*

Almost all crime is opportunistic. That is why victims of violence often know their attackers: the attacker has *easy access*. From a statistical standpoint, a locked door is nearly as good as a barricaded one. A six-foot fence is nearly as good as an impenetrable moat. Criminologist Franklin E. Zimring's work on crime in New York City has made this point abundantly clear.[14] The kind of violence experienced there in the 1970s seemed inevitable at the time, given the combination of economic decline, social pressures, and profits available from the drug trade. If anything, most believed the situation would only get worse. But the New York City Police Department found that making crime even a little bit harder made it much rarer. New York went from being one of the more dangerous cities in the world to one of the safest. It's a shame to see that many of the policies that cleaned up the city and saved thousands of lives are being abandoned in the wake of the George Floyd protests. The skyrocketing rates of murder and violence that have come as a result of the city's newer policies and priorities speak for themselves.

Deterrence works.

If you create a harder target, the balance in the range-risk-reward assessment changes rapidly in the mind of the typical scumbag, and that target is deselected.

You act maturely. You engage and exercise your intelligence. You notice what is happening around you right now, at this moment. And, when you see a threat, like the smart animal you are, you seek to control the distance immediately. If you do these things, violence will be extremely unlikely to find you, but if its beady little bloodstained eyes ever do happen to glance in your direction, it should see the message *fuck off!* Radiate that. Own it.

While there is no shortcut to obtaining presence—it has to be earned—you can set about earning it daily by making the right decisions, using the right words, engaging in the right activities, and making those you love stronger and the world brighter.

Frailty excites freeloaders, so stand up tall and hold your ground.

No matter how anxious, inferior, or shy you may feel, compared to the dirty slugs who like to attack innocent people on the street, you're a superstar.

Act like it.

Determination

If you are unable to maintain distance from a threat and your efforts at deterrence don't work, it is time to be determined. What does determination mean? In the context of self-defense, it means you will do everything in your power to make it out alive. As SBG coach Paul Sharp phrases it, "Option one, I get away. Option two, we get it on. And if they do 'get you,' they should be found dead, close by—that's the mindset." Decide now that this is the type of determination you will have, that if the worst should happen and a predator does get you, you guarantee that the police will find his body next to yours.[15] If the choice is ever between complying with a command that will make you more vulnerable or attacking the assailant, *I want you to fight.*

Like putting gas in your car or taking your blood pressure medication, this is something you need to do *before* it becomes urgent. William Aprill called this "pre-need decision making."[16] Rickson Gracie calls it knowing where your "line in the sand is."

A story involving a small town near where I was raised demonstrates just how powerful this line-in-the-sand principle can be. I grew up in Hollister, California, which is famous for only one thing: in 1947, four thousand bikers, including the Hell's Angels, overran it. For a city whose population was only slightly bigger than that, the event was pretty overwhelming. The event was later dramatized in *The Wild Ones*, a Hollywood classic starring Marlon Brando. Although a lot of people are familiar with the story, what many people don't know is that San Juan Bautista, a much smaller town of two thousand just a few minutes away from Hollister, was almost the victim of a similar event a little over twenty years later.

On receiving word that a gang of bikers planned to overrun the town, the town's sheriff, a Korean War veteran by the name of Nick Agrus, parked his patrol car on the main road leading into San Juan Bautista and sat there alone with his shotgun, awaiting their arrival. Keep in mind that a small dot on the map like San Juan Bautista generally has only two law enforcement officers: the sheriff and his deputy. Think Mayberry, if Mayberry had been an old Spanish mission.

The bikers rode up en masse. Finding the main road blocked by the sheriff's car, one of the gang leaders got off his bike and walked toward the sheriff. At this point, Sheriff Agrus racked his shotgun and said something to this effect: "You can move on down the road to Hollister, but I'm not letting you in here. The first one who tries, I'm going to shoot in the face." He was only one man with one gun, and there were dozens of bikers standing across from him—and hundreds more were coming. But the sheriff was clearly telling the truth. And who wants to be the first one to be shot in the face?

The word spread. The bikers bypassed San Juan Bautista.

Sheriff Agrus had painted himself into a corner. Had the bikers driven around him, would he really have shot one of them simply for entering the city? That would be tough to defend in court. But the point is that he had drawn a line in the sand. It was his town, and that was his line. That's how effective determination can be when it comes to stopping a threat.

Indecisiveness, or a lack of determination when it comes to facing threats, can be devastating. One particular moment in the Petit family's horrifying ordeal at the hands of Komisarjevsky and Hayes illustrates this point well. After the killers entered the residence and hit Dr. Petit in the head with a baseball bat, and before the fatal moment when they lit the still-breathing girls on fire, Hayes took the mother, Jennifer Hawke-Petit, to her bank, where he convinced her to withdraw $15,000. To do that, she had to enter the bank and speak with a teller.

When inside the bank, Jennifer had the good sense and courage to inform the teller of her situation, that she and her family were being held hostage, but she also reportedly told the teller that her attackers were "being nice" and probably "only wanted money." This is what the bank manager reported to the 9-1-1 dispatcher as Jennifer left the bank, where Hayes was waiting for her in a van. Based on the information provided in that call, the police took about an hour and a half to make a direct move against Hayes and Komisarjevsky. They caught them leaving in the Petit family car—after they had sexually assaulted both daughters, raped and strangled the mother, and set them all on fire.

It's easy to second-guess decisions people make in horrible situations, including word choice, but we need to learn from such incidents. We develop foresight by practicing hindsight. If the choice is between complying with a command that will make you more vulnerable or fighting—*always fight*. Compliance is never okay under such circumstances. Do not allow fear or wishful thinking to blur your line in the sand. At every step of the way, I wish everyone involved had fought those two animals with everything they had. Hayes and Komisarjevsky weren't combat athletes or soldiers; they were weak, spineless trash. Yet, there was nothing to stop them from creating such gruesome havoc and horrifying pain that even the jurors needed counseling after seeing and hearing what was shared at trial.

Nothing can change the awful events of that day, but future tragedies can be avoided. Always keep in mind that compliance almost always leads to more horror, not less. Predators like Hayes and Komisarjevsky will profile you. If you look like trouble, they'll probably move on. If you don't, and you look like a high-reward target, they will be more likely to select you. After all, you're in range, and you're low risk. But even if you do everything right and you and your family still come face to face with creatures like Hayes and Komisarjevsky, trapped with no way to escape, know this: regular people—people just like you—successfully defend themselves and others from violent predators every day. They survived by responding the way our ancestors would have; they fought tooth and claw. You need to fight with all the determination you can summon, too. You're from an unbroken chain of survivors, and that's the ultimate goal when a predator is staring you in the face—survival.

20 The Command of Mindfulness

You learn what it means to think with the whole body.

Our ability to accurately predict and intelligently react to violent human behavior depends on our adherence to each element of the MIND acronym. At its core, this means relying on our innate primal instincts and having educated situational knowledge. Taken together, they give us awareness. While awareness is a necessary precondition for staying and being safe, it is only a starting point for achieving an even more powerful state that offers an even greater survival advantage: *mindfulness.*

Mindfulness is awareness without distraction. It is awareness unmoved by internal dialogue—awareness focused not on the past or future but on the *present.* The capacity to be fully in the moment is powerful. It means you have to rid yourself of your internal dialogue and come fully to your senses. And any animal that has come fully to its senses is in its most formidable state of being.[1] To paraphrase Zen master Taisen Deshimaru, this means thinking with the whole body.[2] Although this discussion may sound like a series of deepities, there is nothing false or nonsensical about true mindfulness. Indeed, there are clear, practical, and proven steps for achieving it—steps that are available to anyone with the time and motivation to follow them.

Step One: *Physical Training*

Combat athletics demand a certain level of concentration. You can't wrestle or grapple well if you're lost amid the neurotic thoughts of the chattering mind. Worry, desire, self-conscious ponderings about your social environment, financial stress—that all fades away during a hard roll, which is why so many people find the act of rolling in BJJ (sparring with your partner in a manner that is neither patterned nor contrived) so enjoyable. BJJ offers a shortcut to a clearer and more present awareness. It requires that of you—and that requirement is a beautiful gift.

BJJ and other combat sports aren't the only things that accomplish this. Golf legend Arnold Palmer phrased his experience on the links this way:

> You're involved in the action and vaguely aware of it, but your focus is not on the commotion but on the opportunity ahead. I'd liken it to a sense of reverie—not a dreamlike state but the somehow insulated state that a great musician achieves in a great performance. He's aware of where he is and what he's doing, but his mind is on the playing of his instrument with an internal sense of rightness—it is not merely mechanical, it is not only spiritual; it is something of both, on a different plane and a more remote one.[3]

Any physical activity that requires intense focus can bring its practitioners to such a state of consciousness. But the combat arts have a few specific advantages. First, they involve hand-to-hand combat—something extremely primal that our ancestors had to engage in generation after generation just to survive. This form of physical activity lays the ego bare in a very different way from, say, running. When you're running, you may be alone. In BJJ, you're in competition with another human being who is trying to dominate you physically, just as you are trying to dominate them. That involves a practical reality that can't be easily ignored: one of you has to submit.

Tapping out to your partner means unambiguously conceding defeat. It's one thing to concede to yourself during a run that you can go no farther or faster. It is an entirely different thing to have to admit to another human being that they have beaten you. Most BJJ players have to do this multiple times every practice session and thousands of times over the course of their training. It's part of the improvement process. You can't get good at BJJ without putting yourself through this process. That makes BJJ different from other things that require high levels of concentration—different in a primal, visceral way.

Over the years, I've watched many men begin BJJ, experience rolling for the first time, and quit immediately.[4] Often, the more macho the guy's persona, the faster he flees the mat. This is especially true at SBG, where we have some world-class female black belts. A lot of men can't handle having to tap out to another man. Being forced to tap out to a woman is something even harder for this type of man to face.

The humility required to attain demonstrable skill in BJJ isn't essential in a fantasy-based martial art. In Aikido, for example, you only *pretend* to be thrown against your will. The techniques, like those of most traditional martial arts, work only when both parties cooperate. It is make-believe, a shared delusion. And, like most delusions, it provides plenty of dark places for the ego to hide. A failure to notice that self-delusion betrays a lack of mindfulness. In fact, the more skilled the fantasy-based practitioner becomes at pretending what he does works, the less mindful he becomes.

Combat sports like BJJ, on the other hand, necessitate mindfulness due to their adherence to truth. Dealing with a competitive opponent who is coming at you in an unchoreographed way forces you to focus more in order to be able to respond to the pressure effectively. Dead patterns remove mindfulness from movement, while combat sports training makes it hard to be anything but mindful. BJJ isn't the only combat sport that accomplishes this. You can get it from boxing, MMA, Muay Thai, or any other *real*—that is, competitive—sport or martial art. But many of those sports often come at a cost that extends beyond the body to the brain. While BJJ, just like any sport or exercise, can exact a physical toll, it doesn't come with a price tag labeled *traumatic brain damage.*

Step Two: *Meditation Practice*

There are many apps and podcasts available that can help you improve your meditation practice, as well as actual in-person teachers in most cities. I personally recommend techniques drawn from traditions like Vipassana, Dzogchen, and Zen. But there is no need to wait for a class or to delay until you find the perfect tutorial. The instructions for meditating couldn't be simpler.

It's common to become caught up in our own thoughts, worries, desires, and chatter. When distracted by our inner conversations, we lose touch with what's happening in the moment. And while I've often heard people say that meditation leads to the cessation of that internal dialogue, I think it leads to an awareness of it and an ever-increasing ability to remain unattached to it. This frees up our conscious awareness, allowing for more clarity and focus—two things essential for any warrior or combat athlete.

For many of you, a life lived in a constant state of distraction, anxiety, and desire—in other words, thinking compulsively—may seem normal. You may not even recognize that another state of mind exists. And if you have experienced a meditative state, such as during a hard roll or focused round of golf, how can you re-create at any time and in any place that feeling that occurs effortlessly in those concentrated moments?

Meditate.

Just sit still. Try to think of it as nothing special. It *is* nothing special. Why do it then? To more fully experience what is happening right now. The instructions for basic Zazen, or seated meditation, are simple:

1. Sit with your back comfortably erect: centered, balanced, rooted to the ground, and physically stable. Feel settled here and now.

2. Begin listening. Close your eyes, and allow yourself to hear all the sounds going on around you. Listen to the general sounds of the world as if you were listening to music. Don't try to identify the sounds. Don't put names on them. Simply allow them to play with your eardrums. Then watch them go.

3. Notice your thoughts. Don't try to repress or judge them (that is, after all, just more thought). Trying to control your thoughts is like trying to bite your own teeth. Instead, just witness them arising. Just hear them along with the sounds around you.[5]

Sit, Listen, Notice.
That's all.

And don't overdo it—at least at first. Set a timer for ten minutes at the beginning of each session. Try it once a day for at least ten sittings before adding more time.[6]

While it's probably true that a long Vipassana-style retreat will produce experiences that a shorter, more casual session will not access, as a coach, I've seen students time after time set lofty fitness goals only to fall short. They buy books, watch videos, hire personal trainers, and pursue the toughest workouts. For a short time, the person follows through. But after a while, the habit drops off. The person might continue searching for better workouts and more advanced methods—but because their training sessions are so intense, they become more and more sporadic. Such a person has missed the single most important factor in any workout: *consistency*.

Consistency is essential to progress.[7] Without it, the best workouts, techniques, strategies, and plans will amount to little. Just as I recommend setting manageable workout goals, I also advocate for manageable daily meditation sessions. If you find yourself doing more as the months proceed and can accommodate the extra time, that's fantastic. But don't try to do more only to fall out of the habit. There really is no excuse for that—I should know, as I overshoot on occasion too.

Step Three: *Everyday Life*

Some suffering in life is inevitable because of the existence of sickness, death, and teenage kids. But much suffering is self-imposed: the result of thoughts that arise within the mind. That kind of suffering—whether it manifests as sadness over the past, worry about the future, social anxiety, or general malaise—can come and go with our thoughts. You've experienced this, I'm sure. By becoming aware of and then learning to let go of those thoughts, we can relieve a great deal of that suffering and become safer, clearer, and more aware.

Focused meditation aside, you can calm your mind through any number of daily or weekly practices. You can run, paint, hike, chant, pray, play music, write, lift weights, act, surf, garden, golf, or simply sit. I calm mine through BJJ.

When you roll in BJJ, you'll find neurotic thoughts popping up when you're under pressure; when you're trapped underneath your opponent;

when you're having trouble breathing because you can't expand your ribs; and when your opponent has begun to drag a forearm across your throat. The voice within you is telling you to quit, but you ignore it. You defend your neck. You survive. Eventually, your opponent moves—just a little, just enough. You find the space and moment to escape. You're back to guard. You can breathe. Your opponent is tired. You sweep. You hold. You submit. You've won.

These moments happen. Over the years, they happen a lot. And there are also many moments when you are bested. But in the process, you learn to overcome that little voice in your head. That's a huge part of the benefit of what we do in BJJ. And, as long as you don't give up until you have to, as long as you don't walk off the mat before your opponent has imposed the win or you've overcome him, these lessons in mindfulness, in nonattachment to the negative subvocalization that echoes within our skulls, are inevitable. And that's beautiful.

The pressure of BJJ—and of combat sports in general—is innate to its practice and difficult to replicate with other activities. Whether through BJJ or something else, you need something in your life that is physically demanding, something that makes you occasionally want to give up. This will help create mindfulness.

Compared to physical activity, basic seated meditation may seem boring, pointless, or too easy. But they complement one another. If you're careful and pay attention to your awareness, you may discover that Zazen is one of the hardest things you've ever done. It takes a lot of discipline and energy to achieve the ability to do something without thought or effort. You might even discover that regular meditation gives your mind time to let go of a lot of extra noise and baggage that otherwise clouds your perception of the world around you. With a bit of practice, every act—taking a walk, firing your weapon at the range, preparing food for your kids—can become an act of meditation that translates directly into mindfulness.[8]

True mindfulness isn't found on a mountain. You bring mindfulness to the mountain. To be in a state without distraction in which your body thinks as a whole is Zen. To be gripped by uncontrollable desires and anxieties is to be gripped by distractions. And to see through those distractions, to be free of them, should not be confused with rejecting all forms of thought. Analytical, clear-eyed, rational critical-thinking skills are as vital as ever. An undistracted mind is a fully aware mind. A human being who is not lost in the storms of their own negative thought patterns is a harder human being to hurt.

Modern life makes it especially hard to move through the world without needless distraction, making mindfulness all the more important for our well-being and survival. What's arguably the number one distractor in our daily lives? Our phones. The average adult spends three hours a day staring into theirs. For the average teen, it's seven hours. As author Johann Hari shows, even when we're not looking down at our phones, we're often itching to do so.[9] That's three to seven hours a day when we lack general awareness and are not present in the moment—when we are mindless and vulnerable.

Just as many people use their phones as a ready tool for escaping from their surroundings, so too do many seekers meditate in an effort to suppress negative thoughts. This is a dangerous error, as such thoughts occur naturally and should be acknowledged. The key is to recognize that negative thoughts do not have to result in negative feelings. They have to be believed and focused on for that to happen. Rather than actively trying to suppress such thoughts, you should simply let go of them without emotion. This will greatly diminish their hold over you. Dramatizing your thoughts never adds clarity, only distortion, which can be vulgar. Denying thoughts never gives insight; it only retards the process of discovery. Not dramatizing means clearly recognizing what is present in the moment: all the physical, emotional, and intellectual tension that is currently there. You can't ever let go of what you don't first acknowledge. And you can't get a clear handle on the present moment when you're too busy responding emotionally to your thoughts.

True Zen isn't anti-intellectual; it's anti-bullshit. Your highest state of alertness is a state of mindfulness. That mindfulness manifests as complete focus on the present moment. It is visceral, rapid, and accurate. It is one of the most functional tools you can develop both for avoiding and preventing violence—and for surviving the ultimate challenge, the human experience.

Section Five: Preparedness
How to Avoid and Outsmart Predators

"Freedom from want must never be interpreted as freedom from the necessity to struggle."
—George Washington

21 Thinking the Unthinkable

If you have to fight for your own safety or that of those you love, remember that tenacity isn't just something you can do—it is something you are.

Everything up to this point has focused on avoiding and preventing violence. But what happens when the unthinkable is inevitable? To increase your odds of survival, you must have something to fight for—something that will keep you resisting and battling until the very end. If you know your line in the sand, as Rickson Gracie says, then you know your ultimate motivation.

Rickson tells a story about an experience he once had in Denver, Colorado, when he was attending one of the first Ultimate Fighting Championships. After watching his brother Royce win the event, he was being driven back to his hotel when his driver apparently cut off another car. The enraged driver of the second car started following the car he was in. His car eventually stopped at a red light and the enraged driver aggressively pulled up alongside them on the passenger side, where Rickson was sitting. The enraged driver started yelling and screaming at them. Rickson simply sat there calmly, eyes forward, unengaged. When the light changed, Rickson's driver made a turn, ending the confrontation. The driver, knowing his passenger to be one of the best fighters in the world, asked Rickson why he hadn't responded to the man.

252 • THE GIFT OF VIOLENCE

"Why would I?" Rickson replied.

Born and raised in Brazil, which has one of the highest violent crime rates in the world,[1] Rickson understands true danger. He knows most violent criminal actors are dumb, desperate, and dangerous, and you never know who is carrying a weapon. Having witnessed as a child his father Hélio being nonfatally shot by a gunman,[2] he's long known what was worth risking his life for. "I've drawn the line in the sand," he said. "I know where the line is—I don't have to think about it anymore."[3]

Rickson's approach is simple and intelligent. He's made a pre-need decision. If some young, desperate, and dangerous person with a gun demands his wallet, he can have it. If some young, desperate, and dangerous person with a gun tries to force Rickson's wife into a car, Rickson will fight, even if it means his own death. Nothing in his wallet is worth more than his life, but should he walk away and let someone take his wife, he knows he would never be able to look himself in the face again. He would rather be dead. Threats to the physical safety of his wife and children are where he draws his line. Once that line is crossed, he will fight to the death.

Knowing your line in the sand doesn't just prevent you from acting rashly due to emotion; it also provides you with a practical benefit. When confronted by an extreme and immediate threat, people will generally do one of four things:

1. Run
2. Hide
3. Freeze
4. Attack

These four reactions are mostly self-explanatory, but the third one is sometimes misunderstood. The so-called freeze response is simply a biological response to panic. Panic over what? Panic over the internal debate between fight (attack) or flight (run or hide). When our body is in fight-or-flight mode, but our mind fails to pick one or the other, we can literally freeze in place.[4] This failure to make a decision happens for a few key reasons:

1. *Denial.* We want the situation to be other than it is, so we ignore it. This is a habit often acquired by children of alcoholic or abusive parents. If you recognize this habit of denial in yourself, train yourself out of it. Denial is the most dangerous form of ignorance. Making no decision is usually a terrible decision.

2. *Sensory overload.* When my wife first moved to the United States from Iceland, she found visits to our local grocery store overwhelming because it offered so many choices, far more than she was used to. For some people, more options translate into more anxiety, and it becomes easiest to make no decision at all. When under threat, the same basic effect can happen, but the consequences can be far more severe.

3. *Unfamiliarity with violence.* Having a run-in with a violent criminal who treats you like captured prey can be shocking, especially if you are a cultured and caring human, and so too can being sexually assaulted by someone you know or trust. That shock can manifest physically as freezing.[5]

There is no shame in any of this. The freeze response is simply a biological reaction to what the nervous system is taking in. It is often a product of analysis paralysis, that is, of being forced to make a quick decision about something that you hadn't previously considered or that is completely unfamiliar. This is why engaging in sober contemplation now about your line in the sand, before such a need ever arises, is a responsible exercise for anyone serious about their relationship with violence.

This is an especially important exercise for those who have no confidence in their physical capabilities. In the self-defense courses for women I sometimes teach, I invariably encounter mothers who tell me that their biggest fear is being unable to act when the need arises.

"What if you're being dragged into a car?" I ask. "Won't you defend yourself then?"

More than a few times, I've heard the reply, "I'm not sure I could."

My response in these situations is almost always the same: "What if it's not you they're attacking or trying to drag off, but your child? What would you do then?"

The vivid descriptions of violent dismemberment that the mothers then share match anything Sammy the Bull might have dared dream. Few things in the animal kingdom are as vicious and deadly as a mother protecting her offspring. If you have trouble visualizing harming an attacker, imagine that he is going after your child. And remember that if you let him succeed in harming *you*, he will have taken away the thing your child cares about most in the world: her mom or dad.

That alone should fuel you.

As hard as it might be, visualize a nightmare scenario—and see yourself react. As with the mothers I've taught, this exercise will help prime you to act if such an unlikely event were to ever occur. It'll help you to *not* freeze.[6]

Think of a high dive, which can trigger a similar freeze response. While you are climbing up the diving board, your mind may be whirling up a storm of pure anxiety. Every imaginable thought about why this climb is stupid and why you should stop and slink back down immediately may arise in your brain. Your nerves will be on edge. You may get tunnel vision. Then, even once you make it to the top and walk to the edge of the diving board, you may momentarily freeze before the jump.

This experience can be extremely scary, especially your first time. Being frightened by heights doesn't make you a coward: it's part of our evolution. Your ancestors were frightened of such things as well. That's partly *why* they became your ancestors instead of just another organism that died from a fall before being able to procreate.

So there you are at the end of the board. You're smart and mature enough to recognize that the intense emotions you experienced on your way up are natural. You're not ashamed. You visualize yourself taking the leap.

You jump.

At that moment, as your toes leave the board and your skin, bones, and muscle are pulled down toward the water below, all the anxiety, stress, and apprehension disappear.

For a few fractions of a second, you are free.

The next thing you feel is your body hitting the water and reacting on impact. Your gross motor skills take over. Assuming you can swim (if not, you shouldn't be jumping off a high dive!), you will glide to the edge of the pool without conscious thought or mental strain.

If you've jumped off a high dive before, this may all sound familiar. If you've experienced a fight, you'll recognize not only the similarities but also some key differences. A high dive involves only you, and the goal is simple and easily visualized: you only need to jump. A fight involves you and at least one other person, with any number of other variables. Aside from making a pre-need decision, how can you ever mentally and physically prepare for a situation in which you are being attacked?

Whenever someone is placed in a stressful new environment for the first time, no particular response is guaranteed. Drawing a line in the sand, etched deeply enough to be unambiguous, creates clarity of purpose. But there is another important step that can be taken now to make it even less likely you will freeze under extreme pressure. You can learn to operate under stressful conditions with pressure-adjusted training. Some people may need more preparation than others. Some people naturally charge at a threat. Different people have different reactions. Given the right circumstances, all four reactions—run, hide, freeze, and attack— can have adaptive advantages. The point of training is to help us gain more control over which response we make and when. This is one of the reasons military units always emphasize physical and mental fitness by testing their trainees' boundaries through physical and mental stress.

"Grace under pressure," as Ernest Hemingway called it, is something all combat athletes have to learn.[7] At SBG, we ensure that happens in a physically, mentally, and emotionally healthy way. Our students and athletes are exposed to increasing levels of pressure—enough to challenge them but not so much as to overwhelm them. They learn to use breathing to control pace. They learn that if you can talk yourself into a panic, you can talk yourself out of a panic. This is done through self-coaching, which helps to keep internal dialogue more positive. The mindfulness that combat sports require helps your body learn to react to stress in a way few things can match.

Here are simplified recommendations for optimizing your training:

Expose yourself to stress. For the trainer, simulating the stress of the real-life event as closely as possible is key.[8] Adjusting the pressure to the athlete's level is also very important. The trainee should remember that *we can control effort a lot better than we can control outcome.* We should therefore invest our mental and physical energies in the former rather than the latter. When we do this, the outcome will take care of itself. As John Kavanagh always reminds his fighters, once you step into the cage, the work has already been done.

Control your breathing. There are a few physical things you can do to control your body and mind when you feel anxiety beginning to take over. Controlling your breathing is one of them. In long BJJ matches, controlled breathing helps to control heart rate, which helps you stay in the fight. As you age, this skill becomes even more vital. To beat a younger grappler, the older grappler has to survive, wear the younger person down, *and* attack at his own pace. Coach Cane Prevost, another one of my black belts, uses a very simple technique. If he hears himself breathing harder than his opponent, he slows down. This allows Coach Cane, who is in his fifties, to roll competitively with athletes in their twenties. In addition, for anyone who suffers from panic attacks, controlled breathing is a great tool.[9]

Engage your inner coach. A good inner coach is like a good corner man. The advice you give yourself must be clear, cool, and specific. "Get up!" isn't good cornering advice. "Keep that left foot on the outside" might be. Great cornering is highly specific, immediately relevant, and calmly delivered. Talk to yourself that way.

When a trainee freezes, I talk him through it. I stay positive and inspiring. I run him through the scenario again and again. Climb up to the diving board, walk to the edge, jump. Climb up to the diving board, walk to the edge, jump. Eventually, the butterflies—caused by the release of adrenaline and cortisol—become a familiar guest. As John Diggins, one of my most seasoned grappling competitors, advises: "Embrace them. Learn to welcome them like a friend. Then it won't suck so bad."

When the time comes to make a decision, you must be able to pull that proverbial trigger, whether that means fleeing or fighting. The angst, doubt, and mental distress all occur prior to the first punch, grab, or lunge. But simply *not* freezing isn't enough once violence is initiated. As discussed in chapter 19, you must also be determined to be the one who goes home to your family unhurt. It is here that the type of training described above provides a second benefit: it teaches you exactly what you are capable of. Once things turn physical, you will know you have the skills and knowledge to reach the edge of the pool after you leap off the high dive. You already have your motive, but this awareness will give you even more tenacity.

As a teenager, I briefly had a Kung Fu instructor. He taught mostly forms, but having seen Bruce Lee on screen as a mesmerized thirteen-year-old, I thought all things Kung Fu rocked. My instructor defined *tenacity* as "like the nature of a tiger." The tiger, he taught, is fierce, and it kills well, but not because it's angry or filled with hate, but because that's simply its nature. My takeaway as an impressionable boy was that tenacity is something you *are*, not something you *pretend to be*. I still feel that way forty years later. Most people have no idea what they're capable of. Unless you've undergone some serious trials, such as surviving a concentration camp or war, you probably don't realize just how tenacious you really are. Even if you don't have that direct knowledge, remember that you are the product of an unbroken chain of reproductive success. If you have to fight for your own safety or that of those you love, know that tenacity isn't just something you can do—it is something you *are*.

So how can we become more tenacious in a healthy way that doesn't involve a literal life-or-death experience? I know of no better method than combat athletics. You can click sticks together, perform kata in the air, and execute cool-looking choreographed moves for an entire life-time—and never once really push yourself. But to gain true, functional skill in combat sports like wresting, BJJ, boxing, and Judo, you must endure certain trials. These delivery systems demand you overcome certain challenges and, in the process, reveal your innate tenacity. They teach you about yourself.

One of the toughest and most talented athletes I have ever had the privilege of working with is multi-time UFC champion Randy Couture. At a seminar we once taught together, Randy was asked a question about "street fighting."

"I'm not much of a streetfighter," Randy replied with a smile.[10]

That's a very different attitude from the one you often hear in the boy-speak crowd. But what made Randy's response so telling is he was known for exhibiting that very same smile in the Octagon. This doesn't mean he didn't feel nervous before stepping into the cage. Rather, he was a professional competitor who wanted to be there and knew how to manage those nerves. Based on his years of experience as a wrestler and fighter, he knew what he was capable of, so he remained composed. The cage door would slam shut, and he would smile. There was no anger. No losing control. No temper tantrums—and no quitting. One way or another, he would push the pace. He would move forward. He would grind it out. One way or another, if you were fighting Randy, you were in for a battle. That is tenacity. That is the embodiment of determination—and it is, in a very real sense, the very opposite of the kind of emotionally charged, tempers-flaring, reactive aggression that young men who don't know better mistake for power.

When we find ourselves in unknown territory, fear can set in—and if you're not careful, so can panic. If you have no experience fighting on the ground, a BJJ or MMA fighter can easily elicit this sense of panic in you. They will execute a takedown, mount you (sit on your chest), throw a few well-placed punches or even slaps to the face, and know precisely what you, their frightened, inexperienced opponent who is feeling the helplessness that sets in when you recognize you really have no idea how to escape, will do. You will flop wildly and then roll onto your belly, thereby giving away your neck for an easy choke. From a technical perspective, your life is literally in their hands. In a training situation, they will release the choke once you tap out, but on the street, the choke will mean death if it's held, and by the time the choke is sunk in, there's nothing you will be able to do about it. It's predictable. It's testable. And you can see this pattern occur time and time again in gyms around the world.

Learning how to avoid that fate, how to stay calm when you find yourself underneath a grappler who knows what they are doing, how to just survive—let alone "win"— takes time. It takes exposure. It takes hour upon hour on the mat. It takes losing over and over. It takes all that and more. There is no shortcut, no magic bullet, no secret form, no mystical energy, no easy way out. You have to earn that skill. But here is what I want you to understand—if you have a couple of functioning limbs, *you are 100 percent capable of doing all that.*

It's the fantasy-based martial artist, the huckster, the martial arts conman who claims "some people are fighters and some aren't." (See chapter 23.) Of course, some people are born with a higher aptitude for physical conflict. Different people are born with all kinds of different variations in ability. So what? Anyone can be trained to fight. If you can exercise, if you're capable of movement, you have everything required to step onto the mat.

The outcome on the training mat on any given day isn't really the point. The point is the endeavor itself. The point is the trial by fire of finding yourself mounted, then submitted; of finding yourself mounted, then submitted—over and over again—not in a prearranged form or pattern, but against a living, breathing opponent. Even once you've learned to escape the mount and defend against the choke, you may still occasionally experience a moment of anxiety or even panic during a roll. I certainly have at various times over the decades. Your mind will try to talk you into quitting. "Why the hell am I doing this?" you'll ask yourself. But you keep going. You might still end up tapping out, but you'll also occasionally survive your opponent's pressure, escape from a very dangerous position, and end up winning a match you were certain you would lose. Those matches, those days, teach you so much about both BJJ and yourself. You could label the entire activity an exercise in tenacity.

This brings us back to the core question that may very well determine whether you survive a violent encounter: what *motivates* you?

You have your line in the sand. You've performed the pre-need decision-making exercise. You know what you will and will not fight for. You're capable of making decisions related to your safety and the safety of those you love. You know what you are capable of. And you're building yourself up in a healthy way day by day. But what if, after all that, you're still unsure whether you can overcome the odds in the face of evil?

Remember this: the greatest armies and warriors the world has ever known have been motivated to fight to the death, not because of hatred toward the enemy in front of them. They have been motivated to do so because of the brothers beside them and the loved ones behind them.

Fighting to protect yourself and those you love is far more powerful than fighting out of hate.

Nothing is fiercer than a parent protecting their offspring. Mothers and fathers will risk their safety for their children in ways that they would never consider under other circumstances. Although parents provide a model for what is possible, you need not be a parent to demonstrate this type of courage in the face of a violent threat. Courage is not the absence of fear. Courage is fear overcome by something stronger, something more powerful.

When applying violence, love trumps hate. It will make you more determined and tenacious than the predator you face.

And nothing is more powerful than love. Use it to survive and stay *alive*.[11]

22 Staying *Alive*

There is no timing absent Aliveness,
and there is no fighting skill absent timing.

We've gone deep into the most valuable tool we have for staying safe and managing violence intelligently—our *minds*—and discussed the mindset you need to survive. Now it's time to get physical.

As should be clear by now, there is a right way to prepare yourself for physical conflict and a wrong way. Let's examine first the wrong way: A crowd stands quietly as a martial arts master and his students walk onto the stage. After a short introduction, the master explains that his art has been passed down from guru to pupil for the last thousand years, which started with the system's founder, a one-armed blind monk. The master then turns and faces his student, and with one explosive motion, the student lunges forward to punch the master in the face. Deftly slipping the blow, the master fires back with what seems to be a dozen rapid-fire strikes, culminating with a devastating foot sweep that drops the student to the floor like a rock. The crowd applauds.

This scenario is repeated daily at martial arts demonstrations, schools, and gymnasiums throughout the world—and it is all make-believe.

How can I say with such certainty that it's make-believe? If you watch the student in the demonstration carefully, what you will see is a punch, kick, lunge, stab, or swing that is offered at a predictable angle, frozen in place after being executed, and presented with absolutely no resistance. All of this is designed to make the master look as impressive as possible, and none of this will help anyone learn how to fight against a real attacker.

This lesson was learned the hard way by the few traditional martial artists who stepped into the first UFCs and discovered what happens when a fantasy-based martial art meets a contact sport like BJJ, Muay Thai, or wrestling. Their choreography may be suitable for fight scenes in movies, but it has nothing to do with actual fighting. Bruce Lee said this preprogrammed approach was like dissecting a corpse, and he couldn't have been more accurate in his choice of simile.[1]

The difference between the delivery systems that we all know work well against resisting opponents—boxing, wrestling, BJJ, Muay Thai, Judo, etc.—and the fantasy-based arts that have little to no efficacy in a full-contact scenario can be summed up in one word: *Aliveness*.

Aliveness is the key to discerning fantasy from reality, function from display, and truth from fiction. And a full understanding of Aliveness thus means you will never be confused again about what is a functional and useful method and what is simply a choreographed dance or a dead pattern—a dissection of a corpse.[2]

When I was a young man, I became a fan of James Randi, a magician known as the Amazing Randi who spent decades debunking "woo-woo" and exposing charlatans, such as self-proclaimed psychic Uri Geller, who had managed to fool several world leaders into believing he had paranormal powers. Notably, Geller similarly fooled scientists at the Stanford Research Institute using nothing more than a couple of very simple magic tricks.[3] Yet, within a few short minutes, Randi could demonstrate to general audiences what these smart and educated folks failed to grasp, that *a failure of imagination is not an insight into necessity*, to paraphrase philosopher Daniel Dennett.[4]

It is no surprise that a trained magician like Randi was the one to sort out exactly what Uri Geller was up to. Randi had the requisite knowledge about the creation of magical illusions and the art of deception, and he famously exposed Geller with the help of famed television host and amateur magician Johnny Carson. Just as a highly educated scientist can be easily fooled by simple sleight of hand, so too can an otherwise skeptical, rational person be fooled by a flashy and impressive martial arts demonstration, no touch "knockout," or otherwise "real"-looking show of what is, in actuality, nothing more than the performance of a well-choreographed illusion.[5]

When I first started training in the martial arts, the world was filled with "academies," "institutes," and "schools" that taught traditional martial arts filled with dead patterns, dysfunctional delivery systems, contrived hierarchies, and a whole lot of bullshit. As I explained in chapter 5, I actively trained in Jeet Kune Do, Bruce Lee's "styleless style," which promised something more, but over the years, I saw that his system too had, as a whole, devolved into something that could best be classified as yet another traditional martial art. In other words, it was also dysfunctional. After Bruce Lee's death, the art had become yet one more way to dissect a corpse—a "classical mess," as Lee described arts that were mired in static routines and traditions.[6]

I produced a DVD set many years ago for my friend Burton Richardson, one of the top JKD instructors in the world,[7] in which he honestly discussed his journey through martial arts.[8] In it, Burton said that he had earned a "Full Instructor" ranking from his coach, Dan Inosanto, the man widely considered the leader of the JKD Concepts community, after devoting the better part of twelve years to training in JKD Concepts full time. Yet, he added, despite this certification, the first time he sparred full contact with a good boxer, he was toyed with. The first time he trained with a proper Greco-Roman wrestler, he realized he had little to no functional skill in the clinch. The first time he rolled on the ground with a good BJJ player, he realized he knew nothing about fighting on the ground. And, finally, the first time he sparred full contact with real sticks, he realized he couldn't yet fight with a stick. This led him to question what exactly had he been "certified" in.

Critics of Burton and apologists for poor training methods are quick to blame Burton for any failures in his performance rather than the actual training he received. Might they have a point? Of course not. If a BJJ instructor awards a black belt to a student, and that student lacks fundamental skills and any ability to defend himself when rolling with other BJJ practitioners or wrestlers or judo players, is that the fault of the student, or might that BJJ instructor have a problem with his own understanding of effective grappling and ground fighting?

I've personally awarded hundreds of belts, and I've yet to award a belt to a student who could not defend themselves against others on the same level in live, aggressive matches. Anyone reading is welcome to have a friendly roll with any of my (at the time of this writing) thirty-five black belts. I'm confident you'll find they're all capable of defending that belt well.

So why again is it that other martial artists cannot do the same?

I've yet to meet an able-bodied student I couldn't help reach a proficient level of functional performance. And having known and worked with Burton, I can assure you he was both extremely coachable and athletic.

Anyone coachable can become a competent "fighter." The athletic part is simply a bonus. There are, of course, levels to fighting, just as there are levels to any physical art, skill, or contest. Not everyone can become a competitive UFC fighter, but anyone, and I do mean anyone, who listens to proper coaching and puts in a good-faith effort can learn to become a competent fighter, someone fully capable of defending not only themselves but also those they love. The key is that the training must be Alive.

A competent fighter is, by definition, a tough fighter. Tough isn't how you are born, though—tough is how you perform. And how you perform is a result of scientific training, not simply a genetic throw of the dice. Anyone who says otherwise simply doesn't know how to coach. Indeed, Aliveness is still misunderstood by or unknown to many. And given that this particular epistemology, or answer-seeking method, is at the root of all functional physicality, it's here, with Aliveness, where we must always start our training.

The moment you embark upon the path of Aliveness, you are, by definition, ceasing to pretend to know things you do not know. You are applying an evidence-based approach to your answer-seeking method. In that sense, Aliveness is a process for discovering a certain truth. And it's that truth that helps keep the practitioner sincerely humble.

Ask yourself this question: have you ever seen a form of human inquiry that enforces humility and accuracy better than the scientific process? Though not perfect, the systematic methodology of science is clearly the most honest form of truth-seeking we have. And that it isn't perfect does not mean it isn't best. Any time you hear someone railing against science, ask them for a better alternative for discovering truth.

That question will end the discussion immediately.

So, too, with Aliveness—you won't find a form of physical expression that better fosters humility and accuracy. The competition with your peers, repeated performances, and overall environment of adaptive resistance enforce that mindset. Just as science is our most accurate and honest process for discovering truth in actuality, Aliveness is our most accurate and honest process for discovering truth in combat. Both are tools. Both are epistemologies. They are something you do, not something you know.

Science creates a body of knowledge that has been tested, validated, and studied across cultural lines. Aliveness does the same. In geometry, there is no such thing as a uniquely Canadian or Chinese triangle. Triangles are universal. In Alive training, there is no such thing as a uniquely Canadian or Chinese triangle choke. Triangle chokes are universal.

This doesn't imply that combat sports trained with Aliveness are static, rigid, or fixed. To the contrary, these martial arts evolve over time. Techniques arise as counters to other techniques and movements become more efficient, leading the skill set, the delivery system, and the sport in question to continually advance. Traditional martial arts, on the other hand, are fixed in time and based on myth and revelation. This makes them sclerotic, unchanging, and dogmatic. These two vastly different epistemologies are *not* two halves of a necessary whole. Rather, they are mutually exclusive.

Delivery systems like BJJ are not based on anecdotal evidence. The curriculum is repeated in our version of a lab, the mat, every day, all over the world, by thousands of "scientists." By contrast, traditional martial arts, like religions more generally, claim mythological origins. And both tend to be supported by the same amount of evidence, which is to say none. When pressed for evidence by truth-seeking skeptics, they appeal to ultimate authorities, masters, or prophets. And, as you know, this type of appeal to authority is a common logical fallacy.

When pushed hard enough by educated critics, traditional martial artists, like religious clerics, tend to fall back on a stereotyped response: *what we teach may not be "literally" true, but it is helpful.* But here, too, I disagree. While it's potentially true that any physical movement is better than no movement—assuming it doesn't also lead to delusional decision-making—it's undoubtedly true that the process of Aliveness leads to greater well-being when done properly. It develops humility and confidence, enhances mental and physical health, gives practical lessons in ethics and morality—and does all of this without peddling any form of bullshit along the way. Aliveness has the immeasurable benefit of being based, at its foundation, in things that are factually true.

Any good con artist can fake being a master in a fantasy-based martial art, just as someone can fake enlightenment, start a cult, and collect hundreds of Rolls Royces along the way. But you cannot fake being good in a functional martial art any more than you can fake being good at speaking French. The Alive method does not allow for that kind of deception. Rather, it exposes deception. And that is healthy, because all of us, from time to time, are prone to the seduction of our own egos. All of us can be self-deceptive. Aliveness, like the scientific method, acts as a self-correcting mechanism for that very human flaw. And all of this, every bit of it, is good—good for us as human beings, good for our society, good for our art, good for our families, good for our safety, and good for our well-being.

So what does Aliveness look like in practice?

For training to be Alive, it must contain three key elements—timing, energy, and motion—none more or less important than the other.

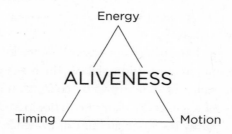

By *timing*, I mean unpredictability. If you drill a pattern or a repeated series of kata, forms, or choreography in a predictable rhythm, then you are not acquiring timing. By *motion*, I mean that the training should not be static. There must be pushing, pulling, clinching, and releasing—there must be unchoreographed movement. And finally, by *energy*, I mean resistance. As far as possible, you must feel the same resistance that you'd feel from an uncooperative opponent. Swing the stick as someone would in real life—don't freeze halfway. Punch with the energy of someone who wants to hit—don't lock your arm out so that your partner can look good performing a strike, throw, trap, or sweep.

Your practice must have these three elements to be *Alive*. The context doesn't necessarily matter.

Here's an example of an Alive process outside of martial arts: When my daughter Anika was eight years old, I began to teach her badminton. We went out into the yard, where I showed her how to hold her racket. Then I stood a few feet away and lobbed the bird at her—slowly. She swung and missed. We tried again. She swung and missed. We tried again. She swung and hit it! The bird flew several feet away. I walked over, picked it up, and lobbed it back at her. We repeated this process as I gradually increased the distance between us. Once she was hitting the bird a good percentage of the time and could reliably hit it back in my direction, I started using my racket as well. And behold: she and I were playing badminton.

That's *Aliveness*.

Let's imagine we had instead used a method drawn from one of the traditional, sclerotic, dead-pattern martial arts: She stands ready with her racket. I put her into a rigid stance, instructing her to root herself. She swings, but her form is all off. Her thumb is pointed in the wrong direction. Her knee is askew. She doesn't turn her hips. I give her a choreographed pattern she can practice by herself in the garage. There is no need for a live bird—after all, she hasn't even learned to stand yet. Of course, she complains that it's boring to stand in the garage, pretending to hit an invisible bird in this robotic way. Within minutes, her attention wavers, her form succumbs to the monotony, and she's begun to lose all interest in badminton. No matter how long we might repeat this nonsense, the moment she faces a live bird, she will be pretty much where she would have been had we started with the Alive method. Worse, she may have even picked up some bad habits along the way without gaining any sense of timing, motion, or energy.

If having someone only ever swing at air sounds like a ridiculous way to teach a child badminton, imagine how silly it would be if you were trying to teach her how to fight. But most traditional martial arts train in a manner just like the one described here. Indeed, most functional martial arts coaches will tell you that it's easier to train a student with no background in martial arts than someone from a fantasy-based martial art, because the raw beginner has the advantage of never having learned the wrong way to perform movements.

If it seems like I'm trafficking in common sense, understand that most traditional martial arts—unlike combat sports—train only through choreography and fixed patterns, and the beautiful simplicity of the Alive method is lost on them. Put simply, the Alive formula necessarily eliminates a great portion of what is considered "training" in the various traditional martial arts.

There are, obviously, times when it's not appropriate to offer resistance. When first learning or practicing a movement, for example, you need to allow your partner time to work out the mechanics. When I was teaching Anika badminton, I first had to teach her how to hold and swing the racket. But in Alive training, this introductory stage is always followed by other stages.

The starting point for understanding the Alive teaching model is the "I" Method. The "I" Method involves a three-stage process that occurs over the course of any given class. You begin with *introduction*, the launch point for any lesson. You then proceed directly into *isolation*, which is the drill stage, and consequently the stage where you will gain the most benefit. And you finish with the *integration* stage, the point at which you take that day's lesson and work it back into the big picture of whatever theater of operations you are working in—grappling, striking, MMA, self-defense, military, law enforcement, etc.

The Introduction Stage

This stage usually takes up no more than a quarter of class—so, assuming a sixty-minute class, anywhere from ten to fifteen minutes. If it takes more time than that, then the instructor may be teaching something for which the class is not yet ready—for example, an escape from a certain choke in a class of people who don't yet know how to do the actual choke. If the material fits the class level, fifteen minutes is generally enough. For example, let's say you are practicing BJJ, something everyone interested in being able to defend themselves on the ground (meaning everyone) should do, and you are working on escapes from the mount position. The instructor would begin by introducing the escape being taught—for example, the bridge and roll. The teacher would demonstrate the move, then point out two or three key details related to how that move works when done properly.

As a coach, I usually try not to point out more than three details at a time, because I don't want to overload the students with too much information. In the case of the bridge and roll, I may talk about the required connection to your opponent, which means how you grab one side of their body to hold them effectively, and the correct mechanical way to roll someone bigger and stronger than you off of your body. The chosen details here matter greatly, and the students need to understand them. This is where having an experienced coach who grasps and appreciates the depth of each fundamental technique matters.

During this stage, students are encouraged to talk to each other, switch back and forth on their own, and work on the material without using any resistance. If there is a limited place for repetition in training, this is it. The instructor walks around, making sure to correct and advise as needed. The objective here is two-fold: first, everyone in class should be able to demonstrate the movement in a manner that is technically correct when no resistance is being applied; and second, every student should understand why and how the movement is meant to work.

The "why" is very important. You can teach anyone *how* to do something. But if they don't really understand *why* that *how* works when it's done properly, *why* it is more efficient, and *why* it maximizes leverage, then they don't really understand the movement—even if their body can perform it. Once the why is understood, the brain can then begin to make the connections between the principles and concepts that operate not only within that particular technique in that particular position but also across other techniques in other positions. We've found that this understanding helps accelerate an athlete's growth and performance. When taught this way, BJJ classes serve as lessons for the intellect as well as the body.

It is important that everyone on the mat *gets it* when no resistance is applied. And by "gets it," I mean that they are able to perform a mechanically correct movement and, as I just described, understand why the technique works the way it does. I have yet to meet a student who was not able to *get it* at the introduction stage, provided the instructor was patient and skilled in communicating the lesson. This is where pithiness helps. The biggest hindrance I see with young instructors at this stage is the tendency to talk too much, explain too much, and, in the process, confuse people.

Once everyone can perform the move properly, without resistance, you should move on to the next stage of class. If this introduction stage takes too long, then the material is inappropriate in terms of quantity or context, or both. One could spend lifetimes just mastering a single aspect of physical conflict. But along the way, each lesson should be simple and make sense.

The Isolation Stage

Once you have completed the introduction stage, you should move straight to the isolation stage.[9] This is what I call *Alive drilling*, the link between the introduction of a technique and the incorporation of the same technique in a live roll against a fully-resisting opponent. This is a critical stage in which you work a specific technique or movement against resistance. It should take up about thirty minutes or roughly half of class. What we do *not* want to do is introduce a new movement or technique, repeat them in some form of dead pattern or repetition, and then go straight to sparring. That is exactly what I am *not* advocating for here. The isolation stage is where you actually begin to acquire technical skill and the critical element of *timing*.

Using our example of escaping mount position (in which someone is sitting on your chest), a simple drill might be one in which one person tries to hold the mount position while the other person tries to escape from the mount position using the technique they just learned. No matter the specific type of drill, it should be Alive, but the exact level of resistance can vary over the course of the session. What kind of resistance should be used? *Adaptive resistance*. That means the pressure can be turned up or down based on the success rate of the students. Some level of failure is not just okay but also expected. As I remind my students at the end of almost every drill, *failure is a necessary part of the process*. If you're not failing sometimes, you're probably not operating under enough resistance. That said, if the instruction given at the introduction stage was solid, most of the students will find themselves actually using the technique they just learned that day, in real time, against a resisting opponent. Such is the power of a functional delivery system.

Timing is not gained from repetitions without resistance. If you walk away from this section on drilling with only one thing that you remember, let it be this: timing *requires* resistance. Timing can only be gained through Aliveness. As such, at SBG we don't refer to any form of repetition without resistance as a drill. All of our drills are done Alive, and there is nothing, I repeat, nothing that cannot be drilled Alive.

Nothing is too deadly.

Nothing is too dangerous.

No one is too old.

No one is too weak.

No one is too new.

Anyone who tells you otherwise, who tells you the reason Alive resistance isn't used is that what they are teaching is just too savage, or that you are just too fragile or a neophyte, is either lying to you or has no idea how to train Alive. Anything related to violence, from harsh words to hand grenades, can be drilled Alive.

Don't forget that.

There are many ways to drill Alive. Indeed, once Alive drilling is properly understood, the number of effective, fun, and functional drills available for any particular movement is limited only by the coach's imagination. In a video podcast I did with Rickson Gracie, we discussed the importance of this type of Alive drilling. He sees focused technique training against resistance as an essential factor in developing technical skill and proficiency in BJJ. As he said, "It's knowledge of technique, yes, but it's also timing that makes the difference in Jiu-Jitsu."

The Integration Stage

You have learned the mechanics of the technique and begun to acquire timing through Alive drilling. Now it is time to put the technique back into the big picture of whatever you are working on at your gym, whether the context is striking, wrestling, BJJ, MMA, self-defense, weapons, law enforcement applications—you name it.

For BJJ, this is relatively simple: it's time to roll, the term we use for sparring. You can start standing or on the ground. If we've been drilling from a particular position that day, I often have the students start from there. No matter the starting point, the end point is clear: you keep rolling until someone submits or taps, and then you start again.

The beauty of this stage is its realism. Nobody is letting anyone get or do anything. Whether you finish your opponent or get finished, the result is earned. There is no substitute for that. None. As SBG Ireland coach John Kavanagh famously says, "We win or we learn."[10]

No matter the class, you're taking the technique or movement that you isolated and drilled with Aliveness, then putting it back into the whole. In a self-defense class, you may end up playing out live scenarios with an aggressive attacker. In a law enforcement class, you may end up trying to take into custody a fully resisting opponent. In boxing or MMA classes, the integration stage can sometimes be trickier, especially when you are working with a group of brand-new students. Indeed, one of the great advantages of BJJ is that you can roll live from day one, but not everyone will, or should, box or spar MMA on day one. This is true even under the gentlest and most welcoming of conditions. No matter the objective or art, the key to becoming more dangerous to bad people is *Alive* training.

Now that you know what Alive training looks like, you are better suited to find good training in your area, and, perhaps more importantly, you'll have a much better *bullshit detector* to help you wade through the ocean of nonsense that is martial arts.

Remember, any physical training can be done Alive.

Handgun retention? Drill it Alive!

Knife defense? Drill it Alive!

Headlock escapes? Drill it Alive!

Slipping punches? Drill it Alive!

Takedown defense? Drill it Alive!

Handcuffing a resisting suspect? Drill it Alive!

Nothing is too deadly. Nothing is too advanced. Nothing ever needs to be in a monotonous, choreographed pattern. When it comes to breaking out of the dead patterns and sclerotic traditions that provide no self-defense value, Aliveness and the "I"-Method will set you free to thrive and survive.

23 Detecting Bullshit

Circumstances will dictate tactics, and plans will change upon contact,
but the skill sets that you develop with Alive training
will largely determine success or failure.

Just as what you train matters, so too does how you train. But if Alive training so clearly leads to increased safety, strength, knowledge, mindfulness, and, as I will show, self-knowledge, you might be asking, why doesn't everyone train Alive?

The simple fact is not everyone is interested in what's true or what works. Having an honest command of a functional skill requires effort and must be earned. A fantasy that promises easy rewards will thus always find an audience. But if you've read this far, my hope is that you will not be similarly duped. You will run into various excuses as to why Alive training isn't or shouldn't be uniformly embraced across the martial arts and self-defense world. Over the last thirty years, I have heard them all, over and over again. None are valid.

Despite the many common myths and misconceptions you might hear from proponents of traditional martial arts about Alive training, the reality is quite different:

Myth 1. *Alive training is too dangerous.*

Reality: Timing, energy, and motion can always be part of training when proper gear, safety measures, and procedures are implemented.

When it comes to hand-to-hand combat, very few things are as dangerous as a knife. According to a multiyear study in Philadelphia, the typical stabbing victim who made it to a hospital had approximately a 7.7 percent chance of dying.[1] The odds of living might be higher than those of a typical shooting victim, but a single well-executed stab with the right blade can be as lethal as any bullet.

Yet many people have absolutely no idea just how dangerous edged weapons can be. This is why you often hear individuals with little to no training or experience question why a police officer was involved in a shooting when the suspect had *only* a knife. My second black belt and good friend, Karl Tanswell, however, understood exactly how dangerous bladed weapons are. He knew well because, in the 1990s, several men tried to kill him in a knife attack. They approached him as he was bouncing at the front door of a nightclub and stabbed him seven times, five times in the body and two times in the head. Luckily for Karl, his fiancée at the time was able to stop the bleeding. He lived.

I'll repeat: knives are incredibly dangerous tools.

Before the attack, Karl had been a lifelong martial artist, and his training had been very similar to my own early training. He had come up through the JKD Concepts world and had just begun to grow disillusioned with much of the hypocrisy and delusion he saw within the community. Like myself, he had begun to focus on stand-up fighting and had started to move away from the system's Filipino martial arts material, also known as Kali or Escrima, because he saw its inherent flaws. After he was stabbed, he stopped teaching the art completely.

Recognizing the heavy responsibility involved in teaching someone methods for defending against a knife-wielding attacker, he knew that he could no longer teach the Kali he had learned from his JKD Concepts instructors. But did that mean no good method existed? Was the only real answer gun or run?

Karl wanted to find out. Once his wounds healed, he went on a quest to find something, anything that might actually work against a knife-wielding attacker. And because he wanted to know the truth, he did it using Aliveness.

Karl grabbed his assistant at the time, stuck a large laundry marker in his hand, told him to attack him, and went through all the possible self-defense options. To make sure his assistant wasn't getting too predictable, he would grab new people off the street, bring them in, and have them go after him. Thick black lines on his face and body denoted failure. And slice after slice, stab after stab, he ended up throwing out just about everything he had learned in his JKD/Kali days.

But then, after countless hours of trial-and-error against a resisting opponent, he stumbled on what did work.

If you think about the best people in the world at striking with their fists, you will be thinking about boxers. If you think about the best people in the world at controlling and finishing people on the ground, you will be thinking about BJJ practitioners. And if you think about the best people in the world at controlling people on their feet and taking them down to the ground, you will be thinking about wrestlers. It is very difficult to block a knife strike. You have to grab the arm that has the knife. Once you have that arm, you have to control it. No one is better at controlling an arm in the standing clinch than wrestlers—no one. Folkstyle, Freestyle, and Greco-Roman wrestlers dominate when it comes to controlling the arms and torso of another human being. They dominate there because that's where they spend their time, in a competitive environment, against resisting opponents. *Competere* made them the best in that position, and that's from where the solution came.

When I met Karl for the first time in Manchester, England, roughly a year after the knife attack, he told me this story. By that time in my evolution, I had already tossed Kali drills out of the SBG curriculum, and I was deeply skeptical of all things related to "knife defense." So I said what you should always say in such a situation: "Show me."

And he did.

We went upstairs to his small second-story gym, which was eerily similar to my own first academy, and he put a training blade in my hand.

"Stab me," he said. And I tried.

For the first time in my life, I saw someone who could actually defend themselves against a blade, using a method that was as practical as it was simple. It wasn't pretty. It wasn't flashy. But it worked.[2]

I invited Karl to the United States to teach our other coaches his system, which he cleverly named STAB: Self-defense Training Against Blades.[3]

Although we lost Karl a few years ago, he was one of the true pioneers of MMA in the United Kingdom—a world-class BJJ instructor, MMA coach, innovator, leader, and mad genius.[4] His loss left a massive hole in the UK martial arts scene, as well as in the hearts of many. Karl's influence, however, will continue to live on through his many students and world-class coaches and through the lives that have been and will be saved along the way. In that, he has a proud legacy.[5]

In all functional fighting systems, the most effective solution to any problem will always seem to be common sense in hindsight. So in response to the fallacy that *Alive training is just too dangerous,* the most honest answer is this: it's just too dangerous *not* to train with Aliveness.

Myth 2. *You must ingrain the body mechanics of a move before introducing any resistance.*

Reality: Timing cannot be acquired through the repetition of dead patterns. Aliveness isn't an optional part of the training regimen—it is the irreplaceable part.

First, going straight to resistance isn't what we do with Alive training. Recall the three stages of the "I"-Method, which begins with the introduction stage. Second, if a living, breathing opponent is completely absent from the training, the element of timing is gone.

Remember my story about teaching my daughter Anika badminton? Let's say it's tennis this time and you're the student. Imagine you want to develop your backhand. You hire a tennis coach. He meticulously walks you through all the subtle movements of the proper backhand swing. He has you execute a backhand swing time and again without the use of a ball, correcting any mistakes in "form" as you go. Because he wants you to "ingrain" the movement, he has you get up every morning and execute five hundred backhands with your racket swatting only air.

Please imagine this training method in your mind, or, better yet, stand up and take a few backhand swings with your hands just to get the feel of it. Short of your coach eyeballing your every move and attempting to correct each angle of your shoulder, elbow, and wrist in accordance with the position of an imaginary ball, you're left simply repeating a dead pattern over and over again. Now, imagine that after a few months of this *movement-ingraining form*—and make no mistake, this is exactly what a kata in the traditional martial arts is—you head onto the tennis court. You're ready to play a game. Your opponent serves. Will your backhand be any better than it was prior to your months of hitting air?

My hypothesis is as follows: your movement *may* have gotten better, but it also may have gotten *worse*. We won't actually know until we test your performance. Why? Because the exercise you were performing in the garage lacked any form of *self-correcting mechanism*. This is a critical concept to understand. You've never once hit a ball, so you have no sense of timing. Further, you might just as easily have developed bad habits as good ones. You have no way of knowing until you test yourself on the court.

Now let's look at how a coach using an Alive method might help you ingrain a proper backhand movement. Yes, at first, the coach may have you swing the racket without a ball a few times, making necessary corrections to your form. But then, and this is likely to happen within minutes, the coach will walk you to the tennis court, stand across the net from you, and slowly begin hitting balls toward you. Your instructions are simple enough: try to hit the ball back over the net using a backhand swing. Your coach knows this isn't a competition but rather a drill. Some element of failure is necessary, as is some measure of success. Each time the ball comes over the net, its angle, trajectory, and force are a bit different. It requires unplanned, unchoreographed movement in order to hit it back effectively. When that timing is off or the movement is technically poor, you either miss or hit the ball in a less-than-optimal way. The feedback is instantaneous, authentic, and never lies. This is the adaptive-resistance phase. If you fail multiple times in a row to hit the ball back, your coach will likely slow it down, soften his hit, place the ball in the ideal spot, and make it easier for you to succeed. As you begin hitting back ball after ball, he might then speed it up a bit, move the ball around the court a bit more, and make it harder for you to succeed—always making sure you're being appropriately challenged.

Having articulated both methods, ask yourself the following question: which player, after a few weeks of training, is going to have a better backhand? Will it be the one who has yet to hit a ball but who has lots and lots of dead repetitions with their racket? Or will it be the one who had very few dead repetitions at the start, perhaps only a few minutes' worth, with perhaps a few more on any given day if the coach noticed something that needed to be adjusted, but who primarily spent their time hitting a moving (Alive) ball back across the court, which came at them at progressively increasing speeds and levels of difficulty? The answer here is obvious. And the understanding of this principle is exactly why some martial arts work and others are simply fantasies.

Some critics are quick to point out that all athletes spend hours repeating a movement. Boxers throw thousands of jabs, and basketball players shoot innumerable free throws. And while that's true, we always need to keep in mind that fighting requires, by definition, the addition of an opponent in order for the element of timing to exist. The distinction between someone with two years of BJJ and someone with twenty years isn't just due to the difference in the number of techniques that they each know. It is also due to the timing the person with twenty years has developed. There is simply no shortcut to developing that. While repetition certainly plays a role in all manner of athletic endeavors, fighting included, you cannot learn to fight at all without lots of exposure to a resisting opponent. Repetition can be helpful when done right, but Aliveness isn't optional—it is required.

Myth 3. *Some people need dead patterns.*

Reality: The notion that "some people are fighters, and some just aren't" is nothing more than an excuse for poor coaching and poor methodology.

Are there some people who are just tougher, more physical, more capable of being comfortable in uncomfortable situations, more apt to keep fighting through pain and injury, and harder to stop or knock unconscious? Of course there are. Does that, therefore, mean that people lacking those traits at birth, or failing to acquire them in their youth, are stuck being softer and weaker forever? Of course it doesn't.

It isn't difficult to make tough people tougher. Making weak people stronger, tougher, and more confident—that's where the true art of coaching really shines. It's done all the time, all over the world, in SBG and any number of other gyms. But the fantasy-based martial arts world, due to its faulty epistemology, creates instructors who are unable to make the weak stronger. As a result, rather than change their training methods, they adopt an excuse—*"Some people are fighters, and some just aren't."* And that excuse then serves as a rationalization for why some people supposedly *need* dead patterns. It's circular reasoning at its most obvious. Don't fall for it.

Also, don't fall for appeals to authority: "My instructor says forms (kata) are and always have been essential." This may or may not be true, but we can't know it's true simply because it is stated by an authority figure. Citing the length of time a particular idea or tradition has been around as some kind of validating proof isn't rational. Astrology charts have been around for a long time, but this doesn't mean you should take them seriously. You should listen to your instructor. But if your instructor teaches dead patterns only, the justifications made by your instructor warrant scrutiny. A lack of honest and sincere questioning is one of the reasons why all forms of superstition, even the pernicious ones, persist.

Don't fall for category mistakes, either. Here's a common one: "Boxers hit bags, football players run tires—all athletes rely on dead training to develop attributes. Why can't martial artists use dead patterns— two-person forms—to do the same thing?" These types of exercises, which also include lifting weights and stretching, help with conditioning, agility, flexibility, or strength-building. They help build the body, the vehicle that executes the fighting techniques, but they do not teach you fighting techniques. If you lift weights properly and consistently for a long enough time, for example, you will become stronger, but you won't learn how to fight. That *doesn't* mean strength isn't very useful. It *does* mean that strength training and fight training are two very different things. Running tires, lifting heavy things, climbing ropes, doing pull-ups, these are all phenomenal tools for improving your body's performance—but they are not *activity-specific* techniques.

Let's go back to my badminton example. Assuming Anika wanted to become a world champion badminton player, she might lift weights, run, do yoga, and engage in a whole host of physical conditioning drills that would help develop her body—her *attributes*—which in turn might help her play better. That's certainly true. However, in order to learn how to hit that bird back at me, she would still have to put in Alive training. She could probably become a pretty good badminton player without lifting weights and running tires. But she would never learn to play badminton at all by only lifting weights and running tires.

Obviously you can incorporate conditioning as part of your fight training. That is, in fact, what most traditional martial artists do. You can even lift stuffed dummies, hit stuffed dummies, and run with stuffed dummies. And in doing so, you can develop your body, challenge yourself, and build a lot of the physical attributes that will help you survive and persevere in a fight. But what you cannot do through conditioning is develop the timing needed to pull off proper technique. As Bruce Lee famously said in *Enter the Dragon*, "Boards don't hit back."[6] Timing, by definition, requires Aliveness. So when someone is rationalizing the use of conditioning-style training methods as a means to develop technical fighting skill, understand they are making a *category mistake*. They are confusing activity-specific skill training with physical conditioning. While one is optional and potentially helpful (*conditioning*), the other is absolutely essential (*activity-specific Alive training*).

Myth 4. *Alive training is only for the young and healthy.*

Reality: This isn't just factually wrong—it's also backward. The less athletic an individual is, the more they need Alive training.

SBG's worldwide network of gyms has, for decades, been helping men, women, and children of all ages and athletic abilities learn functional martial arts through healthy and safe Alive training. My seventh black belt is a woman named Lily Pagle. I first met Lily when she was fifty-one years old, and I was honored to award her a black belt in BJJ when she was sixty. She is, to my knowledge, the oldest woman to receive such a rank. And it was earned. She is tiny, yet she rolls with large, strong, athletic, and aggressive young men and beats them. Roll with Lily and make one mistake, and she will finish you. She is as legit as legit gets. Day after day, month after month, year after year, she worked her way to that level of provable skill by training Alive.[7]

Our academies are filled with people Lily's age and older, as well as people with various levels of physical ability. Everyone trains Alive. This is empirical evidence that demonstrates the lie of this particular myth.

But there is another, more commonsensical way to understand why the notion that Alive training is *"only for the young and healthy"* is nonsense.

As discussed, many traditional martial arts, like all forms of superstition, like to pretend they have "magic bullets," whether they involve mysterious "chi" energy, no-touch knockouts, pressure points, or other secret methods that are claimed to be useful for the old in defending against the young. "The harder, more external styles are for the young," says the old Kung Fu master. "When you get older, you need the 'internal' style." This is, of course, just another defense mechanism for bullshit. If you give it just a few minutes of rational thought, this claim falls apart. Imagine for a moment that there were *special* punches, kicks, throws, or escapes that an older, feebler person could perform on a younger, stronger athlete. Imagine such a thing actually existed. Now ask yourself, why wouldn't the younger, stronger athlete use those methods too?

If a smaller, weaker person discovers a submission or sweep that works well on much larger men like myself, don't you think I'd adopt it in a heartbeat? Can superior timing and technique overcome size and strength? You bet they can. But when timing and technique are equal, do superior size and strength play more of a role? You bet they do. That's why every combat sport has weight classes. A small person highly skilled in BJJ can, and most often will, make a larger, stronger person who has no experience in grappling or BJJ look ridiculous on the ground. But once that larger, stronger person learns what the small person knows and puts in the needed time on the mat to acquire the same timing—it's game on. And there is no magic bullet, no secret spell, no mysterious or hidden technique that will change that reality.

Remember, if you can't effectively use Tai Chi or Silat or Aikido against a resisting opponent when you are younger and stronger, what good will it do you when you are older and less athletic? A functional martial art is a functional martial art no matter who you are, or how old you are. BJJ movements and techniques, for example, can be performed slowly and gently and still be highly effective. What a beautiful thing that is! You will use the same positions, the same movements, and the same delivery systems, no matter your age or strength level. You just have to be wiser in how you train them and, preferably, craftier in how you apply them.

So, how do you safely and intelligently train Alive as you age?

Keep these three things in mind:

1. Stay in shape. (You should do this anyway.)
2. Train smart. (You should do this anyway.)
3. Use progressive resistance. (You should do this anyway.)

Alive training is for everybody.

Myth 5. *You're describing sports. We train for the street!*

Reality: You should never use an inferior training method for a deadly serious event.

If you've heard it once, you've heard it ten thousand times: *"This is for the street, not sports!"* And all manner of bullshit then flows.

Yes, there is much more to managing self-defense beyond physical fighting technique. But even in that preventative and pre-incident arena, when it's all about the MIND (maturity, intelligence, noticing, and distance, deterrence, and determination), combat sports play an essential role. The opponent process and Aliveness training breed maturity, increase applied intelligence, and develop situational awareness, which in turn help you deter character-disordered creeps, stay out of dangerous situations, and gain the confidence needed to survive. And make no mistake, when it comes to preparing for actual physical conflict in the street—the hands-on pushing and pulling, throwing and kicking, clawing and biting, holding and hitting—nothing comes close to the sheer effectiveness found in combat sports—nothing.

Consider the headlock—a simple, visceral technique common in fights. If you've ever been in a fight as a kid, you've probably been in a headlock—or thrown one on. It's natural to grapple in a street fight. Once a blow or two is thrown, grasping, grabbing, pulling, and tackling are commonplace. And in that tussle, gripping the other guy's head is as innate as it gets. So what's your plan when that happens?

"Hit 'em in the balls," the so-called street-training crowd yells.

Easier said than done when you're being dragged to the asphalt headfirst. And even if you pull off a good shot, are you sure they'll let go?

Many years ago, I was involved in an altercation outside my place of work. My attacker seemed to come from nowhere (in truth, I had failed at the N part of the MIND acronym—noticing), and he threw a large, ring-covered fist toward my face. At the time, I was boxing regularly and still teaching JKD Concepts, primarily focused on the most functional aspect they had—kickboxing. I made space. He came at me. I punched him several times, kicked him in the leg several times, and then threw the hardest kick I could into his balls. I was wearing steel-toed boots.

Not only did he not stop—he didn't even pause.

He lunged at me and tried to tackle me to the ground. My BJJ and wrestling were extremely limited at the time, so thankfully, he didn't get me there. He was larger than me, and he was high on something. Being underneath him would not have been good. I managed to catch him in what's known as the "plum" in Muay Thai, a double necktie. Pulling his head down, I threw several hard knees into his face. How many, I am not sure, but there were teeth left on the ground, so more than a few.

After taking several hard knees to his face and skull, he slipped his head out, and finally, thankfully, he backed away. His face was a bloody mess. He brought his hands up to the fresh gap in his mouth and turned to run. As he fled, he yelled that he'd be back—with a gun.

My knuckles were torn up and bloody, so I went to the bathroom and washed, and washed, and washed. Blood-borne pathogens became my concern. After calling the sheriff, I called the HIV hotline.[8] They explained that the virus wasn't likely to transmit in that type of altercation. When I look carefully, I can still see teeth-mark scars on my hand.

I'm neither proud nor ashamed of that incident. It isn't something I ever bring up. I do so here because it offers a vital lesson: my attacker wasn't going to stop unless I stopped him, and a kick to the groin wasn't enough to do so. Had I slipped on his takedown attempt, I am not sure I would have had any way to get him off me. When people take enough meth, crack, tequila, or bath salts, or they're just in the middle of a tremendous adrenalin dump, pain isn't a big deal. And it certainly isn't something you can rely on as an accomplice. Speak with any first responder who's had a few years on the job, and they will tell you stories about people who've suffered major medical trauma—missing fingers, knives sticking out of their heads, ears ripped off—and still keep going. They keep fighting. They keep attacking. They need to be restrained.

They have to be controlled physically. Which is why what saved me in that fight wasn't my ability to punch or knee, though that helped. In the end, what saved me was the double necktie. It kept him from wrapping his arms fully around me and throwing me to the ground. What saved me was what little skill I had at that time in the clinch. What saved me was what controls people—*grappling*.

Someone better at striking than me might not have needed to rely on grappling. Indeed, plenty of fights have ended with a solid punch to the face. But that, too, comes from combat sports. Can you name any art better at punching another human than boxing? Trained boxers have those mechanics down. Still, my ability to defend, survive, and ultimately dominate that short battle came from my time in the gym against a resisting opponent, not from doing energy drills, clicking sticks together, or practicing kata. Whether it is grappling or striking, the skills you will rely upon come from combat sports.

So back to our everyday, commonplace headlock: "Bite them," I hear.

You can certainly inflict a lot of pain when you bite flesh. I've been bitten. But if I am on top of you, and you bite me, that level of pain isn't going to cause me to leap off of you and grant you freedom. It is going to make me mad. It is going to make me want to hurt you. And assuming I am on top of you, and your BJJ skill isn't on a level close to my own, there probably isn't anything you'll be able to do about that.

Now, let's take it to another level. Let's say your attacker, who is now holding you in a headlock, is wearing a leather jacket. Where is your bite now? Let's turn it up again. Let's say that as this leather-jacket-wearing thug is holding you down in a headlock, his buddy is running toward you, and that buddy is going to do what people always do during a brawl when the pack mentality kicks in—he's going to drop kick you in the face.

What now? Bite faster? Bite more?

When skilled BJJ practitioners find themselves in the type of headlock you might encounter in a typical street fight, they find themselves at home. Why? Because once you know what you are doing, those types of basic headlocks are fairly easy to defend. Connected to your opponent, you can move both your bodies as one. You can slip out and take his back, ending him with a choke. Or you can reverse him, take top, release his grip, and begin talking sense to him while keeping him under your control. If he continues to actively resist, you can break his arm or choke him unconscious—or simply stand up and get away. Whether it is one opponent or two, leather jacket or beachwear, mat or concrete, the BJJ practitioner will have the best odds possible of controlling that fight, because she has the best skill set possible for controlling the other person's body. And it is physical control, not pain, that you must learn to rely on when it comes to a self-defense situation.

So now to our final question, which brings the whole *street–versus–sport myth* into clear view.

From a technique standpoint, what is the difference between escaping a headlock held by a big, strong, aggressive guy in the gym and escaping one held by a big, strong, aggressive guy in the parking lot of a Wal-Mart?

The answer: there is zero difference.

Note: I am not saying there is zero difference between these two situations and environments. To be sure, these two situations are very different tactically and very different in terms of the stakes, but there is absolutely no mechanical difference in how a proper escape is performed. There is no magic "street-based" escape for a headlock that is better than a "gym-based" escape, which is why the skill you develop every day on the mat travels with you wherever you go.

Competitive athletes train Alive because they want to win. Change the stakes from a sporting contest to a police officer trying to maintain control over his sidearm while a resisting suspect attempts to take it from him, and winning becomes even more important. While the stakes may change from defending a takedown in a match to maintaining control over a gun on the street, the core skill set remains identical, and the core training method remains essential.

Combat sports are the healthy route for everyone, not just because they develop the root skills in the delivery systems that transcend environment but also because when they are done properly, they are psychologically and emotionally good for people.

Any other related myths you might hear are also easily answered:

"On the street, it's concrete, not soft mats!" Yes, and the mats are there to protect you, not me. As a grappler, I'll be on top.

"On the street, there are multiple opponents!" Yes, and so you would

take a training method that has shown itself to be inferior for training one-on-one and use it for training three-on-one? When multiple opponents are involved, Alive training is even more important.

"On the street, there are weapons!" See above.

"On the street, you don't want to go to the ground!" You can't always choose where you end up. That's why it's called a fight. And remember, no one is harder to take down to the ground than a wrestler.

"On the street, there are no rules! The UFC is full of rules!" Yes, in a venue like the UFC, unlike the "street," you're battling someone who *also* knows how to fight. And besides, if you can't beat us with rules, what makes you think you can beat us without them?

"Why do a fancy grappling technique when you can just slam his head into the concrete?" Because those grappling techniques minimize risk and are faster, safer, and smarter.

As I've pointed out throughout this book, using your brain to its full potential and being able to determine the appropriate level and application of violence is what proper self-defense is all about. Indeed, escalating force when it is unnecessary to do so is both physically hazardous and legally dangerous[9]—to say nothing of the moral questions raised. This is one of the reasons that the "street" instructors who focus solely on things like eye gouges and strikes miss the mark. Not every situation that would benefit from the application of physical force requires gouging an eye or slamming a head into concrete. Sometimes a simple grip on someone's arm will do.

Excessive force is often a sign of poor training. The real *art*, as it relates to the physical application of force, is the ability, or perhaps better stated, the strength—mentally, emotionally, physically, and technically—to apply the appropriate level of force, the *appropriate response*, to a particular situation. This comes from combat sports. It isn't rational to use an inferior training method for a deadly serious event. And while I'm interested in creating combat athletes—not "streetfighters"—it's also true that how we train happens to be the best way to train for the "street."

My coach Chris Haueter has a saying that sums it up well: "Train sport, think street."[10]

* * *

I have heard all of the above and more from instructors who were bus-ily teaching bullshit. I want to say this in no uncertain terms, loudly and clearly: their claims are all lies. Once all the above common myths have been busted—and the superiority of Aliveness training has been demonstrated time and again—advocates of traditional martial arts typ-ically fall back to a more easily defended claim: "All arts have something good," they will mindlessly repeat. Yet this cliché sounds true only in the absence of examination. If by "good" you mean they offer a healthy form of exercise that can improve your strength, speed, flexibility, and coor-dination, then sure.[11] Any local dance school can do that too. But if by "good" you mean they are also functional in a fight, the saying becomes patently false.

When this secondary defense of their traditional martial art fails, they fall back to their last line of defense: they attack the messenger. "Yes, but . . ." they'll say, ". . . you guys lack respect. You only care about fighting, not personal character."

Notice how this works? They start by saying *it works*, then they ac-knowledge that it doesn't work but argue that *it is useful*, and finally, they *attack the messenger*.

The charge that we do not care about character is more than just wrong; it is also backward. Having been involved with martial arts all my adult life, and having been involved with combat sports prior to the in-ception of MMA, I know full well, based on experience, that Alive train-ing and respect for other human beings are never mutually exclusive. In fact, I would take this one step further. When done correctly, Alive training is vastly superior to anything found within traditional martial arts as it relates to the positive effects it has on people in their daily lives.

What benefits as they relate to increased self-esteem and personal confidence could one gain from an art like Wing Chun, Aikido, or any other traditional martial art that one could not gain in even more abun-dance from a functional art like BJJ or any other combat sport? This becomes especially true when we remember that BJJ has one massive advantage: it also happens to be *real*.

It works.

Having skill in BJJ means something tangible in the same sense that having skill at playing basketball, speaking Spanish, or being good at surfing does. They are skills that can be tested and demonstrated in experimental conditions—whether on the court, in a classroom, on a wave, or, in the case of BJJ, on the mat against a noncompliant opponent.

When the ad hominem attacks fail to disrupt truthful discussion about the martial arts or, otherwise stated, truthful discussion about the best methods for managing violence, traditional martial arts advocates make one final appeal: "Well, everyone has to figure out the truth for themselves!"

Sound familiar?

This, in a nutshell, is how a *sophisticated* clergy or *guro* class is created. These are the reactions you get from reasonably intelligent people who, upon receiving an education, realize that what they are teaching, preaching, or repeating is anything but *true*, in the factual sense of the word. As a means of self-preservation—both to save their careers and their standing—they will adopt almost any position that allows them to continue the deception. This often involves blaming the messenger or, worse, their very parishioners—in this case, their martial arts students—for either being too *simple* or for not being *born fighters*.

The core truth is this: if you want to become a competent fighter, you need to spend time with the experts in the three delivery systems—stand-up (boxers, kickboxers); clinch (wrestlers and Judoka); and ground (BJJ). When you do, you'll realize that you're not going to beat a good BJJ purple belt on the ground with "street" tactics any more than you are going to stop a wrestler from taking you down if you have no takedown defense. But remember, too, you don't have to be good enough to beat a young athletic purple belt on the ground or a professional MMA fighter in the cage. You just have to be skilled enough to beat the crackhead or the meth addict or the drunken idiot who makes the mistake of selecting you. You just have to beat the bad guy.

And with functional training from combat sports, you will.

24 The Command of Self

*By training with Aliveness, you take
on the toughest opponent possible—yourself.*

The genius of BJJ as a functional fighting style has been known in the United States since the very first Ultimate Fighting Championship in November 1993, when the unassuming-looking 178-pound Royce Gracie won the eight-man bare-knuckle, no-holds-barred, no-weight-class, no-scorecard event. Featuring a mix of stylistically diverse martial artists, the event had only three rules: no biting, no eye gouging, and no groin shots. Gracie submitted each of his heavier and stronger opponents in a matter of minutes with BJJ techniques that, at the time, appeared magical. But Gracie's feat was no fluke. Although the UFC rule set has since changed a bit, the same general experiment has been run over and over for thirty years now. No practitioner of JKD or Kung Fu or Aikido would ever be expected to win an MMA fight—let alone successfully compete in one—against a trained opponent without also having a solid foundation in grappling or ground fighting.[1]

Only the most delusional traditional martial artists continue to tout the superiority of their particular style when it comes to functionality. The more honest ones will make no such claim, but they will likely call upon one or more of the myths highlighted in the last chapter in an attempt to blur reality. Even those traditional martial arts instructors who readily acknowledge today that dead-pattern training is not an effective methodology for gaining functional martial skills often continue to employ that very methodology in their schools. They justify this by redefining the very terms of the discussion. For them, martial arts are no longer about self-defense but about self-improvement. Like all those who traffic in various forms of superstition, they attempt to find sanctuary by making a vague appeal to the subjective and qualitative and say things like, *"Some things are for self-preservation, and others are for self-perfection."*

In the traditional martial arts world, you will hear instructors appeal to "self-perfection" a lot, though the exact wording can change. The language is often fuzzy, but they are essentially claiming that traditional martial arts are best for bettering oneself while acknowledging that other things (i.e., combat sports) are best for self-defense. Yet, no matter their specific definition of "self-perfection," which in principle is a worthy goal, my question in return is this: would an Alive training method serve the objective of self-perfection just as well as a dead-pattern training method, or perhaps be an even better option for pursuing self-perfection?

When something is serving as a vehicle for self-improvement, it helps if that something also has the benefit of being true, real, and authentic. If you are looking for methods of self-actualization through martial arts, then you will certainly find them in Alive training. This is especially true for one simple reason: how can you aspire to self-perfection if you don't have self-knowledge? If you don't honestly test yourself and learn what you are both capable and incapable of? The mat simply doesn't lie. At its core, *survival* is what BJJ is about. As Rickson Gracie says, "Sometimes, you don't have to win. You can't win. But that has nothing to do with losing."[2] To understand this quotation is to understand the intelligence of BJJ.

Here's what I mean. Toward the end of one of my recent BJJ classes in Portland, I was watching the students to make sure everyone was rolling safely. I noticed one of the newer students struggling. He had only been in the gym for a short time, and a more experienced, aggressive player was smashing him. This newer student wasn't being hurt, but he was being crushed. His arms were trapped, his head was pinned to the side, his cheeks and face were smeared into the mat like butter on bread.

I could see that he was beginning to have trouble breathing. He appeared overwhelmed. I am not sure if he had ever been in such an uncomfortable spot before. Having done BJJ for decades, I have been in that and hundreds of other equally uncomfortable positions thousands of times. For me and anyone else who's trained BJJ for any meaningful length of time, the situation is quite familiar. For him, it was new.

I could see he was on the verge of tapping out ... but then he found a way to catch a breath, move just an inch, and survive a bit longer. As I continued to watch, I saw him struggle again just to breathe as his more experienced opponent adjusted to reclaim his pressure. The newer student now had a look of despair in his eyes—part bona fide panic, part loss of ego—and that look, too, I knew well. His hand was again ready to tap. But then, with a bit of hip movement, he was able to make space and bring his knees to his chest. He got back to guard. Moments later, he swept his larger opponent and ended up on top. And he was surprised. At that instant, I caught his eyes, and I saw a rush of joy. It wasn't the Olympics or the UFC. But, for this guy, it was a huge deal.

I'm sharing one such moment from one class here. That sequence may have been a meaningful one for the student, but the event itself was not unique. In fact, it is to be expected. This is a scene that gets repeated hundreds of times a day in BJJ gyms like mine all across the world. It goes unnoticed by most involved most of the time, because a hard roll is just another day for most of us. But it is an amazing process nonetheless, because it is filled with invisible passages specific to each individual. Much is made about belt ranks across martial arts. BJJ is known for its especially difficult ranking system, which is how we formally recognize a student's progress against her peers and herself. I am always proud to award a new rank, but the internal tests are ultimately the ones that matter most. They are the ones only the individual might ever know about or even recognize

The rush of joy that this new combat athlete experienced didn't come about simply because he survived and ended up in the dominant position. It represented something much bigger. He remembered all the failed and futile attempts that had preceded that moment, and he knew all the hard work and effort he had put in to get to that moment. This wasn't chance or dumb luck. This was well earned. He gained a deeper understanding of himself. The boundaries of what he thought he was capable of had shifted in that moment, and knowing you can shift those boundaries is far more profound than any fleeting success.

After many years of running a functional martial arts gym, I know there is little I have to do for this process to occur over and over again beyond demonstrating the techniques and maintaining a safe and healthy environment. My job is to be present and honor the process. Honor the process, not control, manipulate, take credit for, or own—just *honor*. If I do that, the process, Aliveness, takes care of everything else. And it does so far better than any training method yet discovered.

Safe, healthy, sincere Aliveness—that's enough. Everything profound flows from that. Nothing I demonstrate can ever really be understood without it. This is just as true for me as for my students. I'm continually reminded of what I am and am not capable of. When I first began teaching, I didn't have students who could consistently beat me on the mat. In nine out of ten, nineteen out of twenty, or ninety out of a hundred matches, I would probably get the tap. Unless I was working with a professional fighter like Randy Couture or one of my own coaches, I was usually winning. You can get used to that. Yet, if I stopped teaching altogether today and dedicated myself to nothing but training for the next year, I know I'd have little to no chance of winning a gold medal at the Mundials (World Jiu-Jitsu Championship).[3] I am simply too old at this point. To ascend through the brackets of a major tournament is a process for the twenty- and thirty-year-olds who have been competing for most of their adult lives. Even so, my BJJ feels better than it ever has, and I have little doubt that the BJJ player I am now would make easy work of the one I was twenty years ago.

As time passes, your role within combat athletics will change along with your capabilities. Mine did. I went from sparring partner to teacher to coach's coach. At a certain time in your career, your most useful place might be giving a competitive athlete a tough fifteen-minute round. As you age and slow down physically even more, your most useful place might be providing strategic wisdom from the side of the mat while one of your younger staff members gives a competitive athlete a tough fifteen-minute round.

The job of a good combat athletics instructor, whether in BJJ, Judo, or any other functional martial art, is to teach people how to exceed you. In short, we are creating people who can beat us. If you haven't matured enough to recognize that, then you won't be as useful to others as you otherwise could be—and you won't be aspiring to any kind of meaningful self-perfection. And if your ego can't come to grips with that reality, then your ego will be the thing that prevents you from ever becoming a great coach. That's as it should be. This is true not just for combat athletics instructors like me but also for anyone who has acquired hard-won knowledge in a skill or trade that they want to pass on to a future generation to perfect, whether they're a bricklayer or a pilot, a farmer or a surgeon, or an engineer or a police officer.

By now, you know functional martial arts are, by definition, combat sports. And if you're not currently training in one, please take my strong advice and step onto this path. When you do, you will be confronted with realities you will need to embrace. You'll have to accept being in a room full of people who can beat you. Then you'll have to accept being beaten by them class after class. You'll need to make peace with "losing." Or, as I prefer to put it—learning. Each tap is a lesson, and you will eventually find yourself experiencing small victories, even in defeat. Even after you've climbed up a few rungs in performance, you will feel as though you are climbing an endless ladder with levels that are completely out of your current sight. Your instructor, no matter how smart or tactful, will likely say something at some point that you find disheartening. A functional martial arts coach can casually toss out a particular sentiment and fill a student with joy or give them fuel to hate them forever. It's just the nature of what we do. You will have mornings when you wake up and everything hurts. And you'll have nights where you will travel home after class believing that you'll never get good at *this*—because it's just too hard. You will have days where you want to quit. The vast majority of people quit. You'll notice that, and you might wonder what fun things they're doing right as that heavyweight you least like rolling with is pressing his rib cage into your neck.

All of this, however, leads to your learning to be comfortable in uncomfortable situations. All of it teaches you how to survive. And if you're coachable, all you have to do to get to that place of real, measurable survival skill—both physical and mental—is not quit. And if right now you are thinking, "I don't think I could do any of that," trust me, you can.

As I watched that newer student struggle, I could see those same doubts. He didn't know whether he could survive, let alone win; he didn't know whether he was capable of lasting at all. He questioned himself throughout. But I never did. I knew full well that he was capable of surviving, just as I know you are too. The only one who needs convincing is you.

Combat sports can be a powerful vehicle for self-awareness, self-knowledge, and self-perfection, but they are never a guarantee of such things. Just because someone is phenomenal at a functional martial art doesn't mean they can't also be a jackass. Speaking about one BJJ world champion, my friend and fellow SBG coach Adam Singer once remarked: "Being good at Jiu-Jitsu doesn't make you better than anyone else, and he just hasn't figured that out yet."

I've certainly been a jackass at various times in my life. If you have never looked back in time and slapped your head with an accompanying internal dialogue that sounds something like, "How could I have been so thick-headed?" you probably haven't lived much. But that's no excuse. Today I try to be lenient with others and strict with myself—a precept from the Stoic philosopher and Roman emperor Marcus Aurelius that I remind myself of daily. You can't fake dignity or humility, and the lack thereof is easily betrayed.

Thirty years in combat athletics has helped me become a smarter, kinder, more self-aware human being—to move the needle, at least a bit, toward the maturity end of the scale. And I've seen the same practice transform hundreds of lives. I've witnessed shy, insecure kids turn into strong and assertive young adults. I've seen PTSD victims manage anxiety, rape victims learn to become comfortable again with physical contact, adults struggling from years of childhood abuse learn to relax, and the timid and fragile transform into the assured and vigorous. I've seen success after success like this. And whatever accolades I have achieved due to my own performance or that of my students, it's these sorts of victories that have given me the greatest satisfaction. That's what I love most about my job. And that's why I am ending this book with the suggestion you take up BJJ—or any combat sport.

Unlike most individual sports such as swimming, climbing, tennis, or golf, combat sports like BJJ always require communities, teammates, and tribes in order to produce quality players. While true BJJ is an individual game, it's equally true it requires an entire team to build and mold a skilled individual. And we are social primates. We need contact. We need socialization. We need connection. Our growth, our happiness, and our very well-being are in so many ways connected to the communities we move within. Training in a combat sport can expand your community in a positive way. And the impact of that cannot be overstated.

I dislike the word "spiritual" for the same reason I'm unable to listen to a Buddhist, Vedanta, or yoga lecturer who starts speaking in that special "soft voice." It shuts me down immediately. I think the most accurate word for the kind of process I am describing is maturing. The thing that's had the largest impact on me as a human being has not been any particular mystical experience, focused practice, religious doctrine, or individual teacher. Rather, it has been an ongoing process of ever-increasing levels of self-awareness, compassion, and impulse control that occurred as the natural consequence of overcoming personal challenges. When you have children, loved ones, students, and a community to which you hold yourself accountable, this process should only accelerate. But it isn't automatic.

There is, of course, much more to this journey than just laying down a mat and engaging in the sport. Indeed, skills acquired in the art of violence are never a guarantee of developing a mature, healthy relationship with violence. They are, instead, a necessary but insufficient part of the solution. Necessary because you can't just pretend you don't see something as wicked or glamorous—that clarity has to be authentic. It has to be earned. Insufficient because without the proper environment, the deeper lessons of combat athletics may be unavailable to you. You also need the right culture, values, and goals. If you've read this far, you by now know what's possible, what can be achieved, and what can be gained when training for violence. Done right, training in a functional martial art will not just better equip you to avoid and prevent violence—it will also help you better know and understand yourself. This journey ultimately leads to probably the greatest and most important gift of all: self-knowledge.

While functional martial arts training is the most effective way known to man for developing hand-to-hand combat skills, it also helps you stay in shape, relieve stress, develop mental toughness, foster friendships, overcome fears, gain confidence, control your emotions, understand what physical conflict feels like, and learn what you can and, just as importantly, cannot do. And all of that is more significant in terms of real self-preservation than anything any kind of traditional martial arts or "street-fight" training could ever hope to offer.

So embrace the gift of violence. Seek truth. Be stricter with yourself than you are with anyone else. Lead by example, but don't preach. Keep the negative comments to a minimum—not just those directed to others, but also to yourself. Have enough self-respect to take care of your body and your mind, so you can care for those around you. Become competent in the craft of fighting, and use it to help build up yourself and others. Help the weak become strong. Do and be good. Know your line in the sand. Always win or learn. Take on the toughest, meanest, strongest opponent you have—yourself. And you will be safer, stronger, more knowledgeable, more mindful, and more centered.

As I end this book, I will leave you with one final piece of advice inspired by a quote often attributed to Abraham Lincoln, a celebrated submission wrestler who was no stranger to combat sports: "Nothing is stronger than gentleness."[4]

Be the *gentlest* and *most dangerous* person possible.

Afterword

"Aliveness." The most important concept you've never heard of—until now.

As developed and taught by Matt Thornton starting in 1992, with the opening of the first Straight Blast Gym, Aliveness is a paradigm shift: a completely different way to think about martial arts and, oddly enough, reality. Aliveness helps one figure out what's true.

In the arena of martial arts, Aliveness means that to understand whether a technique or strategy works, you must practice on a resisting opponent. In other words, try it on someone who doesn't want the technique to succeed. Someone who resists. For example, if you want to see if a flying spinning backflip will do what you think it does—say knock your opponent to the ground—then you need to practice a flying spinning backflip on an actual opponent who does not want to be knocked to the ground.

This seems like such an obvious, indisputable proposition that it's almost self-evident. Of course, techniques must be tested on resisting opponents. Yet, across the centuries, in many of the most well-known martial arts, people prepared for combat by practicing kata, which are choreographed, scripted sequences of moves performed either alone or with nonresisting opponents. And many holdouts continue with this practice even today.

Thornton is one of the central figures who helped call attention to the inefficacy of the "fantasy-based, sclerotic" martial arts and usher in a revolution in martial arts based on testing, experimentation, and other related scientific principles. Beyond this, however, Thornton also introduced and popularized the importance of Aliveness in nonphysical domains of thought, specifically in scientific skepticism, critical thinking, and moral reasoning. In each category, he's shown the need for a "resisting opponent," that is, for a way to keep one's delusions in check by creating mechanisms by which one's ideas can be tested. For example, in his frequent guest lectures to one of the university classes I taught in the past, Critical Thinking and Science & Pseudoscience, Thornton would show how it wasn't enough simply to understand and apply critical thinking skills like evaluation, inference, and explanation—one also needed to posit counterexamples as one was thinking through claims. By regularly asking oneself how one could be wrong and braving those conclusions in spirited conversation, the search for truth is brought Alive.

If all this seems very academic, that's because it is. Yet, Aliveness as a martial arts pedagogy has an elegant simplicity to it. But don't confuse this simplicity with triviality or a lack of depth. The odds are that you or someone you know will be faced with violence at some future point, and how you deal with that situation, whether you're facing simple assault or something far worse, is as far from trivial as you can get. Without Aliveness, you cannot begin to "train" for a violent encounter or even truly understand the depths of your own abilities and capabilities.

As a long-time student of Thornton's, I can speak personally to the tremendous gift of Aliveness. But in *The Gift of Violence,* he offers something new: an opportunity for us all to rethink our relationship to violence—what violence is, how to deal with it, what we can do to prevent it, what it means to have a healthy relationship with it, and how to bring Aliveness into our understanding of this primal phenomenon. Thornton offers us a way to figure out what's true and a path forward in a subject most people prefer to ignore. It is a field manual for living and surviving in a modern age that is still largely defined by primitive impulses.

Peter Boghossian
philosopher and coauthor of *How to Have Impossible Conversations*
BJJ purple belt

Acknowledgments

There are so many people that deserve sincere thanks for their help with this book. Here is but a partial list.

Salóme, my ever-patient wife, who managed the kids while I was trapped on the other side of a laptop. Without her, and most importantly, what I've learned from her, this book would never have been written.

Zach Thornton, my brother, who stepped up, took the reins at the gym, and did what needed to be done so I could complete this project.

All those who helped me with the writing process. That list includes Brian, Jon, Robert, and other early readers. And all those who guided me with editing, especially Paul Myatovich, who gave me the confidence to write, and John Frankl, who, without asking, edited the early manuscript by hand.

All those who, through conversation or essay, shared their hard-earned knowledge and contributed to the book in various ways. That list includes Paul Sharp, who is responsible for the "making good people more dangerous to bad" motto—and so much more; Ray Price, who helped immensely with questions that arose; and Adam Singer and Stephen Whittier, whose work will be featured even more prominently in my next book. You have all enriched this project.

Wayne Thornton, my father, whose experiences helped shape this book, and me.

Robb Wolf, who honored me by writing the foreword.

Sam Harris, who suggested the topic to me over a casual lunch. Being told by a writer of his caliber that my own writing was good enough to take on a subject like this motivated me to start the project and develop a manuscript I could be proud of.

Kurt Volkan, my publisher. He believed in this book long before it was done, and he contributed immensely to the final manuscript.

Those of you who provided early reviews—in particular, Michael Shermer, Rickson Gracie, and Steve Salerno.

Peter Boghossian. Your counsel and friendship over these last few years have been truly invaluable.

My coaches—in particular, Chris Haueter and Rickson Gracie. I hope all of you see your own lessons articulated in a way that does them justice.

And finally, the Tribe of SBG. Your questions and thoughts over the years have built this material. I'm counting on all of you to build upon it—and take it further.

Thank you all so very much.

Notes

Introduction: The Gift of Violence

1. Humans and our closest relatives, chimpanzees, are unique not only in the animal kingdom but also among primates for the ways in which we express violence. We both organize and bond over violence, such as in raiding parties to kill members of outside groups, and we both use weapons to harm and kill. For accounts of brutal intercommunity violence and weapons use among chimps, see Jane Goodall, *Through a Window: My Thirty Years with the Chimpanzees of Gombe* (New York: Houghton Mifflin, 1990). Yet, lethal violence against members of the same species is widespread among mammals. According to one study, roughly 40 percent of mammalian species are known to commit lethal intraspecies violence. José Maria Gómez et al., "The Phylogenetic Roots of Human Lethal Violence," *Nature* 538 (2016): 233–237, doi.org/10.1038/nature19758. Some researchers push back against the Hobbesian idea that we humans are a naturally violent species and take a more Rousseauian view. See, for example, Randall Collins, *Violence: A Micro-sociological Theory* (Princeton, NJ: Princeton University Press, 2008), which argues that violence among humans is relatively rare because it goes against our natural wiring. For a critique of this argument, see Richard B. Felson, "Is Violence Natural, Unnatural, or Rational," *British Journal of Sociology* 60, no. 3 (2009): 577–585, onlinelibrary.wiley.com/doi/pdf/10.1111/j.1468-4446.2009.01257.x.

2. The actual quote is: "We must, however, acknowledge, as it seems to me, that man with all his noble qualities, with sympathy which feels for the most debased, with benevolence which extends not only to other men but to

the humblest living creature, with his god-like intellect which has penetrated into the movements and constitution of the solar system—with all these exalted powers—Man still bears in his bodily frame the indelible stamp of his lowly origin." Charles Darwin, *The Descent of Man, and Selection in Relation to Sex,* 2nd ed. (1874), chapter XXI, available at www.gutenberg.org/files/2300/2300-h/2300-h.htm.

3.   It does not, however, come as "speech" or "silence." For more on why referring to speech as violence is not only wrong but also harmful, see Greg Lukianoff and Jonathan Haidt, *The Coddling of the American Mind: How Good Intentions and Bad Ideas Are Setting Up a Generation for Failure* (New York: Penguin Press, 2018), 85–89; Andrew Doyle, *Free Speech and Why It Matters* (London: Constable, 2021); and Sarah Haider, "Violence and Freethought," *Free Inquiry* 38, no. 1 (December 2017/January 2018), secularhumanism.org/2017/12/cont-violence-and-freethought/.

4.   Harvard psychologist Steven Pinker documented the decline of violence over the long and short term in his book *The Better Angels of Our Nature: Why Violence Has Declined* (New York: Viking Books, 2011). While some have criticized Pinker's explanations and conclusions, the data is compelling, particularly when thinking about self-defense implications. People today are far less likely than their ancestors to die a violent death at the hands of another human. For a quick snapshot of the data, see Michael Shermer, "The Decline of Violence," *Scientific American*, October 1, 2011, www.scientificamerican.com/article/the-decline-of-violence/.

5.   United Nations Office on Drugs and Crime, *Global Study on Homicide* (Vienna: UNODC, 2019), 12, www.unodc.org/documents/data-and-analysis/gsh/Booklet1.pdf.

6.   Ibid., 11, 23.

7.   The World Health Organization estimates that one in three women worldwide will experience physical or sexual violence in their lifetime, but unlike homicide, exact rates of sexual violence are hard to measure. World Health Organization, "Devastatingly Pervasive: 1 in 3 Women Globally Experience Violence," March 9, 2021, www.who.int/news/item/09-03-2021-devastatingly-pervasive-1-in-3-women-globally-experience-violence.

8.   Amy E. Nivette et al., "A Global Analysis of the Impact of COVID-19 Stay-at-Home Restrictions on Crime," *Nature Human Behavior* (2021): 868–877, doi.org/10.1038/s41562-021-01139-z; and Antonia Noori Farzan, "The United States Isn't the Only Country Where Killings Quickly Returned after Pandemic Lull," *Washington Post*, April 22, 2021.

9.   See, for example, "Crime in England and Wales: Year Ending September 2021," Office for National Statistics, www.ons.gov.uk/peoplepopula-

tionandcommunity/crimeandjustice/bulletins/crimeinenglandandwales/year-endingseptember2021; and "Crime Returning to Previous Levels in Lothians and Scottish Borders as Restrictions Ease," Police Scotland, August 2021, www.scotland.police.uk/what-s-happening/news/2021/august/crime-returning-to-previous-levels-in-lothians-and-scottish-borders-as-covid-restrictions-ease/.

10. Ryan Lucas, "FBI Data Shows an Unprecedented Spike in Murders Nationwide in 2020," *All Things Considered, NPR*, September 27, 2021, www.npr.org/2021/09/27/1040904770/fbi-data-murder-increase-2020; John Gramlich, "What We Know about the Increase in U.S. Murders in 2020," Pew Research Center, October 27, 2021; Priva Krishnakumar, "10 of the Country's Most Populous Cities Set Homicide Records Last Year," *CNN*, January 4, 2022, www.cnn.com/2022/01/03/us/homicide-rate-us-statistics/index.html; and German Lopez, "A False Choice," *New York Times*, March 2, 2022, www.nytimes.com/2022/03/06/briefing/crime-solutions-ukraine-war-books.html.

11. Heather Mac Donald, "Breakdown: The Unwinding of Law and Order in Our Cities Has Happened with Stunning Speed," *City Journal*, July 1, 2020, www.city-journal.org/ferguson-effect-inner-cities; Aaron Chalfin and John MacDonald, "We Don't Know Why Violent Crime Is Up. But We Know There's More Than One Cause," *Washington Post*, July 9, 2021, www.washingtonpost.com/outlook/we-dont-know-why-violent-crime-is-up-but-we-know-theres-more-than-one-cause/2021/07/09/467dd25c-df9a-11eb-ae31-6b7c5c34f0d6_story.html; German Lopez, "The Rise in Murders in the US, Explained," *Vox*, December 2, 2020, www.vox.com/2020/8/3/21334149/murders-crime-shootings-protests-riots-trump-biden; and Andrew Sullivan, "The Grim Trade-Off of BLM?" *Weekly Dish (Substack)*, June 11, 2021, andrewsullivan.substack.com/p/the-grim-trade-off-of-blm-29d?s=r.

12. For brief histories of Brazilian Jiu-Jitsu and Mixed Martial Arts, see "The History of Jiu-Jitsu," *Gracie Mag*, www.graciemag.com/en/the-saga-of-jiu-jitsu/; "American Jiu Jitsu History Timeline," *BJJ Heroes*, www.bjjheroes.com/editorial/american-jiu-jitsu-history-timeline; and T. P. Grant, "MMA History: The Eras and Fighters That Have Defined a Sport," *Bleacher Report*, December 22, 2010. Please note: Brazilian Jiu-Jitsu should not be confused with traditional Japanese Jiu-Jitsu, which is a separate art. For a brief discussion about the differences between them, see "BJJ vs Japanese Jiu-Jitsu—Key Differences and Similarities," *MMA Channel*, mmachannel.com/bjj-vs-japanese-jiu-jitsu-key-differences-and-similarities/.

13. For examples of the types of submissions used in BJJ, see "Top 20 Submissions in UFC History," YouTube video, uploaded by UFC, November 12, 2013, www.youtube.com/watch?v=HALf3esHQJ0.

14. Shrestha Paul, "List of the Top 50 UFC Salaries 2022, Highest Earning Fighters, Salary Scale Ranking Explained," *Sports Grail*, January 25, 2022,

thesportsgrail.com/list-of-the-top-50-ufc-salaries-2022-highest-earning-fighters-salary-scale-ranking-explained/; and Brett Knight, "The World's 10 Highest-Paid Athletes: Conor McGregor Leads a Group of Sports Stars Unfazed by the Pandemic," *Forbes*, www.forbes.com/sites/brettknight/2021/05/12/the-worlds-10-highest-paid-athletes-conor-mcgregor-leads-a-group-of-sports-stars-unfazed-by-the-pandemic/?sh=658f8abe26f4.

15. For more about Straight Blast Gym, see www.straightblastgym.com/. There you will also find information about my students and the black belts I have awarded.

16. The Internet is littered with videos of fights between Mixed Martial Artists and practitioners of one type of traditional martial art or another. In almost all cases, the MMA fighter makes quick and bloody work of the traditional martial artist. While these videos illustrate well the merits of the charge I make here and throughout this book, I do not generally encourage such challenges or matches for two simple reasons: (1) the traditional martial artist is almost always severely outclassed and thus risks experiencing serious injury and (2) the traditional martial artists featured in such videos often suffer from delusional beliefs and thus aren't operating in reality. See, for example, "Xu Xiaodong MMA vs Wei Lei Tai Chi Master," YouTube video, uploaded by Hung Le Tien, May 19, 2017. For more on the MMA fighter in this video and the troubling backlash he has since faced in China, see Lauren Teixeira, "He Never Intended to Become a Political Dissident, but then He Started Beating Up Tai Chi Masters," *Deadspin*, October 3, 2019, deadspin.com/he-never-intended-to-become-a-political-dissident-but-1838706430. Videos that demonstrate the delusional nature of certain traditional martial artists without the violence are just as damning. See, for example, "Qi Gong Demonstration by Master James Chee in Quanzhou 2010," YouTube video, uploaded by ISWCCA, April 20, 2010, www.youtube.com/watch?v=nVdANNX2zP4. After watching this video, philosopher and author Sam Harris tweeted, "Why is martial arts fraud so instructive? It is faith and self-deception made VISIBLE." @SamHarrisOrg, Twitter, May 24, 2013, twitter.com/samharrisorg/status/338079684120162305.

Chapter 1: The Nature of Violence

1. Numerous books explore the evolution of consciousness, including Todd E. Feinberg and Jon Mallatt, *The Ancient Origins of Consciousness: How the Brain Created Experience* (Cambridge, MA: MIT Press, 2016); Daniel C. Dennett, *From Bacteria to Bach and Back: The Evolution of Minds* (New York: W. W. Norton & Company, 2017); Joseph E. LeDoux, *The Deep History of Ourselves: The Four-Billion-Year Story of How We Got Conscious Brains* (New York City: Viking, 2019); Michael S. A. Graziano, *Rethinking Consciousness: A Scientific The-*

ory of Subjective Experience (New York: W. W. Norton & Company, 2019); and Annaka Harris, *Conscious: A Brief Guide to the Fundamental Mystery of the Mind* (New York: Harper, 2019).

2.   Much has been written about the violence found in scripture. See, for example, Philip Jenkins, *Laying Down the Sword: Why We Can't Ignore the Bible's Violent Verses* (New York: HarperOne, 2012). Violent conflict is also central to the hero's journey, or monomyth, as outlined by mythologist Joseph Campbell. Defining "The Road of Trials" stage of the hero's journey, Campbell writes: "Dragons have now to be slain and surprising barriers passed—again, again, and again." Joseph Campbell, *The Hero with a Thousand Faces* (Princeton, NJ: Princeton University Press, 1949), 90.

3.   Robert M. Sapolsky, *Behave: The Biology of Humans at Our Best and Worst* (New York: Penguin Books, 2018), 3.

4.   Charles Darwin, *On the Origin of Species by Means of Natural Selection* (London: John Murray, 1859), chapter III. The sixth edition is available at www.univie.ac.at/elib/index.php?title=Charles_Darwin_-_On_the_Origin_of_Species_-_1859.

5.   Per biologist Jerry Coyne, "survival of the fitter" might be a more accurate phrase because "natural selection does not yield perfection—only improvements over what came before." Jerry A. Coyne, *Why Evolution Is True* (New York: Viking, 2009), 13.

6.   For a popular introduction to evolution, I recommend Richard Dawkins and Yan Wong, *The Ancestor's Tale: A Pilgrimage to the Dawn of Evolution*, 2nd ed. (New York: Mariner Books, 2016).

7.   Neurobiologist Robert Sapolsky shows how our nervous system unconsciously responds to stimuli and the effects this has on behavior. He also has much to say about violence. Sapolsky, *Behave*.

8.   Much of our understanding of the evolution of aggressive behavior and violence in our own species is based on studies of our closest primate relatives, including those conducted by Jane Goodall. See, for example, her horrifying descriptions of the so-called Gombe war in *Through a Window*, 126–127. More recent studies support her research and findings. See, for example, Gómez et al., "The Phylogenetic Roots of Human Lethal Violence"; and Michael L. Wilson et al., "Lethal Aggression in *Pan* Is Better Explained by Adaptive Strategies than Human Impacts," *Nature* 513 (2014): 414-417, doi.org/10.1038/nature13727. For two short articles on this subject, see Michael Balter, "Why Do Chimps Kill Each Other?" *Science*, September 17, 2014, doi:10.1126/article.22428; and Fiona MacDonald, "Humans Inherited Murder Through Evolution," *ScienceAlert*, September 29, 2016, www.sciencealert.com/humans-inherited-killing-each-other-through-evolution.

9.   We sometimes see this play out dramatically in nature. Most everyone has seen videos of stags challenging other stags for females during rutting season. This typically begins and ends with a roaring contest, with one stag backing down, but sometimes this leads to a fight waged with antlers. An estimated 20 percent of stags suffer permanent injury in such fights over the course of their life. For a stag without a harem, the reproductive benefits of a fight outweigh the individual risks, but stags that already have a harem have less incentive to engage in such fights, so they initiate them less often than their bachelor counterparts. Aside from the risk of injury, the cost of fighting is high for another reason. When two stags are engaged in a tussle, this gives an opportunity for lower-status stags to mate with their females. This behavior from those males is often colorfully referred to as the "sneaky-fucker strategy." Jeremy Cherfas, "The Games Animals Play," *New Scientist* 75 (September 15, 1977), 672–3.

10.   For an evolutionary psychologist's take on this topic, see David M. Buss, *When Men Behave Badly: The Hidden Roots of Sexual Deception, Harassment, and Assault* (New York: Little Brown, Spark, 2021).

11.   Niall Ferguson, *Civilization: The West and the Rest* (New York: Penguin, 2012), 24–25.

12.   Napoleon A. Chagnon, "Life Histories, Blood Revenge, and Warfare in a Tribal Population," *Science* 239, no. 4843 (1988): 985–992, doi:10.1126/science.239.4843.985. See also Steven Malanga, "Welcome to the Jungle: Napoleon Chagnon's Study of Human Nature in the Amazon—and the Academy," *City Journal*, April 13, 2014, www.city-journal.org/html/welcome-jungle-9810.html.

13.   John Horgan, "My Regrets about Controversial Anthropologist Napoleon Chagnon (RIP)," *Scientific American*, Cross-Check blog, September 27, 2019.

14.   As today, levels of violence have varied across time and space due to various societal and cultural factors. See, for example, Timothy A. Kohler et al., "The Better Angels of Their Nature: Declining Violence Through Time among Prehispanic Farmers of the Pueblo Southwest," *American Antiquity* 79, no. 3 (July 2014): 444–464, doi:10.7183/0002-7316.79.3.444.

15.   For a quick breakdown of theories that explain this, see Beth Daley, "Men Are More Likely to Commit Violent Crimes. Why Is This So and How Do We Change It?" *Conversation*, March 25, 2021, theconversation.com/men-are-more-likely-to-commit-violent-crimes-why-is-this-so-and-how-do-we-change-it-157331.

16.   Chagnon, "Life Histories, Blood Revenge, and Warfare in a Tribal Population." For more on the Yanomamö and *unokai*, see Shane J. Macfarlan et al., "Lethal Coalitionary Aggression and Long-Term Alliance Forma-

tion among Yanomamö Men," *PNAS* 111, no. 47 (2014): 16662–16669, doi. org/10.1073/pnas.1418639111.

17. Steven D. Levitt and Stephen J. Dubner, *Think Like a Freak: Secrets of the Rogue Economist* (New York: William Morrow, 2014), 31.

18. As Robert Ardrey famously wrote, "But we were born of risen apes, not fallen angels, and the apes were armed killers besides. And so what shall we wonder at? Our murders and massacres and missiles, and our irreconcilable regiments? Or our treaties whatever they may be worth; our symphonies however seldom they may be played; our peaceful acres, however frequently they may be converted into battlefields; our dreams however rarely they may be accomplished. The miracle of man is not how far he has sunk but how magnificently he has risen. We are known among the stars by our poems, not our corpses." Robert Ardrey, *African Genesis: A Personal Investigation into the Animal Origins and Nature of Man* (New York: Atheneum. 1961), 305.

Chapter 2: The Folly of Pacifism

1. For a deeper discussion of pacifism, see Andrew Fiala, "Pacifism," in *The Stanford Encyclopedia of Philosophy* (Fall 2021 Edition), ed. Edward N. Zalta, plato.stanford.edu/archives/fall2021/entries/pacifism/; and Andrew Fiala, ed., *The Routledge Handbook of Pacifism and Nonviolence* (New York: Routledge, 2020).

2. The term "mama bear" has been widely adopted as a metaphor for a fiercely protective mother for good reason. The most common scenario for a brown bear attack on a human is an encounter with a female and her cub. G. Bombieri et al., "Brown Bear Attacks on Humans: A Worldwide Perspective," *Scientific Reports* 9, 8573 (2019), doi.org/10.1038/s41598-019-44341-w.

3. The International Center on Nonviolent Conflict has developed a video series titled "Pressing Your Case: Nonviolent Movements and the Media" that advises leaders of nonviolent movements on best practices for advancing their cause in the media. It is available at www.nonviolent-conflict.org/resource/pressing-case-nonviolent-movements-media-part-1/. For more on the importance of communication to nonviolent action, see Brian Martin and Wendy Varney, "Communication and Nonviolence," *Journal of Peace Research* 40, no. 2 (March 2003): 213–232, www.jstor.org/stable/3648412.

4. "Just as I have urged Negroes to face the calculated risk involved in resisting injustice non-violently, I implore the white Southerner of goodwill to face the calculated risk that working openly for justice and freedom demand. We Southerners, Negro and white, must no longer permit our nation and our heritage to be dishonored before the world." Martin Luther King,

Jr., address delivered at a Meeting Launching the SCLC Crusade for Citizenship at Greater Bethel AME Church, Miami, Florida, February 12, 1958, kinginstitute.stanford.edu/king-papers/documents/address-delivered-meeting-launching-sclc-crusade-citizenship-greater-bethel#:~:text=Just%20as%20I%20have%20urged,for%20justice%20and%20freedom%20demand.

5. M. K. Gandhi, "The Doctrine of the Sword," *Young India*, August 11, 1920, www.mkgandhi.org/nonviolence/D_sword.htm.

6. Louis Fischer, *The Life of Mahatma Gandhi* (London: Jonathan Cape, 1951), 376, available at archive.org/details/lifeofmahatmagan00loui/page/376/mode/2up.

7. One movement activist wrote at the time, "The civil rights movement is pledged to nonviolence. It is commonly assumed by those of us involved in it that the provocation of violence is alien to its strategy and that violence is simply a calculated risk in trying to achieve its goals. But the facts compel me to question this assumption and to suggest that the provocation of violence is often used as a latent tactic." Jan Howard, "The Provocation of Violence: A Civil Rights Tactic?" *Dissent Magazine* (January–February 1966).

8. Shmuley Boteach, "Repudiating Gandhian Pacifism in the Face of Mass Murder," *Jerusalem Post*, March 31, 2016, www.jpost.com/opinion/repudiating-gandhian-pacifism-in-the-face-of-mass-murder-449885.

9. George Orwell, "Pacifism and the War," *Partisan Review* (August–September 1942), available at www.orwell.ru/library/articles/pacifism/english/e_patw.

10. Lawahez Jabari et al., "Hamas Fires Rockets into Israel as Tensions in Jerusalem Boil Over," *NBC News*, May 10, 2021, www.nbcnews.com/news/world/hundreds-injured-palestinians-israeli-forces-clash-holy-site-jerusalem-n1266812.

11. "Hybrid Threats: Hamas' Use of Human Shields in Gaza," in Sean Aday et al., *Hybrid Threats: A Strategic Communications Perspective* (Riga: NATO Strategic Communications Centre of Excellence, 2019), stratcomcoe.org/cuploads/pfiles/hamas_human_shields.pdf.

12. John Stuart Mill, *Dissertations and Discussions: Political, Philosophical, and Historical*, vol. 3 (London: Longmans, Green, Reader, and Dyer, 1867), 204–205, available at www.google.com/books/edition/Thoughts_on_parliamentary_reform_Recent/ULIYAAAAIAAJ?hl=en&gbpv=1.

13. See chapter 1 ("Violence Is a Tool") in Tim Larkin, *When Violence Is the Answer: Learning How to Do What It Takes When Your Life Is at Stake* (New York: Back Bay Books, 2018).

Chapter 3: The Folly of Bravado

1. In 2018, the American Psychological Association infamously declared "traditional masculinity," which it defined as "anti-femininity, achievement, eschewal of the appearance of weakness, and adventure, risk, and violence," a significant cause of mental health problems among males. *APA Guidelines for Psychological Practice with Boys and Men* (American Psychological Association, August 2018), 3. While I categorically reject this attempt to redefine and pathologize masculinity as something in need of fixing, I acknowledge that the APA is referring to a real problem: boy-speak. Thankfully, numerous psychologists vehemently objected to the framing of the APA guidelines as well, pointing instead to the value of true masculinity: dignity, restraint, courage, confidence, personal responsibility, fortitude, a sense of duty, etc. These characteristics create not only mentally healthy individuals and families but also help preserve and advance societies. See, for example, the short essays in "Twelve Scholars Respond to the APA's Guidance for Treating Men and Boys," *Quillette*, February 4, 2019, particularly the short essay by existential psychologist Clay Routledge titled "A Case Study of Traditional Masculinity," quillette.com/2019/02/04/psychologists-respond-to-the-apas-guidance-for-treating-men-and-boys/; and Pamela Paresky, "What's the Problem with 'Traditional Masculinity'?" *Psychology Today*, March 10, 2019, www.psychologytoday.com/us/blog/happiness-and-the-pursuit-leadership/201903/whats-the-problem-traditional-masculinity.

2. A popular online forum called Bullshido, a play on words of the Japanese term *bushidō*, which means "way of the warrior," is dedicated to calling out bullshit in the martial arts. The group's Facebook page, which has more than 50,000 followers, describes the site thusly: "a rowdy tribe of disgruntled Martial Artists, MMA Fighters, Scientists, and Educators, all fighting a war on BS." For more, see www.bullshido.net.

3. This is true not only of kids. As journalist Jon Ronson has detailed, even the U.S. military has been fooled by martial arts woo and New Age nonsense. In the early 1980s, a traditional martial arts instructor named Guy Savelli was brought in to train Special Forces soldiers at Fort Bragg. He reportedly killed a goat just by staring at it, as described in Jon Ronson, *The Men Who Stare at Goats* (New York: Simon and Schuster, 2004), 53. A movie version of the book with the same title was released in 2009 and stars George Clooney. You can see some of Savelli's techniques on episode 995 of the Joe Rogan Experience (#995) during which Ronson and Rogan watch a series of martial arts instructional videos featuring Savelli. "Joe Rogan Can't Stop Laughing at Fake Martial Artists!" YouTube video, uploaded by JRE Clips, December 7, 2018, www.youtube.com/watch?v=NCDA6LBvyuM.

4. Paul R. Howe, *Leadership and Training for the Fight: Using Special Op-*

erations Principles to Succeed in Law Enforcement, Business, and War (New York: Skyhorse Publishing, 2011), Kindle edition.

5.   For a discussion of why much of reality-based self-defense is fantasy based, see "Reality Based Self Defense Is Fake! Get Real!" YouTube video, uploaded by Funker Tactical—Fight Training Videos, October 14, 2017, www.youtube.com/watch?v=4lUj4njYk1g. Even the editors of *Black Belt* magazine, who curated a book on reality-based self-defense techniques, begin their book with the following warning: "This book is presented only as a means of preserving a unique aspect of the heritage of the martial arts. Neither Ohara Publications nor the author makes any representation, warranty or guarantee that the techniques described or illustrated in this book will be safe or effective in any self-defense situation or otherwise." Editors of *Black Belt* magazine, *The Ultimate Guide to Reality-based Self-Defense* (Valencia, CA: Black Belt Books, 2011), Kindle edition.

6.   Ian Grey, "Blood on the Screen: Violence, Movies and Me," *RogerEbert.com,* July 23, 2013, www.rogerebert.com/features/refn-violence-and-me.

7.   In nature, intimidation itself is sometimes enough to lower prey populations. By triggering costly defensive strategies in prey, predators can reduce prey population density without even killing them. Evan L. Preisser et al., "Scared to Death? The Effects of Intimidation and Consumption in Predator-Prey Interactions," *Ecology* 86, no. 2 (February 2005): 501–509.

8.   Self-conscious emotions such as shame and humiliation have been linked with violence for many years in the theoretical and scholarly literature. See Julian Walker and Victoria Knauer, "Humiliation, Self-esteem and Violence," *Journal of Forensic Psychiatry and Pscyhology* 22, no. 5 (2011): 724–741, doi.org/10.1080/14789949.2011.617542; and Krista K. Thomason, "Shame, Violence, and Morality," *Philosophy and Phenomenological Research* 91, no. 1 (July 2015): 1–24.

9.   It is impossible to read people's intentions 100 percent of the time, so it is always best to assume a verbalized threat is real or at least credible, but there are many other clues that communicate underlying intent. This includes all-important nonverbal cues. See Mark L. Knapp at al., *Nonverbal Communication in Human Interaction*, 8th ed. (Boston, MA: Wadsworth Cengage Learning, 2014). I will discuss this more in chapter 18.

10.   Consider one of our close cousins, the gorilla, which is known for its chest-beating displays in the face of intrasexual competition. The acoustic properties of a gorilla's chest beat communicate body size and thus competitive ability, with lower peak frequencies associated with larger bodies. The act itself may therefore serve as a proxy for a physical fight, which can be costly even to the victor. Edward Wright et al., "Chest Beats as an Honest Signal of Body Size in Male Mountain Gorillas (*Gorilla beringei beringei*)" *Scientific Reports* 11, no.

6878 (2021), doi.org/10.1038/s41598-021-86261-8.

11. Exposure to violence and abuse, especially in childhood, does not just contribute to behavioral, emotional, or learning problems. It may also lead to lifelong physical problems that extend beyond any initial acute injury. See, for example, Terrie E. Moffitt, "Childhood Exposure to Violence and Lifelong Health: Clinical Intervention Science and Stress-Biology Research Join Forces," *Development and Psychopathology* 25, no. 4pt2 (November 2013): 1619–1634, doi:10.1017/S0954579413000801.

12. Aggression is positively associated with physical victimization. See Annis Lai Chu Fung et al., "Relationship between Peer Victimization and Reactive-Proactive Aggression in School Children," *Psychology of Violence* 9, no. 3 (2019): 350–358, doi.org/10.1037/vio0000125; and Caina Li, "Victims Become Covert Aggressors: Gender Differences in the Mediating Effects of Rumination on Anger and Sadness," *Journal of Psychology* 155, no. 4 (2021): 441–456, doi.org/10.1080/00223980.2021.1901254.

13. This is said by the character Gilbert in "The Critic as Artist" dialogue in Oscar Wilde, *Intentions* (London: Methuen & Co., 1891), available at www.gutenberg.org/ebooks/887.

Chapter 4: The Command of Safety

1. "Despite deficiencies in data, the long-term decline in homicide rates between thirteenth-century England (the earliest period for which they can be estimated) and present-day Western Europe and North America is so large and appears so consistently in various places that it cannot be dismissed as an artifact of inadequate records." David F. Greenberg, "Long-Term Trends in Crimes of Violence," *Criminology* 41, no. 4 (2003): 1407. See also Manuel Eisner, "Long-Term Historical Trends in Violent Crime," *Crime and Justice* 30 (2003): 83–142, www.jstor.org/stable/1147697.

2. Many scholars have examined the amount of misalignment between crime statistics and news reporting. See, for example, the chapter titled "Media and Moral Panics" in Yvonne Jewkes and Travis Linneman, *Media and Crime in the U.S.* (Thousand Oaks, CA: Sage Publications, 2018); and Jennifer Silcox, "Youth Crime and Depictions of Youth Crime in Canada: Are News Depictions Purely Moral Panic?" *Canadian Review of Sociology* 59, no. 1 (February 2022): 96–114.

3. Scammers understand this well. They leverage our fears in times of crisis and uncertainty to steal our money. As evidence of this, the Federal Bureau of Investigations put out a public service announcement at the start of the COVID-19 pandemic titled "FBI Sees Rise in Fraud Schemes Related to the

Coronavirus (COVID-19) Pandemic," March 20, 2020, www.ic3.gov/Media/
Y2020/PSA200320.

4.　Pinker, *The Better Angels of Our Nature*, 3.

5.　Although it seems obvious to me that the human capacity to commit
violence is innate—that it is part of our nature as a species—some theorists and
researchers argue that expressions of human violence are a consequence only of
a damaged psyche. Bryn King, "Psychological Theories of Violence," *Journal of
Human Behavior in the Social Environment* 22, no. 5 (June 2012): 553–571.

6.　Kohler, "The Better Angels of Their Nature."

7.　In 2020, 0.93 percent of people over the age of twelve in the United
States were victims of a violent crime (approximately 2.6 million people), a decrease of 15 percent from 2019, when the figure was 1.10 percent (approximately 3.1 million people). Rachel E. Morgan and Alexandra Thompson, *Criminal
Victimization, 2020—Supplemental Statistical Tables*, NCJ 303936 (Washington,
DC: U.S. Department of Justice, February 2022), bjs.ojp.gov/content/pub/pdf/
cv20sst.pdf.

8.　A Bureau of Justice Statistics report from 1987 estimated that the lifetime risk of being a victim of a violent crime in the United States after the age
of twelve was 83 percent. Herbert Koppel, *Lifetime Likelihood of Victimization*,
Bureau of Justice Statistics Technical Report (Washington, DC: U.S. Department of Justice, March 1987), www.ojp.gov/pdffiles1/bjs/104274.pdf.

9.　Over the past few years, there has been a surge of reports about delayed police response times in cities across the United States. Taking my city,
Portland, as an example, see Paul Best, "Portland Police Tell Residents 911 Response Times May Be Delayed Due to Staffing Shortage, Critical Incidents,"
Fox News, December 6, 2021, www.foxnews.com/us/portland-police-tell-res-
idents-911-response-times-may-be-delayed-due-to-staffing-shortage-critical-
incidents; Wright Gazaway, "Portland 911 Center's Average Wait Times Hit
High in 2021, City Plans Improvements," *KATU News*, December 15, 2021,
katu.com/news/katu-investigates/improvements-planned-for-portland-911-
center-as-average-wait-times-hit-high-in-2021; and Maxine Bernstein, "Portland Police Leave 911 Calls on Hold for Hours, then Closed Them without
Response, Records Show," *OregonLive*, January 22, 2021, www.oregonlive.com/
crime/2021/01/911-calls-on-hold-for-hours-then-portland-police-closed-
them-without-response-records-show.html. Most cities have a goal to respond
to high-priority crimes within five minutes, but response times can vary dramatically depending on the city, crime, traffic, staffing, and other factors. See
"Table 107. Personal and Property Crimes, 2008," in *Criminal Victimization in
the United States—Statistical Tables*, NCJ 227669 (Washington, DC: U.S. Department of Justice, 2011), 115, bjs.ojp.gov/content/pub/pdf/cvus08.pdf.

10. For just one example, see Frances Mulraney, "White Protester Screams at Three Black Cops during D.C. Protest Telling Them 'They Are a Part of the Problem' and Yells That She's 'Allowed to Say This to Whoever,'" *Daily Mail*, June 25, 2020, www.dailymail.co.uk/news/article-8457467/White-female-protester-tells-black-cops-problem.html.

Chapter 5: The Search for Truth

1. JKD is sometimes referred to as JKD Concepts. There is a fine distinction to be made between the two terms, but for the purposes of this book, I make no distinction. For more, see Chris Kent, "JKD 'Concepts' vs. 'Original' JKD," JKD London, October 30, 2011, www.jkdlondon.com/jkd-%E2%80%98concepts%E2%80%99-vs-%E2%80%98original%E2%80%99-jkd/.

2. This is an abbreviated version of the more famous quote widely attributed to Lee: "Research your own experience; absorb what is useful, reject what is useless and add what is essentially your own." His daughter Shannon Lee discusses the significance of this longer quote as general guidance for life on the *Bruce Lee Podcast*, "Research Your Own Experience," episode 63, September 12, 2017, brucelee.com/podcast-blog/2017/9/12/63-research-your-own-experience. The quote is sometimes attributed to Dan Inosanto, a student and teacher of Bruce Lee who became the head instructor and thus the face of JKD after Bruce Lee's death in 1973. The full dedication to Bruce Lee's *Tao of Jeet Kune Do* (Santa Clara, CA: Ohara Publications, 1975) reads: "This book is Dedicated to the Free, Creative Martial Artist / *Take what is useful and develop from there.*" Inosanto released a JKD guidebook titled *Absorb What Is Useful* in 1982.

3. In Lee's *Tao of Jeet Kune Do* there are sections on "Kicking," "Striking," "Grappling," and "Studies on Judo and Ju-Jitsu," which map onto this four-ranges-of-combat idea. You will also often hear reference to three ranges: short or close, medium, and long.

4. For an introduction to various philosophical ideas about truth, see Michael Glanzberg, "Truth," in *The Stanford Encyclopedia of Philosophy* (Summer 2021 Edition), ed. Edward N. Zalta, plato.stanford.edu/archives/sum2021/entries/truth/.

5. Daniel Dennett, "Thank Goodness!" *Edge*, November 2, 2006, www.edge.org/conversation/daniel_c_dennett-thank-goodness.

6. Rokas Leonavicius, a second-degree black belt in Aikido who for seven years had run his own Aikido dojo in Lithuania, decided to test his Aikido against an MMA fighter in a sparring match. The results were predictable, but this led him on a fascinating journey in which he went from being a rising star in Aikido to a beginner in functional martial arts. He tracked much of this jour-

ney on his YouTube channel. For the sparring match, see "Aikido vs MMA—Real Sparring," YouTube video, uploaded by Martial Arts Journey, May 1, 2017, www.youtube.com/watch?v=0KUXTC8g_pk. He later traveled to Portland to train at SBG, where I awarded him with a blue belt in BJJ. For more, including the backlash he faced in the Aikido community for speaking honestly, see "Interview with Rokas Leonavicius (Martial Arts Journey on Youtube)," *BJJ Tribes*, October 15, 2020, bjjtribes.com/interview-with-rokas-leonavicius-martial-arts-journey-on-youtube/.

7. See Joshua Landy, "Postmodernism: The Decline of Truth," *Philosophy Talk*, July 15, 2019, www.philosophytalk.org/blog/postmodernism-decline-truth.

8. The original context of the phrase "Truth is a pathless land" is often forgotten. See Jiddu Krishnamurti, from his "dissolution" speech, Star Camp, Ommen, Holland, August 3, 1929, https://jkrishnamurti.org/about-dissolution-speech.

9. See Daniel Dennett, from his "The Evolution of Confusion" speech, Atheist Alliance International, Burbank, California, October 4, 2009; and "Deepity," *Urban Dictionary*, https://www.urbandictionary.com/define.php?term=deepity.

10. For the classic book on the philosophy of science and the logic of the scientific method, see Karl R. Popper, *The Logic of Scientific Discovery* (New York: Routledge, 2002), which was first published in German in 1935.

11. See the discussion on "Appeal to Authority" in Bradley Dowden, "Fallacies," *Internet Encyclopedia of Philosophy*, iep.utm.edu/fallacy/#AppealtoAuthority, which reads:

> You appeal to authority if you back up your reasoning by saying that it is supported by what some authority says on the subject. Most reasoning of this kind is not fallacious, and much of our knowledge properly comes from listening to authorities. However, appealing to authority as a reason to believe something *is* fallacious whenever the authority appealed to is not really an authority in this particular subject, when the authority cannot be trusted to tell the truth, when authorities disagree on this subject (except for the occasional lone wolf), when the reasoner misquotes the authority, and so forth. Although spotting a fallacious appeal to authority often requires some background knowledge about the subject or the authority . . . it is fallacious to accept the words of a supposed authority when we should be suspicious of the authority's words.

12. Charles Darwin, in a letter to A. Stephen Wilson, Down, March 5, 1879 ("Letter 752," *More Letters of Charles Darwin*, vol. 2, ed. Francis Darwin and A. C. Seward, www.gutenberg.org/files/2740/2740-h/2740-h.htm).

13. This is a term Peter Boghossian discusses at length in *A Manual for Creating Atheists* (Durham, NC: Pitchstone Publishing, 2013). He writes, "The word 'doxastic' derives from the Greek doxa, which means 'belief.' I use the

phrase 'doxastic closure'... to mean that either a specific belief one holds, or that one's entire belief system, is resistant to revision. Belief revision means changing one's mind about whether a belief is true or false" (p. 49).

14. "Incredible Kungfu Master," uploaded by Shaolin Kungfu, March 26, 2017, www.youtube.com/watch?v=-F0Q0mS6cBo.

15. "Steven Seagal Great Aikido on 'Tornado' Aikido Festival in Moscow 2015," YouTube video, uploaded by RussianAikidoFederation, December 18, 2015, www.youtube.com/watch?v=269tYaa-Fyg.

16. "Le Kali Escrima au Festival des Arts Martiaux Nord-Europe 2015," YouTube video, uploaded by Karaté Bushido Officiel, December 21, 2015, www.youtube.com/watch?v=n467kDdaQcI.

17. "Top 13 Fake Masters Getting Destroyed—EXPOSED," uploaded by LISTertainment, April 5, 2020, www.youtube.com/watch?v=V33bWVkZTdw.

18. "Worse still, super mental power and spiritual this and spiritual that are desperately incorporated until these practitioners drift further and further into mystery and abstraction." Lee, *Tao of Jeet Kune Do*, 14.

19. For more on why people believe the things they do, see Michael Shermer, *Why People Believe Weird Things*, rev. ed. (New York, Henry Holt, 2002).

Chapter 6: The Power of Method

1. For a good general introduction to epistemology, see Duncan Pritchard, *What Is This Thing Called Knowledge*, 4th ed. (New York: Routledge, 2018).

2. I am speaking specifically about propositional knowledge here, which has two prerequisites: (1) we must believe in a proposition, statement, or assertion; and (2) that proposition, statement, or assertion must also be true. Pritchard gives the following example: "So if you know that Paris is the capital of France, then you must believe that this is the case, and your belief must also be true." Ibid., 4.

3. Ibid., 7.

4. You can learn more about Dan Inosanto and the Inosanto Academy of Martial Arts, located in Marina Del Rey, California, at inosanto.com/.

5. While the axioms of Euclidean plane geometry would exist even if humans never discovered or recognized them (e.g., all right angles were equal before the first human, and all right angles will continue to be equal after the last human), the human mind does seem to be predisposed to recognize abstract geometric concepts. "Geometric Principles Appear Universal in Our Minds," *Wired*, May 24, 2011, www.wired.com/2011/05/universal-geometry/.

6.   See, for example, "Silat Djurus in Chiang Rai," YouTube video, uploaded by Sakan Lam, December 31, 2014, www.youtube.com/watch?v=uKxz-px-ZNQY.

7.   In truth, no one knows the true origins of the oldest Chinese martial arts. See the chapter titled "Genesis: The Origin of Martial Art" in Danny Xuan and John Little, *The Tao of Wing Chun: The History and Principles of China's Most Explosive Martial Art* (New York: Skyhorse Publishing, 2015).

8.   Part of the problem is that traditional martial arts became victims of their own success. With the explosion of interest in traditional martial arts in the 1970s and 1980s, some long-time practitioners who had a military background and saw themselves as hard-contact fighters began to complain about a diminishment in their arts, as new schools popped up everywhere to cater to the masses. In a 1999 interview, veteran Isshin-Ryu Karate practitioner Gary Alexander griped,

> There are too many "friends" out there selling things like phony rank and workouts that are nothing more than aerobics sessions. This is fine for fitness, but you shouldn't slap a black belt on people who do it. If you're going to do martial arts, there has to be impact and conditioning. The word that used to be associated with black belt was "coveted" because not too many people could earn one.

He added,

> How many judo schools do you see out there? How many phony judo black belts? Very few, because you can't pretend to be good at judo. Or boxing. But karate has a certain mystique that allows a lot of wannabe practitioners to say things like, "We can't do this technique because it's too deadly." I don't fall for this or for statements like, "The instructor is such a grandmaster that he can't get out on the mat and divulge all his secret deadly techniques." What you really have is a bunch of snake-oil salesmen.

Gary Alexander, in an interview with Rodney Ley, *Black Belt*, February 1999, 104–107.

9.   For more on this subject, see *No Sacred Cows: Investigating Myths, Cults, and the Supernatural* (Durham, NC: Pitchstone Publishing, 2017); and Michael Shermer, *The Believing Brain: From Ghosts and Gods to Politics and Conspiracies—How We Construct Beliefs and Reinforce Them as Truths* (New York: Henry Holt, 2011).

10.   Much has been written about Karl Popper's so-called paradox of tolerance, which holds that a tolerant society must be intolerant of the intolerant. For a libertarian's take on what both the right and left have gotten wrong about this idea, see Jason Kuznicki, "On the Paradox of Tolerance," *Libertarianism.com*, August 17, 2017, www.libertarianism.org/columns/paradox-tolerance. For a broad defense of tolerance in the context of pluralistic societies, see Jon R.

Bowlin, *Tolerance among the Virtues* (Princeton, NJ: Princeton Univeristy Press, 2016).

11. U.S. Supreme Court Justice Antonin Scalia famously said, "I attack ideas. I don't attack people. Some very good people have some very bad ideas." And if you'd prefer not to quote Scalia, that's fine, because his good friend and fellow justice, Ruth Bader Ginsburg, said it too. Richard Wolff, "Opera, Travel, Food, Law: The Unlikely Friendship of Ruth Bader Ginsburg and Antonin Scalia," *USA Today*, September 20, 2020.

Chapter 7: The Power of the Opponent Process

1. This is a point even members of the U.S. military sometimes miss. While acknowledging the benefits of Mixed Martial Arts, they'll argue you still need a "street-ready arsenal" or say things like, "Mixed martial artists may train for a submission; criminals train for life or death. . . .[I]f you're only training for mixed martial arts-type matches and ignoring the implementation of more brutal (and street valuable) attacks, then you one day may find yourself going for that arm bar while your attacker sticks a finger deep in your eye." Jeff Anderson, "Mixed Martial Arts vs. Street Fighting," *Military.com*, www.military.com/military-fitness/close-quarters-combat/mixed-martial-arts-vs-street-fighting. Contrast this with what BJJ competitor Ryan Hall said when asked what he'd say to those who claim BJJ competition training doesn't transfer to real self-defense situations. "Those people are wrong, to be frank. Anyone who doesn't realize that situation dictates tactics really can't be helped. . . . I don't care if this person tried to eye gouge me or if they bite me, it is irrelevant. If I want to hurt this person, they don't have a prayer in the world." Notably, he said this in an interview *after* a video went viral of him using BJJ techniques to control and subdue an aggressive drunk in a restaurant. T. P. Grant, "Ryan Hall Weighs in on 'Sport vs Street' Debate in Martial Arts," *Bloody Elbow*, March 21, 2012, www.bloodyelbow.com/2012/3/21/2887681/ryan-hall-weighs-in-on-sport-vs-street-debate-in-martial-arts.

2. He continues, "If you are flying to an international congress of anthropologists or literary critics, the reason you will probably get there—the reason you don't plummet into a ploughed field—is that a lot of Western scientifically trained engineers have got their sums right." Richard Dawkins, *River Out of Eden: A Darwinian View of Life* (New York: Basic Books, 1995), 31–32.

3. When science is corrupted or co-opted by ideology, it is no longer a reliable method for discovering truth. Rather, it becomes a tool to validate and serve the ideology's truth and thus is no longer true science. As physicist Lawrence M. Krauss notes and warns, "Whenever science has been corrupted by

falling prey to ideology, scientific progress suffers." Lawrence M. Krauss, "The Ideological Corruption of Science," *Wall Street Journal*, July 12, 2020, www.wsj. com/articles/the-ideological-corruption-of-science-11594572501.

4. Grandmaster Hélio Gracie, who developed Gracie Jiu-Jitsu with the help of his brothers, has an informative chapter on the history of Gracie Jiu-Jitsu in his book, *Gracie Jiu-Jitsu*, rev. ed. (Torrance, CA: Gracie Publications, 2020).

5. You can find more about Fabio Santos and his academy in San Diego here: fabiojiujitsu.com/.

6. Sam Harris, "The Pleasures of Drowning," *Samharris.org*, February 6, 2012, www.samharris.org/blog/the-pleasures-of-drowning.

7. For more about Rolls Gracie, see T. P. Grant, "History of Jiu-Jitsu: The Tragedy of Rolls Gracie," *Bleacher Report*, April 10, 2011, bleacherreport.com/articles/654456-history-of-jiu-jitsu-the-tragedy-of-rolls-gracie.

8. Rorion Gracie, in an interview with James Williams and Stanley Pranin, *Aikido Journal*, August 27, 2011, aikidojournal.com/2011/08/27/interview-with-rorion-gracie-by-james-williams-and-stanley-pranin/.

9. See Pat Jordan, "Bad: Rorion Gracie Is Willing to Fight to the Death to Prove He's the Toughest Man in the West," *Playboy*, September 1989, available at onthemat.com/rorion-gracie-playboy-interview/; and Don Beu, "Gracie Jujitsu: Brazilian Art Is Simple, Fast, Effective, Unorthodox," *Black Belt*, August 1989, 30–33, available at books.google.com/books?id=SdYDAAAAMBA-J&lpg=PA1&lr&rview=1&pg=PA30#v=onepage&q&f=false. An ad for a *Gracie Jiu-Jitsu in Action* video appears in that same issue of *Black Belt* (p. 29), which includes an endorsement from martial artist and actor Chuck Norris that reads: "The Gracie Brothers are the best at what they do. This tape is a must see."

10. The one good thing about the pseudoscience of astrology is that it led to the science of astronomy. There's a great book for kids that helps them discover for themselves how and why astrology is bunk. If you don't yet understand this fact yourself, you might consider trying the experiments and activities recommended in Kimberly Baker, *Horoscopes: Reality or Trickery?* (Farmington Hills, MI: Green Grove Press, 2018).

11. In keeping with the theme of this book, one French study showed that 94 percent of people saw themselves in a personalized horoscope for a serial killer! For more, see Khushi Gupta, "94% of Respondents Believed That a Serial Killer's Horoscope Was Their Own," *Medium*, July 18, 2021, medium. com/@khushigupta_41675/94-of-respondents-believed-that-a-serial-killers-horoscope-was-their-own-28882732a09f.

12. Christopher Hitchens, *God Is Not Great: How Religion Poisons Everything* (New York: Twelve Books), 150. Today this dictum is often referred to as

"Hitchens' Razor." See Jerry Coyne, "Readers' Tributes to Hitchens: The Final Day, with Music," *Why Evolution Is True*, December 25, 2011, whyevolutionistrue.com/2011/12/25/readers-tributes-to-hitchens-the-final-day/.

13. The idea of "devolution" is not a legitimate scientific notion, but I use it here in the sense it is often used in the popular imagination, such as in the novel and film adaptations of *Planet of the Apes*, in which future humans have "devolved" to be more primitive than they are today.

14. As Daniel Dennett once remarked, "I listen to all these complaints about rudeness and intemperateness, and the opinion that I come to is that there is no polite way of asking somebody: have you considered the possibility that your entire life has been devoted to a delusion? But that's a good question to ask. Of course we should ask that question and of course it's going to offend people. Tough." Daniel Dennett, in an interview with Julian Baggini, *Philosophers' Magazine*, May 8, 2017 (originally published March 2010), www.philosophersmag.com/index.php/component/content/article/14-tpm-articles/interviews/31-dan-dennett-and-the-new-atheism?Itemid=101.

Chapter 8: The Command of Strength

1. Researcher Brené Brown describes vulnerability thusly: "Vulnerability is not winning or losing; it's having the courage to show up and be seen when we have no control over the outcome. Vulnerability is not weakness; it's our greatest measure of courage." Brené Brown, *Rising Strong: The Reckoning. The Rumble. The Revolution* (New York: Spiegel and Grau, 2015), 4. See also, Brené Brown, "The Power of Vulnerability" (lecture, TEDxHouston, June 2010), www.ted.com/talks/brene_brown_the_power_of_vulnerability?language=en.

2. People in general are more ignorant than they think they are. We often think we understand how things work but are merely under the illusion that we understand. This provides us with some evolutionary advantages, because it gives us the self-confidence to explore new terrain, but it comes with a price. When confidence scales with ignorance in this way, you're opening the door for very bad outcomes. Ignorant people don't know how ignorant they are until it is too late. For more on this subject, see Steven Sloman and Philip Fernbach, *The Knowledge Illusion: Why We Never Think Alone* (New York: Riverhead Books, 2017), 263; and David Dunning, "The Dunning-Kruger Effect: On Being Ignorant of One's Own Ignorance," *Advances in Experimental Social Psychology* 44 (2011): 247–296, doi.org/10.1016/B978-0-12-385522-0.00005-6.

3. As a product of our own evolutionary history, violence is primal. A lot of young men hunger to be seen as skilled at violence. And a lot of young women are physically attracted to men who behave in a manner that implies a famil-

iarity with methods of violence. Why does the bad boy get the girl? Because he has the mannerisms that signal to other predators to fuck off. And more often than not, she instinctively likes that. That may not be a popular thing to say, but it's true. And it is one of the major reasons men often pretend to know more than they do about violence. For more, see Vinita Mehta, "Why Do Women Fall for Bad Boys?" *Psychology Today*, October 21, 2013, www.psychologytoday. com/us/blog/head-games/201310/why-do-women-fall-bad-boys; Tom Calver, "Roots of Aggression," *Oxford News Blog*, August 12, 2015, www.ox.ac.uk/news/ science-blog/roots-aggression; and "Girls' Perceptions of Boys with Violent Attitudes and Behaviours, and of Sexual Attraction," *Palgrave Communications* 5, no 56 (May 2019), doi.org/10.1057/s41599-019-0262-5.

4.   For more on Rickson, see www.ricksongracie.com/; his book, written with Peter Maguire, *Breathe: A Life in Flow* (New York: Dey St., 2021); and the documentary *Choke* (1999), directed by Robert Raphael Goodman.

5.   As this was well before the age of digital cameras and phones, there is no video from that particular day, but there are videos from other seminars in the 1990s in which Rickson spars with attendees. See, for example, "RARE Rickson Gracie Rolling with 50 People for 25 Minutes at a Seminar in Chicago," YouTube video, uploaded by Riccardo Ammerndolia, June 21, 2021, www. youtube.com/watch?v=qFQiFhL5VXk. Although he's using both hands in this video, his movements and submissions would have felt like magic to those unfamiliar with BJJ. For an example of one-handed and no-handed rolling, see the video of Rener Gracie, Rickson's nephew and Rorion's son, sparring against experienced BJJ practitioners, "1-Handed Rener vs. Purple, Brown & Black Belt at Vancouver Seminar," YouTube video, uploaded by GracieBreakdown, June 18, 2014, www.youtube.com/watch?v=apymToKoRZA; and "Rener Gracie vs. Purple Belt (Both Hands Tied Down)," YouTube video, uploaded by Gracie-Breakdown, June 26, 2012, www.youtube.com/watch?v=z0DIK_bAPJA.

6.   Levels 1 and 2 might also be referred to as "self-aware ignorance" and "self-oblivious ignorance," respectively. The former is a better and healthier form of ignorance than the latter. Massimo Pigliucci, "Platonic Ignorance," *Rationally Speaking*, June 19, 2012, rationallyspeaking.blogspot.com/2012/06/platonic-ignorance.html.

7.   George Orwell, "In Front of Your Nose," in *The Collected Essays, Journalism, and Essays of George Orwell*, ed. Sonia Orwell and Ian Angus (Boiston, MA: Nonpareil Books, 2000), 124. Also available through the Orwell Foundation at www.orwellfoundation.com/the-orwell-foundation/orwell/essays-and-other-works/in-front-of-your-nose/.

8.   In the 1990s, the Gracie Academy in Torrance, California, regularly witnessed such challenge matches. Results were always predictable. See, for example, "CHALLENGE MATCH feat Blue Belt Ryron," YouTube vid-

eo, uploaded by GracieBreakdown, November 28, 2019, www.youtube.com/watch?v=DFrqz2LAUU4; "Jiu-Jitsu Black Belt (Rener Gracie) vs Tae Kwon Do Black Belt Full Contact Match," YouTube video, uploaded by Jiu-Jitsu Times, October 8, 2020, www.youtube.com/watch?v=dZ0h8_hFwlM; and "Gracie Jiu-Jitsu Challenge Match 1996," YouTube video, uploaded by Steve Kardian, December 10, 2010, www.youtube.com/watch?v=QqKV3jZWJJA. Such matches had been occurring for decades in Brazil, where the Gracies had issued an open challenge to martial artists of all styles to fight them in anything -goes (*vale tudo*) matches as far back as the 1920s. For an example, see "Gracie Jiu-Jitsu vs. Karate Team Challenge," YouTube video, uploaded by Sonny Brown Breakdown, September 16, 2021, www.youtube.com/watch?v=JaGDE-C1Yb2k.

9.   Nothing conveys the danger of delusional thinking, especially in the context of physical prowess, than an amusing 2021 survey that asked Americans which animals they think they could defeat in a fight without using a weapon. The results? Seven percent of men think they could beat a grizzly bear in a fight, 8 percent think they could beat a lion, 9 percent think they could beat an elephant or gorilla, and 22 percent think they could beat a chimpanzee. Remarkably, the percentage of women who think the same is not all that different. See "Rumble in the Jungle: What Animals Would Win in a Fight?" *YouGov*, May 13, 2021, today.yougov.com/topics/lifestyle/articles-reports/2021/05/13/lions-and-tigers-and-bears-what-animal-would-win-f.

10.   Although it may sound strange to hear me refer to a choke as "being kind," it is true. Most of the chokes employed in Brazilian Jiu-Jitsu are blood chokes, which will lead to unconsciousness due to cerebral hypoxia if applied properly. Even when they are held long enough for the person to pass out, they do not typically induce any pain or cause any lasting damage or injury. In fact, most MMA fighters will tell you they'd much rather be put to sleep by a choke than knocked out by a punch. Recovery from a brutal knockout can be protracted, sometimes lasting months; recovery from a powerful choke that is released upon inducing unconsciousness is usually immediate. The effects are generally limited to hallucinations and muscle spasms while unconscious. Thomas Lempert et al., "Syncope: A Videometric Analysis of 56 Episodes of Transient Cerebral Hypoxia," *Annals of Neurology* 36, no. 2 (1994): 233–7, doi:10.1002/ana.410360217. Interestingly, one study of elite BJJ athletes not only found no evidence of cognitive impairment in them but also found they had some level of adaptive neuroprotection, either from choke-induced cerebral conditioning or exposure to BJJ-specific high-intensity interval training. Benjamin S. Stacey et al., "Elevated Cerebral Perfusion and Preserved Cognition in Elite Brazilian Jiu-Jitsu Athletes: Evidence for Neuroprotection," *Scandinavian Journal of Medicine and Science in Sports* 31, no. 11 (November 2021): 2115–2122. The one caveat here is that the choke must be released as soon as the opponent is

rendered unconscious, which can occur in a matter of seconds. A choke that's intentionally (or even inadvertently) held for any meaningful length of time beyond that risks causing brain damage, a stroke, or death. There's a horrifying account of a teenager who killed his older cousin while wrestling at a house party by holding a rear-naked choke, one of the most powerful blood chokes in BJJ and thus all of martial arts, for thirty or forty seconds. Rener and Ryron Gracie discussed the incident on their YouTube channel: "Boy Chokes His Cousin to Death with Rear Naked Choke," YouTube video, uploaded by GracieBreakdown, April 5, 2012, www.youtube.com/watch?v=QrsBlDDA0Lg.

11.   There are good scholarly histories of most martial arts available, but most of the myths are inventions that have appeared over time and become a part of the oral tradition within schools and systems. See, for example, the discussion in Benjamin N. Judkins and Jon Nielson, *The Creation of Wing Chun: A Social History of the Southern Chinese Martial Arts* (Albany, NY: State University of New York Press, 2015), 7–13.

Chapter 9: The Real Bogeyman under the Bed

1.   "Cheshire, Connecticut, Home Invasion Murders, 10 Years Later," *USA Today*, July 17, 2017, www.usatoday.com/story/news/2017/07/17/cheshire-connecticut-home-invasion-murders-10-years-later/483863001/; and Manny Fernandez and Alison Leigh Cowan, "When Horror Came to Connecticut," *New York Times*, August 7, 2007, www.nytimes.com/2007/08/07/nyregion/07slay.html.

2.   Hayes did not offer his preferred pronouns in the interview, but he described himself as "feminine" and claimed to have been diagnosed with sexual-identity disorder as a teen. See Steven Hayes, in an interview with Joe Tomaso, *15 Minutes With . . .* , podcast, October 11, 2019 and November 2, 2019, anchor.fm/joseph-tomaso5/; Neil Vigdor, "Connecticut Home Invasion Convict Is Undergoing Gender Transition in Prison," *New York Times*, October 31, 2019, www.nytimes.com/2019/10/31/us/steven-hayes-cheshire-transgender.html; and Jackie Salo, "Notorious Connecticut Killer Undergoes Gender Transition in Prison," *New York Post*, October 29, 2019, nypost.com/2019/10/29/notorious-connecticut-killer-undergoes-gender-transition-in-prison/. For a science-based look at gender dysphoria and gender-ideology claims, see Debra Soh, *The End of Gender: Debunking the Myths about Sex and Identity in Our Society* (New York: Threshold Editions, 2020); Abigail Shrier, *Irreversible Damage: The Transgender Craze Seducing Our Daughters* (Washington, DC: Regnery Publishing, 2021); and Colin M. Wright and Emma N. Hilton, "The Dangerous Denial of Sex," *Wall Street Journal*, February 13, 2020, www.wsj.com/articles/the-dangerous-denial-of-sex-11581638089.

3.   Kate Sheehy, "Home Invasion Killer: I Was Nice to Slain Family," *New York Post*, September 9, 2013, nypost.com/2013/09/09/conn-hostage-fiend-in-sists-he-was-nice-to-petits/.

4.   Regular physical activity can increase your life expectancy up to nearly seven years. C. D. Reimers et al., "Does Physical Activity Increase Life Expectancy? A Review of the Literature," *Journal of Aging Research*, no. 243958 (2012), doi.org/10.1155/2012/243958. For a good summary of the benefits provided by aerobic exercise, see Rhonda Patrick, "Aerobic Exercise," *FoundMyFitness*, www.foundmyfitness.com/topics/aerobic-exercise.

5.   A term has since arisen for martial arts schools that enable and promote this type of culture: McDojos. The first entry for the word on the crowd-sourced online site *Urban Dictionary* was posted on October 19, 2004. "McDojo," *Urban Dictionary*, www.urbandictionary.com/define.php?term=McDojo.

6.   McCain's views toward the sport changed over time. Nick Greene, "How John McCain Grew to Tolerate MMA, the Sport He Likened to 'Human Cockfighting,'" *Slate*, August 26, 2018, slate.com/culture/2018/08/john-mccain-ufc-how-he-grew-to-tolerate-mma-the-sport-he-considered-human-cockfighting.html#:~:text=But%20when%20he%20came%20across,%-2DAmerican%2C%E2%80%9D%20McCain%20declared.

7.   For an interview I conducted with Rickson in which we discuss, among other things, how BJJ can improve lives, see "Rickson Gracie in Conversation with Matt Thornton: SBG Video Podcast Episode 5," YouTube video, uploaded by SBG Portland BJJ and MMA Videos, June 8, 2017, www.youtube.com/watch?v=SQNCz_hw6vc.

8.   At the same time, we need to be honest: obesity is a medical problem. "Obesity," Mayo Clinic, www.mayoclinic.org/diseases-conditions/obesity/symptoms-causes/syc-20375742 (last accessed May 8, 2022). It's also at epidemic levels. The prevalence of adult obesity in the United States has risen from 30.5 percent in 1999–2000 to 42.4 percent in 2017–2018. "Adult Obesity Facts," National Center for Chronic Disease Prevention and Health Promotion, www.cdc.gov/obesity/data/adult.html#:~:text=The%20US%20obesity%20prevalence%20was,from%204.7%25%20to%209.2%25 (last reviewed September 30, 2021). Yet, some people argue that being fat is healthy. This so-called fat activism causes real harm. See Helen Pluckrose and James Lindsay, *Cynical Theories: How Activist Scholarship Made Everything about Race, Gender, and Identity—and Why This Harms Everybody* (Durham, NC: Pitchstone Publishing, 2020), chapter 7. For context, the prevalence of adult obesity in the United Kingdom was 26 percent in 2019 and less than 10 percent in Korea and Japan. "Adult Overweight and Obesity," Statistics on Obesity, Physical Activity and Diet, 2019, NHS Digital, digital.nhs.uk/data-and-information/publications/statistical/statistics-on-obesity-physical-activity-and-diet/statistics-on-obesi-

ty-physical-activity-and-diet-england-2019/part-3-adult-obesity (last edited July 8, 2021).

9. A. C. Shilton, "Why You're Probably Not That Great at Assessing Risks," *New York Times*, June 30, 2020, www.nytimes.com/2020/06/30/smarter-living/why-youre-probably-not-so-great-at-risk-assessment.html.

10. "Leading Causes of Death," National Center for Health Statistics, Centers for Disease Control and Prevention, www.cdc.gov/nchs/fastats/leading-causes-of-death.htm (last reviewed January 13, 2022).

11. In 2019, there were 2,854,838 recorded resident deaths in the United States, making the crude death rate 869.7 per 100,000 population. In 2020, there were 3,383,729 recorded resident deaths in the United States, making the crude death rate 1,027.0 per 100,000 population. The increase in death rate is largely attributed to COVID-19 and the cascading negative effects of the pandemic. Sherry L. Murphy et al., *Mortality in the United States, 2020*, NCHS Data Brief, no. 427 (U.S. Department of Health and Human Services, December 2021), 6; "Deaths and Mortality," National Center for Health Statistics, Centers for Disease Control and Prevention, www.cdc.gov/nchs/fastats/deaths.htm (last reviewed January 13, 2022); and Jiaquan Xu et al., "Deaths: Final Data for 2019," *National Vital Statistics Report* 70, no. 8 (U.S. Department of Health and Human Services, July 26, 2021), 1, www.cdc.gov/nchs/data/nvsr/nvsr70/nvsr70-08-508.pdf. For statistics on causes of death in the United Kingdom and worldwide, see, respectively, "Causes of Death," Office for National Statistics, www.ons.gov.uk/peoplepopulationandcommunity/healthandsocialcare/causesofdeath; and "The Top 10 Causes of Death," World Health Organization, December 9, 2020, www.who.int/news-room/fact-sheets/detail/the-top-10-causes-of-death.

12. Data from the CDC and FBI point to the same trends, but the CDC and FBI draw from different sources, and thus, their homicide figures are not identical. For the purposes of this chapter, I am relying on the CDC's homicide data because I'm placing this data in the context of the CDC's data on all causes of death. Elsewhere in the book, I cite FBI homicide data. For more on the differences between the two data collection systems, see *The Nation's Two Measures of Homicide*, Bureau of Justice Statistics Program Report (U.S. Department of Justice, July 2014), bjs.ojp.gov/content/pub/pdf/ntmh.pdf.

13. In 2020, the percentage of those who died by homicide rose to roughly 0.73 percent, or 7.5 homicide deaths per 100,000 population. The 24,576 homicide deaths in the United States in 2020 represented a 30 percent increase from 2019, when approximately 19,100 people were murdered, equalling 6.0 homicide deaths per 100,000 population. "Assault or Homicide," National Center for Health Statistics, Centers for Disease Control and Prevention, www.cdc.gov/nchs/fastats/homicide.htm (last reviewed January 5, 2022); and "National Vio-

lent Death Reporting System (NVDRS)," National Center for Injury Prevention and Control, Division of Violence Prevention, www.cdc.gov/violenceprevention/ datasources/nvdrs/index.html (last reviewed September 28, 2021). As a point of comparison, the homicide rate in England and Wales for the year ending March 2021 was 0.99 per 100,000 population. "Homicide in England and Wales: Year Ending March 2021," Office for National Statistics, February 10, 2022, www. ons.gov.uk/peoplepopulationandcommunity/crimeandjustice/articles/homi- cideinenglandandwales/yearendingmarch2021#:~:text=The%20homicide%20 rate%20was%209.9,(6%20per%20million%20population). For homicide rates by country and year, see "Homicide Country Data," United Nations Office on Drugs and Crime, dataunodc.un.org/content/homicide-country-data.

Chapter 10: The Predator Next Door (or Already Inside)

1. Obviously, in many unsolved cases, the gender of the offender and the relationship of the offender to the victim are unknown, but in the United States, these three claims are categorically true for those cases in which the offender and victim are both identified. For U.S. figures that support these claims, see, for example, Uniform Crime Reporting Program, "Expanded Homicide," *Crime in the United States 2019*, FBI, ucr.fbi.gov/crime-in-the-u.s/2019/crime-in-the- u.s.-2019/topic-pages/expanded-homicide; and Uniform Crime Reporting Program, "Murder," *Crime in the United States 2019*, ucr.fbi.gov/crime-in-the- u.s/2019/crime-in-the-u.s.-2019/topic-pages/murder.

2. "Expanded Homicide," *Crime in the United States 2019*.

3. This study dates back to the 1980s, when the murder rate was con- sistently higher, so the lifetime risk today would likely be lower than this. As cited in Herbert Koppel, *Lifetime Likelihood of Victimization*, NCJ-102274 (U.S. Department of Justice, March 1987), 1, www.ojp.gov/pdffiles1/bjs/104274.pdf.

4. In truth, strangers are identified as the offender in roughly 10 percent of all murder cases. The 20 percent statistic assumes we include only those cases in which an offender is identified. In up to half of all murder cases, an offender is never identified. See the offender-victim relationship breakdown in "Expanded Homicide Data Table 10," *Crime in the United States 2019*, FBI, ucr.fbi.gov/ crime-in-the-u.s/2019/crime-in-the-u.s.-2019/tables/expanded-homicide-da- ta-table-10.xls.

5. Shannan Catalano et al., *Female Victims of Violence*, NCJ 228356 (U.S. Department of Justice, September 2009), 2, bjs.ojp.gov/content/pub/pdf/ fvv.pdf; and "Expanded Homicide Data Table 10," *Crime in the United States 2019*, FBI, ucr.fbi.gov/crime-in-the-u.s/2019/crime-in-the-u.s.-2019/tables/ expanded-homicide-data-table-10.xls.

6. Matthew R. Durose et al., *Family Violence Statistics: Including Statistics on Strangers and Acquaintances*, NCJ 207846 (U.S. Department of Justice, June 2005), 17.

7. Catalano et al., *Female Victims of Violence*, 3; and Emiko Petrosky et al., "Racial and Ethnic Differences in Homicides of Adult Women and the Role of Intimate Partner Violence—United States, 2003–2014," *Morbidity and Mortality Weekly Report* 66, no. 28 (July 21, 2017): 741–746, www.cdc.gov/mmwr/volumes/66/wr/mm6628a1.htm?s_cid=mm6628a1_w.

8. See Ronet Bachman, *Violence Against Women: A National Crime Victimization Survey Report*, NCJ-145325 (U.S. Department of Justice, January 1994), 7. www.ojp.gov/pdffiles1/Digitization/145325NCJRS.pdf.

9. For a widely discussed op-ed that recommended a possible solution to this problem, see W. Brad Wilcox and Robin Fretwell Wilson, "One Way to End Violence Against Women? Married Dads," *Washington Post*, June 12, 2004, www.washingtonpost.com/posteverything/wp/2014/06/10/the-best-way-to-end-violence-against-women-stop-taking-lovers-and-get-married/. This proposed solution had no lack of critics. See, for example, Erin Gloria Ryan, "Violence Against Women Will End When You Sluts Get Married, Says WaPo," *Jezebel*, June 10, 2014, jezebel.com/violence-against-women-will-end-when-you-sluts-get-marr-1588828277?utm_campaign=socialfow_jezebel_twitter&utm_source=jezebel_twitter&utm_medium=socialflow. To be sure, there are compounding variables (e.g., age, location, education level, class, race, etc.) to consider that might affect the calculus for any given individual. See Mona Chalabi, "The Washington Post Misused the Data on Violence Against Women," *FiveThirtyEight*, June 10, 2014, fivethirtyeight.com/features/the-washington-post-misused-the-data-on-violence-against-women/. Yet, the relationship between family structure and violence-free homes still holds even when accounting for confounding variables. W. Bradford Wilcox, "#YesWomenAndChildren Are Safer Within Intact Marriages," *Federalist*, January 6, 2015.

10. While the danger is real, the exact degree of danger is a matter of debate. One oft-cited study commissioned by the U.S. Department of Justice found that one in five undergraduate women will experience an attempted or completed sexual assault while in college. See Christopher P. Krebs et al., "The Campus Sexual Assault Study," no. 221153, December 2007, www.ojp.gov/pdffiles1/nij/grants/221153.pdf. Such a finding is rightly headline-grabbing, but strong critiques have been made against this and similar studies. See, for example, the points raised in Tessa Berenson, "1 in 5: Debating the Most Controversial Sexual Assault Statistic," *Time*, June 27, 2014, time.com/2934500/1-in-5%E2%80%82campus-sexual-assault-statistic/; and Christine Hoff Sommers, "Rape Culture Is a 'Panic Where Paranoia, Censorship, and False Accusations Flourish,'" *Time*, May 15, 2014, time.com/100091/campus-sexual-assault-christina-hoff-sommers/. Sommers cites

another study that suggests the true figure is closer to 1 in 40 and that shows nonstudents of the same age face a greater overall risk of violent crime: Timothy S. Hart, *Violent Victimization of College Students*, National Violent Crime Victimization Survey, 1995–2000 (U.S. Department of Justice, December 2003), table 1, bjs.ojp.gov/content/pub/pdf/vvcs00.pdf.

11. Neighborhoods with a higher density of on-premise alcohol establishments (bars, restaurants, etc.) have higher rates of police-reported rape. Traci L. Toomey et al., "The Association between Density of Alcohol Establishments and Violent Crime within Urban Neighborhoods," *Alcoholism Clinical and Experimental Research* 36, no. 8 (2012): 1468–73, doi:10.1111/j.1530-0277.2012.01753.x.. Most cases of sexual violence in the United States involve perpetrators using alcohol or drugs. This is true whether the attacker is an intimate partner, acquaintance, or stranger. Kathleen C. Basile, "Victim and Perpetrator Characteristics in Alcohol/Drug-Involved Sexual Violence Victimization in the U.S.," *Drug and Alcohol Dependence* 226, no. 108839 (September 1, 2021), doi:10.1016/j.drugalcdep.2021.108839.

12. The circumstances of each missing child are not always recorded. "2021 NCIC Missing Person and Unidentified Person Statistics," FBI, 2, www.fbi.gov/file-repository/2021-ncic-missing-person-and-unidentified-person-statistics.pdf/view.

13. Katherine M. Brown et al., *Case Management for Missing Children Homicide Investigation* (Attorney General of Washington and U.S. Department of Justice, May 2006), 1, 14, and 18–25, available at www.atg.wa.gov/child-abduction-murder-research.

14. "Kidnapped Children Make Headlines, but Abduction Is Rare in U.S.," *Reuters*, January 11, 2019, www.reuters.com/article/us-wisconsin-missinggirl-data/kidnapped-children-make-headlines-but-abduction-is-rare-in-u-s-idUSKCN1P52BJ.

15. Brown et al., *Case Management for Missing Children Homicide Investigation*, 26.

16. We see a similar phenomenon in other primates. See, for example, this story about a gorilla known as "wonder women" observed by the Dian Fossey Gorilla Fund: "Gorilla Mother Travels Alone to Save Infant," December 20, 2017, gorillafund.org/dian-fossey/gorilla-mother-travels-alone-save-infant/.

17. Charles Q. Choi, "Too Hard for Science? Does Evolutionary Logic Explain Wicked Stepparents?" *Scientific American*, Assignment: Impossible blog, August 23, 2011, blogs.scientificamerican.com/assignment-impossible/too-hard-for-science-does-evolutionary-logic-explain-murderously-wicked-stepparents/.

18. For a short survey of relevant studies, see Diana Zuckerman and Sarah

Pedersen, "Child Abuse and Father Figures: Which Kind of Families Are Safest to Grow Up In?" National Center for Health Research, www.center4research. org/child-abuse-father-figures-kind-families-safest-grow/.

19. See Martin Daly and Margo Wilson, "The 'Cinderella Effect': Elevated Mistreatment of Stepchildren in Comparison to Those Living with Genetic Parents," McMaster University, www.cep.ucsb.edu/buller/cinderella%20 effect%20facts.pdf.

20. See Gavin Nobes and Georgia Panagiotaki, "The Cinderella Effect: Are Stepfathers Dangerous?" *Conversation*, September 24, 2018, theconversation.com/the-cinderella-effect-are-stepfathers-dangerous-103707#:~:-text=They%20analysed%20British%20child%20homicide,the%20US%20 drew%20similar%20conclusions; and Gavin Nobes et al., "Child Homicides by Stepfathers: A Replication and Reassessment of the British Evidence," *Journal of Experimental Psychology: General* 148, no. 6 (2019): 1091–1102, doi. org/10.1037/xge0000492.

21. Grant T. Harris et al., "Children Killed by Genetic Parents Versus Stepparents," *Evolution and Human Behavior* 28, no. 2 (March 2007): 85–95, doi.org/10.1016/j.evolhumbehav.2006.08.001.

22. Timothy Y. Mariano et al., "Toward a More Holistic Understanding of Filicide: A Multidisciplinary Analysis of 32 Years of U.S. Arrest Data," *Forensic Science International* 236 (March 1, 2014): 46–53, doi:10.1016/j.forsciint.2013.12.019.

23. For a textured investigation into why one mother committed "the most unforgivable of crimes," see Nancy Rommelmann, *To the Bridge: A True Story of Motherhood and Murder* (New York: Little A, 2018).

24. Among the largest behavioral differences between males and females are the levels of physical aggression and violence they display. As researcher and author Carole Hooven argues, this is not simply a result of socialization; much of this difference is due to the effects of testosterone. See Carole Hooven, *The Story of Testosterone, the Hormone That Dominates and Divides Us* (New York: Henry Holt, 2021). Notably, this sex-based gap is sizeable by the time children reach puberty. See Lise Eliot, "Brain Development and Physical Aggression: How a Small Gender Difference Grows into a Violence Problem," *Current Anthropology* 62, no. S23 (February 2021), doi:10.1086/711705.

25. Alexia D. Cooper and Erica L. Smith, *Homicide Trends in the United States, 1980–2008*, NCJ 236018 (U.S. Department of Justice, November 2011), 22, bjs.ojp.gov/content/pub/pdf/htus8008.pdf.

26. Some researchers divide violence into only two dichotomous forms: instrumental and expressive. For them, moralistic violence would likely be considered a type of instrumental violence. For a discussion of violence theory,

see National Institute of Justice, "Violence Theory Workshop Summary," NCJ 242216 (summary of a workshop sponsored by the National Institute of Justice, December 10–11, 2002), www.ojp.gov/pdffiles1/nij/242216.pdf. See also, for example, Rodrigo Meneses-Reyes and Miguel Quintana-Navarrete, "On Lethal Interactions: Differences Between Expressive and Instrumental Homicides in Mexico City," *Journal of Interpersonal Violence* 36, no. 1–2 (2021), doi.org/10.1177/0886260517733280.

27. See, for example, Joseph H. Mikalski, "Terrorism and Lethal Moralism in the United States and United Kingdom, 1970–2017," *British Journal of Sociology* 7, no. 5 (December 2019): 1681–1708, doi:10.1111/1468-4446.12635.

28. Between 2014 and 2021, there were, on average, thirty-one fatalities per year due to domestic terrorism in the United States. Seth G. Jones, "The Evolution of Domestic Terrorism," Center for Strategic and International Studies, February 7, 2022, www.csis.org/analysis/evolution-domestic-terrorism.

29. For one harrowing example—the sadistic execution of Daniel Pearl— read Asra Nomani, "This Is Danny Pearl's Final Story," *Washingtonian*, January 23, 2014. He was a perfect target for his killers' perverse propaganda purposes: a Jewish American journalist for the *Wall Street Journal* with family ties to Israel investigating al-Qaeda in Karachi. For more, see the Daniel Pearl Foundation, www.danielpearl.org/.

30. U.S. Department of State, "Travel Advisories," travel.state.gov/content/travel/en/traveladvisories/traveladvisories.html/. Also, be sure to buckle your seat belt, because traffic accidents are the number one cause of preventable deaths when traveling abroad. U.S. Department of State, "Your Survival Guide to Safe and Healthy Travel," wwwnc.cdc.gov/travel/page/survival-guide. As with violence, the road traffic death rate can vary dramatically by country. See World Health Organization, "Road Traffic Deaths, Data by Country," apps.who.int/gho/data/view.main.51310?lang=en.

31. The FBI runs a tipline for exactly these kinds of threats: www.fbi.gov/tips.

32. The 2013 *Diagnostic and Statistical Manual of Mental Disorders* (DSM-V) doesn't include sociopathy or psychopathy as official diagnostic terms and instead classifies antisocial personality disorder. American Psychiatric Association, *Diagnostic and Statistical Manual of Mental Disorders,* 5th ed. (Washington, DC: American Psychiatric Publishing, 2013), doi.org/10.1176/appi.books.9780890425596. See also, "Antisocial Personality Disorder," *Psychology Today*, www.psychologytoday.com/intl/conditions/antisocial-personality-disorder (last updated November 4, 2021); and Andrea D. Glenn et al., "Antisocial Personality Disorder: A Current Review," *Current Psychiatry Reports* 15, no. 427 (2013).

33. Christine Army and Karim Vellani, "Violent Crime Typology and Continuum," *CrimRxiv*, June 22, 2021, doi.org/10.21428/cb6ab371.71ec923d.

34. Catherine Townsend, *Estimating a Child Sexual Abuse Prevalence Rate for Practitioners: A Review of Child Sexual Abuse Prevalence Studies* (Darkness to Light, August 2013), 21, www.d2l.org/wp-content/uploads/2017/02/PREVA-LENCE-RATE-WHITE-PAPER-D2L.pdf. Note: this report explicitly calls attention to a common mistake in reporting on abuse:

> The Adverse Childhood Experiences (ACE) study . . . is the primary source cited for a prevalence statistic by many national and community-based organizations. The ACE study is often cited as the source of the commonly used statistic "1 in 5 adults report that they were sexually abused as children" or "1 in 4 women and 1 in 6 men report that they were sexually abused as children." Unfortunately, this has been translated into "1 in 4 girls and 1 and 6 boys will be sexually abused before they turn 18." Of course, this is not an accurate translation of the statistic. However, it is deeply ingrained in child sexual abuse practice and media reports.

For the initial ACE study, see V. J. Felitti et al., "Relationship of Childhood Abuse and Household Dysfunction to Many of the Leading Causes of Death in Adults. The Adverse Childhood Experiences (ACE) Study," *American Journal of Preventative Medicine* 14, no. 4 (May 1998): 245–258, doi:10.1016/s0749-3797(98)00017-8.

35. David Finkelhor and Richard Ormrod, "Characteristics of Crimes Against Juveniles," *Juvenile Justice Bulletin*, NCJ179034 (Washington, DC: U.S. Government Printing Office, June 2000), 1–11, scholars.unh.edu/cgi/viewcontent.cgi?article=1002&context=ccrc.

36. Howard N. Snyder, *Sexual Assault of Young Children as Reported to Law Enforcement: Victim, Incident and Offender Characteristics*, NCJ 182990 (Washington, DC: U.S. Department of Justice, July 2000), www.ojp.gov/ncjrs/virtual-library/abstracts/sexual-assault-young-children-reported-law-enforcement-victim, 8.

37. "Child Sexual Abuse Statistics," Darkness to Light, www.d2l.org/wp-content/uploads/2017/01/all_statistics_20150619.pdf.

38. Ewlina U. Ochab, "When Is a Girl Ready for Marriage? After Her First Period Says High Court in Pakistan," *Forbes*, May 1, 2020, www.forbes.com/sites/ewelinaochab/2020/03/01/when-is-a-girl-ready-for-marriage-after-her-first-period-says-high-court-in-pakistan/?sh=31c7060b6416.

39. Mais Haddad, "Victims of Rape and Law: How the Laws of the Arab World Protect Rapists, Not Victims," *Jurist*, May 9, 2017, www.jurist.org/commentary/2017/05/mais-haddad-arab-world-laws-protect-the-rapist-not-the-victim/.

40. "Boxed In: Women and Saudi Arabia's Male Guardianship Sys-

tem," Human Rights Watch, July 16, 2016, www.hrw.org/report/2016/07/16/boxed/women-and-saudi-arabias-male-guardianship-system#:~:text=In%20Saudi%20Arabia%2C%20a%20woman's,critical%20decisions%20on%20her%20behalf.

41. "'I Already Bought You': Abuse and Exploitation of Female Migrant Domestic Workers in the United Arab Emirates," Human Rights Watch, October 22, 2014, www.hrw.org/report/2014/10/22/i-already-bought-you/abuse-and-exploitation-female-migrant-domestic-workers.

42. Mary E. John, "Marital Rape Is Rape: Why Modern India Still Won't Accept This," *Indian Express*, May 14, 2022, indianexpress.com/article/opinion/marital-rape-is-rape-why-modern-india-still-wont-accept-this-7913812/.

43. "Nordic Countries: Survivors of Rape Unite to End Impunity for Rapists and Break Barriers to Justice," Amnesty International, press release, April 3, 2019, www.amnesty.org/en/latest/press-release/2019/04/rape-and-sexual-violence-in-nordic-countries-consent-laws/.

44. Sigrún Sif Jóelsdóttir and Grant Wyeth, "The Misogynist Violence of Iceland's Feminist Paradise," *Foreign Policy*, July 15, 2020, foreignpolicy.com/2020/07/15/the-misogynist-violence-of-icelands-feminist-paradise/.

45. "One in Four Women Has Been Raped or Sexually Assaulted," University of Iceland, November 16, 2018, english.hi.is/news/one_in_four_women_has_been_raped_or_sexually_assaulted.

46. European Union Agency for Fundamental Rights, *Violence Against Women: An EU-Wide Survey: Results at a Glance* (Luxembourg: Publications Office of the European Union 2014), fra.europa.eu/sites/default/files/fra-2014-vaw-survey-at-a-glance-oct14_en.pdf.

47. Arsaell Arnarsson, "The Prevalence of Sexual Abuse and Sexual Assault Against Icelandic Adolescents," *Laeknabladid* 102, no. 6 (June 2016): 289–295.

48. Ibid.

49. "Child Sexual Abuse Prevention in Iceland," Blatt Afram, nordan.org/wp-content/uploads/2013/06/Microsoft-PowerPoint-ENSKA_2013-Compatibility-Mode.pdf.

50. For more on Icelandic crime, I recommend the work of Þórdís Elva Þorvaldsdóttir Bachmann, who has become a spokesperson for this problem, and Helgi Gunnlaugsson's book *Wayward Icelanders: Punishment, Boundary Maintenance, and the Creation of Crime* (Madison, WI: University of Wisconsin Press, 2000).

51. World Economic Forum, "Global Gender Gap Index 2015—Rankings," reports.weforum.org/global-gender-gap-report-2015/rankings/.

52. "Burglary," *Crime in the United States 2019*, FBI, ucr.fbi.gov/crime-in-the-u.s/2019/crime-in-the-u.s.-2019/topic-pages/burglary.

53. "Burglary," *Crime in the United States 2019*.

54. Between 2011 and 2020, roughly 63 percent of all home burglaries in the United States occurred during the day. "Burglary Offense Analysis," Crime Data Explorer, FBI, crime-data-explorer.fr.cloud.gov/pages/explorer/crime/property-crime (accessed May 12, 2022).

55. See, for example, Angela Brandt, "FBI Assisting Investigation into High-End Home Burglaries in Area, including Poway and 4S Ranch," *San Diego Tribune*, January 21, 2022, www.sandiegouniontribune.com/pomerado-news/news/story/2022-01-21/fbi-investigating-spree-of-high-end-burglaries-including-poway.

56. Shannan Catalano, *Victimization During Household Burglary*, NCJ 227379 (U.S. Department of Justice, September 2010), bjs.ojp.gov/content/pub/pdf/vdhb.pdf.

57. Catalano, *Victimization During Household Burglary*.

58. Much of this confusion extends into media coverage of "home invasions." Reginald A. Byron et al., "US Newspapers' Portrayals of Home Invasion Crime," *Howard Journal of Crime and Justice* 57, no. 2 (June 2018): 250–27.

59. In response to the Petit family murders, Connecticut Congressman Chris Murphy announced a legislative initiative to make home invasion a federal crime prosecutable in federal court. "Murphy Announces Federal Legislative Package to Address Home Invasion Crimes, Parole and Probation," press release, March 26, 2012.

60. Catalano, *Victimization During Household Burglary*, 2.

61. Some will even dress up and hold a clipboard with a random survey they've printed off the Internet. Kyle Iboshi, "We Asked 86 Burglars How They Broke into Homes," *KGW8*, December 3, 2019 (updated), www.kgw.com/article/news/investigations/we-asked-86-burglars-how-they-broke-into-homes/344213396.

Chapter 11: The Stealth Predator

1. George Simon, *In Sheep's Clothing: Understanding and Dealing with Manipulative People* (Little Rock, AR: Parkhurst Brothers, 2010) and *Character Disturbance: The Phenomenon of Our Age* (Little Rock, AR: Parkhurst Brothers, 2011).

2. A character disorder is an extreme form of a character disturbance.

Simon writes,

> Character disturbance actually exists along two spectra. One spectrum reflects the degree to which a person is purely character disturbed as opposed to having some degree of neurosis. We define character disturbance as the relative absence of neurosis. And neurosis, simply stated, is the ability to experience inner anguish and anxiety as a result of guilt and shame (i.e. conscience). . . . A person's character disturbance can also rise to the level of what's been called a *disorder*. Over the years, professionals have debated just how to best define a disorder of personality and/or character. We all have distinctive, preferred ways of relating to others. And those distinctive "styles" of relating define our personalities. But when our very manner of relating is in itself the source of problems, we call it a personality disturbance. A style of relating to others so rigid, so ingrained, so extreme in its manifestation, and so deviant from the norm of a culture that it severely and negatively impacts a person's ability to function well has traditionally qualified as a disorder.

George Simon, "The Character Disturbance Spectrum," May 6, 2017, www.drgeorgesimon.com/the-character-disturbance-spectrum/. I use the term character-disordered individuals with this distinction in mind.

3. American Psychiatric Association, *Diagnostic and Statistical Manual of Mental Disorders* (DSM-V). For a helpful summary of personality disorders, see Mayo Clinic Staff, "Personality Disorders," Mayo Clinic, www.mayoclinic.org/diseases-conditions/personality-disorders/symptoms-causes/syc-20354463; and Kristalyn Salters-Pedneault, "Cluster B Personality Disorders," *Verywell Mind*, August 28, 2020, www.verywellmind.com/the-cluster-b-personality-disorders-425429.

4. Simon makes this point in the introduction of *Character Disturbance*.

5. Nigel Warburton and David Edmonds, eds., *Philosophy Bites Again* (Oxford: Oxford University Press, 2014). See specifically the editors' interview with Daniel Dennett in chapter 13, "Daniel Dennett on Free Will Worth Wanting," 132.

6. For more on this distinction, see Marcia Sirota, "The Difference Between Being Nice and Being Kind," *Huffington Post*, November 21, 2016, www.huffpost.com/archive/ca/entry/too-nice_b_946956.

7. Covert aggression is not always recognized as a separate type of aggression because it is not expressed violently or physically. Indeed, many researchers make a distinction only between reactive and proactive aggression. See, for example, Julie A. Hubbard et al., "Reactive and Proactive Aggression in Childhood and Adolescence: Precursors, Outcomes, Processes, Experiences, and Measurement," *Journal of Personality* 78, no. 1 (February 2010): 95–118, doi:10.1111/j.1467-6494.2009.00610.x. For the purposes of self-defense, however, it's important to identify covert aggression as a separate and unique category because it is the primary way character-disordered individuals manipulate

and control others. Recognizing and freeing ourselves from this manipulation and control is a major way to protect ourselves and improve our safety, especially with regard to threats from family members and acquaintances. George Simon, "Recognizing Covert-Aggression," drgeorgesimon.com, February 15, 2013, www.drgeorgesimon.com/recognizing-covert-aggression/.

8. Both reactive and proactive aggression is seen in chimpanzees. Richard W. Wrangham, "Two Types of Aggression in Human Evolution," *PNAS* 115, no. 2 (2017): 245–253, doi.org/10.1073/pnas.1713611115.

9. Although I am not aware of any study that specifically examines what percentage of violence is based on reactive aggression and what percentage is based on proactive aggression, we can make this inference based on other quantitative and qualitative research, whether related to the circumstances in which violent crime is committed, the relationship between offenders and victims, the location of violent crimes, and related types of data. For more, see the discussion in chapter 13 on the methods and motives of predators.

10. Laura A. Baker et al., "Behavioral Genetics: The Science of Antisocial Behavior," *Law and Contemporary Problems* 69, no 1–2 (2006): 7–46.

11. When it comes to humans, Matt Ridley makes the point that both nature and nurture explain human behavior but argues that the nature-versus-nurture question is the wrong one to ask. Rather, he promotes a nature-via-nurture view, maintaining that our genes are designed to take their cues from nature. Matt Ridley, *The Agile Gene: How Nature Turns on Nurture* (New York: Perennial, 2003), 3–4.

12. For more on the ethical, social, and legal considerations when asking such questions and conducting such research, see Colleen M. Berryessa, "Ethical, Legal and Social Issues Surrounding Research on Genetic Contributions to Anti-Social Behavior," *Aggression and Violent Behavior* 18, no. 6 (November–December 2013), doi:10.1016/j.avb.2013.07.011.

13. Baker et al., "Behavioral Genetics." See also Laura A. Baker et al., "Genetic and Environmental Bases of Childhood Antisocial Behavior: A Multi-Informant Twin Study," *Journal of Abnormal Psychology* 116, no. 2 (May 2007): 219–235., doi:10.1037/0021-843X.116.2.219.

14. For a quick overview of these parts of the brain, see Olivia Guy-Evans, "Limbic System: Definition, Parts, Functions, and Location," *Simply Psychology*, April 22, 2021, www.simplypsychology.org/limbic-system.html; and "You're Your Brain: Prefrontal Cortex," neuroscientificallychallenged.com/posts/know-your-brain-prefrontal-cortex.

15. Adrian Raine et al., "Reduced Prefrontal Gray Matter Volume and Reduced Autonomic Activity in Antisocial Personality Disorder," *Archives of General Psychiatry* 57, no. 2 (2000): 119–127, doi:10.1001/archpsyc.57.2.119.

16. Kim M. Cecil et al., "Decreased Brain Volume in Adults with Child-hood Lead Exposure," *PLOS Medicine* 5, no. 5 (May 2008): e112, doi:10.1371/journal.pmed.0050112. Of particular note, there's increasing evidence to sug-gest that the so-called lead-crime hypothesis is correct—that higher levels of lead exposure in children correlate with higher future crime rates, including homicide rates. For a discussion of those studies, see Jennifer L. Doleac, "New Evidence That Lead Exposure Increases Crime," Brookings, June 1, 2017, www.brookings.edu/blog/up-front/2017/06/01/new-evidence-that-lead-expo-sure-increases-crime/.

17. Kenneth Abernathy et al., "Alcohol and the Prefrontal Cortex," *In-ternational Review of Neurobiology* 91 (2010): 289–320. doi:10.1016/S0074-7742(10)91009-X.

18. S. W. Anderson, "Impairment of Social and Moral Behavior Related to Early Damage in Human Prefrontal Cortex," *Nature Neuroscience* 2, no. 11 (November 1999): 1032–7, doi:10.1038/14833.

19. M. C. Brower, "Neuropsychiatry of Frontal Lobe Dysfunction in Vi-olent and Criminal Behaviour: A Critical Review," *Journal of Neurology, Neuro-surgery & Psychiatry* 71 (2001): 720–726, dx.doi.org/10.1136/jnnp.71.6.720.

20. Adrian Raine, *The Anatomy of Violence: The Biological Roots of Crime* (New York: Vintage Books, 2013), 67–68. See also Michael Shermer, "Search-ing for the True Sources of Crime," *Scientific American*, June 1, 2013, www.sci-entificamerican.com/article/searching-for-true-sources-crime/.

21. Alexandra Junewicz and Stephen Bates Billick, "Preempting the Development of Antisocial Behavior and Psychopathic Traits," *Journal of the American Academy of Psychiatry and the Law* (January 2021), doi.org/10.29158/JAAPL.200060-20.

22. Steven Pinker, *The Blank Slate: The Modern Denial of Human Nature* (New York: Penguin Books, 2003).

23. Junewicz and Billick, "Preempting the Development of Antisocial Be-havior and Psychopathic Traits"; and Jean R. Séguin, "The Frontal Lobe and Aggression," *European Journal of Developmental Psychology* 6, no. 1 (2009): 100–119. doi:10.1080/17405620701669871.

24. For more, see George Simon, *In Sheep's Clothing* and *Character Distur-bance*.

25. Strains and sprains of arms and feet are the most common diagnoses for BJJ practitioners who have gone to an emergency room for treatment of a training injury. Caroline Stephenson and Matthew E. Robinson, "Brazilian Jiu Jitsu, Judo, and Mixed Martial Arts Injuries Presenting to United States Emer-gency Departments, 2008–2015," *Journal of Primary Prevention* 39 (October 2018): 421–435. Unlike many combat and contact sports, the risk of severe head

trauma due to direct head impact in Brazilian Jiu-Jitsu is low. However, some degree of caution is advised when training certain throws because rapid acceleration or deceleration of the body has been known to produce concussions. Frank Patterson and Matthew Michael Antonucci, "Brazilian Jiu-Jitsu–Related Post-Concussion Symptoms Ameliorated with Neurorehabilitation," *Neurology* 98, no. 1 (January 4, 2022), 525, doi:10.1212/01.WNL.0000801972.10881.A4. In extreme cases, severe brain hemorrhaging can result from excessive throwing. There have been highly publicized cases from Asia in which Judo students died after being thrown repeatedly in class by coaches or older students as punishment. Such cases of abuse generally lead to criminal charges. Regardless, all students of combat sports should be aware of the signs and symptoms of a concussion, and repetitive practice of high-impact throws should be limited for children and adolescents and anyone who does not know how to execute a proper breakfall. See, for example, "Taiwan Boy Thrown 27 Times During Judo Class Taken Off Life Support," *BBC News*, June 30, 2021, www.bbc.com/news/world-asia-57661414.

Chapter 12: The Traits and Characteristics of Predators

1.   Gavin de Becker, *The Gift of Fear: And Other Survival Signals That Protect Us from Violence* (New York: Back Bay Books, 2021), xiv.

2.   This assumes that the first *Homo sapiens* arose 300,000 years ago and that there is a new generation every twenty-five years. For a timeline, see Brian Handwerk, "An Evolutionary Timeline of Homo Sapiens," *Smithsonian Magazine*, February 2, 2021, www.smithsonianmag.com/science-nature/essential-timeline-understanding-evolution-homo-sapiens-180976807/. For an illustrated tour through our evolutionary history, see the chapter titled "Who Was the First Person?" in Richard Dawkins, *The Magic of Reality: How We Know What's Really True*, illus. Dave McKean (New York: Free Press, 2012).

3.   In Rickson's hometown of Rio de Janeiro, the threat from boys and child gangs is especially acute. Referring to the highly acclaimed Brazilian 2002 film *City of God*, which depicts the brutality of Rio's urban violence and the horrors of life in child gangs, a teenager from one of the poorest areas of the city remarked: "It just shows what it used to be like. Now it's much more violent." Alex Bellos, "Where Children Rule with Guns," *Guardian*, January 18, 2003, www.theguardian.com/world/2003/jan/19/brazil.alexbellos.

4.   "The proportion of young men aged 15–34 in fact strongly predicts the incidence of murder, rape, assault, and robbery across all societies of the world." Satoshi Kanazawa and Mary C. Still, "Why Men Commit Crimes (and Why They Desist)," *Sociological Theory* 18, no. 3, 434–447 (2000): 443. This universal constant implies an evolutionary or biological explanation for elements one and

two. Element three assumes the society has a functioning law enforcement and judicial system.

5. The average IQ of chronic adult offenders is 85, or one standard deviation below the mean. For chronic juvenile offenders, it is 92, or half a standard deviation below the mean. See J. Mitchell Miller, ed., *21st Century Criminology: A Reference Handbook*, vol. 1 (Thousand Oaks, CA: SAGE, 2009), 95; and Lee Ellis and Anthony Walsh, "Crime, Delinquency and Intelligence: A Review of the Worldwide Literature," in *The Scientific Study of General Intelligence: Tribute to Arthur R. Jensen*, ed. Helmuth Nyborg, 343–365 (Oxford: Pergamon, 2003). See also Thomas Frisell, "Is the Association between General Cognitive Ability and Violent Crime Caused by Family-Level Confounders?" *PLoS One* 7, no. 7 (2012): e41783, doi:10.1371/journal.pone.0041783.

6. Scott Michels, "Bank Robbery a 'Loser Crime,'" *ABC News*, February 11, 2009, abcnews.go.com/TheLaw/story?id=3432084.

7. Ten of the thirteen people who died in the United States during a bank robbery in 2006 were perpetrators. None were customers. "Bank Crime Statistics 2006," FBI, www.fbi.gov/stats-services/publications/bank-crime-statistics-2006.

8. Jason Koebler, "What You Should Know Before Robbing a Bank," *U.S. News and World Report*, June 11, 2012, www.usnews.com/news/articles/2012/06/11/what-you-should-know-before-robbing-a-bank.

9. See Kelly Dedel, *Drive-by Shootings*, Problem-Oriented Guides for Police Problem Specific Guides Series, no. 47 (U.S. Department of Justice, March 2007), cops.usdoj.gov/RIC/Publications/cops-p116-pub.pdf.

10. Steven D. Levitt and Stephen J. Dubner, *Freakonomics: A Rogue Economist Explores the Hidden Side of Everything* (New York: Harper Perennial, 2009), 79–104. Much of this chapter is based on the eye-raising field research of Sudhir Venkatesh. Venkatesh has written about his experience and findings in *Gang Leader for a Day: A Rogue Sociologist Takes to the Streets* (New York: Penguin Books, 2009).

11. Roughly one in three children is born to a single mother in the United States, and there are roughly three single-mother families for every single-father family. Notably, adolescents in single-father families are more likely to be delinquent than those in single-mother families, but this is believed to be due to single mothers exerting stronger direct and indirect controls. Single fathers are typically also older and less educated than single mothers. See Stephen Demuth and Susan L. Brown, "Family Structure, Family Processes, and Adolescent Delinquency: The Significance of Parental Absence Versus Parental Gender," *Journal of Research in Crime and Delinquency* 41, no. 1 (February 2004): 58–81.

12. Cicero Wilson, "Economic Shifts That Will Impact Crime Control

and Community Revitalization," in *What Can the Federal Government Do to Decrease Crime and Revitalize Communities*, NCJ 172210 (U.S. Department of Justice, October 1998), 11, www.ojp.gov/pdffiles/172210.pdf; and Gretchen Livingston, "The Rise of Single Fathers," Pew Research Center, July 2, 2013, www.pewresearch.org/social-trends/2013/07/02/the-rise-of-single-fathers/.

13. Kay Hymowitz, "The Real, Complex Connection Between Single-Parent Families and Crime," *Atlantic*, December 3, 2012, www.theatlantic.com/sexes/archive/2012/12/the-real-complex-connection-between-single-parent-families-and-crime/265860/.

14. Chris Knoester and Dana L. Hayne, "Community Context, Social Integration into Family, and Youth Violence," *Journal of Marriage and Family* 67, no. 3 (August 2005): 767–780, doi:10.1111/j.1741-3737.2005.00168.x.

15. He first wrote this in 1965 in the aftermath of the Watts riots, and he said it again on the Senate floor in 1992 in the aftermath of the Los Angeles riots. He is making the point that crime, unrest, and disorder stem from issues of class, not race. "Verbatim," *Washington Post*, May 18, 1992, www.washingtonpost.com/archive/politics/1992/05/18/verbatim/5f2908ed-47ae-4044-93af-0631dcafe5da/.

16. Crime rates within racial and ethnic groups also change over time. Barry Latzer, *The Rise and Fall of Violent Crime in America* (New York: Encounter Books, 2016), 266.

17. For good statistics on "nonmarital childbearing" between 1970 and 2016, see National Center for Health Statistics, *Health, United States, 2017* (Hyattsville, MD: U.S. Department of Health and Human Services, 2017), table 4, www.cdc.gov/nchs/data/hus/2017/004.pdf. For more recent statistics by U.S. state, see "Percent of Babies Born to Unmarried Mothers by State," National Center for Health Statistics, CDC, www.cdc.gov/nchs/pressroom/sosmap/unmarried/unmarried.htm.

18. For murder rate by U.S. state, see "Homicide Mortality by State," National Center for Health Statistics, CDC, www.cdc.gov/nchs/pressroom/sosmap/homicide_mortality/homicide.htm. For the murder rate in New Orleans, see Francesca Mirabile and Daniel Nass, "New FBI Data Is In: Murder Rates in U.S. Cities, Ranked," *Trace*, April 26, 2018 (updated September 28, 2021), www.thetrace.org/2018/04/highest-murder-rates-us-cities-list/.

19. For the percentage of births to unmarried mothers by U.S. state in 2020, see table 6 in "Births: Final Data for 2019," *National Vital Statistics Report* 70, no. 2 (March 23, 2021), 21, www.cdc.gov/nchs/data/nvsr/nvsr70/nvsr70-02-508.pdf. For the study on birth rates within New Orleans, see *Child and Family Health in New Orleans* (New Orleans Health Department, December 2013), 26, 125, www.nola.gov/getattachment/Health/Data-and-Publications/

Child-and-Family-Health-in-New-Orleans-December-2013.pdf/.

20. In a 2013 "No Talking Points" segment with chyron that read "Black People. Clean Up Your Act!" CNN host Don Lemon made a direct "tough-love" appeal to black men, offering five commonsensical ways they (or anyone) could help fix the problems plaguing their communities, including violent crime. His number one recommendation was this: "Just because you can have a baby, it doesn't mean you should. Especially without planning for one or getting married first. More than 72 percent of children in the African-American community are born out of wedlock. That means absent fathers. And the studies show that lack of a male role model is an express train right to prison and the cycle continues." This is a message everyone should hear, no matter their race, but if you have any questions about how his comments were received in certain circles, you can find a brief summary here: Tommy Christopher, "Tweetnado: MSN-BC's Goldie Taylor Calls Don Lemon a 'Turn Coat Mofo,'" *Mediaite*, July 27, 2013, www.mediaite.com/online/tweetnado-msnbcs-goldie-taylor-calls-don-lemon-a-turn-coat-mofo/. For the full clip, see Evan McMurry, "CNN's Don Lemon Backs Up Bill O'Reilly: 'He Doesn't Go Far Enough' in Criticizing Black Culture," *Mediaite*, July 27, 2013, www.mediaite.com/tv/cnns-don-lemon-backs-up-bill-oreilly-he-doesnt-go-far-enough-in-criticizing-black-culture/. Incidentally, despite the ugly backlash, Lemon's statement about out-of-wedlock births was deemed true by *Politifact*. Louis Jacobson, "CNN's Don Lemon Says More Than 72 Percent of African-American Births Are Out of Wedlock," *Politifact*, July 29, 2013, www.politifact.com/factchecks/2013/jul/29/don-lemon/cnns-don-lemon-says-more-72-percent-african-americ/.

21. For every 10 out-of-wedlock births per 1,000 births, there is a 5 percent increase in future murder rates. Most of the increase in murder rates during the 1970s and 1980s can be explained by this model. Todd D. Kendall and Robert Tamura, "Unmarried Fertility, Crime, and Social Stigma," *Journal of Law and Economics* 53, no. 1 (February 2010), doi.org/10.1086/596116.

22. As noted, I use the terms interchangeably, though some experts make a distinction between the two—namely, that psychopaths lack a conscience, meaning they feel no remorse, whereas sociopaths might feel some. Kara Mayer Robinson, "Sociopath v. Psychopath: What's the Difference?" *WebMD*, February 14, 2022, www.webmd.com/mental-health/features/sociopath-psychopath-difference.

23. The callous and unemotional traits for which psychopaths are known are evident at a young age. Essi Viding, "Evidence for Substantial Genetic Risk for Psychopathy in 7-Year-Olds," *Journal of Child Psychiatry and Psychology* 46, no. 6 (June 2005): 592–7, doi:10.1111/j.1469-7610.2004.00393.x.

24. Kent A. Kiehl and Joshua W. Buckholtz, "Inside the Mind of a Psychopath," *Scientific American Mind*, September/October 2010, 25, available at:

cicn.vanderbilt.edu/images/news/psycho.pdf.

25. For a list of jobs psychopaths might be particularly drawn toward, see Michael Arntfield, "The Preferred Jobs of Serial Killers and Psychopaths," *Conversation*, May 8, 2018, theconversation.com/the-preferred-jobs-of-serial-killers-and-psychopaths-96173. See also Scott O. Lilienfeld and Ashley Watts, "Not All Psychopaths Are Criminals—Some Psychopathic Traits Are Actually Linked to Success," *Conversation*, January 26, 2016, theconversation.com/not-all-psychopaths-are-criminals-some-psychopathic-traits-are-actually-linked-to-success-51282.

26. Kiehl and Buckholtz, "Inside the Mind of a Psychopath," 24, 27.

27. To score yourself on the original checklist, visit psychology-tools.com/test/pcl-22.

28. Kiehl and Buckholtz, "Inside the Mind of a Psychopath," 25.

29. Robert J. Morton, ed., "Serial Murder: Multi-Disciplinary Perspectives for Investigators," Behavioral Analysis Unit, FBI, www.fbi.gov/stats-services/publications/serial-murder.

30. Raine, *The Anatomy of Violence*, 80.

31. Robert D. Hare, *Without a Conscience: The Disturbing World of the Psychopaths Among Us* (New York: Guilford Press, 1993).

32. James Graham, "Modern Life Has Made It Easier for Serial Killers to Thrive," *Atlantic*, October 2019, www.theatlantic.com/magazine/archive/2019/10/are-serial-killers-more-common-than-we-think/596647/.

33. See Wesley Yang's challenging essay about the deadliest school shooter in U.S. history titled "The Face of Sueng-Hui Cho," in which he draws parallels between his own experiences as a Korean American and that of the Korean American mass murderer Cho, who killed thirty-two people at Virginia Tech. Wesley Yang, *The Souls of Yellow Folk* (New York: W. W. Norton, 2018), 3–28.

34. Michael S. Rosenwald, "The Twisted Minds of School Shooters, and the Anguished Man Who Studies Them," *Washington Post*, July 1, 2016, www.washingtonpost.com/local/the-twisted-minds-of-school-shooters-and-the-anguished-man-who-studies-them/2016/06/30/44987378-2e4e-11e6-9b37-42985f6a265c_story.html.

35. Peter Langman, "Elliot Rodger: A Psychotic Psychopath?" *Psychology Today*, May 28, 2014, www.psychologytoday.com/us/blog/keeping-kids-safe/201405/elliot-rodger-psychotic-psychopath.

36. For more, see Peter Langman, *School Shooters: Understanding High School, College, and Adult Perpetrators* (Lanham, MD: Rowman & Littlefield, 2015). See also Robin M. Kowalski, "School Shootings: What We Know about Them, and What We Can Do to Prevent Them," Brookings, January 26, 2022,

www.brookings.edu/blog/brown-center-chalkboard/2022/01/26/school-shoot-ings-what-we-know-about-them-and-what-we-can-do-to-prevent-them/.

37. David Wilson et al., *Serial Kills and the Phenomenon of Serial Murder: A Student Textbook* (Hampshire, UK: Waterside Press, 2015), 43.

38. "Our findings bring new hope for resocialisation of convicted Mafia members, because they showed significant antisocial traits but they maintained a capacity for emotional connection and greater likelihood of engaging with training and resocialisation programmes than other imprisoned offenders in Italy." Adriano Schimmenti, "Mafia and Psychopathy," *Criminal Behavior and Mental Health* 24, no. 5 (December 2014): 321–31, doi:10.1002/cbm.1902.

39. Peter Maas, *Underboss: Sammy the Bull Gravano's Story of Life in the Mafia* (New York: HarperCollins, 1997).

40. You can find his podcast at sammythebull.com. His YouTube channel is titled Salvatore Sammy the Bull Gravano, www.youtube.com/channel/UC-2qsQ8pUNhhANzMIy6kha2w.

41. Recalling his first killing, he remarked, "Am I supposed to feel re-morse? Aren't I supposed to feel something? But I felt nothing like remorse. If anything, I felt good." Maas, *Underboss*, 36.

42. Both even have their own genre of movie. See Jim Vorel, "The Best Se-rial Killer Movies," *Ranker*, July 29, 2021, www.ranker.com/list/best-serial-kill-er-movies/ranker-film; and "The Best Assassin Movies," *Ranker*, May 14, 2021, www.ranker.com/crowdranked-list/the-best-assassin-movies.

43. In 2019, there were 39,389 firearm deaths in the United States based on verified data. Of those deaths, 23,941 were by suicide, and 417 occurred in mass shootings. A mass shooting is defined here as an incident in which four or more people are wounded or killed. Gun Violence Archive, www.gunvio-lencearchive.org (accessed May 12, 2022).

44. Gun Violence Archive, "Past Summary Ledgers," www.gunviolencear-chive.org/past-tolls (accessed May 12, 2022).

45. Gun Violence Archive, "Mass Shootings," www.gunviolencearchive.org/mass-shooting?sort=desc&order=%23%20Killed (accessed May 12, 2022).

46. An active shooter incident is defined as one or more gunmen actively trying to kill people in a populated area. See "Active Shooter Incidents in the United States in 2021," U.S. Department of Justice, 2, 4, www.fbi.gov/file-re-pository/active-shooter-incidents-in-the-us-2021-052422.pdf/view.

47. Recommendations on the management and treatment of mental health issues fall well outside the scope of this book and my expertise, but for a first-person account from the mother of an infamous teenage mass murderer in which she shares some of the signs and opportunities she missed, see Sue

Klebold, *A Mother's Reckoning: Living in the Aftermath of Tragedy* (New York: Crown, 2016). When asked after the Columbine shootings what she would say to her son, Dylan, if she could, she responded, "I would ask him to forgive me, for being his mother and never knowing what was inside his head, for not being able to help him, for not being the person that he could confide in" (p. xxi).

48. Komisarjevsky's attorneys made the claim that this was Hayes's intention. Judy Hails, *Criminal Evidence*, 8th ed. (Stamford, CT: Cengage Learning, 2014), 112.

Chapter 13: The Methods and Motives of Predators

1. For the purposes of this discussion, I'm using this popular framing, but the necessary elements of a crime from a legal standpoint are: criminal act (*actus reus*), criminal intent (*mens rea*), concurrence, and causation. For more on the legal elements of crime, see Matthew Lippman, *Contemporary Criminal Law: Concepts, Cases, and Controversies*, 5th ed. (Thousand Oaks, CA: Sage, 2019), especially chapters 4 and 5.

2. For the statistics on means of death, see "Murder Victims by Weapon," Crime Data Explorer, FBI, crime-data-explorer.fr.cloud.gov/pages/explorer/crime/shr (accessed May 12, 2022); and "Expanded Homicide Data Table 4," Crime Data in the United States 2016, FBI, ucr.fbi.gov/crime-in-the-u.s/2016/crime-in-the-u.s.-2016/tables/expanded-homicide-data-table-4.xls.

3. More than 32,000 Americans die each year from falls. For statistics on falls, see the wealth of information available at "Keep on Your Feet—Preventing Older Adult Falls," Injury and Prevention Control, CDC, www.cdc.gov/injury/features/older-adult-falls/index.html.

4. They accounted for 77 percent in 2020. Neil MacFarquhar, "Murders Spiked in 2020 in Cities Across the United States," *New York Times*, September 27, 2021.

5. *Gun Crime in the Age Group 18–20*, NCJ 203924 (U.S. Department of Justice, June 1999), www.ojp.gov/ncjrs/virtual-library/abstracts/gun-crime-age-group-18-20.

6. "QuickStats: Rates of Firearm-Related Deaths Among Persons Aged ≥15 Years, by Selected Intent and Age Group—National Vital Statistics System, United States, 2019," *MMWR Morbidity and Mortality Weekly Report* 70, no. 365 (2021), doi:dx.doi.org/10.15585/mmwr.mm7010a5.

7. See P. J. Brantingham et al., "Is Gang Violent Crime More Contagious than Non-Gang Violent Crime?" *Journal of Quantitative Criminology* 37 (2021): 953–977.

8. For the purposes of these figures, a gang-related homicide refers to a murder in which the victim and/or perpetrator were gang members. Arlen Egley, Jr. et al., *Highlights of the 2012 National Youth Gang Survey* (U.S. Department of Justice, December 2014), ojjdp.ojp.gov/sites/g/files/xyckuh176/files/pubs/248025.pdf. An initial analysis of the data put the percentage at 13 percent. "National Youth Gang Survey Analysis: Measuring the Extent of Gang Problems," National Gang Center, nationalgangcenter.ojp.gov/survey-analysis/measuring-the-extent-of-gang-problems.

9. For the overall U.S. murder rate and U.S. cities ranked by murder rate, see Mirabile and Nass, "New FBI Data Is In."

10. Jessica Learish and Elisha Fieldstadt, "Gun Map: Ownership by State," *CBS News*, April 14, 2022, www.cbsnews.com/pictures/gun-ownership-rates-by-state/.

11. The United Nations Office on Drugs and Crime didn't report data for all countries in 2020, including some that would otherwise be at or near the top of the list, such as El Salvador, Venezuela, and Lesotho. For the United States, the UNODC reports a homicide rate of 6.28 per 100,000, which is less than the 6.5 per 100,000 reported by the FBI. "Homicide Country Data," UNODC, dataunodc.un.org/content/homicide-country-data (accessed May 12, 2022).

12. There are crime maps available online for most major cities. For example, to track patterns of criminal activity across the five boroughs of New York City (by precinct), see NYC Crime Map, maps.nyc.gov/crime/; for an official homicide map of Chicago, see "Homicide Map," City of Chicago, data.cityofchicago.org/Public-Safety/Homicide-Map/53tx-phyr; and for a nonofficial murder map of London, see "London Murder Map 2022," murdermap, www.murdermap.co.uk/maps/london-murder-map-2022/.

13. Lawrence W. Sherman, "Cooling the Hot Spots of Homicide: A Plan for Action," in *What Can the Federal Government Do to Decrease Crime and Revitalize Communities*, NCJ 172210 (U.S. Department of Justice, October 1998), 41, www.ojp.gov/pdffiles/172210.pdf.

14. Daniel Trotta, "U.S. Gun Deaths Surged 35% in 2020, Higher for Black People—CDC," *Reuters*, May 10, 2022, https://www.reuters.com/world/us/us-gun-deaths-surged-35-2020-higher-black-people-cdc-2022-05-10/.

15. The fact that people who commit crime tend to be victims of crime presents a unique problem for the police. For a fascinating discussion about this, see F. T. Green, "Victims Are Often Criminals, and That Is a Paradox American Policing Can't Solve," *Outline*, August 6, 2019, theoutline.com/post/7752/victim-offender-overlap. See also Peter Hermann, "Baltimore Murder Victims, Suspects Share Ties to Criminal Justice System," *Baltimore Sun*, January 2, 2012, www.baltimoresun.com/news/bs-xpm-2012-01-02-bs-md-ci-homicide-

analysis-20120102-story.html.

16. This roughly aligns with the loathing, lust, and loot categories as outlined by sociologist Peter Morrall. He adds a fourth, love, to include mercy killings. Peter Morrall, "Murder and Society: Why Commit Murder?" *Criminal Justice Matters*, no. 66 (Winter 2006/7), 36, www.crimeandjustice.org.uk/sites/crimeandjustice.org.uk/files/09627250608553401.pdf. Motives for serial killers are generally more complex and more difficult to determine. See section 5 in Morton, "Serial Murder: Multi-Disciplinary Perspectives for Investigators," www.fbi.gov/stats-services/publications/serial-murder#five.

17. A sense of "disrespect" likely led to one of the most infamous racially motivated murders in U.S. history. Wade Goodwyn, "A Brutal Lynching and a Possible Confession, Decades Later," *NPR*, October 27, 2018, www.npr.org/2018/10/27/661048613/a-brutal-lynching-and-a-possible-confession-decades-later. For other examples, see Steve Fry, "'Mean-Mugging' Leads to Shooting, Death of Woman in Her Nearby Yard, Witnesses Testify," *WIBW*, December 18, 2020, www.wibw.com/2020/12/18/mean-mugging-leads-to-shooting-death-of-woman-in-her-nearby-yard-witnesses-testify/; Ariana Kellend, "Dale Porter Killed over Making Fun, Disrespecting Vikings Motorcycle Club, Says Crown," *CBC News*, February 6, 2019, www.cbc.ca/news/canada/newfoundland-labrador/al-potter-crown-opening-statement-1.5007867; and Dan Rodricks, "The Insanity of Baltimore's 'Disrespect' Killings," *Baltimore Sun*, January 18, 2014, www.baltimoresun.com/maryland/bs-xpm-2014-01-18-bs-md-rodricks-0119-20140118-16-story.html.

18. "2011 Chicago Murder Analysis," Research and Development Division, Chicago Police Department, 27, home.chicagopolice.org/wp-content/uploads/2014/12/2011-Murder-Report.pdf. As it turns out, 2011 marked a relatively low point in Chicago's recent murder rate. In 2020, there were 986 murders in Chicago. Among the victims was a three-year-old boy named Mehki James, who was riding in his dad's car. Sam Kelly, "3-Year-Old Fatally Shot While Riding in Car with Father in Austin," *Chicago Sun-Times*, June 20, 2020, chicago.suntimes.com/crime/2020/6/20/21297973/mekhi-james-austin-3-year-old-shot-killed-man-wounded-central-gun-violence. In 2021, over a thousand people were murdered in Chicago. More than 90 percent of the victims were shot, 90 percent were male, and 80 percent were black, while eighty-six of the victims were under the age of eighteen and twelve were under the age of ten. Cook County Government, "Cook County Medical Examiner's Office Registers Over 1,000 Homicides in 2021," November 30, 2021, www.cookcountyil.gov/news/cook-county-medical-examiners-office-registers-over-1000-homicides-2021.

19. "Disputes Driving Up Homicide Rate," *UPI*, February 12, 2006, www.upi.com/Top_News/2006/02/12/Disputes-driving-up-homicide-rate/5926113 9794019/?ur3=1.

20. Kate Zernike, "Violent Crime Rising Sharply in Some Cities," *New York Times*, February 12, 2006, www.nytimes.com/2006/02/12/us/violent-crime-rising-sharply-in-some-cities.html.

21. "Expanded Homicide Offense Characteristics in the United States," Crime Data Explorer, FBI, crime-data-explorer.fr.cloud.gov/pages/explorer/crime/shr.

22. Ibid.

23. "Expanded Homicide Data Table 6," *Crime in the United States 2018*, FBI, ucr.fbi.gov/crime-in-the-u.s/2018/crime-in-the-u.s.-2018/tables/expanded-homicide-data-table-6.xls.

24. Relevant data in the CDC Wonder system goes back only to 1999, so I could not verify the numbers for earlier decades, but between 1999 and 2020, 275,446 people were killed by firearms in the United States. Of those killed, 154,600 were black and 113,242 were white. "Underlying Cause of Death, 1999–2020 Request," CDC Wonder, wonder.cdc.gov/controller/datarequest/D76.

25. Melonie Heron, "Deaths: Leading Causes for 2017," National Vital Statistics Reports (U.S. Department of Health and Human Services, June 24, 2019), 27, 28, 34, 35, www.cdc.gov/nchs/data/nvsr/nvsr68/nvsr68_06-508.pdf.

26. These are my calculations based on data from appendix table 11 in Rachel E. Morgan and Alexandra Thompson, *Criminal Victimization, 2020*, NCJ 301775 (U.S. Department of Justice, October 2021), 21, https://bjs.ojp.gov/sites/g/files/xyckuh236/files/media/document/cv20.pdf, and from the estimates in table 5 in Rachel E. Morgan and Alexandra Thompson, *Criminal Victimization, 2020—Supplemental Statistical Tables*, NCJ 303936 (U.S. Department of Justice, February 2022), 6, https://bjs.ojp.gov/content/pub/pdf/cv20sst.pdf. It is important to note that these estimates are based on a self-report survey in which respondents report crimes they have experienced. As the survey includes data on crimes not reported to the police, including various forms of assault, the survey estimates are higher than the violent crime figures typically cited in official law enforcement records.

27. These are my calculations based on data in table 5 in Morgan and Thompson, *Criminal Victimization, 2020—Supplemental Statistical Tables*, 6.

28. Morgan and Thompson, *Criminal Victimization, 2020—Supplemental Statistical Tables*, 6. These figures change from year to year, but the share of victimization across races has been fairly consistent for most of the past decade. See, for example, *Race and Hispanic Origin of Victims and Offenders*, 2012–15, NCJ-250747 (U.S. Department of Justice, October 2017), 2, https://bjs.ojp.gov/content/pub/pdf/rhovo1215.pdf.

29. See, for example, "Donald Trump Stated on November 22, 2015 in

a Tweet: Says Crime Statistics Show Blacks Kill 81 Percent of White Homicide Victims," *Politifact*, June 8, 2020 (updated), www.politifact.com/fact-checks/2015/nov/23/donald-trump/trump-tweet-blacks-white-homicide-victims/.

30. This is true whether they are writing from a progressive, moderate, or conservative lens. See, for example, Douglas J. Flowe, *Uncontrollable Blackness: African American Men and Criminality in Jim Crow New York* (Chapel Hill, NC: University of North Carolina Press, 2020); Lauren J. Krivo and Ruth D. Peterson, "The Structural Context of Homicide: Accounting for Racial Differences in Process," *American Sociological Review* 65, no. 4 (August 2000): 547–559, doi.org/10.2307/2657382; Elliott Currie, *A Peculiar Indifference: The Neglected Toll of Violence on Black America* (New York: Metropolitan Books, 2020); Thomas Sowell, *Wealth, Poverty and Politics: An International Perspective* (New York: Basic Books, 1975); Thomas Sowell, *Discrimination and Disparities*, rev. ed. (New York: Basic Books, 2019); Douglas D. Daye, *A Law Enforcement Sourcebook of Asian Crime and Cultures: Tactics and Mindsets* (Boca Raton, FL: CRC Press, 1997); Ramiro Martinez, Jr., *Latino Violence: Immigration, Violence, and Community* (New York: Routledge, 2002); and Katheryn Russell Brown, *The Color of Crime*, 2nd ed. (New York: New York University Press, 2009).

31. Lydia Saad, "Black Americans Want Police to Retain Local Presence," Gallup, August 5, 2020, news.gallup.com/poll/316571/black-americans-police-retain-local-presence.aspx.

32. "Growing Share of Americans Say They Want More Spending on Police in Their Area," Pew Research Center, October 26, 2021, www.pewresearch.org/fact-tank/2021/10/26/growing-share-of-americans-say-they-want-more-spending-on-police-in-their-area/.

33. Linguist John McWhorter refers to this as "woke religion." See his book *Woke Religion: How a New Religion Has Betrayed Black America* (New York: Portfolio/Penguin, 2021). He and others call for a more unifying "antiracist" vision. See, for example, Coleman Hughes, "A Better Anti-Racism," *Persuasion*, August 19, 2020, www.persuasion.community/p/a-better-anti-racism?s=r; and Chloé Valdery, "Revisiting the Teachings of Dr. King in Difficult Times," Theory of Enchantment, mailchi.mp/b4f0d7ab11e8/thepowerofdrking.

34. Admittedly, there is often a heavy price for pursuing the truth wherever it might lead. Consider the case of Roland G. Fryer, Jr., a world-class academic whom I favorably cite elsewhere in this book. I have no special insight into the specific charges made against him beyond what's been reported, but one thing is clear: if your research findings challenge certain orthodoxies and you dare say taboo things from within the system, as Fryer has done, the system will have a powerful immune response that will remain active until you are destroyed or neutralized. For the specific charges against him, see Jim Tankersly and Ben

Casselman, "Star Economist at Harvard Faces Sexual Harassment Complaints," *New York Times*, December 14, 2018, www.nytimes.com/2018/12/14/business/economy/harvard-roland-fryer-sexual-harassment.html. For a different take on the story, see Stuart Taylor, Jr., "Harvard, the NY Times and the #MeToo Takedown of a Black Academic Star," *Real Clear Investigations*, January 29, 2019, www.realclearinvestigations.com/articles/2019/01/27/harvard_the_new_york_times_and_the_metoo_takedown_of_a_black_academic_star.html; "Harvard Canceled Its Best Black Professor. Why?" YouTube video, uploaded by Good Kid Productions, March 9, 2022; and Glenn Loury, "The Truth about Roland Fryer," *Glenn Loury (Substack)*, March 13, 2022, glennloury.substack.com/p/the-truth-about-roland-fryer?s=r. See also Zac Kriegman, "I Criticized BLM. Then I Was Fired," *Common Sense (Substack)*, May 12, 2022, bariweiss.substack.com/p/i-criticized-blm-then-i-was-fired?s=r; Paul Rossi, "I Refuse to Stand By While My Students Are Indoctrinated," *Common Sense (Substack)*, April 13, 2021, bariweiss.substack.com/p/i-refuse-to-stand-by-while-my-students?s=w; and Bari Weiss, "A Witch Trial at the Legal Aid Society," *Common Sense (Substack)*, July 12, 2021, bariweiss.substack.com/p/a-witch-trial-at-the-legal-aid-society?s=w.

35. From Richard Dawkins' foreword to J. Anderson Thomson, with Clare Aukofer, *Why We Believe in God(s): A Concise Guide to the Science of Faith* (Charlottesville, VA: Pitchstone Publishing, 2011), 12.

36. For a review article on the subject, see Nora A. Murphy and Judith A. Hall, "Capturing Behavior in Small Doses: A Review of Comparative Research in Evaluating Thin Slices for Behavioral Measurement," *Frontiers in Psychology* 12, no 667326 (April 2021): doi.org/10.3389/fpsyg.2021.667326.

37. One study found that people can accurately detect pathological traits in others in less than thirty seconds of video observation. Jacqueline N. W. Friedman et al., "Interpersonal Perception and Personality Disorders: Utilization of a Thin Slice Approach," *Journal of Research in Personality* 41, no. 3 (June 2007): 667–688, doi:10.1016/j.jrp.2006.07.004.

38. Although this claim is specifically about behavior, keep in mind this biological fact: "The proportion of human genetic variation due to differences between populations is modest, and individuals from different populations can be genetically more similar than individuals from the same population." See D. J. Witherspoon et al., "Genetic Similarities Within and Between Human Populations," *Genetics* 176, no. 1 (May 2007): 351–359, doi:10.1534/genetics.106.067355; and Michael Yudell, "Taking Race Out of Human Genetics," *Science* 351, no. 6273 (February 2016): 564–565, doi:10.1126/science.aac4951.

39. See Suzanne Leclerc-Madlala, "On the Virgin Cleansing Myth: Gendered Bodies, AIDS and Ethnomedicine," *African Journal of AIDS Research* 1, no. 2 (2002): 87–95, doi:10.2989/16085906.2002.9626548; and Dean E. Mur-

phy, "Africa's Silent Shame," *Los Angeles Times*, August 16, 1998, www.latimes.com/archives/la-xpm-1998-aug-16-mn-13708-story.html.

40. James Alan Fox et al., "Homicide Trends in the United States," Bureau of Justice Statistics, 152, bjs.ojp.gov/content/pub/pdf/htius.pdf.

41. "2011 Chicago Murder Analysis," 13–21.

42. Janet L. Lauritsen and Nicole White, *Seasonal Patterns in Criminal Victimization Trends*, NCJ 245959 (U.S. Department of Justice, June 2014), 8, bjs.ojp.gov/content/pub/pdf/spcvt.pdf.

43. See the graph "Comparing Offending by Adults & Juveniles" in *OJJ-DP Statistical Briefing Book*, Office of Justice Programs, April 18, 2022, www.ojjdp.gov/ojstatbb/offenders/qa03401.asp.

44. For a bit of history on "the Troubles," see Erin Blakemore, "What Were the Troubles That Ravaged Northern Ireland?" *National Geographic*, April 8, 2022, www.nationalgeographic.com/history/article/the-troubles-of-northern-ireland-history.

45. Although questions have recently been raised about the validity of the long-recognized "bystander effect"—that the greater the number of witnesses, the less likely any one person will help someone in distress—the likelihood of a bystander intervening in any given situation is often context specific. For a helpful survey of our best current understanding of bystander psychology, see Elizabeth Svoboda, "If You're in Danger, Will Bystanders Help?" *Greater Good Magazine*, October 2, 2019, greatergood.berkeley.edu/article/item/if_youre_in_danger_will_bystanders_help. See also Shannon Doyne and Michael Gonchar, "Why Do Bystanders Sometimes Fail to Help When They See Someone in Danger?" *New York Times*, September 23, 2019, www.nytimes.com/2019/09/23/learning/why-do-bystanders-sometimes-fail-to-help-when-they-see-someone-in-danger.html.

46. See the discussion on "bystanderology" in Andrew Katrmen, *Crime Victims: An Introduction to Victimology*, 9th ed. (Boston, MA: Cengage Learning, 2015), 21–22.

47. Even when they get there, police officers may fail to act in a prompt or effective manner, whether due to a misreading of the situation or a desire to protect themselves. The former is unfortunate but understandable; humans sometimes make mistakes. The latter is a betrayal of the duties of a law enforcement officer. For example, as Texas law enforcement guidelines state, "A first responder unwilling to place the lives of the innocent above their own safety should consider another career field." Texas Commission on Law Enforcement, "Active Shooter Response for School-Based Law Enforcement," Course 2195, January 2020. Consider the significance of this guideline in the context of the tragic and shocking case at Robb Elementary School in Uvalde, Texas,

in which law enforcement waited for an hour before confronting the murderer of nineteen children and two adults. Joshua Fechter, "After Uvalde School Shooting, Texas Police Wonder How Much Training Is Enough—and Will It Matter?" *Texas Tribune*, June 13, 2022, www.texastribune.org/2022/06/13/uvalde-school-shooting-texas-police-training/.

48. There are some who will slander and libel wholesale all law enforcement personnel. Theirs is an ideological position that not only ignores but also diminishes obvious acts of heroism and bravery. For those interested in seeing evidence of police officers at their best, the Internet is full of dramatic footage of police officers putting their own lives at risk to protect and serve. As one small example, see "Law Enforcement Officer's in Harms Way," *Fox 13*, March 11, 2022, www.fox13news.com/video/1044996.

Chapter 14: The Police as Threat?

1. See, for example, Patrick Sharkey, "Why Do We Need the Police?" *Washington Post*, June 12, 2020, www.washingtonpost.com/outlook/2020/06/12/defund-police-violent-crime/; and Samantha Wilson, "Lizzo, Natalie Portman, & 6 More Stars Who Support Defunding the Police," *Hollywood Life*, June 10, 2020, hollywoodlife.com/feature/celebrities-support-defund-police-4096850/.

2. Kevin McCaffree and Anondah Saide, *How Informed Are Americans about Race and Policing?* Research Report CUPES-007 (Skeptic Research Center, February 20, 2021), www.skeptic.com/research-center/reports/Research-Report-CUPES-007.pdf.

3. "Fatal Force," *Washington Post*, www.washingtonpost.com/graphics/investigations/police-shootings-database/ (last updated May 17, 2022).

4. "Deputy Identified in September Deadly Shooting of Man Whose Family Told 911 He May Kill Someone," *WBRZ*, October 17, 2019, www.wbrz.com/news/deputy-identified-in-september-deadly-shooting-of-man-whose-family-told-911-he-may-kill-someone/.

5. "Statement: KPD Officer 'Violently' Choked, Attacked by Own Taser before Fatally Shooting Man," *WATE*, September 3, 2019, www.wate.com/news/statement-kpd-officer-violently-choked-attacked-by-own-taser-before-fatally-shooting-man/?ipid=promo-link-block3.

6. Eryn Taylor, "Blytheville Officer Won't Face Charges after Deadly Shooting," *WREG*, April 30, 2019, wreg.com/news/blytheville-officer-wont-face-charges-after-deadly-shooting/.

7. Fares Sabawi, "Texas DPS Identifies Man Killed by Trooper after Chase, Fight," *San Antonio Express-News*, April 15, 2019, www.chron.com/

news/local/crime/article/Texas-DPS-identifies-man-killed-by-trooper-after-13769197.php.

8. Mike Hellgren, "Body Camera Footage Released, Officer Identified In Police-Involved Shooting of Kevin Mason," *CBS Baltimore*, March 27, 2019, baltimore.cbslocal.com/2019/03/27/body-camera-footage-released-in-police-involved-shooting-kevin-mason/.

9. Maci Killman, "DA: Officers in Deadly Edmond Teen Shooting Will Not Be Charged," *KOKH*, September 23, 2019, okcfox.com/news/local/officer-who-killed-isaiah-lewis-will-not-be-charged.

10. Marissa Wenzke and Kareen Wynter, "'My Son Was Murdered': Family of Ryan Twyman, Fatally Shot by L.A. Deputies, Responds to Video's Release," *KTLA*, June 20, 2019, ktla.com/news/local-news/my-son-was-murdered-family-of-ryan-twyman-fatally-shot-by-l-a-county-deputies-responds-to-release-of-video/.

11. The deputy, who is black, apparently knew of the suspect's mental health issues and claimed the gun went off accidentally. Youssef Rddad, "Deputy Who Shot East Feliciana Man Fleeing Store with Raw Chicken Will Face Grand Jury," *Advocate*, February 6, 2020, www.theadvocate.com/baton_rouge/news/communities/east_feliciana/article_ef97c4ae-4916-11ea-8578-53e53fd-d6ad5.html.

12. Kevin Foster, "In Josef Richardson Killing, WBR Deputy Won't Be Charged," *WAFB*, March 23, 2020, www.wafb.com/2020/03/24/josef-richardson-killing-wbr-deputy-wont-be-charged/.

13. See Jonathan Capeheart, "'Hands Up, Don't Shoot'Was Built on a Lie," *Washington Post*, March 16, 2015, www.washingtonpost.com/blogs/post-partisan/wp/2015/03/16/lesson-learned-from-the-shooting-of-michael-brown/; Sharyl Attkisson, "Time to Retire Ferguson Narrative," *Hill*, August 12, 2019, thehill.com/opinion/civil-rights/457049-time-to-retire-ferguson-narrative; and U.S. Department of Justice, "Department of Justice Report Regarding the Criminal Investigation into the Shooting Death of Michael Brown by Ferguson, Missouri Police Officer Darren Brown," memorandum, March 4, 2015, www.justice.gov/sites/default/files/opa/press-releases/attachments/2015/03/04/doj_report_on_shooting_of_michael_brown_1.pdf.

14. Arguably the most egregious case involved the killing of a woman, Atatiana Jefferson, who was shot through a window during a wellness check. Just prior to being shot, she had grabbed a lawfully owned gun from her purse, fearing that she and her nephew, with whom she had been playing video games, were under threat. The officer who shot her faces murder charges. Stefan Sykes, "Family of Atatiana Jefferson, Black Woman Killed by Police, Sue City of Fort Worth and Ex-Officer," *NBC News*, November 18, 2020, www.nbc-

news.com/news/us-news/family-atatiana-jefferson-black-woman-killed-police-sue-city-fort-n1248161. In another case, an officer faces manslaughter charges for killing an unarmed man during a traffic stop. "Trial for Former Temple Police Officer Carmen DeCruz Pushed to November," *Fox 44 News*, June 10, 2021, www.fox44news.com/news/local-news/former-temple-police-officer-carmen-decruz-indicted-on-manslaughter-charge/.

15. Jonathan Raymond, "Jimmy Atchison's Family Say They Have New Evidence to Release in His Police Shooting Case," *11 Alive*, May 5, 2021, www.11alive.com/article/news/crime/jimmy-atchisons-family-say-they-have-new-evidence-to-release-in-his-police-shooting-case/85-8fbd39ba-ab6e-4e71-b4c8-170fe4519fd1.

16. There are more than 10 million arrests per year in the United States. "Persons Arrested," *Crime in the United States 2019*, FBI, ucr.fbi.gov/crime-in-the-u.s/2019/crime-in-the-u.s.-2019/topic-pages/persons-arrested. See also Elizabeth Davis et al., *Contacts Between Police and the Public, 2018—Statistical Tables*, NCJ 255730 (U.S. Department of Justice, December 2020), 1, bjs.ojp.gov/content/pub/pdf/cbpp18st.pdf.

17. See table 43A in "Arrests by Race and Ethnicity," *Crime in the United States 2019*, FBI, ucr.fbi.gov/crime-in-the-u.s/2019/crime-in-the-u.s.-2019/tables/table-43; and Allen J. Beck, *Race and Ethnicity of Violent Crime Offenders and Arrestees, 2018*, NCJ 255969 (U.S. Department of Justice, January 2021), bjs.ojp.gov/content/pub/pdf/revcoa18.pdf.

18. As one study finds, "race-specific county-level violent crime strongly predicts the race of the civilian shot [by police]." David J. Johnson, "Officer Characteristics and Racial Disparities in Fatal Officer-Involved Shootings," *PNAS* 116, no. 32 (July 2019): 15877–15882, doi.org/10.1073/pnas.1903856116. A separate study that benchmarked fatal police shooting data against crime rate estimates found "no systematic evidence of anti-Black disparities in fatal shootings, fatal shootings of unarmed citizens, or fatal shootings involving misidentification of harmless objects." Joseph Cesario, "Is There Evidence of Racial Disparity in Police Use of Deadly Force? Analyses of Officer-Involved Fatal Shootings in 2015–2016," *Social Psychological and Personality Science* 10, no. 5 (2019): 586–595, doi.org/10.1177/1948550618775108.

19. "Expanded Homicide Data Table 1," *Crime in the United States 2019*, FBI, ucr.fbi.gov/crime-in-the-u.s/2019/crime-in-the-u.s.-2019/tables/expanded-homicide-data-table-1.xls.

20. "Quick Facts: New York City," U.S. Census Bureau, July 1, 2021, www.census.gov/quickfacts/newyorkcitynewyork.

21. See the NYPD's annual "Enforcement Reports" available at www1.nyc.gov/site/nypd/stats/reports-analysis/crime-enf.page.

22. "Expanded Homicide Data Table 4," *Crime in the United States 2019*, FBI, ucr.fbi.gov/crime-in-the-u.s/2019/crime-in-the-u.s.-2019/tables/expanded-homicide-data-table-6.xls.

23. See table 13 in Rachel E. Morgan and Jennifer L. Truman, *Criminal Victimization, 2019*, NCJ 255113 (U.S. Department of Justice, September 2020), 17, bjs.ojp.gov/content/pub/pdf/cv19.pdf.

24. Keechant Sewell, "Crime and Enforcement Activity in New York City, 2021," City of New York Police Department, 2, www1.nyc.gov/site/nypd/stats/reports-analysis/crime-enf.page.

25. Of the 7,038 police shooting entries in the *Washington Post* police-shooting database dating back to 2015, 334—or roughly 5 percent—were of women (accessed May 17, 2022).

26. "Quickfacts, Population Estimates," U.S. Census Bureau, July 1, 2021, www.census.gov/quickfacts/fact/table/US/PST045221.

27. Of the 7,038 police shooting entries in the *Washington Post* police-shooting database dating back to 2015, 3,024 were white (41 percent), 1,596 were black (22 percent), 1,090 were Hispanic (15 percent), 243 were "other" (3 percent), and 1,419 were "unknown" (19 percent) (accessed May 17, 2022).

28. This fallacy comes with an obvious downside to those who promote it. Whatever god that is called upon to fill the gap gets smaller and smaller with every advance in our scientific knowledge. For a brief discussion of this idea, see Marcelo Gleiser, "What the 'God of the Gaps' Teaches Us About Science," *NPR*, April 8, 2015, www.npr.org/sections/13.7/2015/04/08/398227737/what-the-god-of-the-gaps-teaches-us-about-science.

29. Part of the problem is that the data itself is limited. Collection is not uniform or systematic across all agencies, and data submission is often voluntary. Thus, no conclusions can be drawn with any kind of certainty. For a discussion of the creative approaches researchers sometimes take to determine the role of race in policing, see Lynne Peeples, "What the Data Say about Police Brutality and Racial Bias—and Which Reforms Might Work," *Nature*, May 26, 2021 (updated), www.nature.com/articles/d41586-020-01846-z.

30. See, for example, the tragic circumstances that led to Breonna Taylor's death. Richard A. Oppel, Jr., et al., "What to Know about Breonna Taylor's Death," *New York Times*, April 26, 2021, www.nytimes.com/article/breonna-taylor-police.html.

31. Economist Roland Fryer finds that, when controlling for other variables, black suspects are 27.4 percent less likely to be shot at than non-black and non-Hispanic suspects. Roland G. Fryer, "Reconciling Results on Racial Differences in Police Shootings," *AEA Papers and Proceedings* 108 (May 2018): 228–

33, doi:10.1257/pandp.20181004. If true, a counter-bias effect may account for some of this—in short, white officers might be slower to shoot black suspects precisely because they don't want to be called racist by community members and news media. See Steven M. James and Bryan J. Vila, "The Reverse Racism Effect," *Criminology and Public Policy* 15, no. 2 (January 2016): 457–479, doi. org/10.1111/1745-9133.12187.

32. A black man in the United States is 2.5 times more likely to be killed by police than a white man over the course of his lifetime. No moral person thinks this is a good thing. For some, this is clear-cut evidence that ends the discussion: police are racially biased. Yet, in 2020, black males committed roughly 20.2 homicides per 100,000 black men, while white men committed roughly 2.5 homicides per 100,000 white men. Put another way, black men committed eight times more homicides than white men when controlling for population size. Might this statistic affect the police shooting rate? If so, by how much? If not, why not? If you categorically reject the idea that variables other than racism might explain some of the disparities in police shootings, then you are not conducting an honest search for the truth. Author calculations based on 2020 FBI and U.S. Census data. For the lifetime risk of being shot by police by race or ethnicity, see Frank Edwards et al., "Risk of Being Killed by Police Use of Force in the United States by Age, Race–Ethnicity, and Sex," *PNAS* 116, no. 34 (August 2019): 16793–16798, doi.org/10.1073/pnas.1821204116.

33. In most of the twelve cases from 2019 in the *Washington Post* police shooting database, the officer or officers involved felt threatened in some way before shooting, whether the suspect was in the process of fleeing or fighting. In a few cases, the threat was arguably more perceived than real, and a tragic mistake was made in a fraction of a second. One counterintuitive solution to soften the fight-or-flight response among suspects is to emphasize community policing. While this would invariably increase the number of contacts between police and community members, they would ideally be working in partnership. The hope is that this would not only improve police perceptions of the community and soften any negative biases they might have toward community members but also make members of the community less fearful of police and more prone to cooperate during contacts without immediately fleeing or fighting. For more on the possible benefits of community policing, see Lorie Fridell et al., *Racially Biased Policing: A Principled Response* (Washington, DC: Police Executive Research Forum, 2001).

34. This doesn't come without costs to social and racial justice causes. As economist Glenn Loury warned shortly after Brown's death, "making Brown a poster child around which to organize a movement for social justice might be a profound mistake, for doing so creates a situation where the success or failure of that movement hinges on the facts of his case." Glenn C. Loury, "Ferguson Won't Change Anything. What Will?" *Boston Review*, January 2, 2015, boston-

review.net/forum/glenn-loury-ferguson-wont-change-anything-what-will/.

35. "Kim Potter Is Found Guilty of Manslaughter in the Death of Daunte Wright," *NPR*, December 23, 2021, www.npr.org/2021/12/23/1066012247/kim-potter-trial-daunte-wright.

36. Office of Public Affairs, "Federal Officials Decline Prosecution in the Death of Freddie Gray," press release, U.S. Department of Justice, September 12, 2017, www.justice.gov/opa/pr/federal-officials-decline-prosecution-death-freddie-gray.

37. Rebecca R. Ruiz, "Baltimore Officers Will Face No Federal Charges in Death of Freddie Gray," *New York Times*, September 12, 2017, www.nytimes.com/2017/09/12/us/freddie-gray-baltimore-police-federal-charges.html.

38. There are conflicting findings related to nonlethal use of force by police and race. Some studies find that police are more likely to use non-lethal force against black and Hispanic suspects, while others find no such disparity when controlling for other factors. See, for example, Roland G. Fryer, Jr., "An Empirical Analysis of Racial Differences in Police Use of Force," July 2017, scholar.harvard.edu/files/fryer/files/empirical_analysis_tables_figures.pdf; and Emily K. Weisburst, "Police Use of Force as an Extension of Arrests: Examining Disparities across Civilian and Officer Race," *AEA Papers and Proceedings* 109 (May 2019): 152–56, www.aeaweb.org/articles?id=10.1257/pandp.20191028.

39. See Billy Binion, "Tony Timpa Died After Cops Kneeled on His Back and Joked About It. A Court Says His Family Can Sue," *Reason*, January 6, 2022, reason.com/2022/01/06/tony-timpa-death-dallas-police-kneeled-on-his-back-qualified-immunity-5th-circuit/; Conor Friedersdorf, "A Police Killing Without a Hint of Racism," *Atlantic*, December 3, 2017, www.theatlantic.com/politics/archive/2017/12/a-police-killing-without-a-hint-of-racism/546983/; and Wesley Lowery, "Graphic Video Shows Daniel Shaver Sobbing and Begging Officer for His Life before 2016 Shooting," *Washington Post*, December 8, 2017, www.washingtonpost.com/news/post-nation/wp/2017/12/08/graphic-video-shows-daniel-shaver-sobbing-and-begging-officer-for-his-life-before-2016-shooting/.

40. For a political scientist's debunking of the "hate-crime epidemic" often touted by media, see Wilfred Reilly, *Hate Crime Hoax: How the Left Is Selling a Fake Race War* (Washington, DC: Regnery, 2019). For a discussion of the dishonesty often shown by government and media in response to tragedy, see Douglas Murray, "The Dishonesty of How We Respond to Tragedies," *Spectator*, May 21, 2021, www.spectator.co.uk/article/the-dishonesty-of-how-we-respond-to-tragedies. For a discussion of the overall "invisibility" of Asian Americans, see Jennifer Lee, "Confronting the Invisibility of Anti-Asian Racism," Brookings, May 18, 2022, www.brookings.edu/blog/how-we-rise/2022/05/18/confronting-the-invisibility-of-anti-asian-racism/.

41. For more, see Conor Friedersdorf, "Criminal-Justice Reformers Chose the Wrong Slogan," *Atlantic*, August 8, 2021, www.theatlantic.com/ideas/archive/2021/08/instead-of-defund-the-police-solve-all-murders/619672/.

42. Citizens concerned about public safety have started to push back. See, for example, Seth Moskowitz, "Why Democrats Are Recalling Their Own," *Persuasion*, June 8, 2022, www.persuasion.community/p/why-democrats-are-recalling-their?s=r; and Ronald Brownstein, "Why California Wants to Recall Its Most Progressive Prosecutors," *Atlantic*, April 28, 2022, www.theatlantic.com/politics/archive/2022/04/san-francisco-los-angeles-da-recalls/629701/. For a high-profile example illustrating the problem, see City News Service, "Dave Chappelle Is Not Happy DA Won't Charge Accused Onstage Attacker with Felony," *NBC Los Angeles*, May 9, 2022, www.nbclosangeles.com/news/local/dave-chappelle-hollywood-bowl-attack-charges-gascon-felony-misdemeanor/2888881/. See also Associated Press, "California Is Releasing 76K Inmates Early, Including Violent Felons," *KTLA*, April 30, 2021, ktla.com/news/california/california-will-release-76k-inmates-early-including-violent-felons/; and Peter Nickeas et al., "Defund the Police Encounters Resistance as Violent Crime Spikes," *CNN*, May 25, 2021, www.cnn.com/2021/05/25/us/defund-police-crime-spike/index.html.

43. As journalist Matthew Iglesias notes, the near-term increase in the number of black homicide victims following the #DefundThePolice movement was far greater than the number of black people killed annually by police. Matthew Iglesias, "What Comes after the 'Defund' Fad?" *Slow Boring*, May 25, 2021, www.slowboring.com/p/what-comes-after-the-defund-fad?s=r. See also Conor Friedersdorf, "The Numbers Tell a Different Story about the Police Killing of Minors," *Atlantic*, May 2, 2021, www.theatlantic.com/ideas/archive/2021/05/what-americans-should-know-about-police-killings-minors/618759/.

44. Despite what some claim, these attacks have little if anything to do with white supremacy or Donald J. Trump. Wilfred Reilly, "Crime Against Asians Isn't Due to White Supremacy," *Commentary*, May 2021, www.commentary.org/articles/wilfred-reilly/crime-against-asians-isnt-due-to-white-supremacy/. For more, see Stella Chan and Augie Martin, "Anti-Asian Hate Crimes Increased 567% in San Francisco as Lawsuit Accuses DA of Not Doing Enough," *CNN*, January 27, 2022, www.cnn.com/2022/01/27/us/anti-asian-hate-crimes-san-francisco-lawsuit/index.html; and Oumou Fofana and Jorge Fitz-Gibbon, "NYC Protesters Denounce Spike in Anti-Asian Attacks after Michelle Go's Death," *New York Post*, January 20, 2022, nypost.com/2022/01/20/nyc-protesters-denounce-spike-in-anti-asian-violence-after-michelle-gos-death/.

45. Unless saner voices prevail, we will see more headlines and articles like this: Jacqueline Howard, "US Records Highest Increase in Nation's Homicide Rate in Modern History, CDC Says," *CNN*, October 6, 2021, www.cnn.com/2021/10/06/health/us-homicide-rate-increase-nchs-study/index.html.

46. Kiana Cox and Christine Tamir, "Race Is Central to Identity for Black Americans and Affects How They Connect with Each Other," Pew Research Center, April 14, 2022, 4, www.pewresearch.org/race-ethnicity/2022/04/14/black-americans-place-and-community/.

47. See, for example, Kim Parker and Kiley Hurst, "Growing Share of Americans Say They Want More Spending on Police in Their Area," Pew Research Center, October 26, 2021, www.pewresearch.org/fact-tank/2021/10/26/growing-share-of-americans-say-they-want-more-spending-on-police-in-their-area/.

48. One brave mother is standing up for the victims who are all too often forgotten by mainstream media and policymakers. Rav Arora, "This Mother Is Fighting Black-on-Black Violence—and Wants Police Support," *New York Post*, March 5, 2022, nypost.com/2022/03/05/black-on-black-violence-fighting-mother-wants-police-support/.

49. Just over 12 percent of police officers in the United States are black. However, after years of increasing numbers, it has become harder for departments to recruit and retain black officers post Ferguson, given the prevailing anti-police narrative. As a result, the percentage of black officers has been dropping. This is yet one more damaging effect of the widespread belief that police are actively targeting black people. See Lauren Leatherby and Richard A. Oppel, Jr., "Which Police Departments Are as Diverse as Their Communities," *New York Times*, September 23, 2020, www.nytimes.com/interactive/2020/09/23/us/bureau-justice-statistics-race.html; and David A. Graham, "America Is Losing Its Black Police Officers," *Atlantic*, October 4, 2021, www.theatlantic.com/ideas/archive/2021/10/america-is-losing-its-black-police-officers/620291/.

50. John Wood, Jr., "How We Chose Violence," *Areo*, February 9, 2021, areomagazine.com/2021/09/02/how-we-chose-violence/.

51. For easy access to credible studies on policing and other matters related to race you won't often see highlighted in the mainstream press, bookmark the Google Docs file "Compendium" curated by Free Black Thought (freeblackthought.com) at docs.google.com/document/u/1/d/e/2PACX-1vRP-j5vGVtEK2DZKMo6PZnb3EidgTmVwIqejuJ50_L5hxVyFMSsPruwob-CK1YKvCMb53NLyMiwtHeMKO/pub.

52. Wilfred Reilly, "No, There Is No Coming Race War," *Commentary*, February 2020, www.commentary.org/articles/wilfred-reilly/no-there-is-no-coming-race-war/.

53. Heather Mac Donald, "Breakdown: The Unwinding of Law and Order in Our Cities Has Happened with Stunning Speed," *City Journal*, July 1, 2020, www.city-journal.org/ferguson-effect-inner-cities. See also Heather Mac Donald, "The Myth of Systemic Police Racism," *Wall Street Journal*, June 2, 2020,

www.wsj.com/articles/the-myth-of-systemic-police-racism-11591119883.

54. Data from the *Washington Post*'s police-shooting database (armed includes guns, knives, vehicles, toy weapons, and other unspecified weapons), May 17, 2022 (updated), and "Expanded Homicide Data Table 1," *Crime in the United States 2019*, FBI, ucr.fbi.gov/crime-in-the-u.s/2019/crime-in-the-u.s.-2019/topic-pages/tables/expanded-homicide-data-table-1.xls.

55. As with violence, your age, gender, employment, and location all affect your level of risk. Males between the ages of 15 and 34 account for 41 percent of lightning strike victims, and males account for 80 to 85 percent of deaths. "Lightning: Victim Data," CDC, www.cdc.gov/disasters/lightning/victimdata.html. There are about thirty lightning deaths per year in the United States. John S. Jensenius, Jr., "A Detailed Analysis of Lightning Deaths in the United States from 2006 through 2019," National Lightning Safety Council, February 2020, www.weather.gov/media/safety/Analysis06-19.pdf.

56. Micah Schwartzbach, "Invoking Your Right to Remain Silent," *Nolo*, www.nolo.com/legal-encyclopedia/when-how-invoke-your-right-silence.html.

57. There are an estimated 120.5 firearms per 100 residents in the United States. "America's Gun Culture—in Seven Charts," *BBC*, April 22, 2022, www.bbc.com/news/world-us-canada-41488081.

58. Bureau of Labor Statistics, "Fatal Work Injuries to Police Officers Fell 20 percent in 2019," *Economics Daily*, www.bls.gov/opub/ted/2021/fatal-work-injuries-to-police-officers-fell-20-percent-in-2019.htm (accessed May 23, 2022).

59. Mac Donald, "The Myth of Systemic Police Racism."

60. Thankfully, an increasing number of people are unafraid to say it. See, for example, the work of Michael Shellenberger. Michael Shellenberger, "Why Violent Crime Is Rising," *Michael Shellenberger (Substack)*, December 6, 2021, michaelshellenberger.substack.com/p/why-violent-crime-is-rising?s=w; and Michael Shellenberger, "Why Anti-Police Activism Kills," *Michael Shellenberger (Substack)*, November 24, 2021, michaelshellenberger.substack.com/p/why-anti-police-activism-kills?utm_source=%2Fprofile%2F2255433-michael-shellenberger&utm_medium=reader2&s=r.

61. For example, cases of officer-created jeopardy during traffic stops can be avoided with better training. See the Pulitzer Price–winning visual investigation, "Before the Final Frame: When Police Missteps Create Danger," *New York Times*, October 30, 2021, www.nytimes.com/interactive/2021/10/30/video/police-traffic-stops-danger-video.html.

62. For a brief discussion of possible ways to improve policing, see German Lopez, "Police and the Alternatives," The Morning (newsletter), *New York Times*, March 6, 2022, www.nytimes.com/2022/03/06/briefing/crime-solu-

tions-ukraine-war-books.html.

63. Colin Groundwater, "A Brief History of ACAB," *GQ*, June 10, 2020, www.gq.com/story/history-of-acab.

Chapter 15: The Command of Knowledge

1. Penn Jillette, *God, No!: Signs You May Already Be an Atheist and Other Magical Tales* (New York: Simon and Schuster, 2011), 39.

2. de Becker, *The Gift of Fear*, 116–117, 383.

3. The subject of persuasion has been well studied, particularly as it relates to business practices. There are simple techniques people can employ to increase the likelihood of compliance, whether they are negotiating a deal or selling a product. See, for example, the psychological principles outlined in Robert B. Cialdini, *Influence: Science and Practice*, 5th ed. (New York: Allyn and Bacon, 2008).

4. For more on the methods and motives of con artists in particular, see Maria Konnikova, *The Confidence Game* (New York: Viking, 2016).

5. See, for example, "Baytown Medical Offices Destroyed and Burglarized for More Than $20K," *ABC 13*, March 4, 2019, abc13.com/baytown-burglary-drugs-money/5168093/.

6. For basic safety tips when online, see "Spoofing and Phishing," FBI, www.fbi.gov/scams-and-safety/common-scams-and-crimes/spoofing-and-phishing; and "Best Practices: Safe Social Networking," Information Technology, University of Pittsburgh, www.technology.pitt.edu/security/best-practices-safe-social-networking.

7. It's possible these orphans were the lucky ones. Others are exploited in far worse ways. Martin Lowe, "Children in Asia Exploited by 'Orphanage Trafficking,'" *CGTN*, December 8, 2018, news.cgtn.com/news/3d3d514f-3263544d31457a6333566d54/share_p.html.

8. See, for example, "Teenage Mob Attacks Designed to Distract Police," *CBS News*, April 22, 2019, www.cbsnews.com/chicago/news/teenage-mobs-chicago/; "Chicago Police Say Group of Teens Is Attacking People Downtown," YouTube video, uploaded by CBS Chicago, August 21, 2021, www.youtube.com/watch?v=aHCz-yv6I8o; and "Teen Suspects Arrested in Connection to Mob Street Attack of 15-Year-Old NYC Girl," *NBC New York*, March 8, 2020, www.nbcnewyork.com/news/local/teen-suspects-arrested-in-connection-to-mob-street-attack-of-15-year-old-nyc-girl/2317596/.

9. See Philip J. Cook et al., "Constant Lethality of Gunshot Injuries

from Firearm Assault: United States, 2003–2012," *American Journal of Public Health* 107 (2017): 1324–1328, doi.org/10.2105/AJPH.2017.303837; and Michele Gorman, "Gunshot Wounds Just as Deadly as Always, Despite Data Claims to the Contrary," *Newsweek*, June 23, 2017, www.newsweek.com/gun-data-study-628651. For self-inflicted wounds, the death rate is 85 percent. See Madeline Drexler, "Guns and Suicide: The Hidden Toll," *Harvard Public Health*, www.hsph.harvard.edu/magazine/magazine_article/guns-suicide/.

10. "Prey drive" is a term normally associated with the instinctive hunting behavior of dogs and wolves, but it has been theorized to explain some human violent criminal behavior as well. See, for example, Tiffany Dawn Russell, "The Prey Drive Model of Sexual Violence" (dissertation, University of North Dakota, August 2019), www.proquest.com/docview/2296778711?pq-origsite=g-scholar&fromopenview=true.

11. Peter Nickeas and Priya Krishnakumar, "'It's a Disturbing Trend.' Cities See Large Increases in Carjackings During Pandemic," *CNN*, January 23, 2022, www.cnn.com/2022/01/23/us/carjackings-rise-major-cities-pandemic/index.html.

12. "Carjacking Facts," Jefferson County Sheriff's Office, co.jefferson.tx-.us/Sheriff/crimeprevention/carjacking-facts.

13. Such questions may seem Machiavellian—or even Kissingerian—but that's the point. When you're talking about personal survival, you need to be realistic and pragmatic—not ideological or utopic.

14. Donna Vickroy, "Just Because You Know How to Swim Doesn't Mean You Know How to Survive Drowning," *Chicago Tribune*, June 4, 2019, www.chicagotribune.com/suburbs/daily-southtown/ct-sta-water-safety-st-0606-story.html.

15. The entire point of this book is to provide knowledge that will help keep you safe, whether you're skilled in a combat sport or not. Just as experienced swimmers can sometimes needlessly put themselves in danger, so too can functional martial artists if they don't abide by basic self-defense principles. See, for example, "WARNING (Viewer Discretion Advised) BJJ Black Belt Fatally Shot in Road Rage Incident," YouTube video, GracieBreakdown, May 11, 2018, www.youtube.com/watch?v=sMPPZ02jCmM. *Please note: I mean no disrespect by sharing this video; rather, my hope is that by highlighting the lessons contained therein, lives will be saved in the future.*

16. Surveys of burglars show this over and over. The bigger and louder the breed, the better. See, for example, Iboshi, "We Asked 86 Burglars How They Broke into Homes." But keep in mind that the dogs themselves are sometimes the target. This is particularly true for puppies and small, expensive breeds that might bring in thousands of dollars. See, for example, Melissa Chan, "Lady Gaga

Got Her Dogs Back, but as Criminals Capitalize on the Demand for Pandemic Pups, Others Aren't So Lucky," *Time*, March 12, 2021, time.com/5945294/dog-theft-covid-19-pandemic/; and Sean Salai, "Dog Gone? Pet Experts Warn of Increase in Canine Thefts," *Washington Times*, March 22, 2022, www.washingtontimes.com/news/2022/mar/22/dog-gone-pet-experts-warn-increase-canine-thefts/.

17. "Burglary Prevention Tips," Alliance Police, www.alliancepolice.com/burglary-prevention.

18. At the extreme end of ethical questions related to self-defense is the use of lethal force. Specifically, when is it permissible to kill others in self-defense? There is a strong moral principle that allows the use of lethal force when confronted by someone with the intention and ability to kill you or yours. But there are circumstances and scenarios that do not offer such clear answers and are worthy of careful consideration. See, for example, the discussion in Jonathan Quong, "Killing in Self-Defense," *Ethics* 119, no. 3 (April 2009): 507–537, doi.org/10.1086/597595.

19. Illusionist Darren Brown, who uses his communication skills to trick people for a living, shares a story about how he avoided a mugging by blurting out to a would-be assailant, "The wall outside my house isn't 4 feet high." If this out-of-context and nonsensical line is indeed what enabled him to avoid the attack, it is likely because he had positioned himself as the irrational actor in the encounter. Jenn Selby, "Derren Brown Explains How to Reduce a Mugger to Tears Using Nothing but Words," *Independent*, November 13, 2014, www.independent.co.uk/news/people/derren-brown-explains-how-to-reduce-a-mugger-to-tears-using-nothing-but-words-9859017.html.

20. We intuitively understand the process of de-escalation and have all at one time or another managed to de-escalate a situation, even if a minor one with a friend or family member, but research on de-escalation is relatively new, and the relationship between certain de-escalation techniques and outcomes are not yet well understood. Research is particularly important for developing best practices in acute mental health situations, where effective de-escalation practices would potentially reduce the need for tranquilizers, physical restraints, and seclusion. See, for example, Mary Lavelle et al., "Predictors of Effective De-escalation in Acute Inpatient Psychiatric Settings," *Journal of Clinical Nursing* 25, no. 15–16 (August 2016): 2180–2188, doi:10.1111/jocn.13239; and Alice Fletcher et al., "Comparison of Patients' and Staff's Perspectives on the Causes of Violence and Aggression in Psychiatric Inpatient Settings: An Integrative Review," *Journal of Psychiatric and Mental Health Nursing* 28, no. 5 (October 2021): 924–939, doi:10.1111/jpm.12758.

21. This is an obtainable goal, but the process will be harder for some than for others. As with most behaviors, shyness is partly genetic but environment

also plays a large role. See Ashley K. Smith et al., "The Magnitude of Genetic and Environmental Influences on Parental and Observational Measures of Behavioral Inhibition and Shyness in Toddlerhood," *Behavior Genetics* 42, no. 5 (September 2012): 764–777, doi:10.1007/s10519-012-9551-0; and Sarah Keating, "The Science Behind Why Some of Us Are Shy," *BBC*, June 5, 2019, www.bbc.com/future/article/20190604-the-science-behind-why-some-of-us-are-shy.

22. When it comes to making eye contact, be aware of cultural differences. See Hironori Akechi, "Attention to Eye Contact in the West and East: Autonomic Responses and Evaluative Ratings," *PLoS One* 8, no. 3 (2013): e59312, doi:10.1371/journal.pone.0059312.

23. There's plenty of research that supports the idea that faking it can offer psychological and emotional benefits. See Amanda McCorquodale, "8 'Fake It 'Til You Make It' Strategies Backed by Science," *Mental Floss*, February 1, 2016, www.mentalfloss.com/article/74310/8-fake-it-til-you-make-it-strategies-backed-science; and Ozgun Atasoy, "Your Thoughts Can Release Abilities Beyond Normal Limits," *Scientific American*, August 13, 2013, www.scientificamerican.com/article/your-thoughts-can-release-abilities-beyond-normal-limits/.

Chapter 16: The Importance of Maturity

1. The high rate of youth homicide in the Americas skews the worldwide data slightly. In some European countries that do not suffer from high levels of gang violence, for example, men in their thirties and early forties can experience the highest homicide rates. *Global Study on Homicide* (Vienna: UNODC, 2019), 23, www.unodc.org/documents/data-and-analysis/gsh/Booklet1.pdf.

2. "Violent Crime Victimization," *OJJDP Statistical Briefing Book*, March 31, 2020, www.ojjdp.gov/ojstatbb/victims/qa02601.asp?qaDate=2018.

3. Craig A. Perkins, *Age Patterns of Victims of Serious Violent Crimes*, NCJ 162031 (U.S. Department of Justice, July 1997), 2, 3, bjs.ojp.gov/content/pub/pdf/apvsvc.pdf.

4. Mariam Arain et al., "Maturation of the Adolescent Brain," *Neuropsychiatric Disease and Treatment* 9 (2013): 449–461, doi:10.2147/NDT.S39776.

5. Daniel Kahneman, *Thinking, Fast and Slow* (New York: Farrar, Straus and Giroux, 2011).

6. The effectiveness of proper mentorship has been demonstrated in a controlled study of a dating-violence prevention program (Coaching Boys into Men) that targets male high school athletes through their coaches. See Eliza-

beth Miller, "One-Year Follow-Up of a Coach-Delivered Dating Violence Prevention Program: A Cluster Randomized Controlled Trial," *American Journal of Preventative Medicine* 45, no. 1 (July 2013): 108–112, doi:10.1016/j.amepre.2013.03.007.

7. For more details on this story, see Dean E. Murphy, "South Africa Reins in Its Young Elephants," *Los Angeles Times*, September 18, 1998, www.latimes.com/archives/la-xpm-1998-sep-18-mn-24037-story.html#:~:text=%E2%80%9CThere%20appears%20to%20be%20a,presence%20of%20adult%20elephant%20bulls.

8. This argument typically maintains that Sweden's crime and prison rates are low because the government offers adequate support to mothers and children. See, for example, Tracie Powell, "Prioritizing Education Over the Penal System," *Diverse: Issues in Higher Education*, October 29, 2007, www.diverseeducation.com/stem/article/15085945/prioritizing-education-over-the-penal-system.

9. Jonas Öberg and Klara Hradilova Selin, *Lethal Violence in Sweden, 1990–2017: Trends and Characteristics* (Swedish National Council for Crime Prevention, 2019), 4, bra.se/download/18.62c6cfa2166eca5d70e2a95d/1614334194443/2019_6_Lethal_violence_in_Sweden_1990-2017.pdf.

10. Tino Sanandaji, "Krugman Fundamentally Misunderstands Sweden," *Tino.us*, November 19, 2012, tino.us/2012/11/krugman-fundamentally-misunderstands-sweden/.

11. Ibid.

12. See, for example, Jan O. Jonsson and Michael Gähler, "Family Dissolution, Family Reconstitution, and Children's Educational Careers: Recent Evidence from Sweden," *Demography* 34, no. 2 (1997): 277–293.

13. "Fatherhood and Family Law: The Myths and the Facts," *Liz Library*, www.thelizlibrary.org/liz/017.htm.

14. Levitt and Dunbar, *Freakonomics*, 4. See also John J. Gonohue III and Steven Levitt, "Further Evidence That Legalized Abortion Lowered Crime," *Journal of Human Resources* 39, no. 1 (Winter 2004): 29–49, doi.org/10.2307/3559004.

15. Levitt and Dunbar, *Freakonomics*, 126.

16. Fatherless homes lead to many other adverse outcomes, not just an increase in crime. They include, among other things, childhood obesity, poor school performance, substance abuse, and mental health problems. For a survey of adverse outcomes, see Jerrod Brown, "Father-Absent Homes: Implications for Criminal Justice and Mental Health Professionals," Minnesota Psychological Association, August 4, www.mnpsych.org/index.php%-

3Foption%3Dcom_dailyplanetblog%26view%3Dentry%26category%3Din-
dustry%2520news%26id%3D54. See also chapter 12 of this book.

17. Cynthia Harper and Sara McLanahan, "Father Absence and Youth Incarceration," *Journal of Research on Adolescence* Volume 14, no. 3 (2004): 369–397, www.ojp.gov/ncjrs/virtual-library/abstracts/father-absence-and-youth-incarceration.

18. N. Vaden-Kierman et al., "Household Family Structure and Children's Aggressive Behavior: A Longitudinal Study of Urban Elementary School Children," *Journal of Abnormal Child Psychology* 23, no. 5 (1995): 553–568.

19. Todd D. Kendell and Robert Tamura, "Unmarried Fertility, Crime, and Social Stigma," *Journal of Law and Economics* 53, no. 1 (February 2010), doi.org/10.1086/596116.

20. National Center for Health Statistics, *Health, United States, 2017.*

21. This is from Obama's 2008 Father's Day speech to the Apostolic Church of God in Chicago. The speech is available at "Text of Obama's Fatherhood Speech," *Politico*, June 15, 2008, www.politico.com/story/2008/06/text-of-obamas-fatherhood-speech-011094.

22. See the section titled "Dad-Deprived Boys Versus Dad-Enriched Boys" in Warren Farrell and John Gray, *The Boy Crisis: Why Our Boys Are Struggling and What We Can Do about It* (Dallas, TX: BenBella Books, 2018).

23. A father's presence in a household in an urban, low-income neighborhood places a child at a lesser risk for child sexual abuse. David L. Rowland et al., "Household Risk and Child Sexual Abuse in a Low Income, Urban Sample of Women," *Adolescent and Family Health* 1, no. 1 (Winter 2000): 29–39.

24. Individual teachers, coaches, and counselors can certainly enrich and improve individual lives, but as demonstrated time and again, school systems cannot be relied on to provide each and every student with all the support and guidance they need to succeed. That support and guidance must first come from the home. See, for example, Chris Papst, "City Student Passes 3 Classes in Four Years, Ranks Near Top Half of Class with 0.13 GPA," *WBFF Baltimore*, March 1, 2021, https://foxbaltimore.com/news/project-baltimore/city-student-passes-3-classes-in-four-years-ranks-near-top-half-of-class-with-013-gpa.

25. One group of concerned dads in Louisiana understands this. They work together to protect schools and teach by example. "We're dads. We decided the best people who can take care of our kids are who? Are us," says the group, known as Dads on Duty USA. Joelle Goldstein, "Louisiana Fathers Form 'Dads on Duty' Group to Help Stop Violence at Their Children's High School," *People*, October 27, 2021, people.com/human-interest/louisiana-fathers-form-dads-on-duty-group-to-stop-violence-at-kids-school/.

26. Nicki Crick et al., "Relationally and Physically Aggressive Children's Intent Attributions and Feelings of Distress for Relational and Instrumental Peer Provocations," *Child Development* 34, no. 7 (July/August 2002): 1134–1142, www.jstor.org/stable/3696275.

27. See, for example, Stephen S. Leff et al., "A Review of Existing Relational Aggression Programs: Strengths, Limitations, and Future Directions," *School Psychology Review* 39, no. 4 (2010): 508–535.

28. Just as boys have built-in instincts and behaviors from an unbroken line of evolutionary success that can be destructive or dangerous if left untamed, so too, of course, do girls, including those instincts and behaviors inherited from their female ancestors who successfully shaped the behavior of men and children for the benefit of their families and communities. See Diana S. Fleischman, "How to Train Your Boyfriend," *Psychology Today*, blog, August 5, 2020, www.psychologytoday.com/gb/blog/how-train-your-boyfriend/202008/how-train-your-boyfriend.

29. For a bit more on Rajneesh and how cult leaders manage to exert such control, see Alessandra Potenza, "Here's What Netflix's Wild Wild Country Doesn't Explain about Cult Leaders," *Verge*, April 25, 2018, www.theverge.com/2018/4/25/17275996/cult-leaders-psychology-bhagwan-shree-rajneesh-netflix-wild-wild-country.

30. For an ethnographical study of MMA practitioners and "real" fight training, see Michael Staack, *Fighting as Real as It Gets: A Micro-Sociological Encounter* (Berlin: J. B. Metzler Verlag, 2019).

31. There's a fascinating history to the connection between clothes and crime. Gene Demby, "Sagging Pants and the Long History Of 'Dangerous' Street Fashion," *NPR*, September 11, 2014, www.npr.org/sections/codeswitch/2014/09/11/347143588/sagging-pants-and-the-long-history-of-dangerous-street-fashion.

Chapter 17: The Importance of Intelligence

1. Self-defense training for women has fallen out of fashion since the 1970s. While feminists of that era saw it as a source of empowerment, a newer generation of feminist scholars and activists have come to see self-defense training as implying that women are responsible for stopping violence against them, including rape. Men are the problem, and thus they are the ones who need to undergo training and be taught not to commit rape and violence against women, they charge. This reasoning is silly. It isn't an either-or situation. The feminists in the 1970s had it right. See the discussion in Martha E. Thompson, "Empowering Self-Defense Training," *Violence Against Women* 20, no. 3,

2014: 351–359, doi:10.1177/1077801214526051; Jocelyn A. Hollander, "The Roots of Resistance to Women's Self-Defense," *Violence Against Women* 15, no. 5 (2009): 574–594, doi:10.1177/1077801209331407; and Sarah Brown, "'Empowerment Self-Defense' Programs Make Women Safer. Why Don't More Colleges Use Them?" *Chronicle of Higher Education* 65, no. 31 (April 26, 2019).

2.   See Joanna Williams, "Sarah Everard and the Feminism of Fear," *Spiked*, December 29, 2021, www.spiked-online.com/2021/12/29/sarah-eve-rard-and-the-feminism-of-fear/.

3.   Heather A. Turner, "The Effect of Lifetime Victimization on the Mental Health of Children and Adolescents," *Social Science and Medicine* 62, no. 1, (January 2006): 13–27, doi:10.1016/j.socscimed.2005.05.030.

4.   Constance Smith Hendricks, "The Influence of Father Absence on the Self-Esteem and Self-Reported Sexual Activity of Rural Southern Adolescents," *Pharmacy Practice and Science* 16, no. 6 (2005): 124–131.

5.   It can, however, be improved. There are ways to do this both on and off the mat. Eric Ravenscraft, "Practical Ways to Improve Your Confidence (and Why You Should)," *New York Times*, June 3, 2019, www.nytimes.com/2019/06/03/smarter-living/how-to-improve-self-confidence.html.

6.   Molly Priddy, "Taylor-Made Black Belt," *Flathead Beacon*, September 16, 2015, flatheadbeacon.com/2015/09/16/taylor-made-black-belt/.

7.   Jesse Singal, "How the Self Esteem Craze Took over America and Why the Hype Was Irresponsible," *Cut*, May 2019, www.thecut.com/2017/05/self-esteem-grit-do-they-really-help.html.

8.   Pinker, *Better Angels*, 519–520. Perhaps unsurprisingly, prisoners have been shown to have higher levels of self-esteem than the general population. Tom Jacobs, "Sure, I'm Behind Bars, but I'm Still Morally Superior to You," *Pacific Standard*, June 14, 2017, psmag.com/social-justice/sure-im-behind-bars-im-still-morally-superior-72363.

9.   See, for example, "Zambian Prophet Who Believed He Could Recreate the Resurrection of Jesus Dies after Getting His Followers to Bury Him Alive for Three Days," *Daily Mail*, August 24, 2021, www.dailymail.co.uk/news/article-9922579/Zambian-prophet-trying-recreate-resurrection-Jesus-dies-buried-alive.html. A quick search of the Darwin Awards will yield plenty of other examples: darwinawards.com/darwin/.

10.   The benefits of having the right software have been demonstrated. One Canadian study found that first-year female college students who participated in a twelve-hour training program about assessing risks, acknowledging dangers, and engaging in verbal and physical self-defense had a nearly 50 percent less chance of experiencing an attempted rape over the next year than those who were given only a brochure about sexual assault. Charlene Y. Senn et al.,

"Efficacy of a Sexual Assault Resistance Program for University Women," *New England Journal of Medicine* 372 (2015): 2326–2335.

11. Games aside, you might also introduce at bedtime those classic fairy tales that both offer important lessons to children about dangers in the world and help teach them to deal with uncomfortable emotions like fear. For an interesting discussion about this, see Katelin An, "Why Fairy Tales Are Necessary for Children," *Medium*, June 3, 2019, medium.com/@katelinan/why-fairy-tales-are-necessary-for-children-228e4459dbd.

12. For helpful strategies from a psychotherapist with experience counseling both bullies and bullied, including tips for communicating with school administrators and combating cyberbullying, see Stella O'Malley, *Bully-Proof Kids: Practical Tools to Help Your Child to Grow Up Confident, Resilient and Strong* (London: Swift Press, 2022).

13. For helpful examples of assertiveness (as opposed to aggressiveness), see Clifford N. Lazarus, "Empowerment and Better Health Through Assertive Behavior," *Psychology Today*, June 5, 2015, www.psychologytoday.com/us/blog/think-well/201506/empowerment-and-better-health-through-assertive-behavior.

14. What ultimately matters is how we manage conflict. "Parents: How You Manage Conflict Has an Impact on Your Kids," *ScienceDaily*, September 20, 2017, www.sciencedaily.com/releases/2017/09/170920131717.htm.

15. For more on these and other tips, see "Preventing Family Abductions," Polly Klaas Foundation, www.pollyklaas.org/preventing-family-abductions/.

Chapter 18: The Importance of Noticing

1. Bobby Azarian, "How Anxiety Warps Your Perception," *BBC*, September 29, 2016.

2. Marissa Moore, "How to Overcome Fear and Anxiety," *PsychCentral*, April 7, 2022, psychcentral.com/anxiety/fear-and-anxiety.

3. Dawkins, *River Out of Eden*, 1–2.

4. de Becker, *The Gift of Fear*.

5. See Eli Amdur, "Too Late," *Forbes*, March 11, 2021.

6. de Becker, *The Gift of Fear*, 33.

7. A clenched jaw, flared nostrils, pursed lips, and lowered eyebrows are all potential warning signs. Vanessa Van Edwards, "Aggressive Body Language: 15 Cues and How to De-escalate," *Science of People*, www.scienceofpeople.com/aggressive-body-language/.

8. Nearly 9 out of 10 people are right-handed, which means a hidden weapon will typically be located in the right front waistband. Kevin Porter, *Characteristics of the Armed Individual* (Laurel, MD: Mission in Service Training Section, 2010).

9. While these signs suffice for the purposes of identifying acute threats from a personal self-defense standpoint, police rely on even more indicators when it comes to situational awareness and general threat recognition. See Nathan C. Meehan et al., *Behavioral Indicators During a Police Interdiction*, NRL/MR/5508–15-9598 (Naval Research Laboratory, May 1, 2015), 11–15, apps.dtic.mil/sti/pdfs/ADA620182.pdf.

10. Meehan et al., *Behavioral Indicators During a Police Interdiction*, viii.

Chapter 19: The Importance of Distance, Deterrence, and Determination

1. David Blake, "What Officers Really Need to Know about the 21-Foot Fill Zone," *Police 1*, January 13, 2016, www.police1.com/police-products/firearms/articles/what-officers-really-need-to-know-about-the-21-foot-kill-zone-fhQUJ72iE2aOJpkr/. In season 10 of *MythBusters*, Jamie Hyneman and Adam Savage performed this very type of test in an episode titled "Duel Dilemmas." Adam was able to get off a paintball shot when Jamie charged him from twenty-four feet with a fake knife, but not from twenty feet. You can see the segment here: "Gun vs. Knife Fight," YouTube video, uploaded by Discover, June 16, 2012. www.youtube.com/watch?v=cGzeyO3pGzw.

2. All of Colonel Boyd's briefs and papers are available at "Boyd's Work," *John Boyd Online*, www.colonelboyd.com/boydswork.

3. Robert Coram, *Boyd: The Fighter Pilot Who Changed the Art of War* (New York: Back Bay Books, 2004). See also the videos of Colonel Boyd lecturing available at James M. Brown, "Uploading John Boyd," *Strategy Bridge*, March 10, 2015, thestrategybridge.org/the-bridge/2015/11/16/uploading-john-boyd.

4. "#connection," Rickson Gracie Academy, rickson.academy/en?h=connection.

5. "On Strategy" (1871), as translated in Daniel J. Hughes, ed., *Moltke on the Art of War: Selected Writings* (New York: Ballantine Books, 1993), 92.

6. Mike Berardino, "Mike Tyson Explains One of His Most Famous Quotes," *Sun Sentinel*, November 9, 2022, www.sun-sentinel.com/sports/fl-xpm-2012-11-09-sfl-mike-tyson-explains-one-of-his-most-famous-quotes-20121109-story.html.

7. Meritxell Genovart, "The Young, the Weak and the Sick: Evidence of

Natural Selection by Predation," *PLoS One* 5, no. 3 (2010): e9774, doi:10.1371/journal.pone.0009774.

8. See him talk about his ideas at "William Aprill, Mindset of Criminals and UNTHINKABLE!" YouTube video, uploaded by Practically Tactical, September 9, 2020, www.youtube.com/watch?v=QmkXFWyIDPc. You can find other videos at "William Aprill Tribute Page," Personal Defense Network, www.personaldefensenetwork.com/article/williamaprill/.

9. This is not surprising. As an increasing body of research shows, women with disabilities experience violence at disproportionate rates relative to the general population. Michelle S. Ballan and Molly Burke Freyer, "Self-Defense Among Women With Disabilities: An Unexplored Domain in Domestic Violence Cases," *Violence Against Women* 18, no. 9 (2012): 1083–1107, doi:10.1177/1077801212461430.

10. See the comments by a K-9 services expert in Charles Rabin, "Want to Protect Your Home from Burglary? Get a Dog," *Miami Herald*, April 13, 2016.

11. Betty Grayson and Morris I. Stein, "Attracting Assault: Victims' Nonverbal Cues," *Journal of Communication* 31, no. 1 (March 1981): 68–75, doi.org/10.1111/j.1460-2466.1981.tb01206.x.

12. Sarah Wheeler et al., "Psychopathic Traits and Perceptions of Victim Vulnerability," *Criminal Justice and Behavior* 36, no. 6 (2009): 635–648, doi:10.1177/0093 854809333958.

13. See Janey Davies, "Criminals Reveal 9 Nonverbal Cues That Attract Them in a Potential Victim," *Learning Mind*, October 7, 2020, www.learning-mind.com/nonverbal-cues-criminals/; and Wendy L. Patrick, "How Criminals Find Their Most Likely Victims," *Psychology Today*, August 22, 2020, www.psychologytoday.com/us/blog/why-bad-looks-good/202008/how-criminals-find-their-most-likely-victims.

14. Franklin E. Zimring, *The City That Became Safe: New York's Lessons for Urban Crime and Its Control* (New York: Oxford University Press, 2012). For a short summary, see Franklin E. Zimring, "How New York Beat Crime," *OUP*, blog, June 13, 2012, blog.oup.com/2012/06/zimring-scientific-american-nyc-beat-crime/.

15. This type of determination is what retired U.S. Navy Seal Jocko Willink would call "mind control," which he describes as "declaring martial law on your mind": "Impose what you want on your brain: DISCIPLINE. POWER. POSITIVITY. WILL." Jocko Willink, *Discipline Equals Freedom: Field Manual MK1-MOD1* (New York: St. Martin's Press, 2020), 14.

16. See "PDN Live: Preparing Intuitive Responses in Emergencies," YouTube video, streamed live by PersonalDefenseNet, February 20, 2018, www.youtube.com/watch?v=yGnHv6Q09sU.

Chapter 20: The Command of Mindfulness

1. As Harvard professor and "mother of mindfulness" Ellen J. Langer argues, mindfulness is simply the act of noticing new things. For her, it is a way of being—not a practice—and is the opposite of mindlessness, or being in the world with our brains on autopilot. See Ellen J. Langer *Mindfulness*, 25th anniv. ed. (New York: Da Capo Press, 2014).

2. To bring Zen practices to Western audiences, Deshimaru taught and lived in France for many years. As a result, many of his works were originally published in French. This widely shared quote, which often goes unsourced, comes from Taisen Deshimaru, *Zen et Arts Martiaux* (Paris: Albin Michel, 1983), 81. The full quote in French is: "*Dans le Zen, comme dans le Budo, on doit trouver l'unité directe avec la vérité authentique du cosmos. Car, il faut penser au-delà de la conscience personnelle, avec notre corps entier et non avec le seul cerveau. Penser avec tout le corps.*" The book was subsequently translated into English: Taisen Deshimaru, *The Zen Way to Martial Arts: A Japanese Master Reveals the Secrets of the Samurai*, trans. Nancy Amphoux (New York: Arkana, 1991).

3. As quoted in Michael Murphy and Rhea A. White, *In the Zone: Transcendent Experiences in Sports* (New York: Penguin, 1995).

4. For every ten people who join a BJJ class as beginners (white belt), one or maybe two will reach blue belt, the first awarded belt. This belt typically takes a year or two to earn when training regularly two or three times per week.

5. Quoted and adapted from the words of meditation popularizer Alan Watts. See "The Easiest Way to Get into the Meditative State," YouTube video, uploaded by Your Youniverse, December 17, 2020, www.youtube.com/watch?v=QMswdR9IkAQ; and Alan Watts, *The Way of Zen* (New York: Vintage Books, 1989).

6. There are various positions and breathing exercises to experiment with once you're comfortable with a simple seated meditation. See, for example, "Zazan Instructions," Zen Mountain Monastery, zmm.org/teachings-and-training/meditation-instructions/.

7. If you're the type of person who has trouble with consistency, there are books that offer helpful advice for building good habits. See, for example, James Clear, *Atomic Habits: An Easy and Proven Way to Build Good Habits and Break Bad Ones* (New York: Avery, 2018).

8. For simple advice on integrating mindfulness into everyday activities, see Parneet Pal et al., "Five Simple Mindfulness Practices for Everyday Life," *Mindful.org*, August 27, 2018, www.mindful.org/take-a-mindful-moment-5-simple-practices-for-daily-life/.

9. Johann Hari, *Stolen Focus: Why You Can't Pay Attention—and How to*

Think Deeply Again (New York: Crown, 2022). See also Hari's interview with Bari Weiss, "Honestly: Your Attention Didn't Collapse. It Was Stolen," *Common Sense (Substack)*, April 27, 2022, bariweiss.substack.com/p/honestly-your-attention-didnt-collapse?s=r.

Chapter 21: Thinking the Unthinkable

1.   There were a million homicides in Brazil between 1980 and 2010. Joseph Murray et al., "Crime and Violence in Brazil: Systematic Review of Time Trends, Prevalence Rates and Risk Factors," *Aggression and Violent Behavior* 18, no. 5 (September 2013): 471–483, doi:10.1016/j.avb.2013.07.003.

2.   Gracie, *Breathe*, 19.

3.   Rickson Gracie, in personal communication.

4.   This is generally a temporary mind-body state in which our attention is narrowly focused and we are still connected with our selves. It is not the same as two other possible mind-body states in the defense cascade of humans: tonic immobility (feigned death) and collapsed immobility (fainting). Kasia Kozlowska, "Fear and the Defense Cascade: Clinical Implications and Management," *Harvard Review of Psychiatry* 23, no. 4 (July 2015): 263–287, doi:10.1097/HRP.0000000000000065.

5.   The freeze response is one reason many people are calling for a "yes-means-yes" model of sexual consent. See Lisa Shell, "The Reason Some People Freeze When They're Being Attacked," *Vice*, October 10, 2018, www.vice.com/en/article/kzjk8n/sexual-assault-fight-flight-freeze.

6.   Visualization, or "mental practice," can be a useful tool for improving not only confidence but also motor performance. A. J. Adams, "Seeing Is Believing: The Power of Visualization," *Psychology Today*, December 3, 2009. It is something that has long been used by athletes, including wrestlers, BJJ practitioners, and MMA fighters. See, for example, "Ben Askren—Visualization for MMA Skills," *On the Mat*, March 2, 2013, onthemat.com/ben-askren-visualization-for-mma-skills.

7.   Part of the reason Hemingway's work is so admired is that he placed such great value on characters "who can stand things" in his storytelling. Philip Durham, "Ernest Hemingway's Grace Under Pressure: The Western Code," *Pacific Historical Review* 45, no. 3 (August 1976): 425–432, doi.org/10.2307/3637269.

8.   Although the setting and contexts are completely different, the exposure therapy we employ in the gym is analogous to the exposure therapy sometimes employed in a psychiatric or mental health setting. In the clinical

context, it is available as a highly effective, first-line, evidence-based treatment for anxiety disorders. Johanna S. Kaplan and David F. Tolin, *Psychiatric Times* 28, no. 9 (September 6, 2011), www.psychiatrictimes.com/view/exposure-therapy-anxiety-disorders.

9. For more on how even modest adjustments to breathing can produce profound psychological and physical effects, see James Newstor, *Breath: The New Science of a Lost Art* (New York: Riverhead Books, 2020).

10. Couture says the same thing in his book, written with Loretta Hunt, *Becoming the Natural: My Life In and Out of the Cage* (New York: Simon and Schuster, 2008), 106.

11. Love can make us more formidable and provide us with immeasurable motivation and purpose, but love alone isn't a magical elixir or solution; it always needs to come with practical measures, steps, and action. As human rights activist Ayaan Hirsi Ali writes, "For the perpetrators, the best kind of love is tough love. For the victims . . . the best kind of love is being protected." Ayaan Hirsi Ali, "Will California Ever Be Safe?" *Unherd*, December 13, 2021, unherd.com/2021/12/will-california-ever-be-safe-again/.

Chapter 22: Staying *Alive*

1. "All such things are futile attempts to arrest and fix the ever-changing movements in combat and to dissect and analyze them like a corpse." Lee, *Tao of Jeet Kune Do*, 14.

2. "Alive" and "aliveness" are terms used often by Bruce Lee in *Tao of Jeet Kune Do* to express this idea. For example, he wrote, "When you get down to it, real combat is not fixed and is very much 'alive'" (p. 14); "Forms are vain repetitions which offer an orderly and beautiful escape from self-knowledge with an *alive* opponent" (p. 16; italics mine); and "Mere repetition of rhythmic, calculated movements robs combat movement of its 'aliveness' and 'isness'—its reality" (p. 17).

3. Emma North-Best, "Watch the Video That Sparked a CIA Debate over Psychic Phenomenon," *Muck Rock*, May 9, 2017, www.muckrock.com/news/archives/2017/may/09/cia-uri-geller-video/.

4. The actual quote is: "Philosophers' Syndrome: mistaking a failure of the imagination for an insight into necessity." Daniel C. Dennett, *Consciousness Explained*, illus. Paul Weiner (New York: Little, Brown and Company, 1991), 401.

5. "Magic Smackdown!: When 'Amazing' Randi Humiliated Uri Geller," *Groovy History*, July 15, 2019, groovyhistory.com/amazing-randi-uri-geller-tonight-show.

6. Lee also used the term "fancy mess." See *Bruce Lee Podcast*, "A Fancy Mess," episode 126, November 11, 2018, brucelee.com/podcast-blog/2018/11/27/126-a-fancy-mess.

7. Learn more about him at JKD Unlimited, jkdunlimited.com/.

8. "Being Honest about Your Martial Art," YouTube video, uploaded by SBG Portland BJJ and MMA Videos, May 6, 2020, www.youtube.com/watch?v=j0GApzoGqcA.

9. Isolation drilling is one of the most important things I learned from Rickson Gracie when I first met him. It set in motion the thinking and methodology that SBG is known for today, and it informs everything you read in this section. I am still grateful to Rickson for that, just as I am grateful to my primary BJJ coach, Chris Haueter, and all others who came before me and paved the way for more functional training. Without them, I would not have been able to lay down a roadmap for Aliveness.

10. See John Kavanagh, *Win or Learn: MMA, Conor McGregor and Me: A Trainer's Journey* (Penguin Books, 2017).

Chapter 23: Detecting Bullshit

1. Roger A. Band, "Severity-Adjusted Mortality in Trauma Patients Transported by Police," *Annals of Emergency Medicine* 63, no. 5 (May 2014): 608–614.e3., doi:10.1016/j.annemergmed.2013.11.008; and "Gunshot Victims Require Much More Blood and Are More Likely to Die Than Other Trauma Patients," *Science Daily*, September 17, 2018, www.sciencedaily.com/releases/2018/09/180917082446.htm.

2. For a short glimpse of the STAB system, see "Karl Tanswell—S.T.A.B. Program (Preview)," YouTube video, uploaded by goldstarvideo1, December 1, 2009, www.youtube.com/watch?v=-_ZO17yWi7I.

3. For a review of the STAB system, see Jamie Clubb, "The Return of the 'Alive' Blade!—Karl Tanswell's S.T.A.B. Seminar," *Clubb Chimera*, November 5, 2006, clubbchimera.com/the-return-of-the-alive-blade-karl-tanswells-s-t-a-b-seminar/.

4. For a short documentary on Tanswell's life and work, see "SBG Legacy: Karl Tanswell's Story," YouTube video, uploaded by SBG Legacy, July 14, 2020, www.youtube.com/watch?v=pi4tJC1ynyI.

5. The tributes to Tanswell speak for themselves: John Balfe, "Tributes Pour in for SBG Manchester Head Coach Karl Tanswell," *Mac Life*, January 26, 2018, themaclife.com/sports/mma/tributes-pour-sbg-manchester-head-coach-karl-tanswell/.

6. "Bruce Lee 'Enter The Dragon'—Boards Don't Hit Back," You-Tube video, uploaded by Bruce Lee, April 26, 2013, www.youtube. com/watch?v=3zRsgsUWYks#:~:text='Boards%20Don't%20Hit%20 Back,Scene%20from%20Enter%20The%20Dragon.

7. You can learn more about Pagle here: Stephanie M. Lopez, "Intrinsic Motivation," *Medium*, August 9, 2017, medium.com/@slopez_40898/intrinsic-motivation-c9c6b4dbe3a4.

8. You can find hotline information at HIV.gov, www.hiv.gov/about-us/contact#:~:text=To%20get%20answers%20to%20questions,800%2D448%2D0440)%20or.

9. According to the doctrine of self-defense, criminal force can be justified if there is reason to believe its application is needed to protect against an imminent unlawful attack. Although this doctrine sounds fairly straightforward, there is some grey area here, particularly around the question of "imminence." See Fritz Allhoff, "Self-Defense Without Imminence," *American Criminal Law Review* 56, no. 4 (Fall 2019): 1527–1552.

10. Listen to Haueter's interview with Nick Albin on the *Chewjitsu Podcast*, "BJJ Black Belt Chris Haueter," episode 133, podcasts.apple.com/ie/podcast/episode-133-bjj-black-belt-chris-haueter/id1422970856?i=1000502329188.

11. Beyond the obvious physical benefits, martial arts training has also been shown to improve cognitive self-regulation, affective self-regulation, and prosocial behavior. See, for example, Kimberly D. Lakes and William T. Hoyt, "Promoting Self-Regulation Through School-Based Martial Arts Training," *Journal of Applied Developmental Psychology* 25, no. 3 (May–June 2004): 283–302, doi.org/10.1016/j.appdev.2004.04.002.

Chapter 24: The Command of Self

1. More than a few UFC champions got their start in traditional martial arts as kids or teens before crossing over to MMA, including, notably, Anderson Silva (Taekwondo), Lyoto Machida (Shotokan Karate), George St. Pierre (Kyokushin Karate), and Chuck Liddell (Kempo). Each of these individuals holds high-level black belts in their respective traditional martial arts, but all four are also exceptional in the clinch and on the ground. Silva, Machida, and St. Pierre hold black belts in BJJ, and Liddell was a Division 1 college wrestler who has trained BJJ for years. All have also trained other striking arts, including boxing, and none relied only on their traditional martial art to succeed in the ring. Given the fact that MMA is such a new sport, this type of evolution is to be expected. Prior to the early 1990s, there was simply no real option for BJJ training outside of Brazil, and MMA gyms didn't yet exist. As the years pass,

we will likely see fewer and fewer world-class fighters with a background in a traditional martial art. Rather, we will see more and more athletes who started training MMA and BJJ at a young age.

2.   This quote is widely shared, but I'm not aware of the original source. See, for example, "The Best Collection of Inspirational Jiu-Jitsu Quotes," *bjjee.com*, May 8, 2020, www.bjjee.com/articles/the-best-collection-of-inspirational-jiu-jitsu-quotes/. Other related quotes that closely align with the philosophy of the Gracie family are "To survive is to win" and "If you do not lose, you can only win." See Ryron Gracie, "Helio Gracie Day," *KeepItPlayful (Wordpress)*, October 1, 2012, keepitplayful.wordpress.com/2012/10/01/helio-gracie-day/.

3.   The first one took place in 1996. The annual tournament is run by the International Brazilian Jiu-Jitsu Federation (ibjjf.com).

4.   Although this quote is popularly attributed to Lincoln, I can offer no direct evidence that he actually ever said it. Even if the quote is apocryphal, as someone with functional fighting skill, he certainly would have understood it. For more on Lincoln as a competitive wrestler, see Bob Zeller, "Abraham Lincoln Excelled in Wrestling—What Other Sports Did He Play?" *History.com*, January 21, 2022, www.history.com/news/abraham-lincoln-wrestling-sports#:~:text=Abraham%20Lincoln%3A%20A%20Wrestler%20As%20Young%20Man&text=He%20competed%20in%20wrestling%20matches,in%20the%20sport%20in%201992.

Index

About the Author

Matt Thornton is founder of Straight Blast Gym International, one of the most respected martial arts academies in the world that has dozens of official locations across five continents, including gyms in Australia, Canada, Ireland, South Africa, South Korea, Sweden, the United Kingdom, and the United States. He has been teaching functional martial arts for more than thirty years, and his students include champion MMA fighters and world-class self-defense and law enforcement instructors. He holds a fifth-degree black belt in Brazilian Jiu-Jitsu and lives in Portland, Oregon, with his six children and wife, Salome. He can be found on Twitter @aliveness_ape.